MW00396241

Other Rivers

Other Rivers

A CHINESE EDUCATION

Peter Hessler

Penguin Press
New York
2024

PENGUIN PRESS
An imprint of Penguin Random House LLC
penguinrandomhouse.com

LIBRARY OF CONGRESS CONTROL NUMBER: 2024007384
ISBN 9780593655337 (hardcover)
ISBN 9780593655344 (ebook)

Printed in the United States of America
1st Printing

Book design by Daniel Lagin
Maps by Angela Hessler

for Ariel and Natasha

献给采采和柔柔

Contents

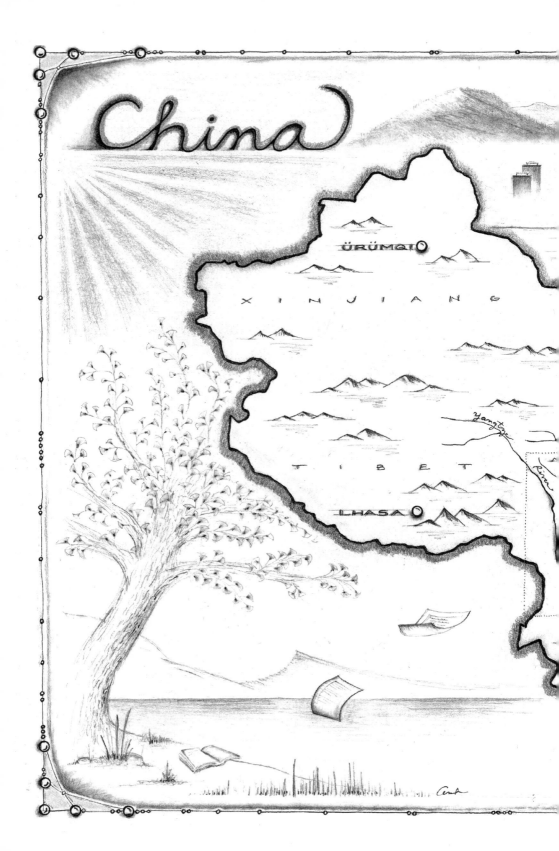

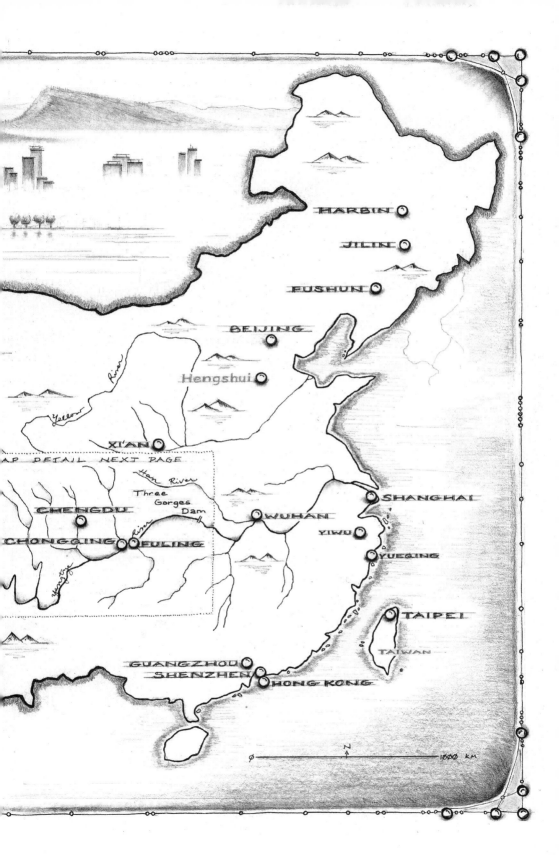

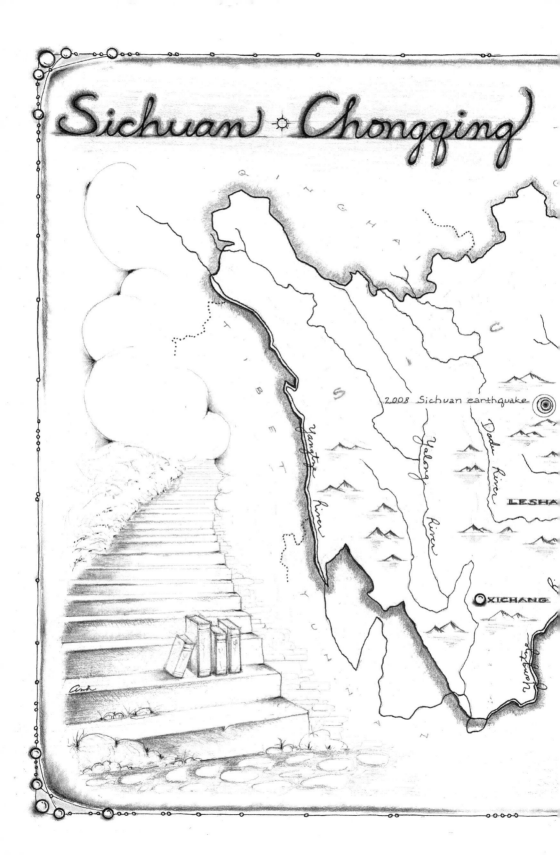

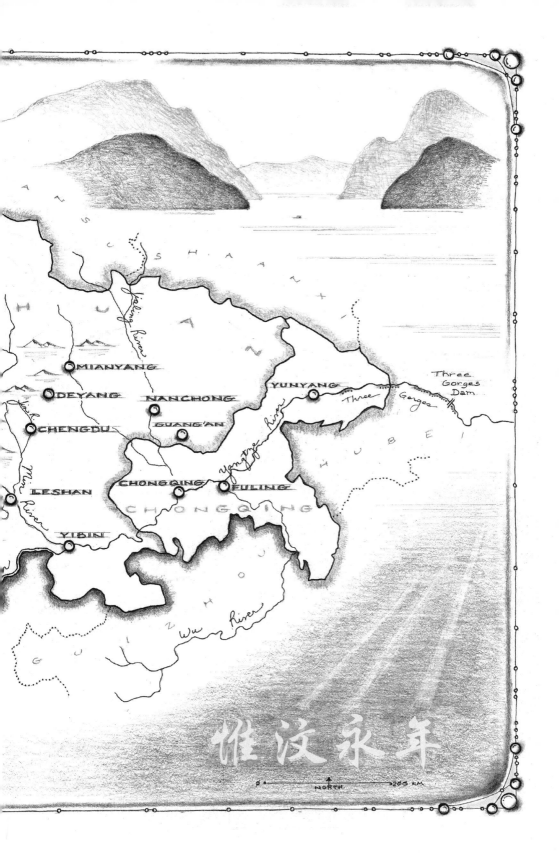

Part I

 CHAPTER ONE

Rejection

September 2019

THE VERY LAST THING THAT ANY TEACHER WANTS TO DO—AND the very first thing that I did at Sichuan University, even before I set foot on campus—is to inform students that they cannot take a class. Of course, some would say that rejection is a normal experience for young Chinese. From the start of elementary school, through a constant series of examinations, rankings, and cutoffs, children are trained to handle failure and disappointment. At a place like Sichuan University, it's simply a matter of numbers: eighty-one million in the province, sixteen million in the city, seventy thousand at the university. Thirty spots in my classroom. The course title was Introduction to Journalism and Nonfiction, and I had chosen those words because, in addition to being simple and direct, they did not promise too much. Given China's current political climate, I wasn't sure what would be possible in such a class.

Some applicants considered the same issue. During the first semester that I taught, a literature major picked out one of the words in the title—*nonfiction*—and gave an introduction of her own:

In China, you will see a lot of things, but [often] you can't say them. If you post something sensitive on social platforms, it will be deleted. . . . In many events, Non-Fiction description has disappeared. Although I am a student of literature, I don't know how to express facts in words now.

Two years ago, on November 18th, 2017, a fire broke out in Beijing, killing 19 people. After the fire, the Beijing Municipal Government began a 40-day urban low-end population clean-up operation. At the same time, the "low-end population clean-up" became a forbidden word in China, and all Chinese media were not allowed to report it. I have not written an article related to this event, and it will always exist only in my memory.

As a student of Chinese literature, I have a hard time writing what I want to write because I am afraid what I write will probably be deleted.

Applicants handled this issue in different ways. I requested a writing sample in English, and most students sent papers that they had researched for other courses. Some titles suggested that the topics had been chosen because, by virtue of distance or obscurity, they were unlikely to be controversial: "Neoliberal Institutionalism in the Resolution of Yom Kippur War," "The Motive of Life Writing for Aboriginal Women Writers in Australia." Other students took the opposite approach, finding subjects close to home but following the government line; one applicant's essay was titled "The Necessity of Internet Censorship." There was also safety in ideology. A student from the College of Literature and Journalism submitted a Marxist interpretation of *Madame Bovary*. ("Capitalism has cleaned up the establishment of the old French society, and to some extent deconstructed various resistances that limit economic and social development.") Another student abandoned every traditional subject—politics, business, culture, literature—and instead produced, in prose that was vaguely biblical, a five-hundred-word description of a pretty girl he had seen on campus:

She was a garden—her shoots are orchards of pomegranates, henna, saffron, calamus and cinnamon, frankincense and myrrh. She was a fountain in the garden—she was all the streams flowing from Lebanon, limpid and emerald, pacific and shimmering. . . .

My first impressions were literary: I saw the words before I met the students. Their English tended to be slightly formal, but it wasn't stiff; there were moments of emotion and exuberance. Sometimes they made a comment that pushed against the establishment. ("I am still under eighteen years old now, living in an ivory tower isolated from the world outside. I'm expecting to change it.") All of them were undergraduates, and for the most part they had been born around the turn of the millennium. They had been middle school students in 2012, when Xi Jinping had risen to become China's leader. Since then, Xi had consolidated power to a degree not seen since the days of Mao Zedong, and in 2018, the constitution was changed to abolish term limits. These college students were members of the first generation to come of age in a system in which Xi could be leader for life.

The last time I had arrived in Sichuan as a teacher was in 1996, when Deng Xiaoping was still alive. While reading applications, I imagined how it would feel to return to the classroom, and I copied sentences that caught my eye:

Only when a nation knows its own history and recognizes its own culture can it gain identity.

Just as Sartre said, men are condemned to be free. We are left with too many choices to struggle with, yet little guidance.

Actually, all of us are like screws in a big machine, small but indispensable. Only when everyone works hard will our country have a brighter future.

The range of topics made it virtually impossible to compare applications, but I did my best. I had to limit the enrollment to thirty, which was already too many for an intensive writing course. After selecting the students, I sent a note to everybody else, inviting them to apply again the following semester. But one rejected girl showed up on the first day of class. She sat near the front, which may have been why I didn't notice; I assumed that anybody trying to sneak in would position herself near the last row. At the end of the second week, when she sent a long email, I still had no idea who she was or what she looked like.

Dear teacher,

My name is Serena, an English major at Sichuan University, and I am writing in hope of your permission for me to attend, as an auditor, your Wednesday night class.

I failed to be selected. I have been in the class since the first week, and I sensed and figured my presence permissible.

I want to write. As Virginia Woolf thought, only life written is real life. I wish to be a skilled observer to present life or idealized images on paper, like resurrection or "in eternal lines to time thou growest." . . . I started to appreciate writers' diction not as a natural flow of expression but careful strategies and efforts, I began to put myself in the writers' shoes, and set out to sharpen my ear as a way to hear the sound of writing—consonance or dissonance, jazz, chord, and finally symphony.

Perhaps I am being paranoid and no one will drag me out. If you can't give me permission, I'll still come to class in disguise until I am forced to leave.

Happy Mid-autumn Festival!

Thank you for your time.

Yours cordially,
Serena

I composed an email, explaining that I couldn't accept auditors. But I hesitated before pressing "send." I read Serena's note once more, and then I erased my message. I wrote:

> The college is concerned about auditing students, because the course needs to focus on those who are enrolled. But I much appreciate your enthusiasm, and I want to ask if you are willing to take the class as a full student, doing all of the coursework.

I was violating my own rules, but I sent the email anyway. It took her exactly three minutes to respond.

When I told other China specialists that I planned to return to Sichuan as a teacher, and that my wife, Leslie, and I hoped to enroll our daughters in a public school, some people responded: Why would you go back there now? Under Xi Jinping, there had been a steady tightening of the nation's public life, and a number of activists and dissidents had been arrested. In Hong Kong, the Communist Party was reducing the former British colony's already limited political freedoms. On the other side of the country, in the far western region of Xinjiang, the government was carrying out a policy of forced internment camps for more than a million Uighurs and other Muslim minorities. And all of this was happening against the backdrop of the Trump administration's trade war against the People's Republic.

It was different from the last time I had moved to Sichuan. In 1996, I knew virtually nothing about China, and almost all basic terms of my job were decided by somebody else. The Peace Corps sent me and another young volunteer, Adam Meier, to Fuling, a remote city at the juncture of the Yangtze and the Wu Rivers, in a region that would someday be partially flooded by the Three Gorges Dam. At the local teachers college, officials provided us with apartments, and they told us which classes to teach. I had no input on course titles or textbooks. The notion of selecting a class from student applications would have been unthinkable. Every course I taught was mandatory, and usually there were forty or fifty kids packed in the classroom. Most of my students had been born in 1974 or 1975, during the waning years of the Cultural Revolution and Mao Zedong's reign.

In 1996, only one out of every twelve young Chinese was able to enter any kind of tertiary educational institution. Most of my Fuling students had been the first from their extended families to attend college, and in many cases their parents were illiterate. They typically had grown up on farms, which was true for the vast majority of Chinese. In 1974, the year many of my senior students were born, China's population was 83 percent rural. By the mid-1990s, that percentage was falling fast, and my students were part of this change. During the college-enrollment process, the *hukou*, or household registration, of any young Chinese automatically switched from rural to urban. The moment my students entered college, they were transformed, legally speaking, into city people.

But inside the classroom it was obvious that they still had a long way to go. Most students were small, with sun-darkened skin, and they dressed in cheap clothes that they had to wash by hand. I learned to associate certain students with certain outfits, because their wardrobes were so limited. I also learned to recognize a chilblain—during winter, students often had the red-purple sores on their fingers and ears, the result of poor nutrition and cold living conditions. Much of my early information about these young people was physical. In that sense, it was the opposite of what I would later experience at Sichuan University. In Fuling, my students' bodies and faces initially told me more than their words.

It took a long time to draw them out. They tended to be shy, and often they were overwhelmed by the transition to campus life. We were similar in age—at twenty-seven, I was only a few years older than my senior students—but none of them had ever met an American before. They had studied English for seven or more years, although many of them had trouble carrying on a basic conversation, because of lack of contact with native speakers. Their written English was much stronger, and in literature class I assigned Wordsworth poems, Shakespeare plays, stories by Mark Twain. In essays, they described themselves as "peasants," and they wrote beautifully about their families and their villages:

> In China, passing an entrance examination to college isn't easy for the children of peasants. . . . The day before I came to Fuling, my parents urged me again and again. "Now you are college student," my father said. . . . "The generation isn't the same with the previous generation, when everyone fished in troubled waters. We have to make a living by our abilities nowadays. The advancement of a country depend on science and technology."

> My mother was a peasant, what she cared for wasn't the future of China, just how to support the family. She didn't know politics, either. In her eyes, so long as all of us lived better, she thought the nation was right. . . . But I see many rotten phenomenons in the society. I find there is a distance between the reality and the ideal, which I can't shorten because I'm too tiny. Perhaps someday I'll grow up.

I felt like we had just gotten to know one another well when my Peace Corps service ended, in the summer of 1998. Before leaving Fuling, I collected the mailing addresses of everybody in my classes, although I doubted that we would be able to stay in touch. Postage to the United States was prohibitively expensive for Chinese in the countryside, and none of the students had cell phones or access to the internet. After graduating, most of them would accept government-assigned positions as teachers in rural middle schools.

Before we parted, students gathered keepsakes: copies of class materials, photographs with me and Adam. They prepared memory books with pictures and farewell messages. During my last week on campus, one boy named Jimmy approached me with a cassette tape and asked if I would make a recording of all the poetry we had studied.

"Especially I want you to read 'The Raven,' and anything by Shakespeare," he said. "This is so I can remember your literature class."

Jimmy had grown up in the Three Gorges, where he would now return. The government had assigned him to a middle school on the banks of a small, fast-flowing tributary of the Yangtze. In the memory book, Jimmy had pasted a photograph of him standing on campus with a serious expression, dressed in a red Chicago Bulls jersey. The Bulls jersey was one of the outfits I associated with Jimmy. This was the era of Michael Jordan, and a number of boys wore cheap knockoff versions of Bulls paraphernalia. My pre-graduation gift to Jimmy and his classmates had been to change the schedule of their final exam, in June 1998. By pushing the exam back a few hours, I made it possible for all of us to watch live while Jordan hit a jumper with 5.2 seconds left, winning his sixth and last NBA title.

Jimmy had never been a particularly diligent student, but he had some Jordanesque qualities: he was a good athlete, and naturally bright, and things always seemed to go well for him. In the memory book, he wrote a message in neat Chinese calligraphy:

Keep Climbing All the Way
Farewell, Farewell, Dear Friend

When Jimmy asked me to record the poetry on the cassette, I was touched, and I promised to do it that evening.

"Also, after you finish the poems," he said, grinning, "I want you to say all of the bad words you know in English and put them on the tape."

When I returned to the United States, I often wondered how things would turn out for my students. For months, I received no updates; all I had were the photographs in the memory book and the characters on my address list. I imagined Jimmy in his Bulls jersey, surrounded by the cliffs of the Three Gorges, listening to the poems of Edgar Allan Poe and William Shakespeare punctuated by strings of curse words.

In 1999, I moved to Beijing as a freelance journalist. I no longer taught, but part of my life continued to operate on the Chinese academic schedule. At the beginning of every semester, in September and in February, I sent out a batch of letters that were hand-addressed to dozens of villages in Sichuan and Chongqing. Now that I was living in China again, it was easy for former students to write back. Their replies arrived in cheap brown paper envelopes postmarked with the names of places I had never heard of: Lanjiang, Yingye, Chayuan. Most students had beautiful handwriting—at the college, they had been forced to spend hours practicing with a traditional Chinese brush. Their graceful script contrasted with the harsh world they described:

> The children show no interest in their studies. Poverty, foolishness are involved in the farmers in our hometown which is far from modern society. Several generations live with working by hand and using animals as labour force instead of tractors. The less they know, the poorer they become.
>
> I often tell the students you must study or you won't change your stupidness. . . . Most of the government cadres are incapable, most of them know little. In your America, that can't be imagined. They only know eating, gambling, drinking, looking for official relations, whoring.

Over time, I was able to stay in touch with more than a hundred former students. Jimmy's brown paper envelopes proved to be among the ones that arrived most regularly at my Beijing office. His postmark read Jiangkou—"mouth of the river" in Chinese. Jiangkou had always been poor and isolated, but soon Jimmy's letters began to describe a life that he had never imagined possible:

> In 1999, a charming girl came into my world, who worked in a res-taurant then. In my eyes, she was so attractive that I fell in love with her, I promised I would love her forever. On March 15th, 2000, I married her eventually. Before we got married, she started to run a grand restaurant of her own. In my opinion, it is a hard work to do business, but she thinks it is a good job, which can develop her abil-ity. At the beginning, we owed our relatives and friends much money. Now we also run a hotel, which cost us 170,000 yuan. To our joy, both restaurant and hotel are going very well. . . . On Sep. 5th, 2001, a baby called Chen Xi (means the rising sun) came into my family, who brought in much pleasure to us.

It was remarkable how quickly the letters changed. By the early 2000s, there were fewer descriptions of poverty, and writers referred to new highways and railroads that were being constructed in their hometowns. Details about money became common: loans, investments, side busi-nesses. Occasionally, a former student sent a message from the factory towns of southeastern China, where so many rural people had migrated:

> I am now going to Fujian. One of my cousins is working in Fujian's Fuding city. He was injured in a toy factory there, so he is having a *guansi* [lawsuit]. And these days we are talking with the boss about the money he should pay for my cousin. I find this place interesting and much richer than Chongqing. And it's easier to find a job with good salary.

Almost none of them had been born with any advantages in terms of family, finances, or geography. But their luck was historical—they couldn't have had better timing. In 1978, when they were a few years old, Deng Xiaoping had initiated his Reform and Opening policy. My Fuling students had grown up alongside these economic and social changes, and they were part of what I came to think of as the Reform generation. Members of this cohort had participated in the largest internal migration in human history, with more than a quarter of a billion rural Chinese moving to the cities. In 2011, China's population officially became majority urban. Since the beginning of the Reform era, an even greater number of citizens—nearly eight hundred million—had been lifted out of poverty.

From a distance, it was hard to grasp what these statistics meant at the human level. But the letters gave me a different perspective. In 2016, a man named David wrote and apologized because back in the 1990s, he had not been a particularly attentive student. It was true—in literature class, David had often slumped over his desk, half asleep. Two decades later, he finally explained the reasons for his malaise:

> For three years, I did not eat and sleep well. I remember in 1996, for half a year, I just had one meal a day. I was a sad man. But now I am happy about my life.

———

Eventually, the brown envelopes gave way to emails and text messages. My own life moved on: for a while, Leslie and I lived in southwestern Colorado, where our twin daughters, Ariel and Natasha, were born in 2010. The following year, we moved to Egypt, where Leslie and I worked for half a decade as foreign correspondents. No matter where I was, I kept the old schedule of sending out a long message at the start of every Chinese semester. I always had a notion that someday, after twenty years or so, I would return to live at the familiar juncture of the Yangtze and the

Wu. I liked the idea of teaching again at the Fuling college, and I was curious about the next generation of students.

In 2017, I inquired about a teaching job. Some of my old colleagues still served on the faculty, and they reported that the college wanted to hire me. I submitted an application, which was sent to be approved by educational authorities in Chongqing, the municipality that administers Fuling. And then—nothing.

There are many kinds of rejection in China. The simplest is financial: in the business world, a denial tends to be direct and blunt. Academics can also be straightforward, especially in the exam-driven culture of Chinese schools. But if the reason for rejection is political, and if a foreigner is involved, there may be no response at all. Nobody mentions a decision, and nobody gives an explanation. The absence of communication effectively means that there is neither a problem nor a solution. It's as if the original application never happened.

After months of silence, I knew that the only chance of clarity was through a personal visit. I made the long journey from Colorado to Fuling, where I met with a well-connected friend. I asked if there was a problem with my writing—in 2001, I had published *River Town*, a book about my two years at the college. But he assured me that this wasn't the reason.

"It's because of Xi Jinping and Bo Xilai," he said. Bo Xilai had been the highest Communist Party official in Chongqing until 2012, when he was involved in an explosive scandal that included, among other crimes, the murder of a British businessman at the command of Bo's wife. Before Bo's fall, he had been seen as a figure with national aspirations and as a potential rival to Xi Jinping. In 2013, shortly after Xi rose to power, Bo was sentenced to life in prison.

My Fuling friend explained that ever since the scandal, Chongqing officials had been under close watch by the national leadership. They were unlikely to approve anything that could be seen as a potential liability, including the appointment of a foreign writer to a teaching job.

"As long as Xi Jinping is in power," my friend said, "you will never teach in Fuling."

His tone was slightly dramatic, as if this were a command that had been issued by the Politburo itself. For a moment we sat in silence. Then I said, "So how is Xi Jinping's health?"

"Hen hao!" he laughed. "Very good!"

During the 1990s, in an undeveloped place like Fuling, people had a distinctive way of discussing the country's most powerful leaders. A former student named Emily, who had spent part of her childhood in a village not far from the city, once described the experience of listening to casual conversations:

> They talked about big people and big events in a way that fascinated me. The big people and big events seemed both remote and near. They were remote because they had nothing to do with the villagers' lives; they were near because the villagers seemed to know every detail.

This combination of distance and intimacy was especially true of Mao Zedong and Deng Xiaoping. Fuling residents spoke about these two figures all the time, and they quoted their sayings as casually as if remembering a conversation from last week. To a foreigner, it felt like living in a new land and learning about the gods that were worshipped there.

But Xi Jinping seemed to represent a new type of god. Early in his tenure, he initiated a strict crackdown on corruption, which appealed to many citizens, including my former students. Over time, as we settled into the rhythm of the semester letters, I started sending periodic surveys, in order to get a better understanding of their lives and their opinions. In 2017, I asked former students to name a political figure whom they admired, and Xi was by far the most popular choice:

> Of course, Xi Jinping is the one I admire. I admire because he has let us benefit a lot, especially the farmers.

> Honestly speaking, Xi is the first political figure in China that I admire. Under his leadership, the officials in the government are having much better service.

> He is the best president in the history. He is strict with the leaders, and the leaders are behaving better now.

While praising Xi, they never mentioned personal characteristics. The old intimacy was gone; now they emphasized the ways in which the system functioned. This was part of what distinguished Xi from Mao and Deng, whose personalities and physical appearances had been central to their appeal. Mao—handsome and aloof, with a poet's sensibility—had made Chinese people feel proud and capable of standing up to the outside world. And Deng, with his diminutive stature and Sichuanese toughness, had tapped into another part of the Chinese mindset, one that valued humility, pragmatism, and hard work. Both men had risen during the revolution, but now, after nearly seventy years of Communist Party rule, the country had reached another stage. The most powerful figure who emerged in this era was essentially bureaucratic—a god of the system.

When I met with my well-connected friend, he reminded me about this aspect of life in China. "You should try Sichuan," he said. "They aren't as nervous as officials in Chongqing."

Originally, Chongqing had been part of Sichuan, but in 1997, the city and its surrounding region, including Fuling, had been designated as a separate political entity. And that was my friend's suggestion: if you're having trouble with Chongqing cadres, just cross the border. After our conversation, I abandoned my dream of living at the juncture of the Yangtze and the Wu. I went west: I applied to teach at an American-affiliated institute at Sichuan University. This time, the application was quickly approved, and in August 2019, I moved with my family to Chengdu.

We rented an apartment downtown, in a building that was situated on the eastern bank of the Fu River. Alongside the Fu, pleasant bike paths were shaded by century-old paper mulberry and white fig trees. The Fu was one branch of a network of small rivers and canals that, in modern times, had been given a lovely name: Jin Jiang, the Brocade River. The various streams of the Jin braided throughout downtown Chengdu, eventually continuing south to join the great rivers of lower Sichuan: first the Min, then the Yangtze. When I looked down from my Chengdu balcony onto the river, it made me happy to think that eventually, after nearly four hundred miles, that same water would flow past the city of Fuling.

Those were among my first lessons from the Xi Jinping era. Along with the new god, a new fear had permeated the government, and cadres were even more cautious than they had been in the past. But Xi remained a god of the system, which meant that the bureaucracy often operated with its own logic and momentum. If a request was rejected, it was worth trying a different office, a different cadre; in a country of such size, there were always other rivers.

At Sichuan University, I taught nonfiction in a section of campus that was still under construction. Our classroom window overlooked a stretch of mud and rubble that had yet to be landscaped, and there was often a pounding sound from workers who were installing cobblestones in a nearby courtyard. Next door, a brand-new building featured a four-story glass facade that was decorated with golden characters that read

"College of Marxism." The college had been designed with a large parking garage in the basement. Once, before an evening class, I wandered through the garage to see what the Marxists were driving to campus. Most of the cars were mid-level foreign brands, although I also saw one BMW and five Mercedes sedans.

The campus itself was enormous. From north to south, it spanned more than a mile, and the grounds were full of yellow and green ride-share bikes, to help the students cope with the distance. In the 1990s, this had all been farmland; back then, Sichuan University occupied a relatively small site on the banks of the Jin River. But the university had expanded into this rural area, which they called the Jiang'an Campus. From my downtown home, it took more than an hour by bus to get to Jiang'an. Suburban campuses had become common in Chinese cities, and Fuling had also constructed a brand-new complex, about ten miles upstream along the Yangtze.

In nonfiction class, there wasn't a single student from the countryside. During the early weeks, I found it hard to identify physical markers among the people in my classroom. It wasn't like the old days, when I could pick out Jimmy by his Bulls jersey, or a boy named Roger by his trademark tattered blue suit jacket, the tailor's label still on the sleeve. At Sichuan University, there was a certain uniformity to students' appearances. They dressed neatly, but not too well; nobody looked obviously poor and nobody looked obviously rich. The girls generally wore baggy jeans or loose skirts, and they almost never dressed in anything that was revealing or form-fitting. Few of them dyed their hair or used much makeup.

The boys' shoes represented one of the few outward signs of prosperity. I never saw girls with flashy jewelry, but some boys wore the kind of high-top sneakers that are prized by aficionados. In every class that I taught, there was at least one student who collected throwback Nike Air Jordans. Often they wore styles that dated to the era of Jimmy and the Bulls knockoffs. But now the gear in a Chinese classroom was authentic:

when I asked one first-year about his retro 1985 Air Jordans, he told me proudly that he had bought the shoes for the equivalent of $450. In non-fiction class, a sneaker-head student used "AJ" as his English name, in homage to Air Jordans.

There were a few other foreign celebrity names in that class. Some were oxymorons: a gentle kid in glasses who called himself Giroud, after Olivier Giroud, the great French footballer; and an owlish boy named Kawhi, after Kawhi Leonard, the preternaturally gifted guard for the San Antonio Spurs. A girl who called herself Giselle, after the Brazilian supermodel, was in fact very tall, very thin, and very pretty. But even Giselle dressed in an understated way. I came to think of the name as an alternative life—perhaps she would have been the glamorous Giselle in a different place, at a different time.

On the surface, the narrow range of appearance suggested a middle-class sameness. But in truth these students had arrived in my classroom from all directions. For our first unit, I assigned personal essays, and many students wrote about mothers and fathers who had migrated from the countryside. Their parents were roughly the same age as the people I had taught in the 1990s; in fact, one of my former Fuling students had a son who was currently a sophomore at Sichuan University. Those Reform-generation parents had worked hard to assimilate to city life, so it wasn't surprising that their children dressed in unobtrusive ways. It reminded me of the United States in the 1950s, when young people had grown up amid a new prosperity. Perhaps the next generation would be more interested in exploring distinctive styles and appearances.

None of my nonfiction students had attended rural high schools, but some had spent parts of their early childhoods in the countryside. These children had often shifted back and forth between rural grandparents and parents who were trying to find their footing in new urban jobs. In some cases, the parents had been separated, not because of discord but because of the demands of a society in flux. Giselle wrote about how, at the age of six, she was sent to live with her army officer father on a military base, because her mother's job required her to be in a different place. Giselle described the day that she arrived at her father's apartment:

> I had no idea about the man who stood in front of me. The only thing
> I knew about his identity was that he is my father. If you wanted me
> to talk more about him, I knew his bed was small and hard and his
> temper was not good.

In Fuling, I had also taught the children of men and women who had been caught up in immense national changes. Those events had been political in nature, with overwhelmingly tragic outcomes: the Great Leap Forward, in which as many as fifty-five million starved to death, from 1958 to 1962; and the Cultural Revolution, which began in 1966 and lasted until Mao's death in 1976. My Fuling students rarely wrote much about their parents' younger lives, because the older people didn't like to talk about it. And most of that history was either censored or glossed over in official texts. There was a blankness to the recent past—the Fuling students could only look ahead.

But family memories seemed different nowadays. The experiences of the Reform generation had been shaped by economics rather than politics, and there was a high degree of agency. People liked to tell stories, and they lingered on details. In one of the composition classes that I taught at Sichuan University, a student named Steve wrote about the experience of eating hot pot with his father. In the story, the older man took a long time in choosing a restaurant, and then, after the food arrived, he insisted on a specific order to the way it was cooked: fatty meat before lean, lean meat before vegetables. This was important, the father explained to Steve, in order to properly flavor the broth. When a waiter arrived with a plate of thin-sliced raw mutton, the father turned it upside down. He told Steve that fresh mutton should stick to the plate.

In the essay, Steve described these meticulous rituals, and he concluded:

My father was born in 1972, when the Great Proletarian Cultural Revolution was going to end soon. The economy of China began to rise again, but was not still good enough. Therefore, he was never starving in his childhood or adolescence, but he seldom felt full in that period of time. He told me that his family could barely eat meat once a week, and there were only a few dishes. In 1990, he started his college life and got his first part-time job. When he got his first salary, he decided to spend half of it to have an excellent meal, which brought him great pleasure.

A student named Fenton compared his parents' stories to superhero films. He used the word *fight*, but not in the Maoist sense of a conflict between social classes or groups. For Fenton's parents, the fight had been to become city people:

My parents were born in rural Shandong in the mid-1970s. Although [they] only have high school education, they didn't want to stay in their hometown and become the next generation of farmers, so they come to the city to fight.

Before I left home and went to college, I had such an interest in listening to my parents' stories about their childhood. Before they graduated from high school and left the countryside, as they said, it was the hardest and happiest time. When my dad was at my age, he worked as a taxi driver and my mother was a woman worker in a state-owned flour factory. I was born in the crossroad of two centuries. Taking advantage of the rapid development of market economy in the coming century, they decided to devote themselves to industry. It can be said that they are [two] of those people who have received the dividend of Reform and Opening.

But these are the stories [from] when they grew up and what I like is that they are the stories of their childhood in the countryside. These stories have a fairly fixed and smooth pattern, which can be

said to be similar to the current [superhero] genre films. "Our childhood living conditions were not good" is always the beginning of this
kind of story. In the middle is something that seems to be easy to realize now but was difficult to achieve at that time. And "you must
cherish everything you have now" is always the end of these stories.

————

Fenton was a friendly kid with round glasses and a crew cut, and he majored in journalism. Like many of my students, he hoped to continue his
education abroad, and he had chosen the name Fenton because it sounded
vaguely like his Chinese name, Huidong. After entering the private economy, Fenton's parents had started a small factory that manufactured
plastic bags. The bag money allowed them to supplement Fenton's education with outside tutors, and he had tested into his city's best public
high school. The bags also must have fed the boy well: Fenton stood over
six feet tall, with a stocky frame.

Most of the boys in the class were taller than me, and so were a few
girls, including Giselle. During our first session, I showed a class photograph from the early months of 1997, when my senior students and I had
stood in front of the Fuling college library. The library had been one of
the most distinctive structures on campus, with bright yellow paint, and
it was often used as a backdrop for photos. In the 1997 picture, I towered
over my students, almost as if they were middle school kids. The image
made the Sichuan University students burst out laughing—I was only
five feet, nine inches tall.

Of all the characteristics of today's young people, their height struck
me at the most visceral level. I felt it in the city, too. In the old days, on
crowded buses, I had been half a head taller than most people around
me; now in a packed Chengdu subway I often found myself looking into
some kid's armpit. In 2020, a study in *The Lancet* reported that out of two
hundred countries, China had seen the largest increase in boys' height,

and the third largest in girls', since 1985. The average Chinese nineteen-year-old male was now more than three and a half inches taller, because of improved nutrition.

They were also far more likely to go to college. My students frequently referred to "985 universities" and "211 universities," classifications that hadn't been used when I taught in Fuling. The numbers 985 refer to a date: the fifth month of 1998, when Jiang Zemin, the leader at the time, had delivered a speech about Chinese education at Peking University. That was near the end of my Fuling years, although I didn't remember any colleagues or students taking notice of Jiang's speech. He was not among the Chinese leaders who were spoken of as gods, but he was shrewd about his limits. A Western-style politician would have begun such a speech by describing his own educational experiences, which, in Jiang's case, were impressive. In 1947, he had graduated with a bachelor's degree in electrical engineering, a rare achievement at that time. As a young man, Jiang worked in automotive engineering in northeastern China.

But Jiang undoubtedly knew that it was risky to elevate details from his own life. And so his speech followed another Chinese narrative genre: the non-personal non-story of a Party man who knows that the system matters much more than any individual. Rather than talk about himself, Jiang connected his message to a god from the past:

> Comrade Deng Xiaoping has repeatedly taught us that science and technology are the primary productive forces. We must respect knowledge and talent. These important thoughts are the theoretical basis of our strategy of rejuvenating the country through science and education. . . . In order to realize modernization, our country should have a number of world-class universities.

This campaign eventually became known as Project 985. Logically, it should have been named after Jiang—he was the first general secretary of the Chinese Communist Party with a proper university degree, and no other leader did more to advance the cause of higher education. But personifying the campaign would have made it vulnerable to politics, which was probably one reason why it was named with a string of numbers. Sichuan University was one of thirty-nine upper-tier institutions that eventually benefited from Project 985, which provided increased funding from the central government. Another campaign was called Project 211, whose numerology was even more obscure: during the twenty-first century, one hundred Chinese institutions would be granted extra support. Along with these national-level programs, there were countless other efforts to improve and expand institutions. When I taught in Fuling, the college had been relatively low on the spectrum of Chinese higher education. But even such a school was highly selective, because there were so few students who tested into any kind of tertiary institution. Since then, the nation's low figure for college entrance—one out of every twelve young Chinese, or 8.3 percent, in 1996—had risen, in the span of little more than two decades, to 51.6 percent. Most people now made it into college, which was why China had constructed so many new campuses.

In nonfiction class, we occasionally looked back at the earlier era. During the unit on personal essays, I assigned a few pages from the beginning of *River Town*. In the excerpt, I described my arrival in Fuling, in September 1996. That month, the college had hosted a series of events and activities to commemorate the sixtieth anniversary of the Long March, the five-thousand-mile trek that Mao and the rest of the Red Army had made across China as part of their struggle to win the civil war.

The Long March had ended in 1935, but Fuling celebrated the sixtieth anniversary a year late. Some students and professors had engaged in a commemorative trek, which took longer than expected; in a remote place, everything seemed to lag a step or two behind the major cities. But the delay had no effect on the enthusiasm of the various Long March commemorations. At every event, Communist Party leaders addressed the crowd with rousing speeches, exhorting the students to love the rev-

olution and the Motherland. One evening, there was a Long March Singing Contest, which Adam and I attended. I described the contest in my
book:

> For the Long March Singing Contest, all of the departments prac-
> ticed their songs for weeks and then performed in the auditorium.
> Many of the songs were the same, because the musical potential of
> the Long March is limited, which made the judging difficult. It was
> also confusing because costumes were in short supply and so they
> were shared, like the songs. The history department would perform,
> resplendent in clean white shirts and red ties, and then they would go
> offstage and quickly give their shirts and ties to the politics depart-
> ment, who would get dressed, rush onstage, and sing the same song
> that had just been sung. By the end of the evening the shirts were
> stained with sweat and everybody in the audience knew all the songs.
> The music department won, as they always did, and English was near
> the back. The English department never won any of the college's
> contests. There aren't any English songs about the Long March.

At Sichuan University, we read this excerpt in the middle of Sep-
tember. I showed some old photographs from the Long March Singing
Contest, and I asked the class if there was anything that struck them.
Somebody from the College of Literature and Journalism raised his hand.

"We just did this last week," he said. He explained that Sichuan University had held a singing competition in honor of the upcoming National Day. October 1 would mark seventy years since the founding of the
People's Republic, and this year's celebration was planned to be especially elaborate. It would be the first major political anniversary under
Xi Jinping.

"It was the same as in your book," he continued. "They also sang only
a few songs, because there aren't many songs about it." Some students
laughed, and he said, "But actually it's not correct that this makes the

judging difficult. If all the songs are the same, then it's easier to tell who is doing a better job. It's easier to compare."

I had never considered that possibility, but it made sense. I told him that maybe I should go back and edit that part of the book. After class, somebody sent a link to a story on the university's website:

PRAISE THE NEW CHINA AND SING THE NEW ERA

Celebrating the 70th Anniversary of the
Founding of the People's Republic of China,

Sichuan University Holds a Faculty and Staff Choral Competition

A series of photographs looked exactly like the old days in Fuling: long rows of singers, all dressed identically, standing against a backdrop of red Communist flags. There was a picture of a stern-faced Party official standing before a podium. The report quoted her speech:

> I hope that in the next choral competition, everyone will integrate their love for the Motherland into their beautiful singing, sing praises for the glorious history of the great Motherland, cherish the historical footprints of the revolutionary martyrs, reflect the character of Sichuan University faculty and staff, and gather together to realize the majestic national rejuvenation.

According to the story, more than twenty-six hundred faculty members had participated. The winners were listed, along with song titles: "My Motherland and Me," "I Love You, China," and "The Motherland Will Not Forget."

In my new life as a teacher, the city was bigger, the campus was bigger—even the students were bigger. Young Chinese were now more than six times as likely to attend college than the students of their parents' generation. Universities had been expanded or rebuilt on a scale that was almost unimaginable, and the per capita GDP was sixty-five times higher than it had been at the start of the Reform era. More than a quarter of a billion farmers had been transformed into urban citizens. But I still taught next door to the College of Marxism, and the university still hosted old-school Communist rallies. The fact that the anniversary numbers were getting higher only underscored how much had stayed the same. Same rallies, same images, same songs—"The Motherland Will Not Forget." Of course it won't forget, not with the same things happening over and over. Even the cadres of the same Party wore the same expressions while giving the same speeches with the same words. For a returning teacher, this was a mystery: How could a country experience so much social, economic, and educational change, while the politics remained stagnant or even regressive?

In nonfiction class, Serena was one of the students who seemed to have missed out on improved nutrition. She stood barely over five feet, and she was small-boned, with a quick smile. Like most of her classmates, she dressed in an informal, nondescript manner: jeans, T-shirts, plain skirts. She had chosen her English name after Serena van der Woodsen, the protagonist of the American teen television drama *Gossip Girl*. In Serena's hometown of Nanchong, a fourth-tier city in northeastern Sichuan, she had studied English by watching *Gossip Girl* episodes online. Now the name embarrassed Serena, who believed that it marked her as a bumpkin, but she felt it was too late to change.

In one essay, she described herself as "low-income class." Neither of her parents had attended university, and they worked middling jobs in Nanchong, which had a reputation for being inward-looking. Online, people mocked it as "Yuzhou-chong," which means, roughly, "Universe-chong," because citizens were so wrapped up in the petty issues of their provincial town. Serena's admission to Sichuan University had been a stroke of great fortune for the family. Anybody who tested into a 985 university paid much less than she would at a lower-tier institution, which was one of many motivations for high school kids to study hard. It was the opposite of the American system, in which elite universities are typically more expensive. Serena's tuition at Sichuan University cost about seven hundred dollars per year.

Admission to the college was one of many ways in which Serena had started to escape the Nanchong universe. Her attitude toward gender issues was another point of departure. Years ago, Serena's mother had temporarily quit working in order to help support her daughter's studies. As far as Serena was concerned, this had been a waste of the woman's talents. She wrote in an essay:

> My mother used to hand in all her money to my dad, stopped working, and became very dependent. She has realized it, regretted it, so there is not much I could say. Sometimes I feel sorry for them because they haven't learned much, sometimes I feel sorry for us [college students] that we are in this "gilded cage."

Chinese college students tend to be cloistered, and the Jiang'an Campus was surrounded by a high wall that ran for more than four miles—twice the length of the famous wall around the Forbidden City in Beijing. Serena was among the students who chafed at the campus restrictions, and she was outspoken in class discussions. Every week, she positioned herself at the front of the room, and she immediately established herself as perhaps the best writer in the group. Her presence as the only rejected student was a constant reminder of my own poor judgment.

One of my goals was to have students undertake reporting projects beyond the campus walls. I had never attempted such a thing in Fuling, and I wasn't sure if it would cause problems at Sichuan University. Fenton told me that even the journalism majors rarely did much reporting.

Their coursework focused primarily on theory, and on the few occasions when students researched off-campus, they invariably worked in groups under close supervision. In the current political climate, Chinese journalists were strictly limited in terms of what they were allowed to cover, and many young people were fleeing the field. On the Jiang'an Campus, it seemed symbolic that the journalism department was in the same building as the College of Marxism.

By week four of the semester, the grounds outside my window had been landscaped with freshly laid sod and a network of cement paths. One day, workers arrived with dozens of trees in flatbed trucks, and by the afternoon the paths were shaded. Working in such an environment made me impatient, and I decided that the students were ready to start reporting. I introduced some techniques for interviewing, and students practiced by talking to workers on campus. When I asked them to submit research proposals, they were more adventurous than I had expected:

[I want to research] a gay bathroom near the Dongmen Daqiao. I know it sounds like a crazy and bold idea, but I also think it has some value. It reflects the living of this sexual minority group and problems that cannot be ignored.

Chengdu Jiuyuan Bridge and bar street. There are many stories happen there, for love, freedom, and sex. I want to talk about the Chengdu bar culture. I like drinking, so I have some experience there, and I heard some stories.

I was in hospital for a long time in my childhood. I changed from hospital to hospital. I met doctors who were irresponsible and left lifelong pain on their patients, and also those devoted and friendly. Hospital is a great place [for research], where you can see how people deal with death, the relationship between patients and doctors, and even, we can see a very small part of China's medical care system.

In Serena's proposal, she wrote:

I want to write about a previous Protestant and now Catholic woman who volunteered to work in church. Depending on the information I can gather, my topic will probably be how religion works in China, like how non-religious people view religious groups, especially inside a family.

———

At the end of every day, my family ate dinner on our balcony. We lived on the nineteenth floor of a forty-three-story building, and our view looked south and east to the Jin River. In late afternoon, the autumn temperature was pleasant, and a soft light reflected silver on the water. It was rare to see more than a few miles into the distance. Chengdu is situated at the western edge of a deep basin, bordered by the high massif of the Himalayas, whose peaks often shed a heavy fog onto the city. On a typical evening, when we ate dinner, the far end of the Jin vanished into the mist, and the great cities of China felt a world away: eight hundred miles to Hong Kong, twelve hundred to Shanghai. We were closer to Hanoi than to Beijing.

Like many parts of Sichuan, Chengdu has a reputation for being self-contained—a city of the basin. There has always been a strong community of artists, poets, and novelists, and during our first month, a group of writers and other literary people invited Leslie and me to dinner. We met in a restaurant that was perched high on a covered bridge above the Jin. At dinner, the hosts complained about the political climate.

"This is the worst it's been for many years," said one man who was involved in publishing.

"You're lucky that your books were already published," another writer said to me. "They couldn't be published now."

My first book to be translated on the mainland had appeared in 2011, the year before Xi Jinping came to power. Leslie's book, *Factory Girls*, had been published in Chinese two years later, when the climate had already started to tighten. Once a book was published, it was rarely yanked from the shelves, but nowadays editors had become more cautious about putting out new material. Earlier in 2019, I had published a book in the U.S. about Egypt, but my Shanghai publisher decided that it was impossible to put out a Chinese translation.

At dinner, I explained that the censors were wary of anything about the Arab Spring. "They don't want the word *zhengbian* in a book, even if it's about another country," I said. In Chinese, the term means "coup d'état."

"I'm not surprised," one writer said. "Especially with the protests in Hong Kong."

The writers were still working on new projects, but they planned to wait for a better moment to publish. It was a common experience for Chinese intellectuals, who were forced to negotiate the ebbs and flows of Party control.

One writer teased Leslie and me about our timing. He noted that we had moved to Cairo in 2011, during the first year of the Arab Spring; we had witnessed the rise of the Muslim Brotherhood, the subsequent military coup, and the massacres that were carried out by the Egyptian security forces. In 2016, we had returned to America shortly before Donald Trump was elected.

"Everywhere you go, something bad happens," the writer said. "And now you've come to China. So something bad is probably going to happen here, too!" All of us laughed, and somebody raised a toast; the conversation moved on. There was wood all over the restaurant and I should have knocked it, but that wasn't something people did in Sichuan.

CHAPTER TWO

The Old Campus

October 2019

I N THE 1990S, FULING TEACHERS COLLEGE OCCUPIED A LUSH, GARDEN-
like campus, which was situated on the steep eastern bank of the Wu
River, about a mile from where the tributary emptied into the Yangtze. Back then, the college was a three-year institution that awarded only
associate's degrees. It was home to around two thousand students, a figure that, in the years since, had increased to more than twenty thousand. Such growth was common among Chinese institutions of higher
education. Many universities in Sichuan and Chongqing had increased
their enrollments tenfold, and a number of teachers colleges, including the one in Fuling, had been upgraded to four-year institutions that
awarded bachelor's degrees. In 2005, as part of this transition, the Fuling college was relocated to a stretch of previously undeveloped farmland on the Yangtze's northern bank. This move followed the lines of the
local rivers—one mile downstream on the Wu, five miles upstream on
the Yangtze—as if the entire institution had been picked up and hauled
away atop some massive ship. Once the college had been reassembled on
the brand-new campus, it was also given a brand-new name: Yangtze
Normal University.

Afterward, a small section of the old campus was sold to developers.

They tore down the gymnasium, the auditorium, and a few other build-ings, replacing them with high-rise apartment blocks. A middle school opened at one end of the site. But there was a long delay in demolishing the majority of the old campus. Locals told me that private developers had expressed interest, but college administrators set a high price. After developers refused to meet the offer, the administrators responded with one of the classic moves in Reform-era bargaining.

In the Peace Corps, we called this tactic "the walk-away." Back then, a volunteer's monthly stipend was the equivalent of $120, but locals sometimes assumed that foreigners had endless supplies of money. Even the simplest transaction—say, the purchase of a bottle of Wahaha-brand water at a kiosk—could grind to a halt because the merchant demanded a 50 percent markup. Occasionally, it was necessary to turn around, take a few steps, and pretend that I was leaving. Almost every time, the mer-chant came running, Wahaha in hand.

It's one thing to execute a walk-away over fifteen cents' worth of Wa-haha, and another thing when the commodity in question is a virtually intact college campus. But that was a basic principle of Reform-era busi-ness: there's no difference between thinking big and thinking small. And so the administrators padlocked the doors of the old college buildings, cut off virtually all maintenance, and abandoned the site. The roads and pathways remained open, and as the years passed, the campus became a kind of pilgrimage for former students. In a country where so many fa-miliar structures had been torn down or remodeled beyond the point of recognition, it was rare to see an unaltered piece of the past. As my Fu-ling students entered middle age, they made nostalgic visits to the old campus, and they often sent beautiful, eerie pictures: vines growing into the windows of our old teaching building, wildflowers covering the cin-der basketball courts where we used to play.

I had always assumed that my former home would be long gone by the time I moved back to southwestern China. But that fall, when I made my first trip back to Fuling, the old campus was still there. In an email, I mentioned offhandedly to my former student Emily that I planned to visit the site, and before I knew it, she had arranged to escort me there with two classmates. Shortly after I arrived in town, they pulled up in a shiny black Volkswagen sedan with heavily tinted windows.

The driver was a man named North. I still remembered the English names that they had used in my classroom: sitting in the back seat of the Volkswagen, next to Emily, was a former student called Jones. The car's interior was impeccably clean, and North had placed a sheet of cardboard atop the passenger-side floorboard. After climbing in, I placed my feet carefully on the cardboard, and I complimented North on the new vehicle. Like anybody who had grown up in the countryside, he instinctively deflected the praise.

"It's not new," he said. "One year old."

North was among the few former students who had become entrepreneurs, and as far as I knew, he was the last one to make the jump to business. A large majority of his peers were still teaching, like Emily and Jones. She was at a local elementary school, and he taught high school English. By now, some of their classmates had as little as a decade left before they reached retirement age for Chinese teachers: sixty for men, fifty-five for women.

A handful of former students had become cadres. In my literature class, all students had acted out scenes from Shakespeare, and certain characters continued to develop over the years, like plays that never ended. One girl who performed Juliet—wearing a red dress, her black hair brushed straight, standing atop a wooden desk in the balcony scene—later worked for the Fuling government bureau that managed the one-child policy. The best Hamlet I ever taught died in Horatio's arms, joined the Communist Party, moved to Tibet, and became a cadre in the Propaganda Department.

And then there were the entrepreneurs. Though there weren't many, they stood out, because Reform business stories had their own Shake-spearean qualities. One boy in my freshman class—clever and mischie-vous, with a grin that usually augured trouble—was later suspended from his government-assigned teaching position in Guang'an, Deng Xiao-ping's hometown. Reportedly, he had struck a student, and after the sus-pension he went west, seeking his fortune in Qinghai province, high on the Tibetan Plateau. He wasn't one of the students who sent letters, but other students sent letters about him. They seemed to take pleasure in the fact that so many good things could come from smacking a pupil. Willy, another former student who had become a teacher, and who also hailed from Deng's home region, wrote about his peer:

> He was sent to Guang'an to teach in 1999. And one year later, he was fined 1,000 yuan and his teaching was suspended for one year be-cause he punished one of his students by whipping the hand with a wooden stick. The student had failed in the exam. Later, [the teacher] started learning to drive and worked as a cab guy for one year. After that he was asked to go back to teach, but he refused and asked for sick leave. The same year he went to Qinghai and worked as a driver again. Two years later he started a private cab service company owning 20 cabs and hiring more than 30 drivers, all from Sichuan. It is said that he also had very tense relation with his wife and he had affairs with a lot of Sichuan girls working in Qinghai KTV centers. Former Fu-ling guys said that he is very *huaxin* [lecherous] and of course he is said to be one of the few millionaires among former Fuling yahoos.

Two of North's college roommates had also become unexpectedly successful. Like North, they had grown up poor, but they entered busi-ness at a time when there was still a frontier quality to the new economy. In the years since, the climate had become notoriously competitive, and now it was rare for a middle-aged person to abandon a stable career in order to strike out as an entrepreneur.

North seemed a particularly unlikely candidate for such a midlife change. As a student, he had been the *banzhang*, or class monitor, a position that generally went to a boy or a girl who was politically reliable. After being encouraged by college authorities, North had dutifully joined the Communist Party, but he didn't seem to care much about politics. He rose to *banzhang* for other reasons: he had good judgment, he was calm, and he was popular among his peers. He had a reputation for being meticulous and risk-averse. He had selected his English name in part because north is the traditional direction of authority in China: faraway Beijing. He had also read in a history book that there was once a British prime minister named North. The history book failed to mention that Lord Frederick North, the Earl of Guilford, was mostly distinguished by having held office during the period in which the empire lost its American colonies.

When it came to making the leap to business, North's thinking was characteristically deliberate. He weighed the disadvantages to starting out as an older person—less energy, less freedom, less flexibility. But he figured there were lots of other Chinese just like him. In 2019, the government identified his cohort, ranging in age from forty-five to forty-nine, as the most populous of any five-year grouping, because they had been born shortly before the implementation of the one-child policy. North believed that his advantage was that he understood his generation. In particular, he understood the rural people who had transitioned to city life, and he knew the things that these individuals would need as they grew older. And one of those things, in North's opinion, was elevators.

He explained the business model while driving the Volkswagen to the old campus. We followed a brand-new road along the Yangtze's northern bank, in an area that used to be farmland. When I lived in Fuling, the urban population was around 185,000, a figure that had nearly tripled in the years since. The most intense growth occurred in the early 2000s, when the government relocated large numbers of migrants from communities that were being flooded by the Three Gorges Dam.

We passed a series of high-rise buildings that had been constructed for dam relocations. "A lot of those buildings still don't have elevators," North said. He explained that construction had often been rushed, because of the scale of the project—across the region, more than two million people had been resettled. "Even some buildings with twelve stories don't have elevators," he said.

North's company specialized in organizing residents, formulating fee plans, and installing elevators. He told me that China's aging population had also factored into his business plan. "A lot of the residents were young when they built those places," he said. "Now they're getting older, so it's harder for them to walk up all those stairs."

We crossed a towering suspension bridge that hadn't existed when I lived in the city. Back then, the Yangtze's surface was broken by waves and rapids, and even from a great height it was possible to sense the power of the river. But today the brown water looked as still and flat as the top of a lake. The road entered a short tunnel and followed the eastern bank of the Wu.

From the back seat, Emily and Jones asked questions about Chengdu: where my family lived, what the university students were like, how Natasha and Ariel were adjusting to Chinese school. But North had his own metric for analyzing my new life in the city.

"What floor do you live on?" he asked while he was driving.

"The nineteenth."

"How many floors are there in your building?"

"More than forty."

"How many apartments per floor?"

"Four."

"How many elevators?"

I had to think for a moment. "Three," I said.

"That must be a very good building," North said. "Usually they would have only two elevators for a building like that."

There was an entrance gate to the old campus, but nobody was on duty. North drove through the open gate, following a narrow road bordered on both sides by overgrown bushes. We passed faded signs with government slogans:

THE PEOPLE'S CITY IS BUILT BY THE PEOPLE
THE PEOPLE'S CITY SERVES THE PEOPLE

BUILD A HYGIENIC CITY
CREATE CULTURED URBAN CITIZENS

The road ended at a courtyard in the heart of campus. On one side of the courtyard stood the college library that used to serve as a backdrop for class photographs. The library's yellow paint had faded, and some of the windows on the lower floors had been broken and replaced with sheets of plywood. Spindly trees grew wild on the roof.

North parked the Volkswagen, and the four of us walked up a stone stairway to the library's entrance. The front door had been secured with a heavy chain and padlock. Above the door hung a weathered nylon propaganda banner of the type that is ubiquitous on Chinese campuses:

BUILD A NATIONAL CIVILIZED CITY
AND A NATIONAL HYGIENIC DISTRICT

I AM AWARE, I PARTICIPATE,
I SUPPORT, I AM SATISFIED

"Look at that old slogan," Jones said. "You don't see that one anymore."

He commented that the message above the library, and most other signs on campus, must have been from the early 2000s, when Fuling was undergoing its most intense urbanization. For an educated middle-aged Chinese, dating propaganda was a kind of political archaeology. The characters themselves could be excavated: sometimes, beneath the surface, a word indicated the opposite of its meaning. The fact that many signs used the term *hygienic* suggested that the city had been dirty at the time. Likewise, repeated references to Fuling as *national* indicated that leaders must have been self-conscious about their provincial status. And whenever a slogan put words into the reader's mouth—*I Support, I Am Satisfied*—it was a sure bet that some citizens had been neither supportive nor satisfied. Probably some of these folks had been riverside residents who ended up in twelfth-floor apartments without elevators.

In the 1990s, the city had been dirty, but the campus was immaculate. Labor was cheap, and Fuling Teachers College employed a large gardening crew. There was never any trash lying around, and bushes and trees were pruned to perfection. It seemed that everywhere I went on campus, I saw workers busy with shears and shovels.

One of Emily's cousins, an uneducated man named Liu, had been part of the gardening crew. She had grown up on campus, where her family lived in the same building as me. Now we headed in that direction, picking our way carefully across a section of broken stairs. We passed a small garden with stone tables and benches that had almost vanished beneath a tangle of bushes.

"Do you remember when we performed the play here?" Emily asked.

I still had faded photographs from that class—a beautiful spring afternoon in 1997. The students had prepared scenes from *A Midsummer Night's Dream*, in which Emily performed the role of Titania. She had always been a good actress, with a calm, confident presence, and she understood literature. She had taken her English name from Emily Brontë.

"I used to play here a lot when I was a child," she said. "We loved being on the campus."

Emily's father was a math professor who was known to be the most decorated academic in Fuling. Unlike most of her rural classmates, Emily had written in some detail about her parents' experiences during the Cultural Revolution. During my first semester, in 1996, she submitted an essay:

> When my parents were of my age, the whole country was in a great confusion: politics went first, intellectuals were said to have the tendency to follow Capitalism, so they were assigned to basic units to accept reformation. My father was one of them. In the following 8 years after he graduated from Sichuan University, he worked in a small coal mine.

The mine was located in a mountainous region south of Fuling, but Emily's father made the best of his circumstances. He helped the mine administrators balance their books, and they appreciated his work and treated him well. As a result, his Cultural Revolution experience turned out to be far better than that of most Chinese intellectuals. The family of his older sister didn't have the same luck. They were sent to another remote place, where the father was beaten repeatedly at political rallies. He died young, and his children were stranded in a poor village where their class background was held against them. This was why Cousin Liu's education ended in middle school.

For Emily, the story of this side of her family was lost in the blankness of the recent past. Once, she wrote about Cousin Liu:

> I don't know much about the history of my cousin's family, because he and his brothers never talk about it. My father sometimes says something, but he is far from a good story teller. So what I know are only some fragments. And when my father tries to start a conversation about the past, my cousins say, "It's the history," and stop at that. Never have I heard them complain about the past.

In the early 1990s, in an effort to support these relatives, Emily's father invited Cousin Liu to live with them in Fuling. The professor also arranged for the job with the campus gardening crew. Cousin Liu always expressed gratitude for his uncle's generosity, but this period had been hard on the boy, who was naturally intelligent. Younger relatives like Emily and her two siblings excelled in academics and eventually tested into universities; meanwhile, Cousin Liu was forced to work with his hands. As with so many lives during this period, it was partly a matter of timing. If Cousin Liu had been the same age as Emily, he would have had better educational opportunities, and his family's class background wouldn't have mattered as much.

All of us lived in the same six-story building, which represented the most elite residence on campus. Emily's father received a spot because of his scholarly achievements, and the Communist Party secretary, the highest official at the college, also resided there. The administration had designated two apartments for Adam and me because we were foreigners. In many ways, the conditions were basic—there was no heat, and the bare cement floors were cold in winter. But the apartments were spacious, and they had beautiful views of the rivers.

Now Emily led us to the old neighborhood. There were around twenty gray buildings, all of them six stories high and arranged around courtyards. In the mid-1990s, most urban Chinese lived in housing that was provided by their *danwei*, or government work units, and this had been the liveliest part of campus. I always loved walking here in late afternoon, when children played in the courtyards while their parents prepared dinner.

Today, nobody was outside in the neighborhood. Like the library, the residential buildings had trees growing from the roofs; in the temperate climate of the Yangtze Valley, it doesn't take long for foliage to overwhelm an abandoned structure. At my old building, departed residents had left potted plants on their balconies, and long branches and vines dangled down the stucco exterior like the hanging gardens of Babylon. Some windows were broken and the front door stood ajar.

We climbed the interior staircase to the top floor. A few holdouts still lived in some of the buildings, but we didn't see any signs of life here. I knocked on the door of my old apartment—no answer. The ground-floor unit that once belonged to Emily's family was also silent. Her parents now lived in another part of Fuling, and I asked her if they missed this area.

"I don't think so," Emily said. "They didn't like being on the ground floor. They always said it was too dark, and we had problems with rats and bugs." She continued, "I liked it, though. I still have dreams that I'm living here. Sometimes I wake up from one of those dreams and I don't know where I am."

Emily had been the youngest in her class, and she had aged well. Her hair was still black, and she had high cheekbones and pretty, arched eyebrows. Her parents had survived the Maoist years relatively unscathed, but they suffered tragedy during the Reform era. Over the years, Emily had written me about their struggles, and I knew that this was one reason she had returned to live in Fuling after some time as a migrant in the south. Today, though, she seemed happy, and she had dressed up for our pilgrimage. She wore white sandals and a pretty flowered skirt, and her hair was tied up in a ponytail. It was easy to recognize the bright-eyed twenty-year-old who had sat in my class in 1996.

We walked around the back of the building, which was shadowed by the campus wall. "Students used to go here at night to *tan lian'ai*," Emily said, laughing. The phrase is a Chinese indirection—literally, it means "talk about love," although it can include making out or even sex. In the 1990s, the Fuling college had strict rules against any romantic behavior. Students were fined if they were caught holding hands, and anybody known to be dating was banned from joining the Communist Party. The few courageous love-talkers usually went to hidden places like the back of our building. "My sister and I would hear them at night," Emily said.

We followed another series of cracked staircases to the teaching building. The front door was padlocked beneath a metal propaganda sign:

THE FULING SPIRIT:
UNIFIED AND PRACTICAL
CULTURED AND HONEST
HARDWORKING AND CREATIVE
UNYIELDING TO OTHERS

We made a circuit of the building, picking our way through the weeds. Through some open windows, we could see a lecture hall with rows of dust-covered desks. Emily, North, and Jones talked about some of the stories we had covered in literature class: *Beowulf, Hamlet*, "The Celebrated Jumping Frog of Calaveras County." Students usually had very detailed memories from this period, because it represented such an important transition in their lives. Now North brought up another lesson.

"Do you remember when you and Adam voted?" he said. "You had your ballots and you showed them to us."

"You voted for Clinton," Emily said.

"I remember that really well," North said.

My memory of the event was also strong, although it always made me a little uncomfortable. "The college wasn't happy about that," I said.

"Of course they weren't happy!" North said, laughing. "I remember that, too."

As the first Americans to teach at the college, Adam and I had been bound to make political transgressions. There wasn't any real context for our presence: nobody in the city could tell me for certain if any Americans had ever lived there. I met a few elderly people who claimed to remember some American residents in the 1940s, but they had no details.

Many years after I left the city, I learned that the memories were partly correct. In the 1940s, there had been a few North Americans in Fuling, but they were Canadian, not American. In Toronto, I met a man named Robert Hilliard, who had been born in Fuling in 1943. Hilliard's father and great uncle were physicians who served in Fuling as medical missionaries under the auspices of the United Church of Canada, a Protestant denomination. Along with others from the church, Hilliard's great uncle helped build and staff Fuling's first modern hospital. The missionaries chose an uncrowded site on the outskirts of town, partway up the steep hillside of the Yangtze's southern bank. They wanted to situate the hospital high enough so that the breeze from the river valleys would alleviate the brutal summer heat.

Fuling's main hospital still occupies the same site today. But what was once the edge of town is now the heart of the central district. The Yangtze breeze is also effectively gone, having been blocked by the forest of high-rises that have been built during the past twenty years. At the Fuling hospital, there's no plaque or memorial commemorating the original founders. Robert Hilliard's family was evacuated in 1944, during the Second World War, when Fuling often suffered from Japanese air raids. In 1941, one of these raids destroyed the Protestant church, which was never rebuilt.

After the Communists came to power, in 1949, virtually all North Americans who remained in the country were sent home. In August of that year, the U.S. State Department issued a white paper that attempted to explain how the United States, which had supported Chiang Kai-shek's Kuomintang government, had "lost" China to Mao's revolutionaries. The document ran for more than a thousand tortured pages, the first of which explained: "This is a frank record of an extremely complicated and most unhappy period in the life of a great country to which the United States has long been attached by ties of closest friendship."

The same month, the State Department recalled Leighton Stuart, its ambassador to China. Stuart had been born in China, the son of a

Presbyterian missionary, and he had served as president of Yenching University in Beijing. In the 1930s and 1940s, Americans who had grown up in China represented important connections to the United States. The author Pearl S. Buck, who introduced China to so many American readers, had also been born to missionary parents.

In 1949, Mao Zedong responded to the American departure with an essay titled "Farewell, Leighton Stuart!" Mao derided American democracy as "another name for the dictatorship of the bourgeoisie," and he took particular offense at one of the key words in the white paper: *friendship*. Mao wrote: "So that's how things stand: the 'international responsibilities' of the United States and its 'traditional policy of friendship for China' are nothing but intervention against China." The essay ended on a triumphant note: "Leighton Stuart has departed and the White Paper has arrived. Very good. Very good. Both events are worth celebrating."

In the 1990s, I had never heard of Leighton Stuart, and neither had any of the other Peace Corps volunteers. But every student in our classrooms knew the name. Mao's essay was part of the national curriculum, with Chinese high school students memorizing excerpts. Years after I left Fuling, Willy described the experience of reading Mao's essay aloud with his classmates. "We sure felt proud at that time," he wrote in an email. "It felt like it was one voice from all the Chinese people. I remember that when we read the text, we were reading in a very passionate and loud voice."

My Peace Corps cohort was known as China 3. The agency has always numbered its volunteer groups, perhaps because it implies a sense of mission. The Peace Corps was founded by President John F. Kennedy, in 1961—the year of Saturn 1 and Sputnik 9. In the same way that the rockets went up in sequence, each Peace Corps cohort was intended to travel to a distant land, build on the work of predecessors, and then return home. And just like the rockets, the Peace Corps was a Cold War endeavor. The program was inspired by *The Ugly American*, a 1958 novel that warned American readers that the Soviets were doing a better job of grassroots work in the developing world. During the Mao era, Chinese propaganda campaigns targeted the Peace Corps, portraying volunteers as tools of capitalists and imperialists.

By the time I signed up, most volunteers were only vaguely aware of this history. Time had moved on, or maybe it had stopped—that was the era of *The End of History and the Last Man*, the 1992 book by Francis Fukuyama, who declared the triumph of Western liberal democracy. Our moment was essentially nonpolitical, because the threat of nuclear war seemed to be over, and terrorism wasn't yet part of the national consciousness. As an ideology, Communism seemed dead. The year that I went to Fuling, the Peace Corps also sent volunteers to Russia, Poland, Romania, and other former Soviet-bloc states that had supposedly transitioned to democracy.

Of the more than eighty countries that accepted Peace Corps volunteers that year, only China still called itself Communist. One reason why the Peace Corps was based in Sichuan province was to curry favor with native son Deng Xiaoping. As part of Deng's Reform and Opening, China was expanding the study of English, which required more instructors. As a result, almost all volunteers were sent to teachers colleges in remote regions. But many cadres remained wary of the American agency. The name "Peace Corps"—Heping Dui in Chinese—had been so tarnished by propaganda that it was a major impediment in negotiations between the two countries. At one point, the Peace Corps even considered calling their China program Xiandaihua Dui, or "Modernization Corps," because the nation's leaders were so obsessed with development. But they finally settled on a different title: Meizhong Youhao Zhiyuanzhe, or "U.S.–China Friendship Volunteers."

But as Mao once wrote, even *friendship* was a loaded word. The Chinese didn't want too many friends arriving at once, so my group of China 3 consisted of only fourteen volunteers. Before joining, none of us had taken a single class in Chinese language, history, politics, or culture. Collectively we had zero experience working in the developing world. One volunteer from Mississippi had never been on an airplane before. Most of us came from the Midwest or the South, where our families had modest means. For a provincial American without a lot of money, the Peace Corps was a good way to go overseas.

Upon arrival in Chengdu, we trained for two months. Peace Corps administrators tried to prepare us for the level of distrust that we were likely to encounter at our teaching sites, but it was impossible to identify every potential pitfall. During the first semester in Fuling, my most powerful classroom experiences involved incidents in which I made a statement that touched, even obliquely, on some sensitive aspect of Chinese history or politics.

At such moments, the room would fall silent, and students would stare at their desks. When I looked up from the lectern and saw the bowed heads, my heart raced and my face grew hot. I found myself stammering, and I tried to change the subject; often, it took a few minutes before the mood returned to normal. Initially, I considered these awful moments to be the times when I felt most like a foreigner. But I came to realize it was the opposite: my body was experiencing something that must be common to young Chinese. The Party had created a climate so intense that the political became physical.

Like all Chinese undergraduates, Fuling students took mandatory political courses every semester. Some of these classes focused on the shameful history of the Opium Wars, when Great Britain and other foreign powers imposed unfair treaties on China. A subject like English—the language of China's original oppressor—was especially charged. The college expected Adam and me to teach about American and British culture, but we weren't provided with foreign textbooks. Instead, every student was given a Party-published book called *Survey of Britain and America*.

The chapter about American history began, naturally enough, with China: "The Indians living in America originated from Asia some 25,000 years ago." After listing some Marxist details about the European discovery of the New World ("it also opened up fresh ground for the rising bourgeoisie"), the text continued to the founding of the United States ("the Constitution of 1787 established the dictatorship of the American bourgeoisie"). A section about contemporary society made some dubious claims. ("Most New Englanders, therefore, are working in factories today. They are good at making watches and clocks.") There were some odd examples of American slang. ("For example, 'draw one' or 'shoot one' means 'pour a cup of coffee.'")

Such details might be questionable, but at least they weren't offensive. The tone changed, though, in chapter 4, "Social Problems":

> Homosexuality is a rather strange social phenomenon that most people can hardly understand. It widely spreads. One reason for this may be the despair in marriage or love affairs. Some people fail in marriage and become disappointed with it. So they decide no longer to love the opposite sex, but instead begin to love a person of the same sex as a return of hatred to the opposite. Another reason may be that some people just want to find and do something "new" and "curious," as the Americans are known as adventurous. So they practiced homosexuality as a kind of new excitement. Through this, we can see clearly the spiritual hollowness of these people and the distortion of the social order.
>
> Drug-abuse is another social problem. . . .

The chapter concluded with a Marxist explanation of why some people become gay:

> The most important reason is the capitalist system of America. In this capitalist society, although science and technology is highly advanced, some people are suffering from spiritual hollowness. Thus they start to look for things curious and exciting.

Initially, Adam and I believed that we could convince students that the book was wrong. How hard can it be to explain to educated people that capitalism does not cause homosexuality? But we quickly realized that this was a terrible idea. In a Chinese classroom, there was no tradition of questioning an official text, and any attempt to do so was likely to backfire. Once an idea was placed in front of students, in print, it tended to stick.

The only solution was to keep our classes as far as possible from texts like *Survey of Britain and America*. During training, the Peace Corps had tried to prepare us for this challenge, which was formidable during a time without internet access. We were told to use realia—objects from everyday life that could be incorporated into lesson plans. Adam and I copied articles from foreign magazines, and we used cassette tapes of American pop music. A couple of times, I structured an entire two-hour class around some pictures or newspaper clippings that my parents had included in a letter.

In the fall of 1996, Adam and I received our absentee ballots for the American presidential election. We both immediately had the same idea: This is perfect realia. One week, each of us took a section of senior students, showed them our ballots, and embarked on a lecture about the U.S. political system. I listed key political vocabulary on the blackboard, and I described the election process. At the end of the lecture, I answered questions, and then I allowed the students to inspect my ballot.

The room became very quiet. One by one, each student took the ballot, studied it, and passed it on to a classmate. There were more than forty students, and by the time I retrieved the ballot and voted for Bill Clinton, the room was so silent, and they were watching with such intensity, that I could feel my pulse thudding in my ears.

Afterward, I waited for the fallout. Two weeks later, a Peace Corps administrator in Chengdu told me that a Fuling official had telephoned to express displeasure with what Adam and I had done. The college left it at that—nobody called us in for a discussion, and we were never told exactly what we could or couldn't talk about in the classroom. With sensitive topics, communication was often indirect. The Fuling cadres assumed that the Peace Corps would pass on the message, and that Adam and I would learn to be more careful.

After Emily graduated, she wrote a letter in which she recalled the semester of the American presidential election:

> Not long after you became my teacher, I read a piece of news comment that said [if] Mr. Clinton took presidency, one of the reasons [why Americans would elect him] was that he would take stronger measure on China. Those days, I hated to see you and Mr. Meier.

She was far more direct than her peers. In class, her opinions often differed from those of the majority, and while she described herself as patriotic, she had never been interested in Party membership. As a young academic, Emily's father had joined one of China's other approved political parties. These organizations often attracted intellectuals who hoped to be part of the system while maintaining some distance from the Communist Party itself. Invariably, such a balancing act was impossible, because the approved parties had no real independence or influence. Even in her twenties, Emily understood the system in a way that her father had not until he was middle-aged. She wrote in another letter:

> I hate political cant because I used to believe in it. The fact that too many people in influential position speak in one way and do in another has been revealed to me with time. I think my father was far more sad than I was when he came to realize this at last in his fifties.

She was among the few students who turned down a government teaching job in order to search for work in the private economy. Usually, these students came from poor families, and they believed that they needed more money than a teaching salary could offer. But there were also some examples from the opposite end of the social spectrum. As a city resident, Emily had the resources, connections, and confidence necessary to make the leap to the private economy. She traveled to Kunming, the capital of Yunnan province, where Cousin Liu had recently established himself. He had left the campus gardening job in hopes of finding something better, although his initial experiences weren't encouraging. In Kunming, he was hired as a ditchdigger for electric lines that were being installed around the expanding city. Over time, Cousin Liu was able to transition to working as a laborer on private construction projects. Then he began to organize and manage his own crew of workers. He had started to become successful by the time Emily arrived in the city, in the summer of 1997.

In Kunming, Emily was joined by her boyfriend, Anry, who was one of North's former college roommates. Anry was among the most athletic students, a handsome, square-jawed boy who came from a remote part of northern Sichuan. His parents were illiterate, but as a child he learned to love poetry, and he became the first from his village to enter college. Like many young literary Chinese in the 1990s, he believed that a poet should be both romantic and angry. For his English name, he dropped the *g*, but Anry remained true to the poetic spirit: he had a quick temper, and he was among the few on campus who were bold enough to "talk about love." He told me later that as a student he had never considered joining the Party because of their restrictions on dating.

Anry was the youngest of four brothers, and he had been designated his family's best hope. This status was common among my Fuling students. All of them had been born before the institution of the one-child policy in 1980, and initially the restrictions were rarely enforced in rural regions. During my last year in Fuling, I taught a section of freshmen who were young enough that their families could have been limited to a single child. But when I surveyed that class of twenty, only one boy had no siblings.

It was far more common for students to have two or more brothers or sisters. In many cases, the families were so poor that parents felt it was necessary to concentrate their resources in the education of the most promising child. Most rural Chinese selected a boy as the chosen one, and often he was the youngest, simply because educational opportunities were improving. It was another example of timing—even members of the same family living in the same village might find vastly different opportunities in the span of a few years. My student Willy had two older brothers who hadn't gone beyond middle school, but everybody contributed to make sure that the youngest made it into college.

In Anry's family, the third brother had also been close to receiving a good education. He entered high school, but his parents decided that they couldn't afford the tuition, and the boy dropped out in order to migrate. He found a factory job on the east coast, where he earned enough to help support Anry's college expenses. The eldest brother also did his part, working for the village government in road construction. This job gave him access to dynamite, and occasionally he took some explosives, detonated them in a lake, and harvested the fish that floated to the surface. Dynamite fishing was illegal in China, but it wasn't uncommon in poor areas. Every now and then, somebody got caught with a short fuse. When this happened to Anry's brother, he was holding the explosives close to his face. He was blinded instantly and both of his hands had to be amputated at the wrists.

The accident occurred less than a month before Anry's graduation. He was still in my class, but it was characteristic that he never mentioned his brother. For rural students, tragedies weren't uncommon, and there was no point in sharing such pain with others. After graduation, Anry reported to his assigned job at a remote middle school, where he spent the first night in the faculty dormitory. The mud-walled building was perched high on a mountaintop, and Anry lay awake, listening to the wind whistle through the cracks in the walls. Ever since the accident, Anry had slept poorly, because his thoughts always turned to his brother, who had a wife and a fourteen-year-old son. Anry knew that now, after years of benefiting from the sacrifices of others, it was his turn to support the disabled brother and his family. The job at the mud-walled school paid the equivalent of less than thirty dollars a month. At the end of that first sleepless night, Anry got out of bed, packed his things, walked down the mountain, and never returned.

He traveled to Kunming to meet Emily. Anry could have worked with Cousin Liu's construction crew, but he wanted something that made better use of his education. Initially, he found a job as a cold-call salesman of dental chairs, working on commission, but he never sold a single chair. He didn't do much better with his next job, which involved selling film for X-ray machines. Next, he tried water pumps. There was no logical connection between these products, and Anry had no idea how to sell things. He walked around the city's newly built districts, carrying brochures and asking questions. Do you know anybody who needs a dental chair? X-ray film? A water pump? At the end of many days, when Anry was exhausted and demoralized, he went to the crowded Kunming train station. He found it calming to sit there alone, watching the migrants come and go.

Emily's job search didn't go much better. She focused on the recruitment centers that were called *rencai shichang*, or "talent markets." But the marketed talents often had little to do with intelligence: many listings for women emphasized height, appearance, and other physical characteristics. Companies often required applicants to stand at least 1.6 meters tall, or five feet, two inches, and Emily was shorter than that.

After weeks of failure, the young couple began to bicker. There had always been some tension: Anry was less interested in politics, and he believed that it was pointless for individuals to try to change the system. He also had more traditional notions about how men and women should

behave. It bothered him that Emily smiled when talking to other men—
Anry told her that she should keep her face completely expressionless.
For a while, she practiced in front of a mirror, trying to learn not to smile.
"At that time I believed everything he said," she told me later.

In the end, they had a migrants' breakup. Connections pulled in different directions: Emily's older sister was working in Shenzhen, in the far
south, whereas Anry knew somebody from his village with a factory job
in Shanghai. Once again, Anry went to the Kunming train station, but
this time, instead of watching the migrants, he bought a ticket and
joined them.

He arrived in Shanghai with less than three dollars in his pocket.
That evening, he slept outside in a public square next to the city's Hong-
qiao station. He couldn't believe how many other young people were in
the square—farm boys and farm girls, and migrants from small cities,
and recent college graduates, all of them sleeping together under the
open sky. Since leaving home, Anry had often recited "Love of Life," a
poem by Wang Guozhen. In the 1990s, Wang was a favorite poet of the
younger generation, so many of whom were on the move:

> *I don't think about success*
> *Since I chose the distant place*
> *Simply travel fast through wind and rain.*

———

In the early years after I left Fuling, former students often wrote about
courtship and marriage. Willy sent a letter from Zhejiang province, where
he had migrated:

> I now know that I had been a frog in a well. There is an awfully
> large distance between Zhejiang and Sichuan province. Here it is
> the Shangrila of the rich. While Sichuan is just the very hell of the

poor . . . There is a great distance between [my girlfriend] and I. I
know we'll never be together if I'm a poor man all my life. Here I
must work hard, hard, and hard.

One of Willy's classmates who had accepted the government-assigned
teaching job wrote:

I'm working in a small village. As you know, I can't make more money
as a teacher in China. But I feel very happy. Because my students
here all respect me and like me very much. . . . Maybe I will have a
girlfriend next year. She is not very pretty and beautiful, but she is
very kind to me.

The people who migrated and the people who stayed to teach often
seemed to describe two different countries. But these disparate experiences were actually connected in the larger system. The teachers in
those obscure Sichuan towns were instructing students who, after completing middle school, often left for the coast with enough basic education to serve as assembly-line workers. All of it was designed for maximum
efficiency, which was why the Fuling college gave out degrees in only
three years, like almost all teachers colleges that hosted Peace Corps volunteers.

In some of the poorest places, the rush to accredit instructors went
all the way to middle school. One of my best students, Linda, had been
the middle school *tongzhuo*, or desk mate, of a quick-minded boy who
tested higher than she did at the end of ninth grade. Because of his
scores, the boy was sent immediately to a three-year institute that specialized in training teachers for primary schools in poor areas. Linda
went on to high school, after which she was selected to enter the Fuling
college. Back then, nobody spoke of algorithms, but clearly there had
been some kind of large-scale calculation. By identifying bright rural
kids and providing them with training that was both narrowed and ac-

celerated, the government produced primary-school teachers who were fully licensed by the age of eighteen.

Of course, these teachers were also bright enough to realize that they were essentially being sacrificed for the sake of the larger system. Linda, by virtue of scoring lower than her *tongzhuo*, had ended up with more education and a better job. But by May 1999, when Linda's first letter arrived at my Beijing office, the *tongzhuo* had fled the remote primary school for better opportunities:

> Nowadays there is a boy who is hunting for me. His name is Huang Dong. He was my classmate in middle school. . . . He only taught in primary school for half a year. After that, he went out and did all kinds of jobs, to be a singer, to be a salesman, and to be vice manager in an investment company in Chengdu. . . . He is kind and brave and aggressive. Most of all, he is very responsible. In a sense, he is trustworth. And above all, he and his family love me very much. Perhaps, he will be my husband in the future.

One of the major contrasts between the two Chinas—the China of the migrants and the China of those who stayed home—was marriage. Traditionally, rural residents married young, and teachers generally followed that pattern. Also like rural Chinese, they generally downplayed any good news. In letters they came across as brutal realists:

> Last winter, I was married with a doctor. He is not very handsome but he is very kind to me. Next spring we will have a baby.

> What makes me happy is that I married an ugly woman who graduated from the math department of Fuling Teachers College.

> [After] graduating Fuling Teachers College, my parents and relatives all wanted to introduce girlfriends to me. . . . So they introduced one

and one, but the one and one passed me and didn't become my wife. There were nearly three dozen girls I knew through their introducing. Some were very fat like pigs; some were so thin that they were the same as flag-sticks and fishing-sticks; some were also very beautiful, but when they saw me, they at once went away and left a word: "The toad wants to eat the meat of the swan." Of course, my family had spent a lot of things and money on my girlfriends.

Now I find a girlfriend finally, she will be my wife after 2000. She isn't beautiful, there are many black points on her face, but I love her, because she has more money than me, maybe I love her money more. . . . I have many things to say, but I can't write out. This letter is typed from my girlfriend's computer.

Migrant marriages were often delayed, and courtships could be complicated. They seemed more likely to suffer breakups, and the breakups were usually permanent. After Emily and Anry parted, they never reunited, although they stayed in touch. A couple of years after Emily moved to Shenzhen, she wrote in a letter:

> I called Anry the other day. I found I was happy to know that he was doing well—he works as the head of Plastic Department in a large factory.

After arriving in Shanghai and sleeping in the public square, Anry had walked six miles to find the contact from his village. The villager gave Anry a place to stay, and every day he visited the gates of factories, inquiring about job opportunities. His degree in English helped him stand out, and within a week he was hired by a Taiwanese manufacturer of plastic computer cases. At the Taiwanese factory, Anry followed the routine of many ambitious young migrants: during the day, he worked, and at night he looked for better work. Soon, he switched to a higher-paying position at a Taiwanese company called DBTel, which produced cordless phones. Every month, Anry sent about a tenth of his salary to his disabled brother.

Anry's college courses had taught him nothing about management, so he began to take night classes and read materials on his own. This was also characteristic of the Reform generation: formal education was important, and so was timing, but nothing mattered more than talent, motivation, and hard work. Occasionally, rejection and missed opportunities turned out to be fortunate. This was true for Linda's husband, who ended up succeeding in private business, and it was also true for the teacher who, after getting suspended for beating his student, made a fortune from taxis on the Tibetan Plateau.

Cousin Liu also benefited from rejection. In Kunming, he proved to have a genius for estimating construction costs. It probably reflected some innate ability for mathematics that ran in the family. Emily always joked that she had missed out on the math gene, but her older sister had it; over time, the sister did well as an accountant in Shenzhen. Their younger brother was perhaps the brightest of the three siblings. He had his father's logical mind, but he struggled to find an outlet, in part because he was socially awkward. As a child, he was bullied by both classmates and teachers—Chinese education tended to be hard on anybody who was different. Nevertheless, Emily's brother tested into college, where he planned to study computers, but he dropped out. After that, he found part-time work as a tutor of *weiqi*, Chinese chess, and he excelled in public competitions of the board game.

Emily worried constantly about her brother's mental health. A couple of times, she asked me to talk to him, but the young man was so withdrawn that it was difficult to carry on a conversation. He seemed traumatized by the intensely competitive routines of his schools, and the family considered seeking psychological help, but such services weren't advanced in places like Fuling. In his spare time, the young man read and reread the ancient philosophical texts of Confucius and Mencius. He often said that he disliked contemporary society. Once, when I asked Emily what she thought was the root of her brother's problem, she said, "He is a victim of modernization."

In contrast, Cousin Liu thrived in the wide-open world of the boomtowns. Kunming builders learned that they could trust Cousin Liu's bids, and soon his construction crew was in high demand. He expanded his operation, started a company, and speculated in real estate. He returned to Chongqing, where he constructed large apartment complexes, and he also had projects in Shaanxi province. By 2010, his net worth was estimated in the tens of millions of dollars, and he sometimes appeared in articles about successful Chongqing entrepreneurs. That year, he donated nearly half a million dollars to charities that supported the poor, an act that was covered in the state press.

Within the genre of Reform stories, there are a number of distinct patterns, themes, and moods. One of the moods is irony. Because Cousin Liu's family background had been considered capitalist, he lost his chance for an advanced education; because he lost his chance for an advanced education, he was forced onto a path that led him to become one of Chongqing's most celebrated capitalists. As a developer, he constructed gleaming new apartment blocks across a broad swath of southwestern and northern China. Meanwhile, back on the campus where Cousin Liu once worked as a lowly gardener, trees grew wild on the roofs of buildings that had been left to rot.

Certain relationships among the Fuling students remained unchanged throughout the years. Emily, Jones, and their classmates still addressed North with the title *banzhang*: "class monitor." In school, North's job had been to collect assignments, arrange study sessions, and convey messages from college leaders. He was an organizer and a connector, and he retained that role after nearly a quarter century. If I wanted an update about a former student, North could usually help.

His information was often elevator-centric. Once, I said that I was about to visit Emily, and North remarked that she lived on the sixth floor of a building on the new campus, and that she had recently inquired about his services. "There are about fifty or sixty residential units, but no elevators," he said of the campus. Another time, I mentioned Grant, a student from a different year. I didn't expect North to know Grant, but his response was immediate. "He lives on the top floor of his building," North said. "He asked me to take a look, but it won't work. There's a car-repair shop on the ground level. You can't put an elevator there."

One day in the fall of 2019, North took me to a project site in Fuling. He had named his business Chuxingyi Dianti Gongsi, or "Travel Easy Elevator Company." North's standard sales pitch was that you should think of an elevator the way you think of a car. He explained this while we walked around the site, which was located in the heart of downtown. It consisted of a twelve-story building that had been constructed in the early 2000s to house migrants from the Three Gorges region.

"In those days, elevators and cars were basically the same," North said. "People didn't have either. But now pretty much everybody has a car. It's a basic tool for transportation. And elevators should still be the same—if you have a car, then you should also have an elevator."

The building had the characteristic look of millennial Chinese construction: aging concrete, small windows, cramped balconies with rusted railings. But a gleaming new glass-and-metal elevator shaft had been attached to the building's exterior, like a splint to a wounded limb. North and I entered the shaft at the ground floor, and he inserted a key into the elevator's console. A set of speakers in the ceiling started playing "Going Home," by Kenny G.

"Going Home" is among the songs that are forever etched into my Fuling memories. Another is an instrumental version of "You Are My

Sunshine," which was played by the low-quality street-cleaning machines that lurched around downtown in the 1990s. The street cleaners looked as if they had been assembled from oversize LEGO sets, with a bizarre assortment of brightly colored brushes and spray hoses that stuck out at all angles. Whenever I heard "You Are My Sunshine," I knew that it was time to find higher ground, because wayward hoses sprayed water at ankle level.

In China, the plot often changed, but the soundtrack did not. In 2019, the first time I returned to downtown Fuling and heard "You Are My Sunshine," my response was pure Pavlovian—I swear that my ankles began to water. But it was all in my mind: now the cleaners were well-designed vehicles with high-pressure hoses that were directed straight down. For more than twenty years, from LEGO-set carts to professional-grade trucks, they had doggedly kept at the street cleaning until they finally got it right. I found it inspiring that throughout this entire process they never stopped playing "You Are My Sunshine."

Kenny G's saxophone had also borne witness to great material progress. "Going Home" had been immensely popular during the 1990s, and over the years it became a tradition to play the song at the conclusion of public events. This was also Pavlovian—in a remarkably short span of time, the most populous nation on earth had conditioned more than a billion citizens to leave events in an orderly fashion the moment they heard Kenny G. When North installed elevators, he always made sure that "Going Home" played on an endless loop. He told me that the song made people feel good about returning to their apartments.

During our visit to the building site, I asked North why it was necessary to use a key to operate the elevator. "It's just like driving a car," he said. He explained that each resident had contributed a different amount toward the construction of the elevator shaft. The price got higher with each floor, so every key was programmed to take the elevator only to the resident's specific landing. It was like owning a car, if your car always went to the same destination while always playing the same song by Kenny G.

North mentioned that one resident on the top floor had refused to pay. As a result, she had to keep trudging up twelve flights in a darkened stairwell where nobody played "Going Home." I asked if anybody ever opted out and then secretly acquired a key from a neighbor.

"It's not common, but I've had it happen," North said. He took out his phone, opened an app, and showed a live video feed: North and me, viewed from above. I looked around and saw a surveillance camera.

"I can watch any of my elevators with this app," he said. He switched the feed to an elevator across town. On the screen, the doors opened and a woman entered. Believing herself to be alone and unobserved, the woman faced the elevator's mirror, leaned close, and began working intently on her makeup. Kenny's sax played while North and I watched the woman fix her face. "See?" he said. "If anybody uses the elevator illegally, it's easy to check. That video stays up for seven days."

North had a partner who handled all of the company's engineering. North's role was essentially that of the *banzhang*: like a good class monitor, he conveyed information to residents, and he negotiated the fee structure for each elevator project. He told me that the process was complicated because, unlike in the past, most buildings no longer belonged to Communist-style work units. For residents who arrived from close-knit villages, a lack of familiarity with neighbors was part of the transition to city life. Elevators were an important part of connecting individuals. "Usually, they haven't even met their neighbors until they start talking about getting an elevator," North said.

During one of my fall visits, I stopped by the new Fuling campus in order to meet the two current Peace Corps volunteers. Officially, the Peace Corps was still called the U.S.–China Friendship Volunteers, and they still numbered their groups. In 2018, Vanessa Gomez had been sent to Fuling as part of China 24, and in the fall of 2019, Austin Frenes arrived with China 25.

Over the years, Peace Corps China had steadily expanded. China 25 consisted of eighty people, nearly six times larger than my cohort. The agency had moved into the less developed provinces of Gansu and Guizhou, where schools often couldn't afford to hire American teachers. Even Fuling, despite its increased prosperity, had difficulty attracting foreign residents. Administrators told me that without the Peace Corps the college wouldn't have had American instructors, because foreigners generally preferred first-tier cities. The volunteers were still paid a monthly stipend, which was one of the few Chinese financial figures that hadn't changed dramatically. Gomez and Frenes told me that they were paid less than three hundred dollars a month.

Another thing that hadn't changed was that the Peace Corps still had political enemies. In the 1990s, Peace Corps administrators feared that hard-core Communist officials would expel the organization, and they advised volunteers to be careful with our personal behavior. The Chinese were so wary that they refused to sign an official agreement with the Peace Corps until the summer of 1998, after volunteers had already been working in the country for five years. In the agreement, the phrase "Peace Corps" appeared only once in a document of several pages. Even the title skirted the issue:

**Agreement Between the Government of the United States of America
and the Government of the People's Republic of China
Concerning the United States Volunteer Program in China**

Nowadays, the Chinese finally seemed comfortable with the Peace Corps, but opposition came from the other side of the Pacific. With China's rapid development, and with increasing tensions over the trade war, some conservative American politicians expressed a desire to end the Peace Corps presence in China. The most outspoken critic was Rick Scott, the Republican junior senator from Florida. On September 5, 2019, Scott demanded that that the Peace Corps permanently relocate all volunteers from China to the Bahamas, in order to assist in the recovery from Hurricane Dorian. Scott wanted this to be accomplished by October 1, the seventieth anniversary of the founding of the People's Republic. The Peace Corps didn't respond to this bit of political grandstanding, and the following month the senator issued another statement: "I'm disappointed that the Peace Corps ignored my request to get out of Communist China. . . . There is no reason the Peace Corps should be using taxpayer dollars to prop up one of our greatest adversaries—a wealthy nation that can fund its own initiatives."

Americans often view the Peace Corps as a traditional development organization, although the agency's goals have never included poverty alleviation. In many ways, the Peace Corps is more like an exchange program: the main purpose is to improve understanding between the United States and other countries. Over the years, as former students became financially successful, I doubted if my teaching had had anything to do with their material rise. I couldn't say that my lessons had helped Anry find his way in Shanghai, or that they showed North how to manage his elevator projects. But I was struck by the little things that students remembered—certain poems from class, or offhand remarks in conversation. Many years after Adam and I had left Fuling, a woman named Andi wrote in an email:

> I didn't even see any foreigners before I went to college. . . . As you know, most of our classmates came from the countryside, including me. We were curious about your drinking bottles, we were interested in your three-dimensional picture books, and we borrowed Adam's color pens again and again, because we had never seen them

before. We were all poor at that time, we were eager to learn, we worked hard at that time.

The memories of our mistakes were also vivid. I never forgot the feeling of stumbling onto some political sensitivity, and I never forgot the terrible silence that descended onto the classroom. When I recalled the lecture with the absentee ballots, it felt like a clumsy lesson by two young teachers who were struggling with a difficult political environment. But this wasn't necessarily a regret. The fact that former students often brought up that same memory simply meant that it was something else we shared.

Once, while visiting Fuling, I ran into a former student named Richard on the street. We hadn't been in contact for years, and he told me that he was happily teaching at a local high school. During our conversation, he mentioned the lecture with the absentee ballots. "That made a deep impression," he said.

Like North, Richard didn't say whether the class had made him feel more positively about American democracy, or if he was inclined to see it, in Mao's words, as "another name for the dictatorship of the bourgeoisie." Either way, the conclusion seemed beside the point. The most important thing was that Richard had been exposed to something new, and he still recalled the class after twenty years.

Following our chance meeting, Richard sent a series of essays that he had written in Chinese about his college experience. One essay described how students had asked Adam questions about American ballads and folk songs. After struggling to describe the music, Adam, who had sung in an a cappella group during college, finally recorded a cassette tape for the students.

When I mentioned this to Adam, he didn't recall the songs or even the act of recording the tape. During that first year, there were so many intense interactions that some incidents vanished from our minds. But Richard remembered. In his essay, he wrote:

In the spring of 1997, Adam gave us a cassette of American ballads that he had learned to sing as a child. . . . There is only one singer and one tone—he sings emotionally from beginning to end. I still have this cassette. Every time I listen, I pay more respect to him who is a teacher, and tears inexplicably fill my eyes.

CHAPTER THREE

The New Campus

October 2019

AT SICHUAN UNIVERSITY, IN ADDITION TO THE NONFICTION CLASS, I also taught two sections of first-year students, who matriculated at a ceremony that was held at the Institute for Disaster Management and Reconstruction. The disaster institute was brandnew, and it had been constructed in the same style as the College of Marxism: light gray exterior, dark tiled roof, upturned eaves. Also like the College of Marxism, the building's entrance featured a golden sign:

SICHUAN UNIVERSITY–HONG KONG
POLYTECHNIC UNIVERSITY

INSTITUTE FOR DISASTER MANAGEMENT
AND RECONSTRUCTION

Before the ceremony, I hadn't met any of the new students. Unlike the undergraduates in the nonfiction class, the first-year students had not applied for my sections. They had been assigned randomly to the half dozen or so teachers who taught the mandatory course called English Composition: Expository, Analytical, and Argumentative Writing. On the day of the ceremony, my department held a short staff meeting for new teachers. We were told that we could prepare our own syllabi, materials, and assignments, provided that the students wrote three papers that fulfilled each of the required types of writing that were listed in the course title.

We were also encouraged to use the two texts that had been provided to each of the new students. One book was *A Writer's Reference*, a style guide that had been published in the United States. The other book was George Orwell's *Animal Farm*. This edition had been published in India, and the front cover featured a drawing of a red-faced pig dressed in a suit and tie and smoking a cigarette. The back cover read:

> *Animal Farm* is, on one level, a simple story about barnyard animals. On a much deeper level, it is a savage political satire on corrupted ideals, misdirected revolutions and class conflict—themes as valid today as they were sixty years ago.

The matriculation was scheduled for two o'clock. We finished the department meeting early, which gave me time to wander around the Institute for Disaster Management and Reconstruction. Inside the front entrance, a "Map of China's Natural Disasters" had been decorated with cartoonlike icons of calamities in different parts of the country: a lightning bolt in western Tibet, a scorched desert in Inner Mongolia. In Sichuan, a panda was accompanied by an inscription: May 12, 2008. That was the date of the Great Sichuan Earthquake, whose epicenter had been less than one hundred miles northwest of Chengdu. The earthquake had had a magnitude of 8.0 and killed nearly seventy thousand people.

A number of the victims were children who died when their school buildings collapsed. Near the map, another large display featured a shocking photograph of a child who had been discovered dead in the wreckage of a school. In the photograph, the boy appeared to be about the age of a kindergartner, and his face, ghost-pale with wide-open eyes, was framed entirely by dirt and rocks. None of the body was visible—it was as if somebody had sliced off a doll's head and dropped it into the rubble. Above the photograph, there was a Chinese national flag and the words:

PROTECT AGAINST RISKS, ELIMINATE
HIDDEN DANGERS, SUPPRESS ACCIDENTS

The ceremony started promptly. It was held one floor above the disaster displays, in an auditorium that had been decorated with a large blue backdrop that read "Welcome to SCUPI 2019." SCUPI—people pronounce it "scoopy"—is an abbreviation for the Sichuan University–Pittsburgh Institute. The dean of the institute, Minking Chyu, began the proceedings with a short speech in which he emphasized diversity, and then he talked about the need for students to speak only English in the classroom.

After the dean finished, a group of six students stood onstage and recited the institute's honor code. One boy read from a printed sheet: "I will contribute to the development of a caring community where compassion for artists and freedom of thought and expression are valued. I will support a culture of diversity by respecting the rights of those who differ from myself." Then a girl spoke about the importance of contributing to scholarly heritage, and another boy mentioned the importance of building "a civil campus environment." At the end, the six students spoke in unison: "This commitment to civility is my promise to Sichuan University–Pittsburgh Institute and to the community of scholars."

All of the speeches were in English. The institute had selected one first-year, a tall, nice-looking boy from the eastern city of Ningbo, to address his classmates. "I had thought about studying abroad after graduation," the student said. "But maybe it would be too hard for me. And staying in China would maybe be too comfortable. I decided that SCUPI would give me a balance between the challenge and the comfort." He continued, "What makes college so memorable? One aspect is freedom. With freedom comes great responsibility."

In the speech, he used the word *freedom* repeatedly. At the end, he said that his favorite poet was Robert Frost, and he recited some lines from "The Road Not Taken."

"Now, my friends, we have chosen the road less traveled by," the student said. "But we can try our best to prove that we made the right choice."

Like so many Chinese public events, the matriculation was highly efficient. All two hundred students wore the same thing—black T-shirts emblazoned with a SCUPI logo—and another fifty or so faculty and administrators attended. The entire ceremony took little more than forty-five minutes, and after it was over, everybody left immediately, without the need for a Kenny G prompt. All of us filed past the Map of China's Natural Disasters and the photograph of the dead child's face. Throughout the ceremony, none of the speakers had referred to the displays, or to the Great Sichuan Earthquake, or even to the fact that the first-year students were celebrating the start of their university careers by gathering in a place whose name included, as a point of institutional focus, the word *disaster*.

When I asked somebody in the administration about the choice of venue, he explained that there was no connection between our program and the Institute for Disaster Management and Reconstruction. It was simply a matter of convenience: SCUPI's campus building had yet to be completed, whereas the disaster institute was ready to host events. And the institute, which had been funded largely by donations from Hong Kong in the wake of the Great Sichuan Earthquake, happened to be located close to SCUPI's temporary headquarters. In the Chinese way, the choice of venue was purely pragmatic, which also meant that during the event, when the speakers found themselves surrounded by images and maps of terrible calamities, there was no reason to say one word about it.

A number of my Sichuan University students had grown up in regions that had been affected by the earthquake. After the disaster, people realized the degree of corruption involved in school construction—they referred to the substandard buildings that collapsed as *doufuzha xiaoshe*, "tofu-dreg schoolhouses." My students had been in primary school at the time of the disaster, and some of them wrote essays about the experience. One girl remembered looking up from her desk and seeing six fluorescent lights swinging crazily from the ceiling. She described the scene after all the children had been evacuated to the schoolyard:

Soon, many pupils began to cry, but no one seemed to comfort them. Maybe their friends were crying now as well. "Why are you crying? What happened?" I asked a girl. She ignored me. That scene left a deep impression on me, as if all the children—who used to pester their mother for sugar, who couldn't stop chattering in class, who liked playing pranks on others, and who were always ready to answer all the questions in class—couldn't speak a single word at this moment. Just then, I saw the top two floors of a teaching building fall on the other side of the playground. Like a toy.

Others wrote about how the earthquake was remembered by the time they reached high school. After a decade, some teachers had reduced the disaster to the most basic lesson for any Chinese child: *You need to work harder*. One girl wrote:

My English teacher even told us a story about her previous student, who ran back to the classroom when the teaching building was shaking violently to take back his English word book to memorize words.

"If you can have his studying attitude, then you might have the opportunity to be admitted to Tsinghua University and Peking University after two years," she told us.

Three days after matriculation, I had my first class of freshmen. There were fourteen, all engineering majors, and they were just as prompt as the disaster ceremony had been. When I entered the room a few minutes early, everybody was already there, waiting patiently. Each of them had brought a brand-new copy of *Animal Farm*.

The students represented the fifth cohort to enter SCUPI. Founded in 2015, the institute was the type of program called a hybrid: a combination of Chinese and foreign education. SCUPI students spent two or three years at Sichuan University, taking all courses in English, and then they could apply to complete their degrees at the University of Pittsburgh or at another school in the United States or otherwise abroad. After graduation, they received diplomas from both Sichuan University and the foreign institution.

There were more than forty hybrid programs in China, reflecting a major shift in education. Back when I had served in the Peace Corps, it was rare for a Chinese student to go abroad: out of the more than two hundred young people whom I taught, nobody went on to study outside the country. In those days, Chinese students who made it to the United States tended to be from elite institutions, and the numbers were relatively small: in 1996, 42,503 Chinese were enrolled at American universities. Many of them were talented graduate students who had been attracted by scholarship offers, and they usually decided to settle in the United States.

After two decades, the situation had changed dramatically. Young Chinese had become far more international, with millennials constituting two thirds of the country's passport holders. The United States was the favorite destination for students: in 2019, there were more than 372,000 Chinese at American institutions. The vast majority of these students paid full tuition, which was a prime motivation for the hybrid programs. Pittsburgh and other universities wanted to create pipelines that directed more fee-paying Chinese students toward their American campuses.

Another change was that these students usually came back to China. According to the Ministry of Education, more than 80 percent of Chinese students returned after completing their studies abroad, which, in historical terms, was unprecedented. There had never been another authoritarian nation in which so many prosperous and educated young people left to study in democratic societies and then willingly came back.

It was also unprecedented for so many American universities to establish programs in a country with such a different view on intellectual freedom. Programs like SCUPI were known as hybrids, but there was nothing mixed about their politics. Despite the claims of the honor code—"freedom of thought and expression are valued"—the University of Pittsburgh could not establish its own political guidelines for the Chengdu program. In terms of legal status, SCUPI was entirely under the umbrella of Sichuan University. The institute's students were required to take the same mandatory political courses as other undergrads, and instructors like me were subject to the oversight of the Communist Party. Our online activities were restricted by the Great Firewall, the government's system of internet censorship and site-blocking. Many commonly used foreign sites, including Google, YouTube, and Facebook, were blocked in China.

The government had started developing the Great Firewall in 1998, the same year that Jiang Zemin initiated Project 985. The pairing of these strategies seemed schizophrenic: If China hoped to develop world-class universities, why restrict the internet? But ever since, the Party followed both paths at once, until the Firewall became part of the basic institutional environment of academia. First-year students were expected to do research in English, so SCUPI provided me with a list of unblocked foreign search engines. A site could be accessed only if it allowed content to be censored by the Chinese authorities, like Bing, or if it remained so lightly trafficked that it didn't draw attention.

I dutifully passed the list on to my classes, although, with the exception of Bing, I had never heard of any of these search engines. They
sounded like obscure rock bands: Dogpile, Yandex, WolframAlpha,
Swisscows, DuckDuckGo. Even this third-tier festival lineup was subject
to cancellation: during week one of the semester, a student could search
on DuckDuckGo, but by week four it was DuckDuckGone. Despite the
site's obscurity, it was deemed important enough to be blocked as part of
the preparations for the seventieth anniversary of the People's Republic.

In the weeks before the anniversary, administrators sent nervous
messages to faculty members. This was another type of schizophrenia:
even while SCUPI handed out lists of unblocked search engines for students, it simultaneously provided each instructor with a subscription to
Astrill, a virtual private network, or VPN. VPNs allowed subscribers to
skirt the Chinese firewall, and they were illegal, which meant that they
generally became less stable in the lead-up to a sensitive date. On September 16, a SCUPI tech administrator posted a VPN update to the
online faculty message board. The administrator avoided any direct reference to the anniversary:

> Dear all, due to recent network situation and some activities, you may
> find many problems with your Astrill clients. . . . Here's a brief list of
> servers [that may be] available. This problem should be resolved
> after one or two weeks, depending on the larger circumstance.

The administrator suggested that during the anniversary period we
should try connecting our VPNs through three American cities: Los An-
geles, Denver, and Fremont, California. The email ended:

> And try not to mention sensitive words on your WeChat, Line,
> QQ, or any other im app. NEVER MENTION IT in your email.
> Thanks.

Students at SCUPI majored in only three subjects: mechanical engineering, industrial engineering, and materials science and engineering. Ostensibly, Pittsburgh's hybrid program focused on engineering because this discipline appealed to many Chinese who hoped to study abroad. But there was also a political dimension. In the original 985 speech, Jiang Zemin had noted that "science and technology are the primary productive forces." The Party generally viewed such subjects favorably, because they were good for economic development and unlikely to inspire political opposition. Sichuan University had been so eager to collaborate with Pittsburgh that the Chinese agreed to invest the equivalent of sixty million dollars in a four-hundred-thousand-square-foot center for the institute, which was still under construction.

I had never taught engineers before, and I wasn't sure whether these students would be interested in writing or literature. On the first day, I asked them to write down their favorite books or authors, along with career goals:

> *Pride and Prejudice*, by Jane. I hope I can try my best to construct my country as an engineer.

> My favorite Chinese author is Lu Xun. My favorite foreign author is George Orwell. I hope to devote myself to scientific research or working in a Chinese tech company to develop new technologies.

> Maybe Charles Dickens and Yu Hua. Engineer for controllable nuclear fusion.

> *One Hundred Years of Solitude.* To be an eminent car engineer. To establish an auto company like Ferrari.

My favorite book is *The Merchant of Venice* and my favorite author
is Shakespeare because his language is very rich. Maybe I want to
be an engineer in the future, use my knowledge to make the world
better.

I quickly discarded a number of preconceptions. These engineers
were highly literate—one boy had even published a science fiction novel
with a commercial press in eastern China. To some degree, their literary
abilities reflected a culture that has always placed great value on the
written word. But it also seemed clear that a number of these students
were not engineers by inclination. When we met outside of class, they
sometimes told me bluntly that they had little interest in their majors.

In many cases, parents had chosen the course of study. Engineering
jobs paid well, and parents sometimes explained that no matter which
direction the Party winds happened to blow, there would always be a
need for engineers and tech specialists. The system's schizophrenic
qualities—increased educational and economic opportunities on one
hand, narrowing political space on the other—produced young people
who were themselves a study in contradictions: the George Orwell
fan who dreams of Chinese tech, the Gabriel García Márquez magical
realist who hopes to work in automotive engineering.

The role that parents played was vastly different from what I remembered in the 1990s. Even a boy like Anry, who had migrated under the immense pressure of family tragedy, never mentioned parental support or
advice. Back then, the older generation often had little to offer, because
they were farmers who knew nothing of the urban world that their children were entering. In 2014, in one of my surveys, I asked my former Fuling students to compare their own child-rearing strategies to those of
their parents:

They raised us like they raised pigs or chickens. We did not get much
love from them. But now our kid is the only hope of us.

I give [my son] all my love and care. I feel bad when I think of my time as a student because our parents gave us nothing. Chinese peasants did not know how to care for their kids at all. I was very often sick and feeling cold but my parents did not care at all.

My kid has a much better life. He has what he wants. . . . We know how to help him study. But my parents knew nothing, and they were illiterate and they were not able to help us at all.

This more attentive approach had also shaped the students in my classroom at Sichuan University. Even if their parents had originally migrated from the countryside, they had long since settled into urban life, and they tended to be savvy about politics. This was another new dynamic—in the past, China had suffered so much instability that political lessons from any particular period quickly became obsolete. But the current parents' knowledge was still relevant, and they knew how to deal with the security state.

At the start of the semester, I asked first-year students to write about some significant incident in their lives, and one boy submitted an essay titled "A Day Trip to the Police Station." The boy—I'll call him Vincent— begins his story with an early morning phone call from the cops. An officer telephones Vincent's mother and informs her that the police need to interrogate her son, who is in high school. The officer doesn't explain what the boy has done wrong. In the story, Vincent racks his brain, trying to figure out if he's committed some crime. He writes in the third person, as if this distance makes it easier to describe his mindset:

He was lost in thought. He was tracing the memory from birth to now, including but not limited to [the time] he broke a kid's head in kindergarten, he used VPN to browse YouTube to see some videos, and talked with his friends abroad in Facebook and so on. Suddenly he thought of the most possible thing that happened two years ago.

In the summer vacation in 2017, he bought an airsoft gun in the Internet, which is illegal in Mainland China but legal in most countries or regions. Although it had been two years since then, he left his private information such as the address and his phone number. In modern society, it is possible to trace every information in the Internet and [especially] easy for police.

Vincent's parents are both Party members with government jobs, and the boy solicits their advice:

He hid his airsoft gun and discussed countermeasures with his father.

"If you are asked about this matter," Dad said, "you just tell him that the seller mailed a toy gun and you were cheated. And then you felt unhappy and threw it away."

Sure enough, two policemen came to his home the next day.

But the interrogation doesn't proceed as expected. Neither officer mentions the forbidden gun; instead, they refer to evidence that Vincent has acquired banned images from the Internet, possibly through VPN use. They accuse Vincent of posting these images and other sensitive material, including terrorist messages, on a website managed by Baidu, a Chinese tech company. Vincent describes the interrogation:

"You posted terrorism videos in your Baidu Netdisk on July 22." One of the policemen showed the summons. "So we are going to take you to the police station for investigation. Please take your ID card."

"That's ridiculous," Vincent said. "I have never browsed such videos, not to mention posted them in the Internet. You must be joking."

"Maybe you didn't post it by yourself," the policeman said. "But the app may back up the video automatically."

"Let me see . . ." Vincent said. "That's possible. I am a member of a WeChat group, and [once] I browsed a terrorism video but I didn't upload it."

"Maybe the app backed up the video itself."

"Oh, no! Damn Baidu Netdisk!!" Vincent said.

The officers escort Vincent out of his home. They proceed across town to a police station, where they enter a department labeled "Cyber-security Police." Seated in an interrogation room, Vincent is impressed by the policemen's politeness. ("It's not scary at all, no handcuffs and no cage.") The officers zero in on the WeChat group:

"What's the group for?" the policeman asked.

"It's my partners who gather to take a live CS game," Vincent responded.

"But how interesting it is!" the policeman said. "They sent porno-graphic videos, traffic accident videos, [breaking news] videos, and funny videos."

"Yes," he said helplessly, "so I am innocent."

"Yes, we believe you," the policeman said. "But you have to [sign] the record because it is the fact that you posted the terrorism video in the Internet, which is illegal."

On one hand, the essay's subject matter was terrifying, but there was also an odd sense of normalcy. The basic narrative was universal: A teen-ager makes a mistake, finds himself gently corrected, and gains a new maturity. Along the way, he connects with the elders who love him. Part of this connection comes from the things they share: the parents, rather than representing authority, are also powerless in the face of the larger system. The narrative ends with a scene of parental advice that could be viewed as cynical, or heartwarming, or wise, or defeatist, or all of these things at once:

"That's why I always like to browse news [but] never comment on the Internet," father said. "Because the Internet police really exist. And we have no private information, we can be easily investigated however you try to disguise yourself. So take care whatever you send on the Internet, my boy!"

From this matter, Vincent really gained some experience. First, take care about your account in the Internet, and focus on some basic setting like automatic backup. Besides, don't send some words, videos, or photos freely. In China, there is Internet police focus on WeChat, QQ, Weibo, and other software. As it is said in *1984*, "Big Brother is watching you."

———

Vincent's favorite author was Wang Xiaobo, a brilliant, short-lived Beijing novelist who had written irreverent and sexually explicit fiction that was banned by the state. Vincent stood over six feet tall, with glasses and close-cropped hair, and he was handsome. During class, he expressed opinions with unusual directness. In our unit on argumentative essays, students selected their own topics, and Vincent chose to oppose the Party's practice of mandatory military training for all students. The Party had instituted such instruction after the 1989 protests in Tiananmen Square, when leaders concluded that young people lacked sufficient patriotism. In the 1990s, the military training focused on university students, but since then it had been expanded to include sessions for middle schools and high schools.

Students grumbled about the training, but it was dangerous to oppose openly. Vincent's argument, though, was clever. Rather than questioning the value of patriotism or the role of the military, he attacked the mandatory training as poorly regulated. He noted that as a high school student he had been charged exorbitant fees that were connected to the training, and he cited Ministry of Education regulations that explicitly prohibited such charges. He also believed that some practices, like a compulsory crew cut for male high school trainees, violated personal freedom. Near the end of the paper, he wrote:

> Moreover, because some instructors have low education and professional quality, some sexual assault events happened. In my grade three [the final year of middle school], my female classmates told me that an instructor entered their room in the morning when they were dressing. And the instructor tickled them. At that time, we didn't think it was a big deal. But after I grow up I know it may be a sexual assault.

At the same time, Vincent didn't strike me as a dissident. When he wrote about his brush with the internet police, he never stated that such monitoring should be prohibited. Early in the semester, we read George Orwell's "A Hanging," which, in the description of an execution in colonial Burma, makes a powerful case against the death penalty. I held an in-class debate about the issue, and Vincent was among the slight majority of students who supported capital punishment. He referred to the death penalty as a human right—in his opinion, if a murderer is not properly punished, such leniency violates the rights of other citizens to a safe society. Vincent was also a proponent of the right to bear arms, which seemed contradictory to his interest in social safety. He told me repeatedly that one of his dreams was to study in the United States and legally purchase a firearm.

I couldn't easily summarize Vincent's politics, other than to say that they were individualistic. Students often described their generation in such terms—they believed that their parents had been much more group-oriented. Nevertheless, these young people seemed remarkably filial; I rarely sensed serious tensions between them and their parents. During one class, Leslie, my wife, visited to talk about some of her past research on youth in China, and she mentioned that young people often seemed willing to be guided by their parents to a degree that would be unusual in America. Vincent raised his hand.

"Do you know why we listen to our parents?" he said.

"No," Leslie said. "Why?"

Vincent smiled. "Because we need their money."

He was, like thirteen of the fourteen students in his section, an only child. That fall, I surveyed all my classes, and nearly 90 percent of the students had no siblings. I learned that when asking this question I had to clarify what I meant by the word *sibling*, because otherwise students might include cousins in their responses. As families shrank, the term had broadened—for many young people, a cousin was a kind of substitute brother or sister.

Three years earlier, in 2016, China changed the policy to allow families to have a second child. In my classes, if a student had a sibling, it was almost invariably a younger child who had been born after a gap of as many as fifteen years. They were a trick-mirror image of my Fuling students, who, in addition to coming from large families, had often been the youngest.

Fenton had a sister who was fifteen years younger. In truth, his parents could have violated the policy much earlier, because as private entrepreneurs they suffered fewer repercussions than people employed by the government. It cost them only a fine, which they could afford, but the real problem had been Fenton's opposition when he was small. Every time the couple mentioned having another child, the boy responded with a tantrum, because he didn't want to see his parents' attention divided. Such behavior was associated with the term "Little Emperors"—since the 1980s, the foreign and Chinese media had reported on the ways in which this generation of only children might be spoiled.

Fenton told me these stories ruefully. He loved his baby sister, and he was embarrassed by his behavior. I said that he shouldn't blame himself—who looks to a child for advice on family planning? But Fenton's mother and father had taken his input seriously. When they finally made the decision to have a second child, they didn't tell Fenton until his mother was five months pregnant. At the time, he felt betrayed—the teenager believed that it had been his right to be consulted. And even though he had failed to stop the pregnancy, there was no question that he had delayed it. "It wasn't my decision, but I influenced them," he told me.

A number of students described similar situations in which they had been consulted about the possibility of expanding the family. This dynamic seemed much more complicated than the notion of Little Emperors bullying their parents with tantrums. It reminded me of Vincent's police essay: parents and children seemed unusually close, in part because of Chinese traditions of filial piety, but also because of the one-child dynamic. And the adults often had little guidance with regard to parenting. Their own fathers and mothers had been poor farmers with virtually no schooling, and now they had to figure out what it meant to be an urban middle-class parent raising a child in the modern world.

Generations in China also interact differently than they do in a democratic society. Even the basic conception is different, because Chinese tend to group age cohorts by decade. People born between 1990 and 1999 are known as *jiulinghou*, or "post-90s," whereas the students I taught at Sichuan University, many of whom were born in 2000 or later, were "post-00s." Such groupings are too short to be truly generational. It's unlike Americans, who are accustomed to thinking about differences and conflicts between generations, in part because each cohort gains a degree of political power through participatory democracy. An important part of the national narrative is the way that generations succeed each other— the notion, for example, that George H. W. Bush was a member of the Greatest Generation, and that he was defeated in the 1992 election by Bill Clinton, who was a Boomer.

But people in China rarely speak of generations in this manner. The country's direction can be shaped by individual leaders—those godlike figures—but they aren't representatives of a specific era or age cohort. The gods are of the Party, and the Party is outside of time. For average citizens, in terms of political participation, there is no real difference between post-00s and post-70s, or between somebody like Vincent and his parents. One quality of an authoritarian system is that it treats everybody like children.

Sometimes, a student essay casually mentioned her mother's abortion. Such matters also seemed to be open topics within a family. One girl described how her mother ended a pregnancy after it had been discussed by no fewer than three generations:

> Actually my mother was once pregnant accidentally when I was in high school. She said they were twins but finally she gave them up, though my grandparents wanted her to keep them. As the single child of the family, I did not have the strong desire to want my mother either to keep them or abort them. My mother once asked me, "Do you want me to bear them?" I think the reason why she said so is because then there was some bad news about the first child's repulsion about the second child. I said, "If you want." I did not know the reason why my mother did not bear them. Maybe I've asked, but the reason [was not] significant [enough] to make me remember.

Such conversations seemed particularly common for daughters. Abortion was widespread among the generation of their mothers, especially the many millions who had made the transition to city life. One Chinese survey from 2014 indicated that nearly a quarter of sexually active migrant women had had an abortion. Very few Chinese held religious ideas about such procedures, which were often viewed as basically a form of birth control, especially during the one-child era. When I asked the student for permission to quote from her essay, she readily agreed. "Abortion is nothing sensitive in China," she wrote in an email. "To be honest, the attitude of some states in the U.S. towards abortion is too much for me." Once, when I was meeting with another student in my office to talk about something else, she offhandedly mentioned that her mother had had around eight abortions. She later clarified her memories in an email:

> I think my mom was pregnant 9 times. For the last one (I was already in college), she mentioned it briefly before and after the operation. But for the others, she told me years later. I remember we went out for a walk, and she was complaining about my dad and then she told me about her abortions. It was a casual mention and we didn't talk much.
>
> I think mentally, she seems fine about abortions. . . . I remember there was one time she just aborted and then went directly back to work.

The student's mother had been born in 1974, the same year as many of the people I had taught in Fuling. In 2016, after the government finally allowed families to have a second child, I surveyed the Fuling cohort, asking if any of them planned to get pregnant. Almost all said no—now that they were in their forties, and with their only children approaching college age, they believed that it was too late. A handful of respondents mentioned other reasons, sometimes with characteristic bluntness:

> No, I will never have another kid. My son is very naughty. He is very bad at study and he is a big troublemaker. He has been making us discouraged. I am afraid of having another copy of my son.

The ones who worked as teachers often mentioned that younger colleagues were preparing for second pregnancies. When these instructors went on maternity leave, their classes had to be picked up by older staff.

This process made my former students even more aware of their unique position in China's social history:

> About 45 of the people around me are going to have a second baby. Many teachers are planning on that now. So they have asked for leave. I have to take many classes instead of them now. It is really bad. We old teachers will have too much work to do if more and more women have a second baby.

> A lot of young teachers will have a second baby. We are jealous of them.

> We are born in the 1970s, we suffer the most in China. We lived a poor life when we were young, we could not have a second baby when young, now [that] we have a good policy we are too old for that. In the future we will have to support four parents who have no money at all when they are old.

A small handful of former students had had a second child in violation of the policy. Virtually none of these violators worked at public schools, where they would have suffered professionally. For people in the private economy, punishment was generally limited to a fine, although they also had to prepare strategies for dealing with the bureaucracy. Willy, the student who migrated to Zhejiang, eventually became a success as an English instructor in private schools. His first daughter was born in 2003, and then, in 2011, he and his wife decided to have a second child. After the birth of another girl, Willy asked me to give her an English name. My family had recently moved to Egypt, so I suggested Nora, after *nour*—"light" in Arabic.

Nora was born in Nanchong, the same city where Serena grew up. Willy's home village was nearby, and his second-eldest brother had good relations with the Party boss at the hospital. Willy used these connections, along with a well-placed bribe, to get Nora out of the birth ward without having her registered. After that, Willy spent a great deal of time cultivating other contacts in the Nanchong government with gifts and dinners. It wasn't until three years after Nora's birth that she was finally documented as a Chinese citizen. Willy wrote in an email:

> I got Nora registered officially at the PSB [public security bureau]. The fine is just ten thousand yuan [around $1,500], which is a small amount compared to the official fine standard. One of my high school classmates is a government official in Nanchong. So this is easy for him to do. But before this was finished, we were worried. We went to the administration of birth control and were told that the fine would be around 100,000 yuan or so.

In another message, Willy wrote:

> By the way, [a former classmate's] wife has a pregnancy of 4 months, and I talked with him, and he was very excited by that. He said that he was learning from me to have more babies.

If Tolstoy had belonged to the Reform generation, he might have written: All one-child families are alike, but every two-child family has the second child in its own way. Willy's former classmate had to figure out his own localized strategy for skirting the policy. After the baby was born, I called to congratulate him. We chatted for a while, and I asked how much the family had been fined. My former student said that they had avoided any penalty.

"We registered her older sister as mentally disabled," he said. "Often those mental problems don't appear until later. So even after a child is a few years old, it's possible to register her in this way."

If a family had a child with a serious disability, they could apply to have a second baby. The previous year, I had visited the former student and spent some time with his eldest daughter, a bright-eyed girl who already spoke good English by the end of elementary school. I asked how anybody at the government office could possibly believe that this child was mentally disabled.

"Of course we didn't bring *her!*" the father said, laughing. "We brought another child."

He explained that it involved a simple commercial transaction. The parents of an actual disabled child made her available for a fee, and she was taken by clients to the government office, where her disability was registered in the name of the clients' child. Then the clients embarked on another fully approved pregnancy. Meanwhile, the parents of the disabled child continued to hire her out to other families. Sometimes, Chinese people described such arrangements with an English phrase that made my heart drop: "win-win."

"But what happens when your daughter gets older?" I asked. "Isn't this going to be a problem when she wants to enter high school or college?"

"It won't be a problem," he said. "At that time, we'll figure out a solution. The government is probably going to change the planned-birth policy anyway. There aren't enough children in China. It doesn't make sense for people like us to wait for them to change it." He didn't sound concerned in the least, and of course he was right: less than four years later, the policy was changed.

At Sichuan University, SCUPI's temporary offices and classrooms were located in the eastern wing of a large building that was devoted to various humanities departments. Our arrangement was compact: walking from my office to the nonfiction classroom took little more than a minute. Along the way, I passed six surveillance cameras. Five cameras were in the hallways, and the sixth was in the nonfiction classroom, where it was mounted on the front wall. When I stood at the lectern, the camera was positioned above my right shoulder, pointed at the students.

I tried to document the cameras that I observed during my daily routines. There was one device on the ceiling of the room where my department held meetings, and three more had been arranged around the lecture hall that was used for larger courses. When I waited for the university shuttle at the campus bus stop, I stood below a white surveillance device that had been mounted atop a pole. It surprised me that there weren't any cameras in the classroom where I taught first-year composition, but perhaps the building crews hadn't gotten around to installing them yet.

Across Chinese cities, digital surveillance had expanded on a scale that was staggering. Some of it was private, like the cameras in North's elevators, but the coverage was especially thorough in government-run public spaces. It took me a long time to count the devices in my local subway station of Dongmen Daqiao: fifteen cameras at track level, forty-seven at the turnstiles, thirty-eight for the various escalators and stairways. The total was a hundred, not to mention the two cameras that were positioned inside each subway car that passed through the station all day long. Who was monitoring all this stuff?

In class, I assumed that somebody kept track of the things I said. This wasn't new: in the 1990s, there weren't any campus security cameras, but the Peace Corps warned us that some students were almost certainly reporting our classroom content to the authorities. In 1997, one volunteer near Chengdu got into an altercation with a taxi driver and was taken to the police station, where a Peace Corps administrator was also called in. In the course of questioning, it became clear that the police had a record of sensitive political comments that the volunteer had made in class during the previous year and a half. That was one reason why Adam and I had been certain that the authorities would find out about our lecture with the absentee ballots.

But we never knew the exact mechanisms by which we were tracked.

Even after more than twenty years, with a high level of trust between me and the Fuling students, I never heard a word about the monitoring. My impression was that the Party was shrewd about recruitment for such jobs, and the vast majority of students remained outside this subsystem. At Sichuan University, some students told me that they heard of classmates who doubled as *xinxiyuan*—literally, "information personnel." But my students didn't know of any friends who did this, and they were just as much in the dark as I was. "It's a waste of time to find out," one nonfiction student told me. She remarked that not only was it dangerous, but it was also bound to be depressing, because *xinxiyuan* were probably rewarded with better government job opportunities after graduation.

For the first-year classes, I was careful with my content during the early weeks. I decided to save *Animal Farm* for the latter part of the semester, when I would know the students better. A number of friends had warned me that the young people in Xi Jinping's China were more narrowly patriotic than previous generations. There was a term for these youths: Xiao Fenhong, or "Little Pinks." They were known for being rabidly pro-Party, making social media attacks on anybody deemed insufficiently patriotic. On college campuses, Little Pinks sometimes reported instructors to the authorities if they said or wrote something that was politically incorrect.

At least in the early weeks, I saw little evidence of either Little—the Pinks or the Emperors. I was pleasantly surprised by a number of independent-minded students like Vincent, and I learned that it was possible to have an active in-class debate. Such activities had been difficult in Fuling, because so many opinions about China were standard, and students were usually afraid to express anything contrary to the Party line. At Sichuan University, there were still many topics that couldn't be broached in class, but students seemed less nervous than I remembered. I asked my first-year classes to debate the death penalty and the system for college admissions, and both topics led to engaged discussions.

As for the Little Emperors, it was true that almost all of these students were only children, and the majority came from comfortable homes. But they were far from spoiled. The fall semester seemed interminable: it began the first week of September and continued until the second week of January, more than a month longer than most American college terms. Chinese students also tend to carry more courses: my first-years spent nearly forty hours in the classroom every week. And yet out of my two sections, for three periods a week, over seventeen weeks of term, there wasn't a single student who missed a single hour. One boy had to travel to Beijing for a family emergency, but he insisted on making up the class by attending the other section. It was hard for me to imagine more diligent students, which wasn't surprising. After all, they had had the kind of teachers who tell children that if there's an earthquake and the school is about to collapse, the good student is the one who runs inside and grabs his English text.

They also weren't complainers. After my nonfiction classes undertook off-campus reporting projects, I decided to try the same thing with my first-years. These engineers could have perceived it as unfair—none of the other composition sections were required to do interviews away from Jiang'an. But there was no resistance, and the first-years diligently trooped off to their projects: one to a Buddhist temple, another to the Chengdu Zoo, another to a McDonald's near campus. Vincent went to the People's Park in downtown Chengdu. Inside the park, nestled among a grove of trees, was something known as "Marriage Corner"—a meeting place for people looking for mates. They listed their attributes on flyers and hung them from a wall. When Vincent visited, he was perplexed by all this talent on paper:

What confuses me is why these people have [such] excellent conditions but can't find lovers. For males, they are almost all handsome and well-featured. Besides, they all have a good salary and have a good career. Moreover, they have 1 to 3 apartments and a car. For females, they are beautiful and graceful. And they all have a stable work like teachers or government officials. Are they lying? Do they make up information? It must be a joke if they really have such conditions but can't find a mate.

At the Marriage Corner, Vincent met a number of parents who were searching for partners for their children. One woman told him about her daughter:

"My daughter is 29 years old," the lady says. "She is very beautiful." At the same time, she opens her phone to show us her daughter's photo. Not so beautiful, but above the average appearance for women. In this talk, I learn that her daughter graduated from Xiamen University—a top-20 university in China, and she also got master's degree from Arizona State University. She majors in economics and accounting. Because she spent too much time studying, she didn't find a boyfriend in school. Now she works in an investment bank and her family has their own company. Now she can't find a suited man to become a mate, because her own condition is so excellent and there is no male who matches her for marriage. So, because of this reason, she has to try a method which is not so romantic: Go to the marriage market.

Vincent's conclusion was simple: young people in China study too much, and there's no proper sex education. He noted that parents and teachers often try to prohibit dating among high school students. In Vincent's analysis, the natural outcome is a generation of people who are highly educated, highly motivated, and highly skilled at almost everything—except connecting with a lover. They are also highly susceptible to scam artists. At the Marriage Corner, Vincent met another individual:

His name is Heng Dashuai, which means handsome in Chinese. Now he is 65 years old and his job is a matchmaker. . . . He used to be a miner and lost his left eye because of a fight. In 2014, he helped to look for a mate for his nephew. And he found it not easy to find an appropriate mate because both online and offline marriage markets are full [of] fake information and even cheating. As a Christian, he is glad to help others and he decided to do this. Now he has a notebook filled with non-married people information and a huge WeChat group for matching them.

The ancient miner, his good eye glittering, regaled Vincent with tales of treachery and deceit in the wilds of the People's Park. He warned the young man not to trust listings that looked too perfect: they were probably created by agencies, which then demanded fees to arrange dates. For dates, the agencies sent young employees who had been dressed up and handed bogus résumés from 985 universities. The whole thing was energized by hordes of terrified parents, each of whom was burdened by the thought of an only child like an albatross around the neck. Vincent concluded his essay with a marriage-corner manifesto:

Because of one-child policy and traditional ideology, many parents consider their children as their treasure which belongs to the parents instead of the children themselves. . . . We are all respective individuals. We belong to no people, and no people belong to us. We spend a romantic life pursuing love. I hope the future Chinese children can have genuine liberty.

———

The research projects were the highlight of that first semester. The students were curious and observant, and the grind of high school had left them with extremely high capacities for boredom, which is one of the lesser-known secrets of effective journalism. One freshman interviewed forty-seven customers at a bubble tea shop—it amazed me that the management didn't kick him out. The boy who wrote about McDonald's entered the restaurant at eight o'clock in the evening, sat down at a booth, and eavesdropped on conversations until seven the following morning. Late at night, two women in revealing clothes sat in the next booth, complaining to each other about low rates for sex work. A table of street buskers showed up with their guitars and ate without saying a word, possibly to save their tired voices. Motorcycle deliverymen used the nighttime fast-food restaurant as a kind of dormitory. They had worked out an arrangement with the McDonald's shift workers, who allowed the deliverymen to sleep in booths when business was quiet.

The student observed that the daytime franchise was patronized by citizens who were middle class or higher, but after midnight it became a refuge for the social classes that had largely missed out on China's boom. At two o'clock in the morning, a pair of drunk men arrived, ordered soft drinks, and sat down near my student. For three hours, one of the drunks unburdened himself to his companion. His girlfriend had just left him; his job was terrible; he didn't see the point of living. The student wrote:

> His friend just sat [beside him] listening to his words and patting his back now and then. . . . But three hours later, when they were leaving, I saw a subtle shining in [the drunk man's] eyes: the earth is still rotating regularly, and life is still going on. He clearly realized that life and work might be tough, but that was the only way to survive in this cruel society.

For young people from comfortable backgrounds, the students had few illusions. They were alert to corruption and abuse, and they were sympathetic to individuals who felt trapped by the system. A number of students gravitated to people or groups who were searching for some deeper meaning in Chinese society. At a Catholic church, Serena got to know a group of believers so well that they invited her to attend a five-day retreat in southern Sichuan. This was the kind of event that usually gets shut down by the Party, but the priest didn't inform anybody from the government. He also requested that attendees not post anything about the retreat on social media. When Serena asked the priest about this request, his gnomic response sounded like a lesson from a Daoist fable. "Even if you post it, nonbelievers won't come," he told her. "Even if you don't post it, believers will come."

At the retreat, nobody from the security forces showed up, but Satan did. The priest engaged in faith healing: he laid on hands and prayed while the attendees, mostly older women, shouted and wept. On the final day, when everybody had been worked into a frenzy, one woman collapsed as if possessed. Serena's essay described the reactions of other attendees:

"The devil came!"

"How powerful the devil is! He dares to come to the church, when all of us are here."

"True. How scary! In the daylight! In the church!"

[The priest] waved his hands, indicating that it was nothing serious and hinting that people should give the woman space. But the crowd didn't disperse—some wishing her peace, some praying, some discussing the devil. . . .

The music master led the congregation to sing Hallelujah. He was like a rock star, swinging to the beat; the believers were like fans, waving their arms and clapping with the beat. "My hands are numb." "My voice is hoarse." I heard people saying these things with pride. . . .

In the afternoon, [a woman named Wang] led the congregation to pray. "Close your eyes and pray. Think about your burden. Let it go for the five days. We are going to come close to Jesus." As she went on, Wang wiped her tears and sobbed. Tears even rolled down my cheek.

––––––

After spending time with the Catholics, Serena decided that her next project would focus on a gay bar called Hunk. This transition wasn't as abrupt as it may seem, because Chengdu was known for both its Christian and its gay communities. In America, such a pairing would defy logic—Chattanooga and San Francisco, together at last. But Christians and queers both represent fringe communities in China, and they are more likely to flourish in a place like Chengdu, far from the nation's political center. Sometimes, people jokingly refer to the city as "Gaydu."

At home, I still had a copy of *Survey of Britain and America*, with its lessons about homosexuality. ("In this capitalist society, although science and technology is highly advanced, some people are suffering from spiritual hollowness.") In an odd way, the book's warnings had come true: as Chinese society became more capitalist, more prosperous, and more technologically advanced, many people sensed that spiritual fulfilment was elusive. They also became more comfortable with individuals who identified as LGBTQ. In 1997, the national government abolished the criminalization of "hooliganism," a law that had often been used to target gay people. Four years later, homosexuality was removed from China's official list of mental disorders. Sichuan became so relatively open that the Peace Corps sent a same-sex married couple as part of the China 21 cohort. The American couple served for two years at their site, where colleagues and students politely referred to them as "sisters."

Under Xi Jinping, China had cracked down on all sorts of NGOs and advocacy groups, including many that pushed for LGBTQ rights. But this official retrenchment didn't seem to be reflected in the attitudes of the young people I taught. In first-year classes, I conducted periodic surveys, in part to see which topics might work for debates. One semester, I asked if gay marriage should be legal in China. Such a change had never been seriously discussed in the People's Republic, although Taiwan legalized gay marriage in May 2019. In my classes, the response to the survey question was lopsided: 79 percent of my first-year students believed that gay people should be allowed to marry. Originally, I had worried that the topic might be too edgy for an in-class debate, but I abandoned it for the opposite reason. For too many students, it was already a nonissue.

They described LGBTQ topics as among the relatively few points of contention between them and their parents. "They're open-minded in many things, but conservative in many others," one student wrote of her mother and father. "They think homosexuality is against nature and sometimes show a kind of implicit disparagement for LGBTQ groups." In 2021, in my annual survey of former Fuling students, I asked if gay marriage should be legalized. Of the respondents, 84 percent said no—an almost perfect reversal of the percentage in my current Chengdu classroom. A number of Fuling respondents included comments:

I am a traditional man. My answer is NO.

I will say no. It is disgusting for two same sex persons to be together.

It makes us feel sick when we think of two same sex persons get married, live together and. . . .

There wasn't much difference by gender: of the women who responded, 75 percent opposed legalization. One woman wrote: "I don't mind it, but if my son does that, I'll disagree with it." Even relatively liberal middle-aged people seemed baffled by the issue. During one of my Fuling visits, a former student named Grant told me that he had recently taught a high school class that included two boys who fell in love. They often spent the night at each other's homes, and they liked to wear matching clothes to school. Chinese teachers frequently report student relationships to parents, because they are seen as distractions to academic focus. In the case of the two boys, Grant dutifully told the parents, but none of the adults believed that a same-sex relationship was even possible. "They insisted that it's just friendship," Grant said.

Grant finally called the boys into his office. "I told them that in America they can marry, but it's not like that here," he said. "They didn't deny it—they were proud to be gay. I said that if you are gay, in traditional China it's a problem." Grant told me that he didn't have any personal issue with homosexuality; he was simply concerned about the children's future. But the boys showed not the slightest bit of fear or shame.

In nonfiction class, a senior named Yidi lived off-campus with her girlfriend, a hip foreign music producer and DJ who performed in clubs around China. Yidi was one of the few students who wore stylish clothes, cultivating a distinctive appearance in a way that wasn't common for female undergraduates. She had tried to start an LGBTQ support group at her public high school in Beijing, posting flyers around the campus, but they were quickly removed by school administrators. Yidi had come out to her mother, which was still unusual in China. In Serena's essay on the gay bar, she cited a 2016 report based on surveys by Peking University sociologists, who noted that less than 15 percent of gay Chinese were fully open to their families. Yidi said that her mother had accepted her sexuality, albeit somewhat sadly. "She said that it's her problem, not my problem," Yidi explained.

Yidi had dated both boys and girls. My impression, though, was that most of my students had never had a romantic relationship. Unlike in the past, Sichuan University and other Chinese colleges no longer restricted dating, but the current students seemed nearly as romantically inexperienced as the previous generation had been. This contradicted the notion of a more individualistic generation, but students often told me that their personal development had been stunted by the intensely competitive environment of high school. A couple of freshmen wrote angry essays about how their teachers had secretly photographed them with partners and sent the images to their parents.

Like Vincent, many students described such patterns as damaging. But their response rarely seemed to involve open resistance or even an attempt to loosen up. If anything, their instinct was to find a way to make dating seem like work—this seemed to be their comfort zone. There were college courses that helped young people approach romance with the same diligence that they applied to academic subjects. One nonfiction student had recently taken a class called Economics of Love and Marriage, which was taught by a professor in the school of public health. Each Economics of Love student had to fulfill two assignments, one of which was to develop an organized and detailed plan, presented via PowerPoint, that illustrated how he or she would pursue an individual who was sexually attractive. The other assignment involved another PowerPoint presentation that focused on market development for regional matchmaking services. My student, who described himself as shy and inexperienced, seemed to like this approach. He believed that after formally studying the Economics of Love, he could go out and apply this knowledge to some young woman.

He had also taken a course called Family Inheritance Law. The class was taught by a law professor named Zhang Xiaoyuan, who had been nicknamed the Prince of Civil Law. Zhang was in his late forties, the same age as the people I had taught in Fuling, and he was charismatic and outspoken. When we met, he told me bluntly that he was pessimistic about marriage in China. "I don't believe that it's natural to stay with somebody for so long," he said. Zhang himself had been married to the same woman for twenty years, and when I asked if this was a contradiction of his beliefs, he laughed. He said that he and his wife were as pragmatic as most members of their generation. "It's for our child," he said.

For years, Zhang had taught courses on law, marriage, and sexuality at Sichuan University. He often surveyed his students, and recently he had given a questionnaire to a large first-year class. Of the 229 respondents, only 18 percent had had a sexual relationship. Zhang observed that students were so inexperienced that they were often unsure of basic desires. Only 3 percent identified as gay, but 11.9 percent said they were bisexual. Another 9 percent answered that they were unsure if they were straight, gay, bisexual, or something else. "They don't know!" Zhang told me, shaking his head. "I think that that's something to worry about."

It didn't surprise me that one of the few students who had embarked on an active dating life was also willing to do edgy research. When the non-fiction class proposed subjects for profiles, Yidi chose her VPN dealer. That was the term she used—it was like sourcing drugs. "I've been paying him on WeChat for a while, so I want to find out who he is," she said.

That first semester, I began to notice clear patterns for VPN use. At the beginning of term, few freshmen seemed to rely on such services, and their English-language research was limited to whatever they could find on Swisscows or WolframAlpha. Sometimes they showed up at my office hours just to ask me to google something. A few kids inquired about *fanqiang*, or "climbing the wall," the term for evading the government's internet controls. They wanted help signing up for the same VPN service that I used, but I didn't know how to do it without an overseas credit card. There were many Chinese VPNs that charged via WeChat, but I didn't know which ones were reliable.

Over time, I learned that the best advice was: Talk to an older student. Along with the various mandatory political classes, learning how to *fanqiang* was essentially part of the curriculum at Sichuan University. Most of my juniors and seniors used Google and other blocked sites, and it was an open secret that many departments and institutes, including SCUPI, helped instructors arrange VPN services. Serena described it as almost like a game. She majored in English, whose faculty needed full access to the internet. Serena told me, "Whenever they ask us in class to google something, some students say, 'We don't have a VPN, so how can we google? Can you tell us how to use a VPN?' And they said, 'Sorry, we have support, but we're not allowed to tell you.'"

During Yidi's interview, she learned that her VPN dealer was neither a hardened criminal nor a dissident, nor even a tech guy. He had developed an online course in art history after attending graduate school in Europe, where he became accustomed to a free internet. Back in China, he was frustrated by the firewall, so he set out to find a good VPN service. In the process of shopping around, he realized how easy it would be to set up such a business. That was an old story: the user who becomes a dealer.

When Yidi asked how much the business cost to run, the dealer hesitated. "If I tell you, you will probably ask for a refund," he said. But he went ahead: for three hundred yuan a year, a little less than fifty dollars, he could rent a Vultr virtual private server overseas, which could handle up to fifty Chinese customers, each of whom paid the dealer an annual subscription fee of three hundred yuan. And then he scaled it up: fifty times three hundred, minus the minimal overhead, as many times as he pleased. He said the hardest part was dealing with sensitive dates like the seventieth anniversary of the founding of the People's Republic. At such a time, the firewall became more rigid, and he had to cope with angry customers. It was like a drug dealer who can't get the good stuff for a couple of weeks after the supply chain has been interrupted by a major bust.

Yidi was a gifted writer, with a breezy, funny voice. Her story had no sense of surprise or outrage, which reminded me of essays by Vincent and others. These young people were clearly accustomed to contradictions and mixed messages; after all, they lived on a campus full of security cameras where faculty tacitly encouraged undergrads to contract with illegal VPN dealers. In the same way, Yidi wasn't shocked when one of those dealers turned out to have a sideline in art history. She wrote:

The business is operated on WeChat, one of the most meticulously monitored social-media platforms in the world, and I was concerned that such an approach is tantamount to distributing anti–sexual harassment leaflets on public transportation during International Women's Day. But my dealer dispelled the myth. "Hundreds of millions of Chinese are getting around the wall, you think the state will punish them all?"

The dealer was exaggerating the numbers, but his point was that the Party probably wanted some holes in the firewall. People in the export business needed access to Google and other useful online tools, and scholars and researchers depended on full access to the internet. Yidi thought that more than half the students she knew at Sichuan University used a VPN, which was similar to other estimates I had heard. In society at large, the figure was much lower, especially among older people. During my 2017 survey of former Fuling students, I asked whether they used VPNs, and only one out of thirty responded in the affirmative. For most Chinese, the hassle and the expense served as adequate deterrents. But VPN use was much more common among the young, the elite, and the educated. Yidi's dealer told her, "It's a good business, the gray market of China."

Whenever I received a particularly good paper, I asked the student to read it aloud in class. But I wasn't sure if Yidi's subject matter was too sensitive. In first-year composition, I hadn't shared Vincent's story about the police interrogation. I also asked him to submit his final draft directly via email rather than use the SCUPI online system, where monitoring was more likely.

I felt more confident about the older nonfiction students, who had chosen to take my course. It seemed that most of them used VPNs, so I figured they would benefit from Yidi's research. When I asked if she would share the essay, she agreed without hesitation.

At the beginning of class, Yidi stood up and read while I showed the text on a projection screen. Her pronunciation was excellent, with a slight British accent. There was some laughter at funny parts near the beginning, but then the class quieted. The students stopped fidgeting; they sat still and listened. By the time Yidi introduced the dealer, the room was silent except for the sound of her voice.

As the students got quieter, my pulse began to race. I felt my face flush—suddenly, it was as if I were back in the 1990s classroom. I looked around, and the students wore expressions of curiosity; they didn't appear to be offended. But I knew that it took only one or two individuals to start a problem. Yidi stood directly in front of the security camera, and by the time she was halfway finished, I was convinced that I had put her at risk. But now it was too late to stop. Her voice was clear to the end of the story.

CHAPTER FOUR

Chengdu Experimental

November 2019

A T 7:01 A.M. ON SEPTEMBER 2, MORE THAN AN HOUR BEFORE MY twin daughters were scheduled to begin third grade at Chengdu Experimental Primary School, the first message appeared on the WeChat group for parents. The group name was Class Six, and every time somebody posted a message, my phone beeped. The initial beep came from somebody called Number 16 Zhou Liming's Mama:

Regarding today's weather, is it fine to wear shorts?

It took less than a minute for the next beep. This time, the writer was Number 35 Li Jialing's Mama:

We are wearing shorts, it's not cold.

Each message appeared in the standard WeChat format: a time stamp, the sender's name, an avatar, and the text within a bubble. The bubbles scrolled down the screen like the dialogue of a play in which characters had been both named and numbered:

7:08 AM

Number 13 Zhao Fan's Mama:

There will be lots of people inside the classroom,
it won't be cold.

7:17 AM

Number 16 Zhou Liming's Mama:

Fine, then we will also wear shorts. Thank you,
dears @Number 35 Li Jialing's Mama and
@Number 13 Zhao Fan's Mama.

For Leslie and me, getting our daughters into Chengdu Experimental had been a long and mysterious process. In the spring of 2018, the two
of us had traveled to Chengdu to visit schools. We had a good impression
of Chengdu Experimental, which is considered to be perhaps the best
public primary school in the city. But administrators were noncommit-
tal about admitting Ariel and Natasha. The school had no recent tradition of educating foreigners, and if the twins were to attend, they would
be the only Westerners in a student body of about two thousand.

They would also be the only children who didn't speak Mandarin.
Leslie is Chinese American, and we met while working as journalists in
Beijing. When Ariel and Natasha were born, they were given proper Chinese names. But the twins had never used these names, and Leslie and I
hadn't tried to teach them Mandarin. We always had the idea that someday I would return as a college professor in China, and the girls could
learn the language through immersion.

This remained our plan when we moved to Chengdu, three weeks
before the fall semester. Initially, we had stayed in a Sheraton across the
street from Chengdu Experimental, and a tutor came every morning to give
the girls a crash course in Mandarin. Leslie and I tried to reach administrators and teachers at the school, mostly without success. At one point,

somebody requested that the dean of my institute make a call to the educational authorities, to vouch for my status at the university. Finally, with only four days until the start of the semester, just when we were starting to panic, a teacher informed us that the girls were welcome to attend. But it was never clear to us exactly how or why the twins had been admitted.

During registration, I was instructed to join the other parents on WeChat. Some WeChat groups develop their own distinct language, and in Class Six the standard pronoun was first-person plural, as if parent and child had merged: *We are wearing shorts. We have finished our math homework.* For usernames, parents identified themselves by their children, and often they included the school-assigned student numbers. (I have changed the names and numbers of other children, for privacy.) In exchanges, people politely referred to one another by their full usernames— Number 35 Li Jialing's Mama, Number 42 Zhu Zhentao's Baba—as if these were formal titles.

Along with the Mamas and the Babas, there were a few Nainais and Yeyes: grandmas and grandpas. A user in a WeChat group, in order to prompt a response, can double-tap somebody's avatar, which is called "tickling." Any tickle is documented, like a stage direction that everybody else can see. In addition to being the most popular app in China, WeChat may also be the most passive-aggressive. Chinese tend to monitor the app obsessively, and they get impatient if a message goes unanswered. I often wondered if anybody else in Class Six found humor in the late-night postings:

9:11 PM

Number 07 Chen Qilan's Grandma tickled Number 26
Liu Peiyu's Mama

If I had followed the standard format, my own title would have been the longest: Number 54 Zhang Xingcai and Number 55 Zhang Xingrou's Baba. Ariel and Natasha were the only twins in Class Six, and as latecomers they had been assigned the highest numbers. We hadn't had time to buy uniforms, so on the first day we borrowed two sets from the school: dark plaid skirts and white button-up shirts embroidered with the school insignia. When we entered the classroom, we saw that all the other students were also wearing red scarves, the mark of the Young Pioneers, the Communist Party's organization for schoolchildren. Natasha and Ariel seemed nervous but composed when we said goodbye. A large sign hung on the classroom wall:

THE ENTIRE NATION CELEBRATES THE 70TH GLORIOUS BIRTHDAY OF THE PEOPLE'S REPUBLIC

That day, Leslie and I were moving into our apartment beside the Fu River. We hired a van to transport luggage from the Sheraton, and then Leslie took a cab across town to IKEA, in order to buy some furnishings. While I was unpacking, my phone beeped periodically, and I checked in on the Class Six dialogue. I noticed that parents also referred to their spouses by the children's names, which created even more opportunities for WeChat passive-aggression:

11:58 AM

Number 16 Zhou Liming's Mama:

May I ask what time in the afternoon we are supposed to pick up the children?

Chen Qilan's Mama:

Yesterday at the parents' meeting Teacher Zhang said that they should pick up their children at the main gate at 3:40

Number 16 Zhou Liming's Mama:

@Chen Qilan's Mama—Oh, thank you. Zhou Liming's
Baba went to the meeting but he didn't tell me.
[weeping-and-laughing-while-covering-eyes emoji]

Shortly before three o'clock, Number 54 Zhang Xingcai and Number 55 Zhang Xingrou's Mama called me to explain that because of various IKEA-related delays, she would be unable to make it to school for pickup. [weeping-and-laughing-while-covering-eyes emoji] I waited alone in front of the gate. When Class Six marched out of the schoolyard, Teacher Zhang walked at the front of a neat line of children, and Ariel and Natasha were at the end. The twins held it together until they reached me.

"I feel so stupid!" Ariel said. She burst into tears, pressing against my side. "We didn't understand anything!" Her sister was also sobbing: "I don't want to go back!"

A few parents looked sympathetically in my direction, and Teacher Zhang hurried over. She was middle-aged, with large, alert eyes and a gentle manner. "I think that it was difficult for them," she said.

I thanked her for her patience, and I said that we would continue to work on Mandarin at home. I waited for Natasha and Ariel to calm down before we walked to the subway station. On the way, we passed a large red sign:

CHENGDU EXPERIMENTAL PRIMARY SCHOOL
(FOUNDED IN 1918)
EXPERIMENTING AND RESEARCHING TO GUIDE THE REGION

———

Chengdu Experimental had no other American students or teachers, but the school's early history had been heavily influenced by ideas from the United States. At the end of the nineteenth century, John Dewey, the American philosopher and educator, had pioneered the concept of the experimental, or laboratory, school. For most of his career, Dewey had no special interest in China, but in the spring of 1919 he was invited to deliver a series of lectures in Japan. When Dewey was in Tokyo, a delegation of Chinese scholars visited and persuaded him to travel to China.

Dewey's trip happened to coincide with a critical historical moment. For the past two millennia, the Confucian emphasis on learning had been a strength of Chinese culture. The imperial examination system, which had been institutionalized in the seventh century, lasted for about thirteen hundred years—the world's oldest standardized test. But the purpose of education had always been narrow: to prepare men—and only men—to pass the exam and become government officials. In 1905, after the Qing dynasty had been weakened by the Opium Wars and other conflicts with Western powers, the examination system was abruptly abolished. Intellectuals were left with an existential question: What should be the purpose of schooling in a modern China?

On May 4, 1919, three days after Dewey arrived in China, thousands of university students gathered in Beijing to protest the terms of the Treaty of Versailles. The students were upset that the victorious allies planned to give German concessions in eastern China to the Japanese. Their protest expanded to address other political, social, and educational issues, eventually becoming known as the May Fourth Movement.

The title of Dewey's first lecture in China was "Democratic Developments in America." More than a thousand attended, and soon the American was being hailed as a "second Confucius." He extended his visit to last for more than two years, and he delivered some two hundred lec-

tures around the country. *The Chinese Students' Monthly*, an expat publication based in New York, described the reception:

> Bankers and editors frequent his residences; teachers and students
> flock to his classrooms. Clubs compete to entertain him, to hear him
> speak; newspapers vie with each other in translating his latest utter-
> ances.

Dewey emphasized pragmatism and experimentation, and he warned
his audiences against blindly importing any single Western model of
schooling. China needed, in Dewey's opinion, "a new culture, in which
what is best in western thought is to be freely adopted—but adapted to
Chinese conditions." Dewey believed that education should prepare students to participate in democracy, an idea that was welcomed by the
May Fourth Movement, which promoted values that students personi-
fied as Mr. Democracy and Mr. Science. Such notions were radically
different from Chinese tradition. Because of the imperial examination
system, education in China had always been closely tied to political authority, unlike in the West, where higher learning in premodern times
generally came out of religious institutions. Elizabeth J. Perry, a historian at Harvard, has described the ancient Chinese system as effective
in producing "educated acquiescence." People who were schooled within
the Chinese political system were less likely to oppose it, which, in Perry's
opinion, contributed to the stability of dynastic China.

After this system collapsed, there was a sudden influx of ideas from
the West, which had a tradition of educated individuals opposing political authority. The Chinese Communist Party was one outcome of these
new ideas. In an essay titled "Educated Acquiescence," Perry writes, "The
early leaders of the CCP, Mao Zedong included, were educated intellectuals who had been politicized in large part by their exposure to Western
learning." They were also exposed to American philosophers like John

Dewey. In 1920, a young Mao Zedong mentioned in letters that he was studying Dewey's works, and initially the young Communist was swayed by the American philosopher's stance against violent revolution. In an early essay, Mao wrote, "Thus we will not provoke widespread chaos, nor pursue that ineffectual 'revolution of bombs,' or 'revolution of blood.'"

A number of educators who attended Dewey's lectures and classes subsequently tried to incorporate his ideas into Chinese schools. One of these figures was Hu Yanli, who eventually became the principal of Chengdu's most important primary school. In homage to Dewey, the school's name was changed to include the word *shiyan*—"experiment, test."

Hu Yanli led Chengdu Experimental for a dozen years, and the school still celebrates this period. On the twins' first day, in the main courtyard, we passed a series of prominent commemorative displays. One featured a black-and-white photograph of Hu and other teachers gathered on the site of the current school. Another listed a quote from Hu, along with a reference to the most famous student who was educated under his watch:

> "In order to make it easier for other schools to adopt these concepts, we didn't do anything capricious, but we consistently emphasized self-motivated study, and in particular we emphasized the fostering of a democratic spirit. We hoped to adapt to the individuality of each student and fully develop their genius."
>
> From 1935 to 1939, Li Peng, the former premier of the State Council, studied at Chengdu Experimental Primary School.

———

The school agreed that in the beginning, Ariel and Natasha would be responsible for only their math homework. For *yuwen*, or language class, it was impossible for them to jump in at grade level, but there was no mystery about what they had to do. In the earliest grades, Chinese writing is itself a kind of math: an exercise in basic addition, as characters are memorized one after another.

Across China, all first graders begin the march to literacy with the same character: 天, "sky; heaven." From there, during the fall semester, the children learn 299 more characters, and they add 400 in the spring. The pace accelerates in second grade: 450 each semester, with the final lesson ending on 坟, "tomb." All this is laid out in a series of four textbooks that are accompanied by boxes of flash cards, published by the Ministry of Education. In order to become proper Chinese third graders—to go all the way from heaven to tomb—Natasha and Ariel needed to memorize a total of sixteen hundred characters.

They started with ten a day. Leslie organized our system of home study, and every afternoon when the twins returned from school, she handed them a new stack of flash cards. For each set of ten, we quizzed them twice: first on recognition, then on writing. The flash cards outlined the correct stroke order, and the twins wrote the characters over and over in dozens of cheap brown exercise books that scattered like autumn leaves around the apartment. There were pencils everywhere; after our first electric sharpener wore out, Leslie bought another. Each textbook had to be acquired in a set of two, and these twinned materials also colonized our home. The opening page of the language text featured an image of the Chinese flag, a crowd of happy children from various ethnic groups, and Beijing's Tiananmen Gate with its famous portrait of Chairman Mao. The top of the page said, in large characters:

我是中国人

(I AM CHINESE)

That semester, the twins spent 30 percent more days in class than they would have at their Colorado public school. There are few school vacations in China, and the only significant break in the fall is for National

Day, on October 1. In 2019, all schools in China had five days off for the holiday, but they were required to make up two of those days on weekends. Ariel and Natasha's class was also given thirty-six pages of math homework that had to be completed during the break.

Leslie and I often felt overwhelmed, but even the parents of children who had been there since first grade seemed to be playing catch-up. Virtually all of Ariel and Natasha's classmates were enrolled in private supplemental courses, and it was hard to imagine parents more attentive to their children's education. On the first day of school, I counted forty-nine beeps from the WeChat group. There were seventy more on the second day. Day three clocked in at 237: an average of one beep every six minutes for a span of twenty-four hours. That was also the day that I figured out how to mute the alerts on WeChat.

Parents wrote at any time of the day or night. Once, when Leslie and I were uncertain about a math assignment, I posted a question, and in less than ten minutes the parents of two different children had sent photographs of the homework. The school relied on the parent group to handle certain administrative duties, like distributing official notices and collecting fees for uniforms and lunches. Occasionally, a parent visited a class in order to photograph the children's activities. Late one evening during the first week, Tang Zhiyun's Mama began posting pictures that she had taken during science class. Each image was perfectly focused on an individual child wearing a white lab coat; I found Natasha in the thirty-first frame and Ariel in the seventy-third. Finally, after midnight, and after 107 photographs, the WeChat dialogue came to a temporary halt:

12:10 AM

Number 42 Lei Hejia's Baba:

@Tang Zhiyun's Mama, you still haven't gone to bed?
Hard-working

12:15 AM

Tang Zhiyun's Mama:

I have a lot more, but I can't send them all right now.
Tomorrow. . . .

Sure enough, ten hours and eleven minutes later, Tang Zhiyun's Mama posted another seventy-six images of children in lab coats.

At afternoon pickups, I looked at the faces around me and marveled at the apparent normalcy. Most parents seemed like typical middle-class urban Chinese: they didn't dress in expensive clothes, and many of them took the subway, like us. When we talked, they reminded me of the students I had taught in Fuling. Many of them had grown up in working-class or rural families, but they had attended mid-level or lower-tier universities in Sichuan. They were among that early cohort of college-educated provincials, and now, with their children in one of Chengdu's top schools, they were aiming for something better for the next generation.

The parents referred to the twins as Cai Cai and Rou Rou. In China, it's common to simplify a three-part name by doubling the last character, and the twins had been nicknamed almost immediately. Given the lack of foreigners, it was remarkable how quickly the school incorporated Ariel and Natasha into the system. On the second day, Teacher Zhang found two students who spoke some English, and each child shadowed a twin. At the end of the first week, a school rally celebrated Chengdu International Poetry Week, a local festival. The WeChat group distributed a poster with an image of the rally, at which all students had been seated in rows on the sports field. The children wore white uniform shirts and red Young Pioneer scarves, and they held blue volumes of a Chinese classic, *Three Hundred Tang Poems*, against their chests.

When I looked closely, I saw that Natasha and Ariel had been positioned in the front row. Somebody must have loaned them the scarves, and they clutched books that they couldn't yet read. Like everybody else, the twins were waving their right arms at a forty-five-degree angle. Also like the other children, and like many Chinese in photographs, Ariel and Natasha were not smiling. If it weren't for the classical-poetry books, the scene could have been a Maoist rally, and it gave me a strange sensation. But that was all part of what we had signed up for—the characters, the poetry, the nicknames, the rallies. *I am Chinese.*

Like some Chinese American couples, Leslie and I had given our daughters different family names to be used on each side of the Pacific. In English, the twins were Hesslers, but their Chinese family name—Zhang—came from Leslie. The first character of their given names—Xing—had been selected more than a century before their birth, by one of their maternal great-great-grandfathers. He was a native of northeastern China, the region once known as Manchuria. Throughout most of history, the northeast had been remote and lightly populated, but it started to develop at the end of the nineteenth century. During this period, some of China's earliest railroads began to open new trade routes to coastal and overseas markets.

The twins' great-great-grandfather capitalized on these changes by acquiring an oil press and flour mill. Soon, he became the largest landowner in his village, and he established the foundation for what he hoped would become a great clan. He married four wives, built an impressive family compound, and opened a primary school for his offspring and some other local children. For good measure, he named the next twenty generations of Zhangs. These names were arranged in a poem that read, in classical Chinese:

凤立同兴殿   *Feng li tong xing dian*
鸿连毓宝朝   *Hong lian yu bao chao*

万传家庆延　　*Wan chuan jia qing yan*
九锡国恩昭　　*Jiu yang guo en zhao*

The members of each generation would adopt one character in their names, following the lines in succession—a poem that, in human terms, would be finished in approximately five hundred years. As part of the fourth generation, Ariel and Natasha were given Xing, the fourth character, which means "prospering." The poem connects the family's success to that of China:

The phoenix stands in the palace of prospering together
The swan connects and nurtures the dynasty of treasures
Ten thousand generations pass on the continuing family celebration
Nine ornaments display the favor of the nation.

The Zhang patriarch believed in Confucian values, but he was also open to some of the new ideas that were spreading in China. At the family school, he had his daughters educated alongside his sons, which in previous eras would have been unheard of. He decided that his first wife's second son—the twins' great-grandfather—should be prepared to enter the modern world. The boy was sent to the first middle school in Jilin province that followed a curriculum called New Learning. The school taught the Chinese classics, but the top priorities were mathematics, history, geography, and the natural sciences. The boy excelled, and in his late teens he won a scholarship to study in the United States.

At some point after arriving in America, in 1920, he marked the transition by adopting a new name: Zhang Shenfu. The last two characters come from a classical phrase that means "many diligent men drafted into service." Shenfu belonged to one of the first significant waves of Chinese students to come to the U.S., and this was also when John Dewey was spreading his ideas across China. In America, young Chinese tended to major in pragmatic subjects that they believed would be useful in their homeland. More than a third of the Chinese students who went to the United States between 1905 and 1924 became engineers.

Shenfu had intended to study literature, but he switched his major to mining engineering. He attended the Michigan College of Mines, near the Canadian border, and after graduation he worked a variety of jobs across the U.S. In his diary, he describes his work experience in terms of patriotic responsibility:

January 26, 1926

China still does not have a person who manufactures machinery. To have it begin with me in the future would be a most wonderful thing.

February 4, 1926

Harbin's transport is very convenient; I would like to do some work there. But its railways are all in the hands of foreigners. This is a hateful thing.

June 4, 1926

If China wants to become prosperous and strong, it must develop its steel industry; otherwise it cannot resist the encroachments of foreign nations. Right now its machinery relies entirely on imports. If a war begins and resources from the outside world are cut off, then China will surely be defeated.

Shenfu often exhorts himself to self-improvement, and he admires American technology and many aspects of the political traditions:

March 8, 1926

President Wilson thought that at the founding of America there were the most talented people, like Madison, who drafted the constitution, and Franklin, who had so much morality and philosophy. Because of these people, America's constitution was able to be effective. In China, everyone is seeking his selfish interests with no sense of civic morality and the internal conflicts are never-ending. This is terrifying to people.

But he seems wary of democracy, and he often notes examples of corruption in elections. Mostly, though, he is distressed by certain aspects of American culture:

January 1, 1926

My personal conduct must be honorable and in my dealings I must be more frugal.

I had lunch with my landlord, Harry Weart. His neighbors, an old couple, like to play with dogs and birds and they spoke of their pets. I am disgusted by this kind of talk.

January 9, 1926

The youth society in America is all about dancing and cars. Family life has been completely destroyed. The women pursue dissolution and the men seek idleness as pleasure. Thefts and murders are increasing by the day. Morality is regressing. . . . China must take America as a forerunner of what is to come.

In the 2000s, when Leslie was researching her book *Factory Girls*, which includes some sections on family history, she translated entries with the assistance of a Chinese graduate student. In the diary, rows of Chinese characters are punctuated by English names of industrial enterprises: Sincerity Coal Company, in Herrin, Illinois; International Lead Refining Company, in East Chicago, Indiana. Shenfu tries factory jobs, engineering jobs, mining jobs. He complains about foremen who make racist comments about Chinese, and sometimes, in these hard-edged towns, he feels unsafe:

April 26, 1926

In the morning I went to the factory to work. The night before, two blacks killed a white guy with a knife. Yesterday the whites set fire to a black church. The situation on the streets is very nervous. Tonight the whites have chased all the blacks out of the area. I packed my luggage and will go to New York tomorrow.

This fear seems to have passed quickly, or maybe the excesses of the Roaring Twenties were a distraction. They must have seemed nearly as bizarre to a mining Manchurian as they would have been to a Martian:

May 22, 1926

In the morning I went into the No. 72 mine and looked at the rotary dumps.

Since I started work here, I have gotten up every morning at 6:15. I am full of energy. People should get up early and not oversleep.

A theater operator in New York ordered a woman to take off her clothes before five hundred guests and stand in a giant bottle of alcohol, then he served the alcohol to the guests. There is a lawsuit about this.

In 1927, after seven years in America, Shenfu returned to China. His father—the man who had named twenty generations of Zhangs—welcomed his son with a grand celebration in the village. The following day, the patriarch pummeled Shenfu on the backside with a traditional wooden rod called a *jiafa*. The ritual beating was carried out because, on the other side of the ocean, the young man had changed his major without requesting permission from his father. The beating was so serious that Shenfu had trouble sitting down for days. Nearly a century later, in the People's Republic of high-speed trains and 985 universities, it would seem incredible: a Chinese parent who beat his son for switching from literature to engineering.

Given that numbers are universal, Leslie and I had thought that math would be relatively manageable for the girls. But we quickly realized that Chinese textbooks often bury digits beneath a pile of words. In the twins' math textbook, many problems included long paragraphs of background information, some of it apparently designed to distract:

> In 2009, the total number of migrant workers in our country was 230 million, and the construction and development of the cities are inseparable from their industrious labor.
>
> Grandma: "Every month I receive a subsidy of 185 yuan."
>
> Liang Liang [the grandson]: "Baba and Mama are working in the city, where every month they can send back 800 yuan."
>
> 1. Liang Liang and Grandma spent 745 in August. How much did they have left over?
>
> 2. In September, the surplus was 260 yuan, and in October the surplus was 30 yuan less than it was in September. What was the total surplus for these two months together?

Many problems involved money. Migration often cropped up, along with logistics. Much of Unit 1 was dedicated to problems that involved seating large numbers of people on buses, trains, and boats. There were also questions about schoolyard rallies:

> The class has 18 boys and 18 girls who will participate in drill performances and group calisthenics.
>
> Naughty: "During drill performances, we classmates stand in 4 lines."
>
> Smiley: "During group calisthenics, one pattern is formed by a set of 3 boys and 3 girls."
>
> In drill performances, what's the average number of people standing in each line?
>
> During calisthenics, how many patterns can be formed by 36 people?

Problems were often conveyed through dialogues between cartoon characters, some of whom had loaded names: Naughty, Little Sloppy, Clever Dog, Wise Old Man. Occasionally, a mistake was deliberately inserted into a word problem:

> While multiplying one two-digit number by another two-digit number, Little Sloppy misreads 22 as 25, and as a result his answer is higher than the correct answer by 69. What is the correct answer?

After a long day at Sichuan University, the last thing I wanted to do was clean up Little Sloppy's second digits. But Leslie and I plowed through, dictionaries at hand. Sometimes we came across a word that we didn't know even in English. In Unit 7, we learned *run*, or "intercalary," which, according to *Merriam-Webster*, means "inserted in a calendar." The twins kept missing questions about *run* years, until we read the fine print on page 69:

[Every four years] there is a year that adds 1 day in February, for a total of 366 days, and these are called *run* years. It is also stipulated that if a year ends in double zeros, it must be divisible by 400 in order to qualify as a *run* year. So the year 2000 is a *run* year, but the year 1700 is not a *run* year.

If Leslie or I had ever learned the divisible-by-four-hundred rule about leap years, we had long since forgotten. After all, it would be personally relevant only if we lived until the year 2100, when, at the age of 130, we would need to make plans for a February with twenty-eight days. But Chinese third graders needed this information now:

Out of 1900, 1996, 2018, and 2016, how many *run* years are there?

Out of 1800, 1960, and 2040, which is not a *run* year?

Children also had to memorize the number of days in each month, and certain questions were devious:

Ping Ping: "I was looking through a calendar and saw that there was one year when November had five Saturdays and five Sundays."

Huang Feifei: "So what day of the week would November 1st have been that year?"

Was this really math? As a language teacher, I had always observed a tendency toward rote memorization. Students studied long lists of English vocabulary words, writing them over and over, a pattern that came from the ways they learned characters. I had assumed that math would involve repetitive worksheets, but the subject was far more dynamic than that. Even the problems had problems—students had to figure out what the question was really asking, and which information was extraneous. They were required to show how they arranged equations, and grading was strict. At the end of the first semester, when parents gathered for a conference at the school, the math instructor concluded her talk with a statement on values. "Math is virtue," she declared. "Math is a way to cultivate yourself."

It also seemed designed for a hypercompetitive society in which citizens needed to be alert. One guiding principle behind Chinese third-grade math could be summarized as: Don't be a sucker. Leslie said that when you read an American exam you can tell that the writers of the exam want children to get things right. But Chinese exams are aiming for wrong answers.

Our favorite question that semester appeared on page 56 of the math text. There was a drawing of a mirror, and inside the mirror was an image of a clock. The question read:

> Long Yiming started to do his homework after he got home from school. In the mirror, he could see that his wall clock (which had only graduated markings, no numbers) said the time was 6:30. After Long Yiming finished his homework, he turned on the television, and "Dragon Gate Story," which is broadcast at 18:30, was just beginning. How is this possible?

Those were typical distractions—the digressive grammar, the confusing use of both "6:30" and "18:30," the sneaky detail of a clock without numbers. But the principle remained the same: Don't be a sucker. If an image is reversed, an hour hand that appears to be to the left of six o'clock is actually to the right. Natasha scrawled the answer in her fledgling characters:

> He saw "6:30" in the mirror, but the time was really 5:30. So he did homework for one hour.

———

Shortly after the twins' Chinese great-grandfather studied in the United States, one of their American great-grandfathers made his own academic journey. Frank Dietz—my mother's father—traveled across the Atlantic rather than the Pacific. But Frank eventually settled on a different version of Zhang Shenfu's dream: to study in the West and then apply that knowledge in China.

Like his Chinese counterpart, Frank had grown up in a provincial town in a country that was being transformed by railroads. In early-twentieth-century America, though, this process was far more advanced than it was in China. Many members of Frank's extended family worked for railroads in the South, and his father was employed by a train line in Pine Bluff, Arkansas. The rails brought prosperity, but occasionally they also carried more dangerous by-products of the modern world. In 1917, Frank's father died suddenly, at the age of twenty-nine, probably after being infected by an early wave of the virus that became known as the Spanish flu. Frank, the eldest of three brothers, was only six.

His mother pawned her wedding rings and found an office job, but eventually she realized that she couldn't raise the boys alone. She enrolled them as boarding students at Subiaco Abbey, a Benedictine monastery in west-central Arkansas. Frank excelled, and the monks encouraged his interest in the priesthood. In 1929, the Benedictines sent him to study as a monk at Sant'Anselmo all'Aventino, an abbey in Rome.

As part of the transition, the eighteen-year-old changed his name to Frank Anselm Dietz. In Rome, he kept a diary, which, like the journals of Zhang Shenfu, has been passed down by descendants. Sometimes these two young men—one writing in classical Chinese, the other in English—comment on the same things. Both wrote about Benito Mussolini on anniversaries of January 3, 1925, the day on which he had assumed the powers of a dictator:

[Zhang Shenfu]

January 3, 1926

Since Mussolini's rise, Italy's social situation has improved and the ambitions of its citizens have increased and recovered very much. This will create more problems for the rest of Europe.

[Frank Dietz]

January 3, 1931

Read Mussolini's good-will speech to America. I think about half of it is "boloney."

Both diaries describe poor health, undoubtedly from the stress of living in strange environments. Language was part of the challenge. Shenfu learned English, and Frank battled with Latin, Italian, and Hebrew. One patch of common ground between Confucians and Benedictines is self-flagellation, and the tone of certain Shenfu entries—*in my dealings I must be more frugal*—is echoed by Frank:

January 12, 1931

Am dreadfully lazy and "sleep in" for the first time this year, and *Deo volente*, the last time.

January 24, 1931

Can't get any interest in any of my classes and don't do any work all day. This can't go on!

But the writers have vastly different orientations toward their home countries. China's poverty and political chaos represent personal burdens for Shenfu, whose entries are full of distressed references to warlords, race traitors, and foreign aggressors. Frank, on the other hand, almost never comments on news from the United States. His boat docks at Naples the same month of the stock market crash of 1929, but he never refers to that event or to the Depression. The American economic downturn was probably minor compared to the various traumas suffered in China. In any case, national issues are not Frank's struggle, and he often seems to lack direction. Then, in the spring of his second year at the monastery, there's a sudden spark of life:

March 18, 1931

Dom Francis Clougherty, chancellor of the Catholic University, Peking, arrives here to-day on his way back to China. A big strapping Irishman.

March 22, 1931

Fr. Clougherty is very interesting to listen to. According to him the University is under a perfectly solid foundation and he has received promises to come out to China from a considerable number of very capable teachers, both Benedictine and otherwise.

March 23, 1931

All small talk among Americans is now about China.

March 25, 1931

Pontifical High Mass this morning and Solemn Vespers before dinner. . . . Talk to Hugh and Donald about China upon my return.

Fr. Clougherty had a big day to-day but came down to Donald's room and gives Donald, Hugh, Edward and me an inspiring talk. We are so wrought up that when Clougherty leaves at 12 o'clock Donald, H, and I stay up and talk it over till almost 3 A.M. I believe that this is the turning point in my life and I am going to sign up for China. God be with us!

The Catholic University of Peking, known in Chinese as Fu Jen, had been established by Benedictines from Pennsylvania in 1925. Like many foreign projects of the time, the university sought to combine pragmatism and faith, science and God. Pope Pius XI issued a proclamation: "You should supply the University at Peking on the one hand with the men best fitted to govern, to teach, and to bring up souls in piety, and on the other hand to provide the equipment and instruments to teach the sciences properly."

Father Francis Clougherty—the "big strapping Irishman"—was actually Irish American, from Pennsylvania. His visit to Rome was brief, but he inspired Frank and other young monks to change career plans. That spring, Frank's diary tracks their progress as they negotiate the formidable Catholic bureaucracy. Some Church titles would not have been out of place in the future People's Republic:

March 27, 1931

Everything is China at present. I breathe, eat and sleep <u>China</u> and I think that is about the case with all of our "China group." Fr. Clougherty is sick in bed this morning. . . . He & Donald have an interview with Cardinal Van Roseum, Prefect of Propaganda, this afternoon.

May 8, 1931

Raph receives very encouraging letter from his senior at Washington saying that he has no objection to Raph's changing his vows for China.

May 24, 1931

> Hugh approaches his Abbot on the subject of his going to China
> & receives, as usual, an evasive answer. Martin has made a rough
> draft of his letter to his Reverendissimo and will send it in a few days.

In 1932, Frank returned to the United States, where he planned to be ordained as a priest. He told his Benedictine superior that he had received a call from God to serve as a teacher at the Catholic University of Peking. The superior replied that occasionally God gives a false call, in order to test a young man's obedience to his earthly superior. And in this case, the earthly superior expected Frank to teach the next generation of schoolboys at Subiaco Abbey, in rural Arkansas.

By the middle of November, Ariel and Natasha had memorized more than five hundred characters, and they understood most of what was spoken in class. Leslie and I had worried about the twins becoming a burden, but Teacher Zhang never expressed frustration, and we quickly realized that she was a remarkable instructor. I couldn't imagine handling two foreigners along with fifty-three other third graders, especially in the Chinese way. There were no groups or divisions: all fifty-five moved through the material at the same pace. At one conference with the parents, Teacher Zhang talked about the *weibade wenti*, "the problem of the tail." Using a PowerPoint slide, she showed us how, during the previous semester, seven students had failed to reach 90 percent in the final exam. This term, the number of sub-ninety children had been reduced to four. "These are the students that we spend the most time with," she said.

Whereas American education often values small classes, the Chinese system focuses on efficiency and specialization. A typical American primary-school teacher handles all subjects, but Teacher Zhang taught only language. She was assisted by a teacher in training, who was also a specialist. Another instructor came to the classroom for math, another for English, and so on across the subjects. Through the day, children hardly moved from their seats. Lunch was wheeled into the classroom on a metal cart, and the kids ate at their desks, like little workaholics. During class, they sat with both feet on the floor and their arms crossed neatly atop the desks. If a teacher called on a student, the child stood up before speaking. In math, whenever a student drew a line in an equal sign, a minus sign, or a division sign, she was required to use a ruler. For a while, the math instructor tolerated Ariel and Natasha writing these symbols freehand, but then she started deducting points, and the twins quickly adjusted to using rulers. This discipline was part of the emphasis on efficiency: if children were orderly, they wasted less time.

The system also maximized parental support while minimizing input to effectively zero. Parents were discouraged from entering the front gate, with the occasional exception of photographers or others with special business. On WeChat, Mamas and Babas busily engaged in fee collecting and other administrative duties, and they exchanged thousands of messages about homework, uniforms, and virtually every other topic under the sun. But I never saw a parent post advice for Teacher Zhang. There were no suggestions, no complaints, and no criticisms. The school's message was clear: We are in charge.

And the "we" of the chat group—the way parents were subsumed by their children—was also true in person. Parent-teacher conferences were held with everybody at once, and adults sat in their children's assigned desks. Only Leslie and I attended as a complete Mama-and-Baba set, because having twins gave us the right to two seats. Every other couple had to select one parent to attend.

The moment the adults occupied the desks, their body language changed. They kept their eyes on the front, and they didn't fiddle with their phones except to take pictures of PowerPoint slides. The conferences could last for two hours, but parents remained fully attentive. In four semesters, nobody asked a single question. That message was also clear: You are here to listen.

Another Chinese educational strategy involves a strict hierarchy of academic priorities, almost to the point of triage. At Chengdu Experimental, everything revolved around language and mathematics, which produced almost all homework—usually, a total of between two and three hours a night. The teachers of these two subjects enjoyed the highest status, and their textbooks were also the best. In particular, the math book was brilliantly organized.

But some of the other texts could have been tossed together by Little Sloppy and his cronies. In the government-published English book, the second unit introduced body-related vocabulary through a series of dialogues about accidents, injuries, and medical care. Children got bitten by dogs, smashed their heads on rocks, and sustained serious injuries while playing soccer. Even eating was dangerous—one page featured a little sour-faced boy who said, "At lunch time, I bit my tongue. It really hurts." That was one English word that the children learned quickly: *hurts*. On another page, a quartet of kids sprawled out on hospital beds with English labels:

Bill—8 years old—foot hurts

Ben—10 years old—leg hurts

Lily—9 years old—ear hurts

Jane—10 years old—arm hurts

Was this a good way to inspire language learning? And who the hell puts a nine-year-old in the hospital because her ear hurts? In the 1990s, my Chinese students and colleagues had attitudes toward health that impressed me as somewhat fearful. It wasn't surprising, given China's long history of poverty, epidemics, and natural disasters. Since then, the nation had become dramatically safer and more prosperous, but old mindsets endured, especially in families that were limited to a single child.

There were more catastrophes in Morality and Rules, the political class that was supposed to teach third graders to behave well and to love the Communist Party and the nation. In that textbook, careless children often drowned in rivers and ponds, and they were abducted by apparently friendly aunties who turned out to be predators. One chapter told the story of Mo Mo, a nine-year-old who plays with his father's cigarette lighter in a vacant field. The good news is that the dedicated staff at the hospital save Mo Mo's life. The bad news:

> But he suffered extensive burns all over his body, resulting in permanent disability. Blind curiosity and careless experimentation have brought great misfortune to Mo Mo, his family, and society.

It was telling that the nouns *curiosity* and *experimentation* were both connected to negative adjectives. If one guiding principle of Chinese primary education was "Don't be a sucker," another seemed to be: "Fear everything outside the classroom." This was one of many contradictions at an institution whose name included the word *experimental*. The school's beautiful campus included basketball courts, a soccer field, a jungle gym, and a track. But I rarely saw children playing outdoors, and strict rules forbade any child below sixth grade to touch the jungle gym. Ariel and Natasha found it ridiculous—they said that the jungle gym would seem tame for any Colorado kindergartner.

Near the displays about the school's history, there was a sign with the heading "Rules for Primary School Students." The guidelines ran for nearly three hundred characters, organized into nine parts, from the Party to Polonius and beyond:

1. Love the Party, love the Country, love the People. . . .

6. Be honest and keep your promises. Ensure that you are as good as your word, don't lie or cheat, return borrowed things on time, correct your mistakes. . . .

8. Cherish life and keep safe. Stop at red lights and go at green lights, avoid drowning and don't play with fire. . . .

The rules didn't mention individuality, self-motivated study, or other virtues that had been extolled by Hu Yanli, the John Dewey acolyte. In the schoolyard, the sole reference to "democratic spirit" was the one that appeared on the same sign as the name of Li Peng, the former premier. Nearby, there was a short biography of Li and a display of his calligraphy. Of course, none of these materials mentioned that in June 1989, Li Peng had reportedly advocated for the use of force to suppress the student and worker protests in Tiananmen Square. In the wake of the massacre, in which at least hundreds of people died, the most famous alumnus of Chengdu Experimental was nicknamed the Butcher of Beijing.

The Tiananmen protests represented the last echoes of a movement that began when John Dewey was still in China. After May 4, 1919, Chinese students often played a prominent role in political uprisings. This role ended, though, with the 1989 crackdown. Some of the change can be attributed to post-Tiananmen campus policies, ranging from the political courses to the mandatory military training that Vincent wrote about in my class. But it was also a matter of China returning to a much older tradition of education in service to the state. In "Educated Acquiescence," Perry observes that this tradition has remained strong even as Chinese universities expanded both their enrollments and their contact with foreign scholars and ideas. "One might have expected," she writes, "that opening China's ivory tower to an infusion of scholars and dollars from around the world would work to liberalize the intellectual climate on Chinese campuses. Yet Chinese universities remain oases of political compliance."

Even in the early decades of the twentieth century, there were signs that foreign influence might not have expected outcomes. After Dewey's lecture tour, he never returned to China, and most of his ideas failed to gain traction there in the long run. Mao quickly turned against the principle of nonviolence, although he continued to value Dewey-style pragmatism and experimentation, at least in the early years of the revolution. In his home province of Hunan, Mao researched local peasant movements in a systematic manner, and his observations contradicted dogmatic Marxists. Mao concluded that support for Communism was more likely to come from rural regions than from the urban working class, an idea that proved instrumental in the victory of the Chinese Communist Party. Nevertheless, after Mao rose to power, he initiated political campaigns attacking Dewey and his Chinese followers.

This was a common pattern for early educational exchanges between the U.S. and China. It was largely a history of missed connections and lost opportunities; from the American perspective, it often seemed as if China took the pragmatism without the democratic values, the science without the faith. In the case of Frank Dietz, the China dream ended quickly. His first false call from God was also his last: without the option of going to Beijing, Frank decided to leave the Benedictines. He enrolled in law school, married, had two children, and eventually ran a small insurance agency.

Later in life, my grandfather rarely talked about his decision to decline ordination. He remained a devout Catholic, and I never learned about his interest in China while he was alive. In my midtwenties, not long before I joined the Peace Corps, my mother gave me Frank's diaries. I often wondered what would have happened if he had joined the other Benedictines at the Catholic University of Peking. Father Clougherty—

the "big strapping Irishman"—spent more than two decades in China. During the Second World War, he directed relief work in support of Chinese soldiers who were fighting Japan. Within an hour after the attack on Pearl Harbor, the Japanese arrested Father Clougherty, who spent the next four years as a prisoner of war. He survived and eventually had a long retirement in the U.S. In Beijing, after the Communists came to power, they took over Catholic University, assigning its facilities to Party-run institutions. Another version of the university was founded in Taiwan, where today it's known as Fu Jen Catholic University.

Zhang Shenfu's working life was also shaped by war. During the fight against Japan, he used his American education to oversee Chinese mines on behalf of the Kuomintang government. Accompanied by his wife, Xiangheng, Shenfu moved frequently, and all of the couple's five children were born in remote mining towns. Shenfu continued his diary:

July 17, 1940

These few years have passed quickly without much meaning. First, I have no friends, because I have lived so long in the mountains, separated from the outside world. Second, I have no ideas in life, knowing only about mines and mining work. What is the ultimate aim of life? I have not decided yet. Forty-two years have passed in this way. This is worthy of pity and regret.

After Japan surrendered, in August 1945, the Kuomintang needed to regain control of valuable mines. But Chinese Communists were building support in the northeast, often with the help of Soviet troops. The following January, the Kuomintang assigned an official to inspect an important coal mine in Fushun, a site in Liaoning province that was known to be dangerous. The official had a reputation for playing politics, and he was able to maneuver out of the assignment. The mission fell to Shenfu. Unlike Frank, Shenfu had never taken a monk's vow of obedience, but his patriotism seemed as powerful as any religious faith. He accepted the Fushun assignment.

At the mine, local Communist and Soviet agents prevented Shenfu from carrying out a proper inspection. He tried to return to the provincial capital, but a band of armed soldiers boarded his train at a deserted station. At nine o'clock on a bitterly cold evening, the men marched Shenfu and six other Kuomintang mining engineers to a nearby hillside, where, with their hands bound behind their backs, they were murdered with bayonets. Shenfu was stabbed eighteen times. A Chinese newspaper reported his last words: "To die for my duty, I have no complaints."

Shenfu's second son was only nine. His name was Zhang Ligang—Li was the second character of the patriarch's poem. The family fled the mainland in 1949, and the boy became a standout student in Taipei. For graduate school, he made his own journey across the Pacific. He studied engineering and physics in the United States, where he married another science student from Taiwan. Eventually, they became American citizens. With the births of Leslie and her brother—Tonghe and Tongyi—the family poem inched forward another character.

Back in China, the official who had declined the Fushun assignment abandoned the Kuomintang, joined the Communist Party, enjoyed a long career in government, and lived to the age of 102.

Nobody in the Party took credit or responsibility for Shenfu's assassination, and they never explained why they had targeted a civilian. For Shenfu, the Communists had always been mysterious. In America, almost twenty years to the day before he was killed, he had written:

January 19, 1926

Those people who sing the praises of communism, it is hard to know what they are really thinking in their hearts. Lenin and Trotsky have endured many sufferings without changing their orientation. They

have good morality. But China's Communists, I don't know what their
morality is like.

———

When Leslie and I moved to Chengdu, friends warned us about the political indoctrination in a public school. After all, Ariel and Natasha's
great-grandfather had been killed by the Communists, and now they attended a school whose rules began with the words "Love the Party." But
many Chinese separate the political and the personal. In the 1970s, when
China and the United States began to take the first steps toward normal-
ized relations, Leslie's father, Ligang, joined some of the earliest delega-
tions of American scientists who traveled to the mainland. After retiring
from his career in the U.S., Ligang served as a university dean in Hong
Kong. In other parts of the world, the son of a martyr would probably
have behaved differently—it's hard to imagine a Cuban exile participat-
ing in similar exchanges with the Castro regime. But Ligang believed
that his deepest ties to China transcended politics: they were personal,
cultural, intellectual, and emotional. For him, education was sacred, and
he had faith in the value of exchange.

We sent Ariel and Natasha to Chengdu Experimental with a similar
faith. I believed that Teacher Zhang and other instructors were more
likely to view the twins as individual children, rather than strictly Americans, and I wanted the girls to learn the language and experience a different system. In truth, there were things about education in both places
that I liked and disliked. It wasn't completely different from John Dewey,
who believed that there was much to be learned from Chinese traditions.
In *John Dewey in China*, the historian Jessica Ching-Sze Wang emphasizes that the American philosopher's view of reform was far from one-
dimensional. Of course, things didn't turn out exactly as Dewey might
have wished, which was typical of the long and troubled history of

U.S.–China exchanges. When people traveled across the Pacific in hopes of combining the two traditions, they almost never came away with what they had expected.

Nevertheless, I knew that instructors like Teacher Zhang were deeply committed, a pattern that I also recognized among my former students who had become teachers. From my surveys, I estimated that more than 90 percent of the people I had taught in Fuling were still employed as teachers. In the 2021 survey, I asked how many jobs they had had since graduation, and the average for teachers was only 2.1. More than a quarter had worked at the same school for nearly twenty years, which seemed remarkable given all the changes of the Reform era. I doubted that one would find such stability among a similar cohort of Americans who had been trained as teachers in the mid-1990s. But educators in China enjoy high social status, and their salaries have increased at appropriate levels over the years. When I asked my former students to rate their job satisfaction on a scale of 1 to 10, the average response for teachers was 7.9.

But they could be scathing about the state-mandated material that they had to teach. "China's education is like junk food," one woman responded on a survey. Another wrote, "I think China's education is rubbish. No creativity, too much work, pressure, and most of what the students are learning at school is useless in the future." In 2017, I asked former students to identify China's biggest success in the previous decade, and everybody mentioned something related to economics or development. The most common response by far was improved transportation. Out of thirty people who answered, nobody mentioned education.

Emily was the only former student who taught in a primary school. In Shenzhen, during the early 2000s, she had done well as a migrant, and eventually some of her friends started successful businesses of their own. Emily could have joined them, but in 2009 she moved against the tide of migration and returned to Fuling. In her hometown, it would have been easy to rely on her father's academic connections to find a job at one of the best local schools. But Emily made a point of avoiding such networking. In an email, she described her job interview at an obscure school in Fuling's rural outskirts:

> I decided not to use "guanxi" any longer to gain my own benefit. . . . [The school] was not an important one, so things were easy. On September 1, I went to the new school, 40 minutes bus-ride away from where I lived. . . . The sight here was quite different. In the middle of the school there was a broad playground, and there was an opening on one side, where I could see farmers working in a field. "This is where I want to stay," I thought to myself.

During the interview, various administrators tried to nudge Emily toward more prestigious positions. Primary-school teachers weren't paid as well as those who taught in middle and high schools, and the key subjects of math and language were also more respected. Emily described the interview:

> "Would you like teaching in the middle school?" a thin old man came in and asked.
> "There's a middle school here?"
> "Yes."
> "Sorry, I prefer primary school."
> The old man went out.
> "Would you like teaching Chinese or Math?" a thin young man came in and asked.
> "I'd like to teach English. I've been teaching English for years in Shenzhen and I'm good at it."
> The young man went out.

Two years after Emily started the job, her school was officially incorporated into the city system, because of Fuling's rapid growth. For most people, this would have represented a welcome sign of progress, but Emily wrote in an email:

> Yesterday afternoon, when I saw students in my school are lined up and led by their class teachers to go out of the school, I feel sad. From this term, my school is no longer a countryside school, it's a "city school" now. Many things are changing, and there will be more discipline and rules. It will be more like a factory than a school.

She was perhaps the most idiosyncratic and thoughtful of my former students. She often talked about Cousin Liu, who had become wealthy beyond imagination and yet still seemed dissatisfied. "He doesn't really care about money," Emily told me once. "He wants something else, but he's not sure what it is." In Cousin Liu's home village, he built a mansion for his elderly mother, but the woman continued to live largely like a peasant. She spent hours laboring in the fields beside the grand house, tending plots of rice and vegetables. Emily said that her aunt was motivated to work in part because she feared that the new wealth might be a mirage. "She says that anything can disappear at any time," Emily explained.

In China, people rarely had time to observe the small details of everyday life. But Emily wasn't in a rush, and everywhere she went in Fuling, she watched and she listened. Her messages described small moments in the city:

> One day on a bus I heard a conversation between a mother and a son and I feel sad.
>   Son: Mum, it's holiday, I can play now.
>   Mother: No, Son, it's not the time to play. You should study

hard. You can play after you go to college. (The boy looked no more than ten.)

Over the years, there was only one extended period during which Emily fell silent. It happened to coincide with some major life changes for me: in 2006, Leslie and I married, and the following spring we moved from Beijing to southwestern Colorado. During these transitions, it took a while to register that I was no longer hearing from Emily. After reaching out a number of times, I finally heard back, and we exchanged a series of long emails. At one point, I asked how Emily's brother was doing. Her response was quick:

Dear Mr. Hessler,

How are you?

It's very hard for me to sit back in front of the computer and write you back. Last time you asked about my brother. And I didn't know how to reply. He is no longer with us. Three years ago he jumped off a bridge in Chongqing. . . . Sorry, I think I still can't go on writing. Maybe I should talk to you next time.

Sorry for telling you this.

Emily

In China, a family tragedy is not a story to be shared. To some degree, this is a matter of basic decency, because sadness is a burden best lifted alone. *Sorry for telling you this.* Even when a tragedy is public, and when there is no sense of shame, it's best to keep emotion within the family. The death of Leslie's grandfather was, in many ways, a national event:

the funeral was attended by more than ten thousand people, and a Beijing tram line was named after Shenfu. But the family rarely talked about it. When his wife, Xiangheng, first heard the news, she gathered her five children, told them about their father's death, and wept. Then she promised that this was the last time the children would ever see her cry. In the months that followed, Xiangheng's hair quickly turned gray, and she began to smoke heavily, a habit that would follow her to the grave. But she never wept in front of her children again.

A generation later, when Leslie was growing up in New York, she wasn't told the story of her grandfather's death. She had no idea that he had been killed by the Communists, or that he had been designated a martyr. It wasn't until Leslie was in her midthirties, and already working as a journalist in the People's Republic, that her father finally explained to her and her brother that their grandfather had been assassinated. When he finished the story, he wept. Like his own mother, that was the first and the last time he cried in front of his children.

I never learned other details about the death of Emily's brother. My own brief encounters with the young man had left a deep impression, both of his sweetness and of his pain. Emily had been fiercely protective, which must have made the suicide even more shattering. She had moved back to Fuling within a year of the death, partly in order to be close to her parents. But the family avoided talking about it. In conversations with Emily, I was careful not to mention her brother.

But I could see that the loss informed her teaching. She resisted narrow-minded ambition because she felt that her brother had suffered from the competitive environment of Reform-era China. When she wrote about her work, she rarely fixated on academic success: for her, the most important lessons to impart to children were social and emotional. She was frustrated that her father, who had built a career on achievement and status, failed to understand why his daughter dedicated herself to students from modest backgrounds. In one email, she wrote:

I feel sad every time after calling my father. I'm just too ignorant before him. I don't have enough knowledge to share with him on mathematics, or history, or geography. . . . I want to share with him my
happiness when receiving flowers from my students; when they
say, "I like you, Miss Emily"; when one little girl finally raised her
hand asking to join in the play after being silent for one and a half
years in kindergarten (her former teacher told me so); when one
aggressive boy admitted his fault, and tried to be nice to his fel-
lows; when one gloomy boy from a broken family found his safety
around me; when the children try to behave when I have a sore
throat. . . . I want to share with my father all these things which I
truly value.

In her spare time, Emily read widely about schools and child-rearing.
Like Chinese educators from the previous century, she often searched
for values and practices from overseas. One year, she read *Summerhill*,
the 1960 book by A. S. Neill, a Scottish headmaster who had advocated
for a democratic education that freed children from adult pressure. After
that, Emily studied Marva Collins, a Black American educator whose
ideas had been influential in the 1980s. Emily wrote in an email:

Neill believed that "not to interfere" was the best way to manage
the children. While Collins interfered a lot, of course in a positive
way. I think maybe they were different because they had different
background. Collins and her students were mostly black people.
And at that time black people were mostly belong to lower class. So
education was the way to change their social status. They needed
to work hard and go to college and then get a noble job. Neill was
white and so were most [of] his students. Changing status was not
the main goal. What they cherished was creativity and being themselves.

In China, most people take education seriously, because it's the way of getting a better life. But I have doubt about the importance of school education when I get to know more about it. This year I shared the same office with Grade One and Grade Two Chinese and Math teachers. I've been sick to listen to complaints about how stupid some of the children and their parents are. Sometimes they telephone the parents and criticize them for not checking the children's homework. Sometimes they criticize the children badly in the office for mistakes in their exercise books. I think I would never want to go to school if I were the children.

Emily believed that Chinese education was long overdue for a change. For many citizens, the drive to escape poverty was over, but there was still something desperate about how hard people worked and the ways they pushed their children. After my daughters enrolled at Chengdu Experimental, Emily and I often talked about the things I observed. She told me it was a good sign that the school no longer ranked students by exam scores—the more progressive Chinese institutions were trying to get away from this kind of pressure. Chengdu Experimental had also developed curricula that it shared with schools in undeveloped parts of Sichuan. Even if the institution no longer publicly identified with the ideas of John Dewey, it still tried to innovate in whatever small ways were possible in the Chinese system. And I appreciated that the school had been bold enough to accept my children. At a politically sensitive moment, there was a risk associated with any foreign writer, but administrators seemed to believe that there was some value in having American students.

Emily's son, Tao Tao, was three years older than the twins, and he attended a Chongqing school that also had a reputation for experimentation. In the Chinese climate, though, there were limits to how far educators were willing to push reforms. The tradition of "educated acquiescence" remained strong, and parents were well aware of the potential risks to any child who became too creative and free-thinking. Sometimes this became a point of tension between Emily and her husband, Yunfeng.

Yunfeng had grown up in the countryside, where his education was modest. But he was intelligent, and he had thrived in the factories around Shenzhen, where he rose to become a skilled technician and then a manager of production lines. One reason why the couple had been able to move to Fuling was because Yunfeng found a good job at a foreign-owned plant that manufactured batteries for electric cars.

Tao Tao was the spitting image of his father. He had the same wide eyes, strong build, and slightly coarse features. But his mind came straight from his mother. He had a thoughtful, deep intelligence—years ago, in my classroom, Emily had often taken a long time to answer questions, because she considered different angles before speaking. Her son had a similar patience, and, also like his mother, he had a tendency to come up with unconventional opinions.

Sometimes, when Emily described her son's ideas, I felt the same way that I did when a student at Sichuan University made a brave comment or wrote about an edgy topic. For a teacher or a parent in China, the most inspiring moments can also be the ones that make you look over your shoulder. In one email, Emily wrote:

> Last Saturday when we were having dinner, Tao Tao asked some difficult questions about history and the country's political leaders. I was thinking about how to answer, but his father's voice came first, telling him not to ask such things.
>
> "It's impossible to have a conversation with you!" Tao Tao was annoyed.
>
> "Your questions are very interesting; maybe you can ask your history teacher." I tried to make it up.
>
> "Tao Tao is encouraged by his school to think independently,

why do you do the opposite?" I asked Yunfeng when we were taking a walk afterwards.

He said, "I deliberately said that; I must stop him thinking that way. Do you know what happened to those college students who said things against the Party on the Internet? They won't have their diplomas, which means they will have no future in China!"

CHAPTER FIVE

Earthquake

December 2019

A T CHINESE UNIVERSITIES, WHEN A STUDENT REPORTS A PROFES-
sor for political wrongdoing, the verb used to describe this action is *jubao*. It happens rarely, but the possibility is always
there, because potential infractions are both undefined and extremely
varied. A student might *jubao* a teacher for a comment about a sensitive
historical event, or a remark that seems to contradict a Communist Party
policy. Ambiguous statements about Xi Jinping are especially risky. In
2019, the same year that I started teaching, a literature professor named
Tang Yun offhandedly described the language of one of Xi's slogans as
coarse during a lecture at Chongqing Normal University. After students
complained, Tang was demoted to a job in the library.

Other problems can involve course materials. Once, I met a law-
school teacher from another institution in Sichuan who had gotten into
trouble after developing a syllabus with some sensitive content. The syllabus included *Animal Farm*, but the teacher told me that Orwell wasn't
the problem. The controversial material consisted of *Disturbing the Peace*,
a documentary that the artist Ai Weiwei made about his encounters
with the Chinese judicial system. For two years, the law-school instructor used the film in class without incident, but then, partway through
another semester, some students decided to *jubao*. Within a week the

teacher had been replaced with a substitute. But the process can be slower, and much less predictable, if an initial complaint is made on social media, which was how it happened to me.

On the evening of December 11, a few minutes before I was scheduled to start nonfiction class, Leslie called. A friend had just forwarded her a tweet by Peidong Sun, a historian at Cornell University:

American writer and journalist Peter Hessler, under Chinese name Ho Wei . . . who moved to China with his family in Aug. 2019 to teach Non-fiction writing at Sichuan University, has possibly been reported for his behavior/speech.

Sun's tweet referred to a message on an internal bulletin board at Sichuan University. Somebody had taken a screenshot of the message and then posted it to Weibo, the Chinese version of Twitter. On Chinese social media, people often distribute screenshots, which are more difficult for censors to monitor. In this case, the screenshot was too blurry to read on my phone. Leslie's friend said that the report was spreading quickly on both Chinese and American social media. "I wanted to warn you before you started class," Leslie told me.

I checked my watch—there wasn't enough time to look up the original posts. I thought about whether anything in recent days might have triggered a student to *jubao*. Only a week earlier, Yidi had stood in front of the class and read her paper about the VPN dealer. At the time, I felt panicked, but afterward nobody in the class seemed upset, and since then Yidi and I had corresponded about other things. I figured that she would have told me if somebody had started trouble.

For the semester's final projects, a few students were researching off-campus subjects that might be considered sensitive. Serena was interviewing gay activists, but we hadn't discussed her work in class. My freshman composition sections had started reading *Animal Farm*, but the book had been approved by the university. I couldn't think of a definite reason for somebody to *jubao*, so I decided to begin the evening session as normal.

When I entered the classroom, Yidi was sitting in her usual place in the center of the group. She didn't appear to be agitated, and Serena also looked normal. I glanced at the security camera at the front of the room. I don't know what I expected to learn; the device had no lights, and there was never any way of knowing whether it was actively recording. I turned my back to the camera and arranged my notes at the lectern.

After I started to call roll, I heard some students whispering. A few were showing phones to their neighbors. Finally, a girl near the front said, "Mr. Hessler, have you seen this?"

She handed me her phone. She had pulled up screenshots of seven comments that had been posted on the university's bulletin board. The first one read, in Chinese:

To have Ho Wei teaching in our institute is truly treasonous.

The room was quiet while I scanned the other posts. "I know where this is coming from," I said, after I had finished. "It's from another class. It doesn't have anything to do with you."

Hoping to change the subject, I asked an engineering major named Tim to read a draft of his research paper. Tim had studied an online community that called itself the Federation of Stingy Men. Federation members were obsessed with living solely off the interest from their savings and investment accounts, even though many of them were well employed or even wealthy. They shared strategies: one member explained that three millimeters is the smallest amount of toothpaste necessary for brushing your teeth, and another man, who was a millionaire, documented how he traveled to the Chengdu airport, with all his luggage, on a free bike-share. In conclusion, Tim wrote, "There are some people who have been living this kind of abnormally thrifty life . . . because of the habits they developed when they were poor."

A number of research projects touched on the ways in which Chinese citizens responded to sudden prosperity. I had already planned that the following week we would proceed from Tim's cheapskates to a Porsche salesman who had been the subject of a profile by a classmate named Anna. Like most students, Anna had no previous experience as a reporter, but she proved to be a natural. She had a friendly, open demeanor, and she visited a Porsche dealership near campus and convinced a salesman to let her shadow him. One afternoon, she watched the dealer unsuccessfully try to convince a potential customer that the age of fifty was not too elderly for the purchase of a Porsche. In China, the first significant generation of wealthy people was reaching middle age, and they were trying to figure out how they should behave.

Such topics always interested the nonfiction class, and they enjoyed Tim's paper. But during the breaks I saw students checking their phones, and a couple of them came up to tell me that they hated the *jubao* behavior. At the end of class, I told them not to worry, and I promised that we would meet as scheduled the following week. But in truth I wasn't certain. The bulletin-board posts had claimed that I was *xile*—roughly speaking, the term means "finished," but it can also be read as a death threat. One Twitter user translated the last line into English:

[Ho Wei] spoke w/o restraint only b/c he considered himself a big writer; I think he's gonna die soon.

It was after ten o'clock by the time I got home. Leslie and I sat down at the dining room table and talked about how things might proceed. I had already been contacted by a few journalists, both Chinese and foreign. Our fear was that I might be suspended or even forced to leave China, and we decided that I should avoid making public comments until I knew more about the attack and the university's response. The timing couldn't have been worse: we had just finished transitioning to our new life in Chengdu, and Ariel and Natasha were finally becoming comfortable in the classroom.

That evening, I stayed up late, checking comments on Weibo. The majority of responses seemed to support me, with users complaining about Xiao Fenhong, the Little Pinks:

This generation of young people is impossible.

The students at Sichuan University should just smash the school's sign themselves.

The students who reported Ho Wei not only blind themselves, they also blind the public. It's like Lu Xun said—to awaken somebody in an iron house is a painful business.

A few posts referred to Xi Jinping, although, in the dance of Chinese censorship, they found ways to avoid writing the leader's name:

The main reason is not that the teacher cannot disagree with the student's thinking, it's that no one can disagree with <him>.

I took a poetry appreciation class in my sophomore year. In the class, the teacher satirized °°° in front of more than 100 students, and nothing happened. Later, microphones were installed on the ceiling of the classroom.

Others pointed out the lack of clarity and due process:

Each person has different values, and these people feel that they have done something right and prevented a wrong by reporting it.

The real problem is: Why is this kind of *jubao* made, who will adjudicate it, and who will interpret it?

Below that, the writer switched to English:

Real problem is Big Brother.

———

The next morning, the director of my program at SCUPI, who was an American, telephoned. He sounded worried, and he said that we might have to go to a police station downtown. Later he called and asked me to come to the campus instead, in order to meet with the dean. By now, I was almost certain that the attack was not connected to my teaching materials or to anything that had been said in the classroom. All indications were that the problem had started with comments I had made on a draft of a freshman's argumentative essay.

As a teacher in China, I had always dreaded this type of essay. In the 1990s, Fuling students were provided with a state-published text, *A Handbook of Writing*, which included a unit on "Argumentation." The model essay in this unit was titled "The Three Gorges Project Is Beneficial." It followed a standard structure: introduction, argument, counterargument, and conclusion. In the counterargument paragraph, the writer listed some reasons to oppose the Three Gorges Dam: flooded scenery, lost cultural relics, the risk of an earthquake destroying the structure. "Their worries and warnings are well justified," the essay continued, and then proceeded to the transition: "But we should not give up eating for fear of choking."

In Fuling, I found it hard to teach this argumentative essay for a number of reasons. First, nobody was allowed to argue about the Three Gorges Dam. Information signs about the project were all around Fuling: in low-lying parts of the city, the government had painted red lines that marked the water level of the future reservoir. Another red line, figuratively speaking, was the topic of the dam itself. When I lived in Fuling, it wasn't possible for a Chinese scientist to openly oppose the project. The dam was politically sensitive, and it was known to be a pet project of Li Peng, the premier and Sichuan native who was the most famous alumnus of Chengdu Experimental Primary School.

An infinitely smaller problem, but one that occupied infinitely more of my own energy, was that transition sentence. Traditional Chinese education emphasizes the use of set literary phrases, and my Fuling students often tried to do the same thing in English. They diligently incorporated the transition sentence into their own argumentative papers, and then it infected other writing: personal narratives, dialogues, literary essays. I might be reading a paper about *Hamlet* when suddenly a voice would boom out, more startling than the dead king's ghost: "But we should not give up eating for fear of choking." The words are a direct translation of *yinyefeishi*, a Chinese literary phrase. Over and over, I tried to explain that no matter how beautiful the characters are in Chinese, they sound terrible in English.

At Sichuan University, I occasionally received a first-year argumentative essay that choked up the same phrase. I admit that I felt a tiny spark of nostalgia, but that was also the problem: more than twenty years had passed, but I was still teaching the same essay form under the same restrictions. A handful of courageous students, like Vincent, used their papers to criticize a government policy, but most first-years knew it was best to be safe. Even if a student took a pro-government stance on a sensitive topic, he couldn't fully engage with a counterargument.

Meanwhile, any teacher who played devil's advocate ran a significant risk. One of the first-year students—I'll call him John—submitted a draft of an essay arguing that it's necessary for the government to limit free speech. John wrote that "in a civilized country with the rule of law," citizens aren't allowed to question national sovereignty. In the comments section, I responded:

> It's not accurate to say that in a civilized country with rule of law, people are not allowed to make statements that challenge national sovereignty and social stability. In the United States, Canada, Europe, etc., anybody can make a statement claiming that some part of the country deserves independence.

This comment may have been blunt, but it didn't directly criticize China or the Party. On the Sichuan University bulletin board, though, my words had been twisted into something else:

> In class, a student gave a speech saying that the country's sovereignty cannot be violated.
>   Ho Wei asked why it's allowed to be violated in Quebec, Texas, California, and Scotland. People violate their national sovereignty every day.

The posts continued in this vein. Using a few details from my editing comments on John's paper, the author created a scene in which I argued aggressively with students. All of the dialogue was fabricated wholesale:

> Some students said CNN, NBC, and the Voice of America are anti-Chinese media organizations.
>   Ho Wei responded, How many of their articles have you read?

The original posts had been made anonymously. Shortly after the attack, the comments had reportedly been removed, probably by censors. But screenshots had been bouncing around Weibo, where they might stir up more trouble. Now I remembered that the freshman classroom was the only place I taught that did not have a surveillance camera. If the administration investigated, there was no digital proof that the argument had never occurred.

John was quiet, and his academic performance was somewhere in the middle of his class. We had never had an unpleasant interaction, and I had a good impression of his cohort. But unlike the nonfiction students, the first-years had not chosen to be in my section, and I generally knew little about their politics. Had John posted the attack? Or another student from the class? Or Little Pinks elsewhere in the university?

When I reviewed my comments on John's paper, there was one in particular that seemed likely to cause trouble. In the essay, John addressed a hypothetical situation in which a major event occurs and the government lies about it. He wrote:

> I have to say that this possibility does exist, but it is very small, because if such a big event really happens, it must be the government that informs the people in the first place. I think that official information is always timelier and more accurate than that of the individual.

I edited the essay on December 7, 2019. At the time, a mysterious virus had already started to spread in Wuhan, more than six hundred miles east of Chengdu. But the earliest public reports had yet to appear, and I had no idea that we were about to witness a cover-up. Instead, my editing remarks referred to the 2003 outbreak of severe acute respiratory syndrome, or SARS. Back then, foreign journalists had been the first to report that the Chinese government initially lied about the true number of infections. In my remarks, I wrote:

> One of the functions of the media anywhere in the world is to report on things that the government might want to hide. We have seen over and over, in countless countries, that official information is not always accurate or timely.

———

Even with prior experience in China, it was hard to gauge the political climate at Sichuan University. Thus far, students had never reacted to a sensitive subject in the way that I remembered from Fuling, when the classroom fell silent and all the heads dropped. But this didn't mean that the Sichuan University students weren't offended by some of the things I said. Over time, I realized that they were better at hiding their reactions, which, in some ways, could be more dangerous for a teacher.

Long after the fall semester, Serena told me about an incident that occurred during October, when Leslie visited the nonfiction class. Leslie talked about her experiences as a Chinese American journalist, and at some point, during a description of her family background, she casually used the English phrase "China and Taiwan." Without realizing it, she had stumbled into a forbidden zone. In the People's Republic, those two proper nouns can be linked by history, culture, geography—but never by the conjunction "and." Even the act of connecting these places linguistically implies that they are separate politically.

In an email, Serena described the class's reaction:

> I remember once Leslie said the words, [a classmate] turned to look at me and wanted to interrupt Leslie's speech. (I think she already held out her hand, ready to speak, but just needed a little bit of encouragement from Chinese classmates.) I think I said something like, "外国人这样想很正常" ["It's very normal for foreigners to think this way."] I mean, I do believe theoretically Taiwan is part of China (I take it as a thing to remember), but I just don't like arguing or even just seeing that kind of argument. And that wasn't what Leslie's speech was about anyway, and it appeared just that once. I didn't want the speech interrupted.

In response to three words, all of these things happened at once: the raised hand, the rapid communication between students, the calculation about whether or not to speak. But neither Leslie nor I noticed anything. When we read Serena's description, we couldn't even recall the larger context of Leslie's remark. It seemed amazing that these young people could care so much about Taiwan—I wasn't sure if anybody in the class had even visited the island.

On the other hand, Leslie's family had fled to Taiwan after her grandfather was bayoneted to death by the Communists. If anybody in that room deserved to have a hair-trigger response to the word *Taiwan*, it was Leslie. But she had been born and educated in the United States, where nobody had instructed her how to respond emotionally to comments about an island in the Pacific Ocean. This was always one of the hardest things to convey to people in China. Freedom wasn't only the right to say and write things without fear of repercussions. It was also the ability to determine your own relationship to your country, your identity, and your past.

When I taught in Fuling, the political courses had titles that included "Mao Zedong Thought" and "Building Chinese Socialism." Since then, another two decades of Communist history had piled up, and the names of mandatory classes at Sichuan University seemed to be getting longer: "Introduction to Mao Zedong Thought and Theoretical System on Socialism with Chinese Characteristics," "Research on Xi Jinping Thought on Socialism with Chinese Characteristics for a New Era." If these titles seemed ungainly, things got even worse when students opened the texts:

Only by taking the socialist core values as a major task with basic internality and targeted norms can we realize these core values while enhancing the people's self-confidence in the path forward, theoretical self-confidence, institutional self-confidence, and cultural self-confidence, in order to ensure that socialism with Chinese characteristics is always moving in the right direction and constantly showing stronger vitality.

It was appropriate that the term *self-confidence* was repeated four times in a single sentence. That was a fundamental problem: the Party lacked the confidence necessary to allow young people to think for themselves. In the old days, the indoctrination had seemed mostly effective; I remembered how Fuling students generally believed even a text as ridiculous as *Survey of Britain and America.* But my initial impression at Sichuan University was that the tools of "educated acquiescence" no longer worked quite as well. For one thing, there was too much outside material; VPNs were widespread, and course readings often included foreign texts like *Animal Farm.* Many young people were well traveled, and they seemed too sophisticated for crude propaganda. In fact, I became aware of the sentence about self-confidence because it was quoted in the argumentative essay of a first-year student, whom I'll call Scott.

Scott happened to be in the same section as John. In class discussions, Scott rarely said much, but he wrote well. On the day that I assigned the argumentative essays, he approached me after class. There were usually a few students who chatted after the bell, but Scott waited patiently until all of them were gone. Once we were alone, he said, "Will other people see our essay?"

I asked what he meant by "other people."

"Other teachers," he said.

He explained that he wanted to argue against the mandatory political courses. I told him that he didn't have to post the paper on the SCUPI system; he could either hand it to me directly or send it from a private email account. That seemed to satisfy him, and during the weeks that followed, he visited several times during office hours.

He quickly realized that by choosing a sensitive topic, he had made his project much more difficult. "When I search on Baidu, I can only find the counterpoint of my argument," he said during one visit. "Or I find people who say things like 'I don't care if I'm brainwashed, as long as it gives some benefit to us.'" Scott believed that most useful sources had been removed by censors or blocked by the firewall. "All of the opinions online are the same," he said. "I don't want to be a reactionary. But if the opinions are always the same, then I think it can be dangerous."

In his paper, Scott described the experience of attending the mandatory Party class:

> In our institute, every political course has about 100 students. But in fact, there are only 40 students present [at] every class on average. . . . And what else is interesting is that you can find there are few people sitting in the front and a lot of students gathering at the back of the room. They are trying to keep distance [from] this course. Then, what's more interesting about this course is what students do here. Once, I counted the number of students. There were 43 in total, but just 5 or 6 of them were focusing on the teacher. The rest of them were playing cell phone or just sleeping.

I could tell that the project made Scott nervous, and I told him that it was fine to change topics. But he seemed driven to write about the subject, probably because he was so frustrated by the political classes. In his essay, he wrote:

> The trend of today's society is to become more and more open both in economy and thought. The students now like something [to be] more individual, and they expect a personalized life. Everyone now wants to live with a clear mind, and [they] don't prefer to be collectivized as before.

During Scott's research, he learned how to install a VPN, because he needed to climb the Great Firewall in order to gather evidence. After he had the VPN, he used it to open a foreign-based Gmail account, which allowed him to communicate outside the SCUPI system. For the Communist Party, there was no question that the mandatory courses and other forms of propaganda had succeeded in creating a highly politicized environment for the young. This was clear in the reaction to Leslie's talk—students had been trained like hawks to be alert to certain words and phrases. But there was also some part of the young Chinese mind that had been trained to tune out those same words and phrases. *I just don't like arguing*, Serena had written in her email. *I didn't want to see the speech interrupted.* It occurred to me that for Scott, the most lasting political lesson from his first semester probably wouldn't come from the mandatory Party class—it would come from learning how to use a VPN and a Gmail account. But I couldn't tell how many students were like Serena and Scott, and how many were Little Pinks. And it took only one extremist to cause a problem.

By the time I met with the director of my program and Minking Chyu, the SCUPI dean, it was early afternoon. Party officials at the university had already interviewed a number of my students, to try to learn the truth about what had happened. Chyu told me that the students all said the same thing: they hadn't witnessed any classroom exchange like what had been recounted on the bulletin board and Weibo.

In the hybrid arrangement at Sichuan University, Chyu represented the University of Pittsburgh. Originally from Taiwan, he was now a citizen of the United States, where he had begun his career as a professor of engineering and later became an administrator. His Chinese was fluent, but as a foreigner, he couldn't be directly involved in any Party investigation. Officials communicated their findings to him, and during our meeting, Chyu told me that the cadres seemed satisfied that the classroom argument had not occurred.

I had brought a copy of John's essay. I gave the paper to the dean, and I showed him the page with my comment about SARS.

"This was the only part that was critical of the government," I said. "Otherwise I was just pointing out mistakes in his reasoning."

The dean pushed the paper aside. "That's not important right now," he said. He explained that nobody had formally started the *jubao* process. As long as a complaint was not formally filed, the university didn't need to take further steps. The dean said that it was in our best interest to stay quiet and hope that the controversy blew over.

I explained that journalists had contacted me, and if I remained silent, people would assume that I was in trouble. "I think that I should issue a statement," I said. "I can say that in fact I have not been reported, and that the posts were not accurate."

The dean thought for a moment and agreed. After the meeting, I made a statement to an NPR correspondent, who posted it on Twitter. Almost immediately the social media conversation started to die down.

Later that month, my department held a meeting about the incident. All foreign teachers were asked to attend, along with a SCUPI associate dean and a Communist Party official from the university. When I entered the room, I instinctively looked for cameras—there was one in the middle of the ceiling.

At the start of the meeting, I was asked to tell the story of the incident. Afterward, the associate dean, whose name is TsunZee Mai, spoke. Like Chyu, Mai had grown up in Taiwan but became an American passport holder. "We need to respect the country's laws, and their laws prohibit us to talk about political issues," Mai said. "Try to avoid any political issues or political opinions."

An American professor spoke up. "Is there anything that is explicitly forbidden?" he asked.

The Party official took out a prepared statement and read aloud, in English. "Content and styles of lessons are encouraged to vary," she said. "However, certain topics should not be broached by either teachers or students. These include sex in a graphic or degrading manner, political opinion that may not be generally agreed upon, religious material, promoting or degrading the tenets within, and topics deemed politically sensitive. Topics in class should be kept neutral."

On the surface, the statement seemed detailed, but in fact there were few specifics. Cadres often avoided drawing clear lines, which might encourage teachers to go to the edge.

"Sometimes we have discussions and students raise topics themselves," the American professor said. "And they might raise a topic that seems borderline. To what extent do we interrupt?"

This time, the Party official answered in Chinese. "It's better not to talk about it," she said. "Because this is still a Chinese student. You don't know if that student will *fanguolai.*"

The term means "turn it upside down." That seemed to be something the official feared—the volatility and potential deviousness of the young.

Throughout the various meetings, nobody said that I had done anything wrong. But neither did they say that it was a violation for a teacher's editing comments to be twisted and then posted on social media. This was another way in which SCUPI wasn't really a hybrid: if we had been at Pittsburgh or another American institution, and if private academic correspondence had been made public in a way that threatened an instructor, there would have been a proper investigation. But now there seemed to be no interest in learning who was behind the attack. If Party officials had spoken with John, and if they knew more about what had happened, they kept their findings to themselves. The response was to proceed as if nothing had occurred, which meant that five days after the attack had been posted on the bulletin board, I was scheduled to teach John and his cohort again. We still had three weeks together in the classroom, along with George Orwell.

When I discussed my case with the law-school teacher who had been disciplined after using the Ai Weiwei documentary, he explained that fear typically ran in two directions. Administrators were afraid of what students might do, and they also feared higher officials. After the incident with the documentary, the head of the law school quickly reassured superiors that he would discipline the teacher. The punishment, though, was relatively light. The teacher was suspended from that class, but he was allowed to continue with his other courses. He told me that a larger scandal would have reflected poorly on everybody. "They were protecting me, but they were also protecting themselves," he said.

My case had a similar dynamic. In a normal situation, I would have talked directly to John and other students, but I decided it was too risky. I was still new to the university, and my family was vulnerable. Someday, when things felt more stable, I would try to learn more, but for now my calculation was similar to that of most people within the system. It was in all of our best interests to stay quiet.

The law-school teacher told me that he had learned that his *jubao* came from students in the College of Marxism. But he didn't know the specific students, and he didn't care. "I know what's the root cause," he said. "It's the nation's educational system." He continued: "The problem wasn't the students. They don't understand. They don't know that they are doing something wrong. They don't know that they are being hurt themselves. They don't know that they are being enslaved by certain ideas."

The incident had taught him not to push the envelope. "Afterward, I discovered that I'm not a very brave person," he said. He mentioned some well-known human rights lawyers who had gotten in trouble recently. "Their children's studies are affected, their wives have lost job opportunities. They've had financial costs. I can't take on this kind of burden. So I became more *chenmo*."

Chen means "to sink," and *mo* is "silent"—to sink into silence, to become reticent. The teacher continued, "I'm not angry at the students," he said. "I'm angry at the system."

For the first class after the attack, I arrived early. John was already in the room, along with two others. He didn't make eye contact when I greeted the students.

We were supposed to discuss *Animal Farm* that day. But I had grown more nervous as class approached, until finally I decided to delay Orwell for a week. Instead, we talked about some sample papers, and then we did an editing exercise. I had hoped to gain a better sense of the group's dynamics, but as the class reached the final hour, I still didn't know if anybody was aware of what had happened with John's paper. Even John was a cipher. He didn't participate in the discussions, and there were moments when I thought he might be avoiding my gaze, but he had always been shy. It was similar to what I had observed with my nonfiction class: in terms of politics, today's students were much harder to read than the people I had taught in the 1990s.

I felt relieved to hear the final bell. A few students seemed disappointed that we hadn't talked about *Animal Farm*, and they lingered after class. One boy remarked that he had found the novel to be even more depressing than *1984*. "Because Winston has his happiness," he said. "At least he has a moment. Here the animals don't even have that."

Another student brought up *Brave New World*. He commented that Aldous Huxley's fictional society is quite different from Orwell's. "But the end is very similar," he said. "It's also very negative."

"Big Brother," the first boy said. "Some students want to be Big Brother."

John was still in the classroom, and now I was careful not to look in his direction.

"What about you?" the boy said to me. "Do you want to be Big Brother?" He said it lightly and laughed; I couldn't tell what he meant by the comment.

Of the many things that were banned, blocked, or censored in China, the novels of George Orwell did not make the list. Our apartment was a few blocks from Xinhua Winshare, one of the largest downtown bookstores that were overseen by the Party. When I visited the store, the first display featured a large table with stacks of books that documented the career and theories of Xi Jinping in mind-numbing detail. There were twenty different titles, including:

Xi Jinping's Seven Years as an Educated Youth

Stories of Xi Jinping and Poverty Alleviation

Xi Jinping in Fuzhou

Xi Jinping in Xiamen

Xi Jinping in Zhengding

Xi Jinping in Ningde

Less than thirty feet away, another large table was dedicated to a set of books marketed as "The Dystopian Trilogy": *1984*, *Brave New World*, and *We*, a novel that was banned in the Soviet Union after it was written, around 1920, by Yevgeny Zamyatin. Directly above the Dystopian Trilogy table, a security camera hung from the ceiling. The cover of *1984* declared, in large characters:

WAR IS PEACE.

FREEDOM IS SLAVERY.

AND BIG BROTHER IS WATCHING YOU.

The display also featured a Chinese version of *Animal Farm*. A publisher in Shanghai told me that translations of *Animal Farm* generally sold around a hundred thousand copies every year, and *1984* sold twice as many as that. Despite the political climate, there was no campaign to censor Orwell, whose works remained on many university reading lists.

Less than two weeks after the Weibo attacks, some students from another department at Sichuan University invited me to attend their dramatic performance of *1984*. When I arrived at the lecture hall, the professor greeted me warmly. He asked only that I not mention the name of the class in anything I wrote. Other than that, nobody seemed concerned about my presence. I sat at the back of the room, near a security camera. There was another camera at the front.

The assignment had been for groups of students to prepare and perform a new version of a classic foreign story. The first group gave a rendition of *Eugene Onegin*, by Alexander Pushkin, and then another group performed *Crime and Punishment*. For that play, girls dressed in red capes that were reminiscent of *The Handmaid's Tale*. They were followed by the Orwell group, whose players wore beige jumpsuits with ID numbers across the breasts, like factory workers in the Maoist years.

The play began with Winston, the hero of the novel, casually discussing a recent public hanging with a colleague. They were interrupted by the Two Minutes Hate, during which the jumpsuited students shouted curses in Chinese:

> *Fangpi!* [Fart!]
> *Yangliande zhu!* [Sheep-faced pig!]
> *Yangliande luozi!* [Sheep-faced mule!]

At the end of the Two Minutes Hate, the students chanted *wansui*, "ten thousand years," or "long live." During the Cultural Revolution, the phrase had often been connected to Mao Zedong's name. Now the students shouted:

> *Ten thousand years to Big Brother!*
> *Ten thousand years to Big Brother!*
> *Ten thousand years to the British News Agency!*
> *Ten thousand years to the British News Agency!*

After that, the play focused on Julia, the woman who becomes Winston's lover. In the novel, Julia is a highly sexualized figure who hates the control of the state, and the students included explicit material:

> Winston: When I first saw you, I wanted to rape you, kill you, and climax at the end of the Two Minutes Hate. And she, she would be just . . . "fulfilling our duty to the Party."
> Julia: Can you guess how many other men I've had?
> Winston: It doesn't matter. The more men you've had, the more I love you.

After applying makeup to Julia's face, Winston gazed at her. "You are a woman, Julia," he said. "Not a Party Member." From there, the script departed from Orwell's original story. In the novel, there isn't much to Julia apart from sexualized resistance; she is a profoundly unintellectual character who gets bored whenever Winston talks politics. But the Sichuan University students had reimagined the woman as a secret Party agent. She is assigned to entrap Winston—but then, in the act of carrying out her mission, she can't stop herself from falling in love. Her feelings are shattered when Winston gives her up under torture.

After that, Julia renews her dedication to the State. The play ends with her reporting to O'Brien, her superior in the Party, who gives her the name of another target for seduction. The target's name is a play on

Yan Lianke, a contemporary Chinese author whose satirical novels have often been banned. The script read:

> O'Brien: Comrade Julia, congratulations on accomplishing this task. Your next mission is Ye Lianke.
> Julia: [makes a sound of agreement]
> O'Brien: Answer again, clearly!
> Julia: Received, officer!

After the performance, I met one of the undergrads who had written the script. She explained that she had expanded Julia's role because Orwell's original character seemed underdeveloped. It impressed me as a sophisticated reading—the student had recognized a strain of misogyny that runs throughout the novel. She had taken risks with the material; the sexualized content alone was more than enough to draw a rebuke from the Party. But their teachers had encouraged them to be free and creative, and the students were proud of their work. I felt heartened by their bravery—a bright point at the end of a long month.

Earlier in the semester, Serena had come to my office with bad news. Because she had been admitted late to the nonfiction class, there had been some mix-up in paperwork, and now she realized that she wasn't properly registered. I sent pleading messages to the administration, but the wheels of the bureaucracy wouldn't budge. The university informed me that it was impossible for Serena to receive credit for the class.

Her response to the nonfiction experience—first rejected, then denied credit—was to ask politely if she could take the course again in the spring, this time on the books. She had some ideas for new reporting projects, and she didn't care if any course material was repeated. That was heartening, too: despite the political climate, and despite the ugliness of the *jubao* culture, there were still many young people who did whatever they could to learn.

In December, I traveled to Fuling to see a former student named May and her husband. May had grown up in the city, and after graduation she found a teaching job at a local vocational school. Back then, it was hard for former classmates to stay in contact. Anybody who wanted to travel from Fuling usually did so on the large passenger ferries, which took more than eight hours to go upstream to Chongqing, the nearest big city.

In those days, if I received news from a former student, I included it in my next semester letter, as a way of keeping everybody updated. In spring of 2000, May wrote:

> I'm glad you told me so much information about my classmates. Because I didn't get in touch with them, I knew nothing about them. I hope you and our classmates come to Fuling and hold a get-together someday. That's wonderful. Maybe we will be old at that time. We become a mother or father, aunt or uncle. Today we get married, tomorrow we have a baby. The day after tomorrow, we are old. . . .
>
> Perhaps this year or next year I'll get married. I don't think too much about this. Sooner or later is the same thing.

Like her rural classmates, May downplayed good news. In truth, there had never been any doubt about whether she would marry. During college, she had already been in a serious relationship with a boy named Lu Yong, who had been her middle school classmate. Not long after May sent the letter, they held a wedding, and their son was born the following year. May had been right about how quickly time would move, in ways both good and bad, and in 2016, as the couple approached their midforties, Lu Yong was diagnosed with stage 4 lung cancer.

In December, I told May that I planned to visit Fuling. I explained that I understood if she didn't want to meet or talk about the illness. In China, people often avoided such topics, for the same reason that they didn't discuss other tragedies—there was no point in burdening friends. But May had always been straightforward, and she was still determined to host a get-together. She wrote back:

> We can meet at my home. I can also get other classmates in Fuling together. My husband is outgoing, you can talk to him about the prognosis, he doesn't mind it.

Early on a Saturday, I caught a high-speed train from Chongqing to Fuling. The old passenger boats had gone out of business years ago, because the fast trains had reduced the journey from eight hours to thirty-eight minutes. At the Fuling station, Lu Yong was waiting in a Skoda sedan. He wore the same heavy black-framed glasses that I remembered, although now they seemed even bigger. The skin around his face had tightened, and his cheekbones jutted out; he must have lost thirty pounds. His close-cropped hair was the color of steel bristles.

He said it was the first time he had driven in months. "I usually go for a walk in Forest Park every day, if the weather is good," he said, while we crossed one of the new Yangtze bridges. "Otherwise I don't go out much."

The couple and their teenage son lived with Lu Yong's parents in a high-rise apartment complex across from the park. Lu Yong's father had had a successful career in government, and the spacious apartment sprawled across two stories. After we arrived, Lu Yong escorted me to the rooftop balcony to look out at the Yangtze. The winter river was gray-brown beneath shrouds of fog.

He remarked that the Yangtze's surface was currently 170 meters above sea level. The height of the river was documented every day on a website, and Lu Yong checked it regularly, out of habit. His job had been with the City Management Bureau, where he was in charge of cleaning the river around Fuling. Standing on the balcony, he reminisced about what it was like when he started, in 2000. "In those days you could almost walk across the river on all the trash that used to gather near the dam," he said, referring to the Gezhouba Dam, a smaller structure that had preceded the Three Gorges Project. "Here in Fuling there were always a lot of trees and branches, especially after rain. And animal corpses. Usually it was pigs or dogs, although occasionally we'd find a human body."

As the city's funding improved, Lu Yong's department acquired a fleet of fourteen boats, and they had dramatically reduced the volume of trash. Lu Yong had stopped working two years earlier, after the diagnosis. "I had had a pain in my chest for a while," he said. "Finally I went to see the doctor and they did tests. The doctor said, 'You should have come earlier.'"

He continued, "It was too late. The cancer was already at an advanced stage, and they couldn't do surgery. Now it's spread to my back, and you can see this place on my neck. And there's another one here on my head."

He touched two bumps. They bulged beneath taut, papery skin, like his cheekbones. He coughed periodically, and his complexion looked pale. But he was animated, and speaking about the cancer didn't seem to make him uncomfortable. He said that the original prognosis had given him only three to six months, but he had already exceeded that period by almost two years. "They didn't do chemotherapy," he said. "Right now I'm on an experimental drug. There's no hope of curing it; it's just a matter of delaying things. Look at Steve Jobs—even somebody like that couldn't get rid of cancer."

Like many Chinese men of the Reform generation, Lu Yong had been a heavy smoker. Lung cancer was now the leading cause of cancer death among Chinese. Lu Yong told me that after the diagnosis he had continued to smoke cigarettes for a couple of weeks, mostly out of shock. Then he finally quit, and he hadn't smoked since.

"Probably it was the cigarettes that caused it," he said. "But the doctor can't say for sure. China has more lung cancer than anywhere else. A lot of the people who get sick are smokers, but some of them aren't. It could be the air pollution."

Even in the early stages of my former students' careers, they had often complained about the health costs of *guanxi* networking. Teachers and others in government jobs were expected to attend banquets that involved rich food, gifts of cigarettes, and frequent toasts of baijiu, strong, sorghum-based alcohol. Such rituals were particularly common for anybody involved in business. Not long after leaving Fuling, Jimmy had written about meeting his wife. At the time, she worked in a restaurant, but this unassuming waitress turned out to be a dynamo. In 2002, I made a trip to the Three Gorges and visited the couple, who had a one-year-old daughter. They owned a small hotel and restaurant, and business was thriving. They still lived in Jiangkou—"the mouth of the river"—but the town was scheduled to be inundated the following year, when the first stage of the Three Gorges Dam would be completed.

Jimmy had settled into the body of a prosperous provincial. He was twenty or so pounds from the days of the Bulls jersey, and now he often dressed in a suit and tie. He was still teaching, but he also helped out with his wife's business. Later that year, he sent a letter updating me on their progress. He acknowledged that even a successful business had drawbacks:

> Everything has two sides, on the contrary, my health is very bad because of too much wine and beer. So I usually carry much medicine on me at present.

As former students entered their thirties, they sometimes referred to more serious health problems. In 2003, one man wrote:

> I have to take medicine two or three times a day, and stop drinking beer or wine. When I have meals with my colleagues and leaders, they always ask me to drink, otherwise they think I'm a bad-mannered

man. But I don't want to tell them the truth. I am afraid they will [exclude me]. Some of them are not friendly.

When I was in the Peace Corps, coercive drinking was such a health risk that our training included special sessions on banquets. We learned about the various set characters who dominated such events: the bullying department head, the shot-glass lieutenants, the Party-hack wingmen who could swoop in at any moment and demand rat-a-tat toasts with a sodden foreign volunteer. In all of Sichuan, the most notorious banquet site was Yibin, a Yangtze city upstream from Chongqing. Yibin produced Wuliangye, a famous baijiu brand, and local officials never missed an opportunity to drink. The Peace Corps had endless problems with Yibin banquets, culminating with one volunteer becoming so ill that he had to be evacuated to Hawaii for treatment. After that, there was a period when the Peace Corps refused to send male volunteers to the site. Only brave Corpswomen, the Amazons of the Upper Yangtze, were allowed to serve in Yibin, because cadres were less likely to bully women into drinking.

Fuling was no Yibin, but we still had plenty of alcoholic banquets. Later, whenever I visited, friends and former students organized long meals with endless shots of baijiu. But all of that changed after 2013. As part of Xi Jinping's anti-corruption campaign, government bureaus were banned from hosting lavish dinners. When I first read the news, I couldn't imagine people in Sichuan and Chongqing obeying. But the change was as complete as if somebody had thrown a circuit breaker. During my first semester at Sichuan University, there was a grand total of one banquet, at which not a single drop of alcohol was served. The department chair told me that the rules were so strict that I couldn't even order a beer and pay for it myself.

Nowadays, when I met up with middle-aged friends, it sometimes felt like everybody was involved in a nationwide detox. People still organized dinners, but they rarely drank much. At meals, I was often struck by how much the men had aged. Many of the women I had taught in Fuling had hardly changed, but most men had gained significant weight, and their faces sagged from years of too many cigarettes and baijiu shots. Among my former students and their spouses, Lu Yong was the first lung-cancer patient, but I feared he wouldn't be the last.

After we sat down to lunch, Lu Yong's mother said, "I'm so happy that you drove today." Other than that, nobody mentioned the cancer. The guests were all friends from the 1990s, and they had been in frequent contact with May and Lu Yong throughout their ordeal. Grant and Caitlyn had met as students at the Fuling college, and later they married. They were joined by another couple, Linda and Huang Dong, who had known each other since middle school. Huang Dong had been the *tongzhuo*, or deskmate, that Linda had mentioned in her 2000 letter about their courtship. Each of these three couples had been together for more than twenty years.

In the early 2000s, the marriages of my former students usually seemed rushed. Most of them had no dating experience, and they described spouses in ways that seemed dismissive. *He is not very handsome. What makes me happy is that I married an ugly woman who graduated from the math department.* But the vast majority of these rapid-fire courtships turned into marriages that lasted. In my 2016 survey, I asked about marital status, and only one out of thirty-three respondents had been divorced. I asked the question again in 2021, and the figure was one out of thirty-two. Some added comments:

I am a good man, I am married.

I am sure married. I think divorce is a trend for many young people born in the 1980s or in the 1990s.

I have my wife. Not many people around me are divorced. Teachers cannot afford to do that.

We are married now. We are very traditional Chinese. We don't
think it is good to divorce.

Their experiences contradicted larger trends. China's divorce rate
has more than tripled since 2000, and it's now higher than in the U.S.
But most of the people I taught had grown up in rural communities that
looked down on divorce, and the students retained these values even as
they became urban people. Another rural quality that endured was a
tendency to maintain an even keel. In the same way that former students
downplayed good fortune, they were unfazed when things became difficult.
In 2001, one woman wrote a letter and mentioned that she had been dating:

I have a boyfriend, not a *laotou* [old man, or husband]. It seems that
we can not get along well. We often quarrel, quarrel, quarrel. I don't
want to marry. It is too *xinku* [hard].

Despite her comments, they married. Five years later she sent an update:

My husband works as a policeman in a prison. They are often free
and at weekends always go out for playing cards, while I'm very busy
and painstaking. So I often feel angry at that.

In 2021, she sent an email in which she referred to a new car, a new
apartment, a new salary—and the same old husband:

My husband is a prison policeman, who has a bad temper. We often
quarreled in the past. I have adjusted myself. Now I'm better although sometimes we still quarrel.

Nothing had changed; everything had changed—that combination
often seemed like a contradiction. But over time, I sensed that certain

anchors, like my former students' marriages and their teaching jobs, helped keep them stable amid other sweeping transformations. To some degree, I felt the same way. On every trip back to Fuling, there were moments when I lost my bearings: the Yangtze had become a reservoir; the sleepy river town had turned into a booming city; the eight-hour boat ride had been replaced by thirty-eight minutes on a high-speed train. But some essential quality of the people stayed the same. It was comforting to share a meal with these couples who had known each other since middle school.

Before the trip, I had printed out some old photos. At lunch I gave them to the students, and Lu Yong told me that he had some pictures of his own. He took me into his home office and turned on his computer.

"These are from my *danwei*," he said, opening a file of digitized images. "We were recording things from the river, and these were photographs that they collected. I made a copy. These were all taken from 1997 to 2000."

The images featured the old colors I remembered, the brown city and the gray air, everything pixelated by pollution. The streets looked empty: in those days, there were few cars, and bicycles had never been common in the hilly city. At the end of the file, Lu Yong came to a set of photographs from the summer of 1998, when Fuling had experienced the last serious flood of the pre-dam era. Back then, the lower part of downtown had yet to be demolished in preparation for the Three Gorges Project, and the Yangtze inundated many streets and ground-floor apartments. There were photographs of residents wading up to their thighs in coffee-colored water. Many of the men were shirtless, and they were small, with ropelike muscles. I realized that nowadays I never saw city residents who looked so sinewy. And I couldn't help but think that, of all the men I knew from the 1990s, Lu Yong was the only one who had become physically smaller.

He wanted to copy the pictures, but he said he needed to review them again for political sensitivities. Despite his absence from the office, he still had the careful habits of a *danwei* employee. He flipped patiently through the images, eventually choosing four to be deleted. Two were pictures of unsmiling government cadres lined up for a group photo after some special meeting about the flood. The other pictures featured the photographers who had been commissioned to record the natural disaster. After these images had been erased, Lu Yong copied the rest onto a USB drive. "This is all part of Fuling history," he said. "I thought you would want to have it."

By the time we finished lunch, sunshine had penetrated the Yangtze fog, and some of us went for a drive. With Lu Yong behind the wheel, May, Linda, and I headed across the river to the mountain of Beishanping.

In the 1990s, city residents occasionally took weekend trips to Beishanping. They caught a ferry across the Yangtze, and then they climbed hundreds of stone steps up the mountain's southern face. The long, flat summit was forested with pine trees, and there were beautiful views overlooking the city and the two rivers. There were no paved roads atop the mountain, where the farmland was remote and poor. It took so much effort to climb the steps that relatively few people visited.

Since then, the government had constructed new roads on both sides of the mountain, which had become the site of a number of development projects. Lu Yong followed the eastern route, which switchbacked up the steep slope. Near the top, he passed a new housing complex of about a dozen apartment buildings. He said that the buildings had been constructed as part of the compensation for farmers whose land had been taken for the various projects. But relatively few people actually lived there, because the site was inconvenient for city jobs. Most owners kept the empty apartments as investments while they rented housing downtown or in other places where they worked. While driving past, I didn't see anybody outside.

"Everything on Beishanping is a failure," Lu Yong remarked. He explained that part of the problem was the way the Chinese system posts city leaders for five-year terms and then rotates them to other parts of the country. This was an old tradition—in imperial times, the central government had been careful not to let local leaders get too entrenched. In Fuling, during the intense development of the Reform era, each successive Communist Party secretary had tried to leave his mark on a different part of the city. "The first one started all the projects in Lidu," Lu Yong said, referring to an area along the Yangtze that was the site of the Fuling college's new campus. "Then the next Party secretary wanted to develop Jiangdong. The Party secretary after him came here to Beishanping. Now we have a new Party secretary, and he's back in Lidu, doing more projects there. Each of them has five years to do whatever he can. That system is supposed to reduce corruption, but it also means that people don't think long-term." Of all the new sites, Lidu was the most successful, because it was situated along the Yangtze, whereas Beishanping had been doomed by its remoteness.

Past the summit of the mountain, Lu Yong drove through another development. This one was much larger, and it was arranged around a golf course. But there was nobody outside here, either. We passed a series of billboards that paired poetic Chinese phrases with English versions that had the ring of bad machine translation:

RIVER TOWN GOLF

THE 20,000 INTERNATIONAL HEALTH SPA

FRAGRANT AND CONSERVATION OFFICIAL GAS

KEEP A MENTAL AND PHYSICAL

RIVER TOWN GOLF

AS THE WORLD'S TOP LUXURY FACHJTIES

THE DEFINITION OF THE HUMAN FUTURE

Along the road, dozens of banners were decorated with a coat of arms and the English words *River Town Golf.* The coat of arms featured a cursive letter *R*, a lion rampant, and a golden golf club. I commented that the font used for the "River Town Golf" signs was the same as the one that appeared on the cover of the UK edition of my first book.

From the back seat, May asked if I had ever talked to people at the golf development about their name, and I said that I had.

"What did they say?" she asked.

"They said that it had nothing to do with my book."

Everybody laughed. "Of course not!"

When I lived in Fuling, nobody called the city *jiangcheng*—"river town" or "river city." Chinese cities often have nicknames with historical roots, and *jiangcheng* famously describes Wuhan, which sits at the juncture of the Yangtze and the Han River. Li Bai, perhaps China's greatest poet, was the first to refer to the area around present-day Wuhan as *jiangcheng*, in a poem from the Tang dynasty, more than twelve hundred years ago. It would have been presumptuous for Fuling to use the term. Instead, the city went by the much more modest Xiao Shancheng: Little Mountain City. Chongqing was nicknamed Mountain City, and Fuling, with similar geography but a much smaller population, was given the diminutive.

After I decided to call my book *River Town*, I knew that Fuling natives would correct me. I also knew that I would never be able to explain how bad *Little Mountain City* sounds in English. In any case, I didn't expect Fuling residents to enjoy the book, because there was a long tradition of Chinese responding negatively to foreign depictions of their country. These reactions were often justified: throughout history, many outsiders had described China in ways that were prejudiced, unfair, or just plain wrong. But even when a foreigner knew her subject well, and wrote about it sympathetically, she was likely to be attacked. The Chinese intelligentsia had been largely dismissive of Pearl S. Buck, whose novels like *The Good Earth* reflected deep personal knowledge. Buck had grown up in Zhejiang province, where she learned both the dialect and classical Chinese, and she spent nearly forty years in the country. Nevertheless, one of the first Chinese translators of *The Good Earth* criticized Buck for making China look bad, asking rhetorically whether her perspective was one of "white superiority."

Nothing bothered Chinese readers more than a foreigner who described the country as poor or backward. In 1998, when I started writing my book, I knew that I couldn't avoid the issue, because poverty and isolation had shaped the city and virtually everybody in my classroom. I decided that the only solution was to be direct, and on the first page I wrote:

> There was no railroad in Fuling. It had always been a poor part of Sichuan province and the roads were bad. To go anywhere you took the boat, but mostly you didn't go anywhere. For the next two years the city was my home.

After finishing a draft at the end of 1998, I sent it to Emily. I had quoted some of her writings, and I wanted to make sure that she approved. I was also curious to hear her thoughts about my depiction of her hometown. She read the first two chapters and then wrote:

> I think no one would like Fuling city after reading your story. But I can't complain as everything you write about is the fact. I wish the city would be more attractive with time.

She sent updates while reading. Sometimes she enjoyed a section, but her next note might express frustration or shame. She was particularly embarrassed by any description of the city as dirty or chaotic. After completing the book, she wrote:

In the first chapters, I saw a foreigner in an advantageous position showing curiosity and sympathy for Fuling and its people. He did ok as a foreigner [coming] from an advanced country. But maybe I'm too sensitive to be completely comfortable with all his curiosity and sympathy.

As I read, I gradually began to like the foreigner. Especially when he showed his affection to the countryside. . . . I was happy to see a man of 29 also appreciate the beauty of the poor place.

I was unlikely to find a more open reader than Emily. I assumed that if her reaction was mixed, most Chinese, and especially those who lived in Fuling, would dislike the book.

River Town was published in 2001, and in subsequent years, when I visited Fuling, people made some of the remarks that I had anticipated. They often told me that everybody in China knows that "river town" refers to Wuhan. When the Fuling college commissioned an unofficial translation of the book, for school officials to read, they changed the title to *Jiangpan Cheng*—Riverside Town. People also pointed out errors, including that I wrote the mountain's name as "Baishanping" instead of "Beishanping." In the dialect, both words sound the same, and I had relied on a local map that misprinted the characters.

But there were surprisingly few complaints about descriptions of poverty and isolation. By the time of publication, some of those blunt page-one sentences were already obsolete: the first highway had been completed, and a passenger rail line was under construction. In the years that followed, four additional new expressways were built, along with two more railways. The book was finally published in an official mainland Chinese translation in 2012, before the censorship began to tighten under Xi Jinping. This happened to be a moment when a number of foreign books about China became unexpectedly popular. Among educated Chinese, there was a new curiosity about how outsiders viewed the country, and readers seemed more confident than in the past. They were also nostalgic. People often told me that the Reform years had been so demanding that they never had time to record what was happening, and they appreciated having a portrait, even if it came from a foreigner. If anything, they enjoyed reading about the hard times, because it reminded them how far they had come. Ten years after the book was published, Emily reread it and sent a message:

> With a distance of time, everything in the book turns out to be charming, even the dirty, tired flowers. . . . Thank you so much for having recorded those fond memories.

Eventually, more copies were sold in China than in the United States. As the years passed, young American readers seemed more likely than the Chinese to be uncomfortable with the notion of a white male foreigner writing about a remote city in China. They also may have distrusted the Peace Corps more. On review sites like Goodreads, millennial American reviewers sometimes dismissed *River Town* as an anachronism:

> I would never have picked up this book on my own, mostly due to the fact that I've never met a peace corps alum who wasn't one of those white missionary adjacent wide-eyed liberals who thinks they're not part of the problem BECAUSE they are liberal and yet can't see themselves centering their own narrative rather than the people they are trying to help.

> Some of the ethnocentric views and biases stood out to me. He criticized the politics of the citizens and some of their views.

> I heard it's kinda cringe to enjoy Peace Corps memoirs, but I enjoyed this one.

––––––

The first time I learned about River Town Golf was in 2014, when I made a trip back to Fuling. After seeing signs for the new development, I hailed a cabbie and asked him to take me to the site. At the top of Beishanping, we passed dozens of half-finished luxury villas and condominiums arranged around a golf course. Brand-new billboards featured machine-generated English:

MELTING IRON ARK OF MOUNTAINS
THE SPIRIT OF AGREGNOTES HANGSHAN
THE GAS OF THE NATIVE FOREST

I paid the cabbie and proceeded on foot. The golf course greens were closely trimmed, but the holes had yet to be installed, and I couldn't see any indication of recent play. I followed a road to a small arcade of shops. Out in front, there was a life-size bronze statue of a Spanish bullfighter sweeping his muleta in front of a charging bull. The shop doors were locked, and a nearby sign read: "The Next Generation of Fuling City."

A quarter mile up the road, in the center of a roundabout, a massive European-style ceremonial arch had been built out of concrete. I walked slowly around the structure, trying to figure out what it represented. Later, I looked at pictures online and realized that the arch was a replica of Munich's Siegestor, the victory monument that King Ludwig I had commissioned during the 1850s. The River Town Golf Siegestor was slightly smaller than the Munich version and it did not include the original German inscription: *Dem Bayerischen Heere*, "To the Bavarian Army."

I returned the following day for an interview with Li Piaohai, the marketing director for the Fuling Beishan New City Comprehensive Development Co. Ltd. Li told me that the company was owned by a larger state-owned corporation, and the total investment in River Town Golf was expected to be ten billion yuan, or about $1.6 billion. As part of the project, they had relocated more than six thousand farmers from this part of Beishanping, some of them to the housing compound that I later visited with Lu Yong. The centerpiece of River Town Golf would be a Marriott hotel to serve golf tourists.

I asked about the English name. Li was in his thirties, dressed in a dark suit and tie, and he explained that the name had nothing to do with the title of my book. "It just means that this is a small town with a river and with golf," he said. "That's all. And the English name is different from the Chinese name."

The Chinese name consisted of four literary characters, *Yu Lin Jiang Shan*, which translates as "The Emperor Looks at His Empire." I asked why the names were different.

"You can't translate it directly," Li said. "And if you say 'river town' in Chinese, people will think you're talking about Wuhan. They don't use that name for Fuling."

I didn't want to get sidetracked by my misappropriation of Wuhan's nickname, so I changed the subject. I asked why none of the signs used the word *golf* in Chinese.

"This is the first golf course to be built on the banks of the Yangtze River," he said. "But there are lots of other things that are going to be here as well, like hot springs. So we call it a *tiyu zuti gongye*—'sports group industry.'" Li continued, "We don't specifically call it 'golf.'"

I asked if this was because the Party had recently targeted the sport in anti-corruption campaigns. In fact, the Chinese government had banned the construction of new golf courses back in 2004, but during the freewheeling environment of that era, most provinces ignored the restrictions. Now the rules were actually being enforced under Xi Jinping— the Emperor was Looking at His Empire. Li acknowledged that this had become an issue.

"The central government doesn't encourage the use of arable land for new golf courses," he said carefully. "So we emphasize that this is about sports in general, not just golf." He told me that River Town Golf was confident that the government would eventually allow them to proceed with opening the course. "For this kind of mountainous land, what's the value?" he explained. "It was hard for farmers to make a living here."

During that trip, I met some former residents who were wandering around the site. They grumbled about the terms of their relocation, saying that they hadn't been compensated fairly for the land they used to farm. They were much blunter than Li about the prospects for River Town Golf. "They're never going to finish it," one farmer said. When I asked why, he mentioned the old Chongqing bogeyman. "This project was approved under Bo Xilai," the farmer explained. "So after Xi Jinping came, there was no way it could continue."

After that trip, whenever I returned to Fuling, I checked in on River Town Golf. Four years later, in 2018, there still weren't any holes on the course, and the fairways were no longer being mowed. Some farmers had returned to plant corn and vegetables along the edges of the course. The villas and the Marriott hotel were still unfinished shells of concrete. In front of the empty arcade, the bronze bull and matador were frozen in their interminable *tercio de muerte*.

That year, at the main office, I met another manager, named Gary Xia. Xia confirmed that the central government had forbidden the local authorities to open the course. "They said the reason was because it's a waste of land," Xia told me. "But it's also because of Bo Xilai." He explained that when an official gets arrested for corruption, that also means trouble for any projects that were approved under his watch. After all the investment on this mountaintop, and all the relocations, nobody had ever played a single round of golf.

But they kept the English words *River Town Golf* on all banners and billboards. Gary Xia told me that Marriott had pulled out of the hotel deal, but his company hoped to proceed with the luxury development anyway. "We're going to build an amusement park here," he said. "It's a branded park for *Xiong Chumo*."

Xiong Chumo was a popular children's cartoon that featured two bear brothers. I had trouble seeing how cartoon bears fit in with golf, the Spanish bullfighter, and the Bavarian Army victory arch, and sure enough, by December 2019, when Lu Yong drove me and the others around Beishanping, the developers had given up on *Xiong Chumo*. Now the golf course was used primarily for picnics. On a former putting green beside the Siegestor arch, vendors had set up plywood stalls that sold mutton kebabs, noodles, beer, and other refreshments. Parents lounged in the sun while their children ran around the abandoned fairways.

During our tour of the various mountain failures, Lu Yong and the others didn't seem to find any of it remarkable. Over the years, I had never been able to get answers to certain questions about River Town Golf. Was anybody upset about the waste? Why didn't the relocated farmers complain more? What does a bullfighter have to do with either Fuling or golf? And who was the genius who had decided to build a replica of the Siegestor triumphal arch atop a remote mountain beside the Upper Yangtze?

Similar questions could be asked across China. By 2019, it seemed that virtually every city had some equivalent of River Town Golf—an ill-advised development project, usually half-built and abandoned. It was part of the nationwide detox, or maybe a hangover. Things had happened so fast that memories were blurred, as if everybody had been a little drunk for a couple of decades. It felt like only yesterday that I had worried about my book's descriptions of poverty; then the Fuling developers co-opted the title as a luxury brand; now the unfinished River Town Golf condos stood like memorials to past excess. It wasn't surprising that locals didn't waste much energy trying to figure out exactly what had happened. They were much more inclined to wait for a sunny afternoon, buy some mutton skewers, and picnic beside the arch that marked the glory of the Bavarian Army.

On the last day of 2019, the Chinese government notified the World Health Organization that Wuhan was experiencing an outbreak of severe pneumonia of an unknown type. That same morning, officials in Wuhan shut down the Huanan Seafood Wholesale Market, where the majority of known cases had occurred thus far. The Wuhan police announced that they were investigating eight individuals for spreading rumors about the outbreak, and the government gave the impression that there was no reason for panic.

During the first week of 2020, news continued to trickle out of Wuhan. On January 6, *The New York Times* reported that fifty-nine people in the city had been infected, although, at the time, it was believed that nobody had died. The story quoted an expert on infectious diseases in Singapore, who speculated that the virus was probably not spreading from humans to humans, because Chinese reports claimed that health workers had not gotten sick. In the print edition of the *Times*, the story appeared on page thirteen.

Like most people, I didn't register the potential risk of the virus. For me, Wuhan remained the same as it always had been—the other river town. In the sporadic journal that I kept about daily life in Chengdu, on January 6, I made no reference to the *Times* report, or to the virus, or to Wuhan. Instead, I recorded a math problem that I had worked on with the twins that evening:

Big Sister and Little Brother want to buy the same book. But Big Sister's money is 2.4 yuan short, while Little Brother's money is 3.6 yuan short. Together their money is enough to buy the book. How much does the book cost?

January was a month of everyday distractions, of long-distance news that was easily ignored. On the ninth, I turned in my grades at Sichuan

University; that same day, for the first time, Chinese authorities publicly confirmed the outbreak of a new coronavirus. On January 10, a man who had gone regularly to the Huanan Seafood Wholesale Market became the disease's first official fatality, according to the Wuhan Municipal Health Commission. That was also the day on which Ariel and Natasha sat the final exams that were standardized for all Chengdu third graders: seventy minutes for math, seventy minutes for Chinese. In the twins' short lives, that had been their longest semester: a total of ninety-one days in the classroom. But all those hours at Chengdu Experimental had paid off. Natasha and Ariel could now communicate well in Mandarin, and they had a cohort of a half dozen good friends in the class. When Leslie and I picked up the girls after the final exams, we chatted with other parents about getting together during what everybody expected to be a normal Lunar New Year holiday.

On the morning of January 17, shortly before I was scheduled to speak to 140 current Peace Corps volunteers in downtown Chengdu, there was an unexpected announcement that the China program was ending. The news had nothing to do with the coronavirus. For months, the senators from Florida, Rick Scott and Marco Rubio, had repeatedly called for the Peace Corps to leave China, although few people had taken them seriously. The Senate has no authority over where Peace Corps volunteers are posted, and it's a long tradition that the agency should be removed from political spats. Throughout the nearly sixty-year history of the Peace Corps, the U.S. had never ended a program because of a diplomatic conflict.

In the past, whenever the Peace Corps determined that a country no longer needed volunteers, the program was "graduated." This process typically took two or three years, involving frequent meetings with representatives from the host country, to make sure that the departure was handled well. But there had never been any communication with the

Chinese government about shutting down the Peace Corps program. When the announcement was made, it didn't come from the agency or from the Trump administration. The senators from Florida broke the news on Twitter.

"For too long, Beijing has fooled organizations such as the World Bank and the World Trade Organization," Rubio wrote. Scott chimed in: "I'm glad the Peace Corps has finally come to its senses and sees Communist China for what it is: the second largest economy in the world and an adversary of the United States."

The tweets appeared early on the morning of January 17, China time. In Chengdu, the Peace Corps was in the midst of an in-service training for all current volunteers. As an alumnus from the early years, I had been invited to speak about my experiences. But by the time I arrived at the training site, in a hotel in downtown Chengdu, nobody was in the mood for nostalgia. The American volunteers, most of whom were in their twenties, looked stunned; some were red-eyed from crying. At the back of the room, more than a dozen Chinese staff members stood with stoic expressions. Some had worked for decades for the American agency, and they had just learned that their jobs were ending. Behind the Chinese staff, somebody had hung a red nylon banner in honor of the in-service training. It was the same style of sign that was used for propaganda in China, and today it seemed equally tone-deaf:

WELCOME TO IST 2020
BE THE TREE YOU WISH TO SEE IN THE WORLD

From the expressions of the American staff, I knew that the last tree anybody wished to see right now was a journalist. A Peace Corps administrator approached and said, as tactfully as possible, that I was no longer invited to the lunch that had been scheduled to follow my talk. Later, when I wrote an article about the program's closure, neither the director of the Peace Corps nor anybody else at the agency would agree to an interview.

The only person who talked was Senator Rick Scott. During our phone interview, the senator acknowledged that neither he nor anybody on his staff had spoken with a single current or former China volunteer in order to learn more about the program. When I mentioned the possibility of the program contributing to American diplomacy, the senator said, "I asked the Peace Corps about that. They didn't know of one person who had ever gone to the State Department from the Peace Corps."

I explained that twenty-seven former China volunteers currently worked in the State Department, and I asked if this knowledge might have changed his mind. "I'd have to get more information," he said.

In the early years of Peace Corps China, volunteers were warned repeatedly about the program's vulnerability. Chinese hard-liners especially hated the idea of young Americans being posted deep in the country's interior. Many years after I served, a former colleague at my college told me that the Fuling volunteers were originally supposed to be sent to Wanxian, another Yangtze city with a teachers college. But Party officials were concerned that Wanxian was too close to the construction site of the Three Gorges Dam, where foreigners might learn sensitive information. So the cadres pushed us 130 miles upstream, to Fuling.

Of course, I ended up writing about the dam anyway. At some level, it didn't matter which river town you chose: if you sent young, open-minded Americans to remote parts of China, they were bound to learn about their surroundings, just as they were bound to teach new ideas. They were also bound to stumble—the job included plenty of failure and frustration, which wasn't a bad thing. The experience forced volunteers to consider other perspectives, which is one of the most useful lessons anyone can learn, especially when young.

Despite the small size of the program, it produced dozens of alumni who went on to China-related careers. Adam Meier, who had taught with me in Fuling, later went to work at the State Department, where he helped administer the Fulbright program and other international exchanges. There was also a disproportionately high number of writers and journalists. Volunteers from the first ten groups published at least eleven books about China, and they worked as correspondents for a range of news organizations, including National Public Radio, *Newsweek*, and *The New York Times*. One correspondent even came out of Wanxian, the river town that made the Party nervous. In 2000, the Chinese finally invited the Peace Corps to Wanxian, and the first volunteer was a twenty-six-year-old named Jake Hooker. Despite having no background in Chinese, Hooker learned the language to a remarkable fluency. In 2008, as a reporter for *The New York Times*, Hooker won a Pulitzer Prize for exposing how rural Chinese factories were exporting toxic ingredients for use in pharmaceutical products around the world.

None of this had been in the interests of the most conservative elements in the Party. The reactionaries celebrated isolation and self-reliance, which was why Chinese schoolchildren had been forced to study Mao's famous essay, "Farewell, Leighton Stuart!" In the Reform era, reestablishing contact with the outside world had been a slow, painful process, and it took decades for the Peace Corps to feel stable. But now all of that had ended in a flurry of tweets by politicians who knew virtually nothing about the program. It was another version of the old pattern, the U.S.–China exchange that somehow leaves both sides dissatisfied.

After the Florida senators broke the news, a conservative Chinese publication called *Guanchazhe* published an homage to Mao's essay. The new version was titled "Farewell, Peace Corps in China, We Won't See You Off," and it was written by a columnist named Pan Gongyu. Pan wrote, "After twenty-seven years in China, the U.S. diplomatic offices intended to 'raise wolves,' but ended up with a litter of huskies." Conservatives across the Pacific also celebrated. In the 1990s, the Chinese had worried about volunteers possibly serving as intelligence agents, and now the same paranoia had taken root in the U.S. In the *Washington Examiner*, a commentator named Tom Rogan wrote approvingly of the Peace Corps closure, in part because he believed that some American volunteers may have become Chinese spies:

> We must thus ask how many of the more than 1,300 previous volunteers in China may have been recruited by the MSS [the Chinese Ministry of State Security] during their time there. The number is likely very small, but unlikely to be zero. How many of those volunteers then returned home to take up employment in the State Department or another U.S. government agency?

The Peace Corps had promised that current volunteers would finish their terms of service before returning home, but everything was changed by the new coronavirus. On January 28, five days after the entire city of Wuhan had been placed under quarantine, the Peace Corps evacuated all volunteers from China. The following day, the U.S. embassy in Beijing and the various American consulates around the country, including one in Chengdu, began to send nonessential personnel home. On the morning of the thirtieth, the State Department issued an advisory telling Americans not to travel to China.

By the last day of January, China had an official total of 11,791 confirmed cases, along with 259 deaths. But it was clear that there had been a cover-up in Wuhan, and most experts believed that the actual toll was much higher. For Leslie and me, there were no longer any distractions; the long-distance news had finally arrived at our doorstep. On January 31, Chengdu tightened its lockdown policies, which had first been issued a week earlier.

Most of our foreign friends with children had already left the country. During the final week of January, there had been a spasm of panic-buying at Chengdu grocery stores and pharmacies. But now virtually nobody was outdoors. In early evening, the windows of the high-rises were illuminated, but the neighborhood was dead silent. Chengdu felt like a city suspended—every sign of life had been swept off the streets, and whisked up stairways and elevators, and now residents stayed inside, waiting to see what would happen next. Leslie and I decided that there was little chance of catching a virus in this environment, and in any case, we had worked too hard to get our family settled in the city. Neither of us looked at flights out of China.

On the eleventh day of the lockdown, February 3, at five minutes and forty-three seconds past midnight, and shortly after I had gone to bed, an earthquake struck the northeastern outskirts of Chengdu. I heard the quake before I felt it. First there was an uneven knocking, muffled and faraway, like a construction crew working on an upper floor. Then the noise grew louder—it seemed to descend from above, as if the tremor had started in the sky.

Later, I realized that the earthquake felt upside-down because the building was swaying. Our forty-three-story structure, like every properly engineered high-rise that had been built after the Great Sichuan Earthquake of 2008, had been designed to move during a tremor. The higher the floor, the farther it swayed, and the more it created tension in walls and other supports. There were also dampers—big shock absorbers designed to handle a quake—which made the knocking sounds. Initially, these noises and vibrations were most intense on the upper stories, and then they rippled down to the middle levels. I had been listening for a while before my own windows rattled and the bed began to shake. I sat upright. By now, Leslie was also awake. It seemed like a long time before either of us spoke.

"Is it over?" she said.

Fifteen seconds, half a minute—I couldn't say how long the tremor had lasted. I got up and checked the twins' room. They slept in a heavy wooden bunk bed, and I shook each of the supports: solid. Nothing in the room had fallen down. I could hear the girls' heavy nighttime breathing when I closed the door.

I went to my study and turned on the computer. Online reports soon identified the epicenter as outside Deyang, a small city about forty miles from Chengdu. There didn't seem to be much damage; the magnitude was measured at 5.2. But I knew that sometimes a small quake represents a foreshock. In the spring of 2008, a series of minor tremors around Chengdu had preceded the one that killed almost seventy thousand people.

I stepped outside onto the balcony. The view was clear to the far bend of the Jin River, its surface slick with city lights. There were no signs of activity in the high-rises around us. I assumed that most residents had slept through the tremor; probably, they would read about it in the morning. Traditionally, an earthquake in China represents a bad omen, but there was no point in thinking about that now. Leslie and I had made our decision; we were here in our home on the nineteenth floor. Like everybody else in the city suspended, we would wait.

Part II

CHAPTER SIX

The City Suspended

February 2020

O N THE TWENTY-SEVENTH DAY OF THE CHENGDU LOCKDOWN, five masked men appeared in the lobby of our building carrying a hundred-inch TCL Xclusive television. It was late morning, and I was taking Natasha and Ariel outside to get some air. The three of us were also wearing surgical masks. I had never seen such an enormous TV; it arrived in an eight-foot-long box that weighed more than three hundred pounds. Two of the masked men stood inside an elevator with a tape measure, trying to figure out whether the box would fit. Otherwise, it was going to be a long haul up the stairs. An address scrawled atop the box noted that it was to be delivered to a customer on the twenty-eighth floor.

The deliverymen had been admitted into our compound with special passes. The complex consisted of nine high-rise buildings arranged around a central courtyard, and, like many housing blocks in China, everything was enclosed by a high wall. In normal times, there were three entrances, but two of the gates had been chained shut on the last day of January. Since then, all residents, visitors, and deliverymen had been funneled through a single checkpoint. Anybody who arrived at this gate was greeted by an infrared temperature gun to the forehead. The gun was wielded by a government-assigned volunteer in a white hazmat suit, and, behind him, a turnstile led to a thick plastic mat soaked with a bleach solution. A sign read "Shoe Sole Disinfecting Area," and there was always a trail of wet prints leading away from the mat, like a foot-bath at a public swimming pool.

Compared with many other places, our compound's restrictions were relatively light. We could leave as often as we pleased, provided that we carried passes that had been issued by the *juweihui*, the neighborhood committee, the most local level of the Communist Party. When I corresponded with former students in other parts of Sichuan and Chongqing, it seemed that the majority of them were limited to one individual per household going out every two days. Often, that person had to inform the authorities where she was headed. At our compound, we didn't have to explain our destination, but even so, few residents ventured beyond the gate. Nearly all restaurants, government offices, and shops had been closed, and schools had been suspended indefinitely. When the Chengdu government issued the stricter lockdown regulations on January 31, it even banned "every sort of group dinner party."

Many residents could purchase necessities without leaving their buildings. This was true in urban areas across China, where e-commerce had been popular even before the coronavirus, which was now known as COVID-19. Throughout the lockdown, my neighbors had been ordering things on Taobao, the country's biggest e-commerce site, and they got their food delivered from Hema Fresh, a nationwide grocery chain that had a branch nearby. Both Taobao and Fresh Hema were owned by the Alibaba Group, one of China's largest technology companies. All day long, motorcycle deliverymen handed off items to my compound's security guards, who trundled through the courtyard with dollies and shopping carts, dropping off an unbelievable number of boxes and bags, all of them marked with apartment numbers in black ink. In my lobby, the most packages I counted at any time was 125.

Whenever I went out, I stopped in the lobby to study the deliveries.

On the morning that the Xclusive TV arrived, the other packages re-inforced the impression that folks had settled in for the long haul: two electric power strips for apartment 1101, three bottles of Omo laundry detergent for 3003, a huge box of fresh ginger for 3704.

I tried to strike up a conversation with one of the TV deliverymen. He was standing near the elevator door, and he wore his surgical mask in the position that the twins and I called "the holster." This was when a man kept the straps around his ears but pulled the mask down beneath his chin, usually so that he could spit or smoke a cigarette. I asked the deliveryman what he would do if the TV wouldn't fit inside the elevator.

"It'll fit," he grunted. "No problem."

He unholstered the mask and pulled it back over his face. He didn't seem friendly, and the men weren't making much progress with the TV, so the twins and I went outside. Next to the river, a row of bike-shares had hardly been touched for weeks, and I used my phone to unlock one. The twins liked the challenge of riding the adult-size bikes, and they took turns wobbling along the empty riverside path.

When they got bored, we proceeded to the zombie subway station be-side our compound. The station was still operating, but it was silent ex-cept for a public-service message, played on an endless loop, that warned nonexistent passengers to watch their step. On the ticket level, all thirty-eight security cameras were still in place, recording everything that didn't happen in the empty station. Ariel and Natasha visited each entrance, laughing while they ran up and down the escalators in the wrong direc-tion. This had become part of our daily lockdown routine, an easy way for the girls to release some energy. They hadn't seen another child for nearly a month.

After we returned to the compound, and had the infrared gun pointed at our foreheads, and sloshed through the bleach footbath, the deliverymen were returning with the empty TV box on a dolly. The man I had talked with earlier explained that they had been forced to remove the top half of the box in order to fit it into the elevator. He still wasn't eager to talk.

These days, people seemed especially wary of strangers. If I got in the elevator with another resident, he often turned his back to me. Most people were probably aware that our compound was, at least by local standards, a hot spot. On the various government apps that mapped Chengdu's COVID cases, our compound lit up bright red. There had been a positive test somewhere in the complex—the only one in our neighborhood.

Security guards told me that the case involved a man who had visited family near Wuhan. Wuhanphobia was rampant, because contact with somebody from that city, or even from Hubei province, could trigger a quarantine. Near the end of January, after Chengdu had locked down, a Party official at SCUPI had distributed a message to the WeChat accounts of all teachers and administrators:

Dears,

As part of the procedures to contain the novel coronavirus outbreak, please let us know if you have been to Wuhan, Hubei Province for the past month. If you do or have interacted with someone from Wuhan or Hubei Province, please quarantine yourself for 14 days and closely watch your health situation.

Within minutes, and without further prompting, teachers and staff began to post testimonials. First, Chinese instructors sent messages, because they immediately understood what the Party wanted, and then the foreigners followed suit. There was something ominous about watching my colleagues' statements pop up on WeChat, one after another:

I haven't been to Wuhan and have not had any contact with Wuhan personnel. I will be in Chengdu all the winter holiday.

I haven't visited Wuhan or contacted anyone from Wuhan in person after January 9th. I will stay in Chongqing during the winter break and will try to stay at home as much as possible.

I have never been to Wuhan or been in touch with anyone from Hubei in person. I'm currently in Chengdu, Sichuan and am staying home as much as possible.

———

From the day that the Huanan Seafood Wholesale Market was closed, on January 1, to the day that a Chinese official publicly acknowledged for the first time that the virus was spreading through human transmission, on January 20, there had been nearly three full weeks of official inaction and misinformation. In Wuhan, a number of individuals had known better, and some of them had tried to warn others. On December 30, an ophthalmologist named Li Wenliang, who worked at the Central Hospital of Wuhan, saw a medical report for a patient who appeared to have SARS. Li posted a screenshot of the report on a WeChat group of about 150 former classmates from medical school. He wrote, "7 confirmed cases of SARS were reported from Huanan Seafood Market and they are isolated in the emergency department of our hospital." Later that day, he sent an update and a correction: "The latest news is, it has been confirmed that they are coronavirus infections, but the exact virus strain is being subtyped."

Somebody in Li's WeChat group took screenshots of the warnings and posted them on social media. These screenshots followed the common pattern of sensitive information in China, spreading for a while before the censors caught up. After Li's warnings were scrubbed from the internet, the police came to his home. He was forced to sign an apology, and the cops gave him a written warning for "publishing untrue statements."

Others in Wuhan were also reprimanded for spreading rumors, and officials continued to deny that the virus could be transmitted between humans. Even well-respected scientists participated in what later seemed like a cover-up. Wang Guangfa, a prominent respiratory expert at Peking University, traveled to Wuhan as part of an inspection delegation organized by the National Health Commission. On January 10, Wang told Chinese state media that the virus had little capacity to cause illness, and that the outbreak was under control. (Later, he revealed that he had been infected.) For the next ten days, prominent Wuhan officials continued to downplay the outbreak.

After the entire city was quarantined, a number of residents wrote angrily about the cover-up. The most prominent commentator was Fang Fang, a sixty-five-year-old novelist. Fang Fang was the writer most closely associated with Wuhan; for decades she had published fiction about the city's history and culture. During the quarantine, she began posting daily reports on Weibo. On January 25, she analyzed the government's failure:

> But right now what I want to say is that what you saw from those government officials in Hubei is actually what you would expect from most government cadres in China. . . . If this outbreak had happened in another Chinese province, I'm sure the performance of those officials wouldn't be much different than what we are seeing here. When the world of officialdom skips over the natural process of competition, it leads to disaster; empty talk about political correctness without seeking truth from facts also leads to disaster; prohibiting people from speaking the truth and the media from reporting the truth leads to disaster; and now we are tasting the fruits of these disasters, one by one.

As lockdowns were instituted across the country, Fang Fang's reports became immensely popular. At one point, she had more than fifty million readers. She wrote every day, and she had a novelist's instinct for subject and tone. "The only things I can pay attention to and experience are those little details that are happening around me," she explained in one post. Among the details, she described feeding rice to her sixteen-year-old dog, because it was hard to acquire dog food in the quarantined city. Many of Fang Fang's posts appeared after midnight, and she mentioned that she took sleeping pills every evening, because of stress.

Even in the best of times, Wuhan is not an easy city. The weather is notorious—brutal heat in summer, choking fog in winter. The floods are even worse than those of most river towns, because Wuhan is situated on a low, swampy plain where the Han River joins the Yangtze. In addition to this natural crossroads, the city is home to one of the two largest rail hubs in central China. Throughout modern times, disruptions of many types have converged in Wuhan: diseases, armies, political movements. The violent uprising that eventually finished the last imperial dynasty, the Qing, began in Wuhan, in October 1911.

The Wuhan lockdown was unlike that of any other city in China. The term used to describe it was also unique: *fengcheng*, or "sealed city." Within the sealed city, residents couldn't go for walks or bike rides the way that we did in Chengdu, and they were strictly prevented from leaving Wuhan. The scale of the quarantine was unprecedented in human history. A total of more than nine million people had essentially been restricted to their apartments and housing compounds.

Fang Fang described the profound isolation, but she also wrote about Wuhan with affection. This was part of her appeal: after succeeding as a writer, she had never abandoned her hometown for Beijing or other eastern cities that tended to be favored by creative types. In one quarantine report, she quoted something she had written many years ago for a documentary:

> The reason I like Wuhan starts with the fact that this is the place I
> am most familiar with. If you line up all the cities in the world before
> me, Wuhan is the only place I really know. It is like a crowd of people

walking toward you and amid that sea of unfamiliar faces you catch sight of a single face flashing you a smile that you recognize. To me, that face is Wuhan.

As a successful author, Fang Fang could be bolder than most citizens. On Weibo, she criticized officials by name, and she commemorated the deaths of prominent residents who had been infected, including Li Wenliang, the ophthalmologist. Less than a week after Li was interrogated by the police, he caught the virus at work, and he died on February 7. He was only thirty-three, and he left a widow and two small children. On the evening of Li's death, Fang Fang wrote, "Right now everyone in this city is crying for him. And I am heartbroken."

This post, like many of the things that Fang Fang wrote, was subsequently removed from Weibo. But she kept writing, and sometimes she addressed the censors directly:

> To my dear internet censors: You had better let the people of Wuhan speak out and express what they want to say! . . . If you won't even allow us to release some of our pain, if you can't even permit us to complain a little bit or reflect on what is happening, then you must be intent on driving us all mad!

———

Every day in Chengdu, before noon, I was required by Sichuan University to send a form testifying that I had had no contact with anybody from Wuhan or Hubei. I also had to submit my body temperature, along with a confirmation that I was not suffering from fatigue, cough, or difficulty in breathing. As the lockdown wore on, I sent the same figure every day: 36.2 degrees centigrade, which is the equivalent of 97.2 degrees Fahrenheit. And every day, I submitted the same COVID mantra:

I have not had contact with people from Wuhan today. I have not had contact with people from Hubei province today.

In the manner of so many things in China, the noon deadline was not really a noon deadline. It inched forward day by day, undoubtedly because somebody was pressuring the poor administrator who had been tasked with collecting the forms. She sent a series of messages that, with textbook WeChat-style passive-aggression, made it clear that I needed to be quicker about wrapping up my Wuhan-free mornings:

February 22, 2020 11:37 AM

Hi Dr Hessler,

How is everything going today? Just checking before submitting the daily report.

Cheers,

February 26, 2020 11:12 AM

Hi Dr Hessler,

How's everything going today? Enjoy the sunshine. [smiley-face emoji]

Best,

February 27, 2020 10:58 AM

Hi Dr Hessler,

How's everything going today? Have a lovely day. [smiley-face emoji]

Best,

Our semester began the last week of February. I was scheduled to teach the same classes as the previous term, with new students. But now nobody was allowed to return to campus, and the administration told us that classes would be remote for the indefinite future. My department hastily prepared an online platform, and all teachers were given an hour-long training session. Across the country, China planned to educate more than twenty-two million college students online, along with an estimated 180 million schoolchildren. Because China was the country where the virus first spread, it was also the first to attempt remote learning.

Beginning at eight o'clock every morning, these tens of millions of users started logging in. My home internet connection often became unstable, and I quickly learned not to be ambitious with the technology. This was true across China: the Zoom-style course, with everybody appearing onscreen, wasn't used by any of the teachers I knew. My students were invisible: if a camera was turned on, it featured only the instructor, although even that could be problematic. In nonfiction class, I attempted to live stream the first lecture, but the system failed so many times that I gave up. After that, I avoided video. For each class, I prepared low-resolution images and documents to share on-screen, and my students and I communicated only through audio and text.

In three sections, I taught nearly sixty students, only one of whom I had met in person: Serena. For the rest, all I had were their voices in my headphones, their words on the screen, and their English names. In the 1990s, it would have been easier to imagine faces, because that was the era of rural students who, with little awareness of the outside world, had named themselves with Sino-Dickensian flair. Along with Anry and North, I had taught Youngsea, Silent Hill, and Soddy. There was a girl named Joy, and a boy named Joy. One student called himself Tirana, after the capital of Albania, and another boy—quiet, serious, idealistic—was named Marx. A trio of farm kids from a poor county north of Fuling called themselves Lazy, House, and Yellow.

Twenty years later, I wondered if you could track China's rise through English names. For my online sections of freshman composition, most students had selected old-school white middle-class standards: Agnes, Florence, David, Andy, Charles, Steve, Peter, Brian. Whenever these names popped up on-screen, I couldn't help but envision kids I had grown up with in Missouri—in 1980, there were three Brians in my fifth-grade class. When was the last time any American named his kid Brian? But nowadays the Chinese were making Brians in Sichuan and Chongqing. I figured that in the next generation, if China started to decline, it would begin with the Caitlyns, the Aidens, the Madisons.

I was glad to have a Sisyphos in my nonfiction class. He was a senior, and on the first day, I asked students to list their hobbies. Sisyphos's terse response—"Physics, finance, and economics"—made me envision a weary young man gazing up at a boulder. There were still a handful of unusual names, although nowadays they often reflected international sophistication rather than isolation. One first-year section included a sports fan who called himself Curry, after the Golden State Warriors guard, and there was a rap aficionado named Rakim. In my mind's eye, Curry always wore blue and gold and fiddled with his mouth guard during online class, and I envisioned Rakim as Black. For one of Rakim's early papers, he analyzed a reality show called *The New Rap of China*, which, at the command of some Party genius, had banned any Chinese contestant who wore dreadlocks. Rakim wrote: "In my point of view, this rule is not only an insult to Black Culture, but also an offense to the rights that participants should have." I was impressed by his orthography—despite being stranded in eastern Hunan, Rakim was aware that the word *Black* should be capitalized. He was doing this weeks before it became official style at *The New York Times*.

My students were scattered across more than fifteen provinces and municipalities, ranging from Yunnan in the far southwest to Jilin on the North Korean border. Despite the geographic diversity, their situations were broadly similar. During week one of the semester, I asked if students personally knew anybody who had been infected with COVID, and all of those who answered—fifty-six total—responded in the negative. They remained under lockdown restrictions, and they tended to be cautious. Nearly a third reported that they had not stepped outside their housing compounds in a month. Like me, they were required to submit daily temperatures and testimonials to the university. *I have not had contact with people from Wuhan today. I have not had contact with people from Hubei province today.*

For the first week, I assigned John Cheever's "The Enormous Radio." The story describes a New York City couple who acquire a radio that allows them to eavesdrop on conversations in other apartments in their building. After reading it, my students mentioned things that they had noticed about their neighbors during the lockdown. They described how quickly rumors spread between apartments, and the ways in which people avoided each other. One boy wrote:

> I was reading news when a notice which was published by the government caught my attention. It was a [list of people who had been quarantined], and I saw a name which belongs to my next door neighbor. The reason why she was isolated is that there was a confirmed case of COVID-19 in her company. In order to ensure the safety of our community, she was taken to live alone for 14 days. As far as I'm concerned, it was fine for the government to do so, but what happened next was a bit unexpected.
>
> I couldn't count how many calls my dad received that morning. Those so-called old friends of my father, they missed my father at the same time. They would talk something about my family at the beginning, and then pretend to mention our neighbor casually to get some information. Some of the friends even wanted my father to give them a time table about when our neighbor went out of the house.

———

On the thirty-ninth day of the lockdown, the packages in my lobby included a box of houseplants for 3703 and some flowers for 2903. It was now March, and sometimes I saw people tending plants on their balconies. But it was still rare for residents to leave the compound. When women went downstairs to pick up packages, they were often dressed in pajamas, even in the afternoon. In the lobby, management provided a spray bottle of 75 percent alcohol solution, and sometimes I saw a masked, pajama-clad resident standing in a puddle of the stuff, spraying her hands, packages, shopping bags, whatever.

People rarely spoke in these situations. There were no greetings, no jokes, no moments of shared commiseration. Part of it was the masks. On my floor, residents wore them even if they were merely dropping off garbage ten feet from their door. Outside, I often saw motorcycle deliverymen, helmetless and fiddling with their phones at thirty miles an hour, their masks safely in place.

In addition to the masks, some people in my compound wore see-through plastic gloves and surgical booties. These costumes of the quarantine, along with all the other restrictions, turned citizens inward, and people directed their energy toward whatever space was left to them. Among the packages in my lobby, I noticed many home furnishings and cleaning implements: a Pincai-brand storage cabinet for 602, a Deema vacuum cleaner for 2304, a giant carpet, wrapped in tape and plastic, for 303. There was home-office equipment (wireless mouse, 4201; file cabinets, 301). By the forty-fourth day, somebody in 3704 had felt the need to buy an electric footbath machine from Kosaka. (Slogan: "Powerful by Dreams.")

From what I could tell, my neighbors' lockdown diet was healthy: lots of fresh vegetables and fruit. I never saw evidence of alcohol going anywhere other than 1901: my apartment. The government strategically allowed cigarette and alcohol shops to remain open, but when I talked to store owners in my neighborhood, they said sales were terrible. There are many types of loneliness in this world, but it's a special isolation to feel that you are the only individual in a forty-three-story building who is drinking his way through a lockdown.

I almost never saw children. I knew they were up there: a game called Mini Table Football to 2703, a Huanqi toy box to 1804. The compound printed out documents on request and left them in the lobby, and I noticed homework assignments for kids who were attending online school: for 2102, a chapter on chemistry; for 3802, a handout on poems from the Northern and Southern dynasties. But children didn't even venture outside their doors, because parents were so frightened of the disease. For a very brief period, Leslie and I allowed Ariel and Natasha to play alone in the courtyard, but it horrified the security guards and others—they would rush up to the girls and ask if they were all right. I realized that I had to accompany them at all times.

By this point, scientists were starting to believe that the virus was less dangerous for children, and that there was little risk of transmission outdoors. In any case, the total number of infections in Chengdu was remarkably low. By March 1, in a city of sixteen million, only 143 cases had been reported, including the one in my compound. But some people distrusted the government numbers, which, given everything that had happened in Wuhan, was not surprising. Mostly, though, people's behavior reflected a deep-rooted fear of illness. It was similar to the material in the twins' schoolbooks—after a long history of epidemics, disasters, political unrest, and high mortality rates, Chinese tended to be terrified of disease and injury, especially with regard to children. Even the young people I taught—boys and girls in their late teens and early twenties, suddenly confined with parents and other elders—didn't seem to push boundaries. Often my students reported staying inside much longer than the rules required.

Rakim wrote an essay about spending the lockdown with his seventy-eight-year-old grandmother. After a period of weeks without any infections, the local government began to lift restrictions. Rakim's grandmother told him that she planned to rejoin her elderly friends who danced every night outdoors in a public square. Rakim described his response:

"What?" totally shocked by what she said, I asked. "You are going to participate [in] these public activities again?"

"Yes, I am," said nan in anger. "These activities have been suspended due to the virus for a long time. It's time to get back to routine."

"Fine, then take care and wear your mask," I said helplessly.

Even before the pandemic, I had noticed a cautious quality to my students. I thought it probably reflected the intense pressure and responsibility that they felt as only children. In Rakim's essay, the generational roles were reversed, with Grandma playing truant while the young man fretted at home:

At about ten-thirty, I went to the living room to quench my thirst. However, I noticed that no one except me is in this house! My grandma has not come home yet! I called her instantly, worrying that something bad had happened. After a few seconds, she picked up, "What's wrong boy? I'm still playing."

"Seriously?" I said anxiously. "Do you know what time it is? I thought you [got] into trouble."

"Don't worry about me," said grandma. "I will come home before twelve o'clock."

———

At night, I went for long bike rides. I liked the empty streets, and I liked looking up at the high-rises with their rows of illuminated windows. The people were still there, waiting; for the first time, I thought of a Chinese city as patient. Usually, Chengdu evening streets are heavy with the smell of hot pepper and *huajiao*, or prickly ash, the characteristic spices of Sichuanese cuisine. But with all restaurants closed, the scents had vanished from the streets. Their absence felt like part of the city's silence.

While riding, I passed countless walls and gates with government-assigned volunteers in hazmat suits. The Chinese tendency to enclose residential areas with walls turned out to be an advantage in the government's control of the virus. Entrances could be sealed off, turning compounds into little forts, which also made it easy to survey residents. During the lockdown, volunteers from the neighborhood committee stopped by our apartment on three different occasions. They always asked the same questions: *Does anybody here have a fever? Has anybody been to Wuhan? Hubei?* The volunteers were friendly and talkative, and part of the purpose seemed to be to convey information and put people at ease. At one point, a volunteer informed me that the positive case in our compound involved a resident of Building Nine who had a connection to Wuhan.

After that, during my journeys outside, I always detoured past Building Nine. I began to notice people behaving in ways that seemed unusually vigilant. Once, a woman wearing pajamas, a mask, plastic gloves, and surgical booties walked past me holding a delivery package, a bottle of disinfectant, and a cotton swab. Like many people during this time, she avoided eye contact. With the pajamas, the protective gear, and the thousand-yard stare, she looked like a sleepwalking surgeon. She entered the lobby of Building Nine, where she gingerly used the cotton swab to call the elevator. Even her gloved hand didn't touch the button.

I was curious about what was happening in Wuhan, and a friend put me in touch with a pharmacist who worked in a hospital in the sealed city. Nearly every day, we exchanged WeChat messages. The pharmacist, whom I'll call Zhang, had found himself on the front lines of the crisis, and a dozen of his close colleagues had fallen sick. One was in critical care. Zhang's messages often expressed anger at the government:

My personal opinion is that the government has always been careless and they suppressed dissent. Those are two of the causes.
Because of this, they lost the golden opportunity to control the
virus. . . . I don't believe the state-run media or read their reports.
On the contrary, I pay more attention to what my friends say. You
asked about my first reaction? In fact, even now I am not very frightened by the disease. I just take necessary precautions. But I am worried sick that if I get it I might infect my family.

Zhang was roughly the same age as my Fuling students, and he had
the phlegmatic character that is common to the Reform generation. He
had considered checking into a hotel to isolate himself from his wife and
daughter, but the few places that remained open in Wuhan required special approval. I avoided giving too many details about my own family's
daily life, because so many things that we enjoyed—the long walks, the
piles of packages—were impossible in Wuhan:

> Our basic needs are met (at least food and clothing are enough). It
> feels like the era of planned economy when I was little. . . . There are
> barely any cigarettes, alcohol, tea, snacks, drinks, or pet food avail-
> able. Maybe things will get better later, who knows?

His daughter was eleven, and we exchanged pictures of our children.
Zhang described his struggles to keep the girl engaged:

> People who spend a lot of time in a confined space tend to become
> lazy and depressed. It's not easy to motivate them. I'm now teaching
> my daughter to practice Ping-Pong against the living-room wall. My
> childhood school didn't have so many Ping-Pong tables. We used to
> do that a lot. Now she is quite skilled at it. Other times, I encourage
> her to stand up and play the guitar, moving to the beat, like a real
> band guitarist.

On March 5, a message from Chengdu Experimental was distributed in the WeChat parents' group:

> The situation is still grim in terms of preventing and controlling the epidemic. The school requires each family to report the child's physical condition to the class group every day. The school will also collect some data according to the requirements of the relevant department, which requires everyone's cooperation.

After that, the twins' temperatures and daily whereabouts had to be submitted, along with the usual testimonials. *I have not had contact with people from Wuhan today. I have not had contact with people from Hubei province today.* Despite Chengdu's low case numbers, the authorities had not set a date for children or university students return to in-class instruction. Like most Chinese elementary schools, Chengdu Experimental did not attempt simultaneous instruction, and Teacher Zhang and other instructors posted short videos about lessons. Leslie and I decided to skip the videos, and instead we doubled the twins' daily ration of characters—now they memorized twenty every morning. In the afternoon they battled word problems in the math text:

> Ping Ping: I calculated a three-digit number that was divided by a one-digit number, and the quotient was 104, with a remainder of 5.
> Huang Feifei: Why did you think that the divisor was 9 instead of 6?
> What is the correct answer?

The Ministry of Education estimated that more than 220 million children and adolescents had been confined to their homes. As time passed, I heard increasingly negative reports from former Fuling stu-

dents who taught in third- and fourth-tier cities. "As for the classes online, it couldn't be much worse," one high school teacher wrote. "The
students can't control themselves." His students typically followed lessons on mobile phones, which seemed common in smaller cities, where
households rarely had a spare computer.

As March progressed, certain aspects of the lockdowns eased in cities around China, and some people began to return to work. But schools
weren't part of this process—the emotional fear of disease and children
seemed to outweigh the scientific evidence. This meant that many children remained alone at home after their parents went to work. I often
corresponded with Willy, who estimated that 80 percent of his ninth-
grade pupils were unaccompanied during the day. The parents often
complained to him about their children's behavior during this time.

"People say their kids are *shenshou*," Willy said, using a term that
means, roughly, "mystical beasts." He continued, "They say, 'We want the
mystical beast to go back to the cage.' The cages are the school." Willy's
own two children also followed classes on phones, and he had noticed a
rapid deterioration in his teenage daughter's behavior. "We don't know
exactly when she is having class and when she is using the mobile phone
to chat or play games," he said. "She is right now out of control."

During the fourth week of online classes, a friend in Fuling reported
that a middle school student in Beishanping had jumped out of his fifth-
floor apartment. The student had been fighting with his father, who was
trying to get him to focus on online lessons. My friend sent a cell phone
video taken by somebody who lived nearby.

The apartment was located in one of the housing developments for
farmers who had been relocated for River Town Golf. In normal times,
few residents occupied these apartments, but some families had retreated
there during the pandemic. In the video, two people crouch over a motionless form at the base of a building. Police cars have arrived, along
with an ambulance; three men in masks approach the motionless form
with a stretcher. Bystanders engage in a terse dialogue:

"The feet hit the ground first."

"How can the family take this? My God! This is so sad."

"Jumped from the fifth floor, right?"

"The fifth floor."

————

In China, suicide is the leading cause of death among young people aged fifteen to thirty-five. I sensed that the isolation of the pandemic was driving even more young people to take drastic measures, although it was hard to find evidence. In March, I saw one report of a suicide in Hebei province, where an elementary school student had been scolded for using his phone to watch videos instead of attending remote classes. That boy, like the Fuling middle school student, had jumped from his building.

The report from Hebei was subsequently removed, and it seemed likely that the vast majority of such incidents were kept out of the press. A friend in Fuling told me that the boy eventually died from his injuries, but nothing appeared in local news. If anything was posted on social media, it was quickly taken down. In the months after the pandemic, a number of other former students talked to me about suicides and attempted suicides in their communities. I estimated that there must have been hundreds of these incidents nationwide, but the Party removed them from the pandemic narrative. One former student explained, "The online classes are like a campaign that we have to win, just like we must defeat the virus. So this kind of thing should not drag it down."

The suicide of Emily's brother had made her highly sensitive to issues of mental health, and she had also heard about the death in Beishanping. She told me that Tao Tao had weathered remote schooling relatively well, but she was concerned about her students. "Some of them have been terrified by the intense atmosphere, especially when they are alone," she wrote near the end of February. A couple of weeks later, she sent an update:

I was optimistic about the online classes at first. I thought it was a new experience if there was no other choice, and it was better than playing electronic games, at least. But now I realize I was too optimistic. Some students stay at home alone without an adult during daytime, and some adults are not qualified parents and don't have good communication with their children when they are both under great pressure.

For all the ways in which Chinese were protective of children, worrying about accidents and disease, they often lacked the same sensitivity to mental health. Intense pressure was simply accepted as a normal part of childhood. Emily wrote about how quickly the Beishanping suicide vanished from daily conversation:

When I told my colleagues about the incident, it didn't receive too much attention. Maybe there have been too many cases like this these years. When everybody is busy trying to catch the fast-moving train, no one has time to care about somebody who got off. And if you don't hide your soft heart, it's really hard to move on.

———

At the entrance to my compound, the neighborhood committee erected a series of information boards. One board displayed an organizational chart for an entity called the Communist Party Service Team for Home Quarantine, and it included headshots and cell phone numbers of seven government officials. In the past, I had never seen such information posted in public. As a journalist, I knew that it was usually a waste of time to try to interview cadres, who avoided the media.

One afternoon, I called the number at the top of the chart. The quarantine-team leader picked up immediately, and after I introduced myself, she promised to arrange an interview. Within an hour I received a call from the neighborhood committee's Party secretary. He told me to stop by his office the following morning, which was a Saturday.

In Chengdu, there was a total of 1,685 neighborhood committees. Every Chinese city was divided into such units, which played a key role in disease control. In Wuhan, an estimated ten thousand contact tracers worked during the initial period of the sealed city. They were divided into teams of between five and seven, with each group directed by an individual with training in public health. But other members often had no previous health experience. Many of them came from neighborhood committees whose members understood local dynamics. Their survey work provided some of the earliest details about how the virus moved. Even in the first weeks, Wuhan contact tracers noticed that people often seemed to transmit the virus before they showed symptoms.

Sheer manpower made a difference during this period. Much of the neighborhood committee work was wasteful—the bleach footbaths, for example, served no purpose. But other early efforts turned out to be critical. In February, just weeks after the worst mistakes had been made in Wuhan, it became clear that the situation was turning around. Even critical voices began to support the government's approach. On February 13, Fang Fang posted from the sealed city:

> But one thing clear is that the government actions taken to control the outbreak are proving to be increasingly effective. Over time, they are also gradually finding methods that are more humanistic.

The information boards in my neighborhood were part of this human-oriented effort. When I met with the local Party secretary, he answered my questions with an openness that I had rarely seen among Chinese cadres. His name was Wang Yi, and he was in his forties, a serious man in a blue blazer with a safety-pinned armband that read "Party Member Service Team." He had grown up in the neighborhood, where his father had also worked for the government. The old man had come out of re-tirement to don a hazmat suit during the outbreak—he was one of the volunteers who checked temperatures in front of apartment buildings. In truth, all of these individuals were paid a reasonable day wage, but they were referred to as *zhiyuanzhe*, or "volunteers." Some were small-shop owners whose businesses had been closed by the lockdown, and working for the committee helped them make ends meet.

Party Secretary Wang told me that he had slept on a couch in his of-fice for the first two weeks of the lockdown, when he worked from eight o'clock in the morning until midnight every day. His team consisted of thirty-eight people, most of them recently hired volunteers. The com-mittee oversaw a jurisdiction of around six thousand residents. All of their hard work in surveying the district had turned up exactly one case: the resident in Building Nine.

"He had been in Hubei," Party Secretary Wang told me. The resident had traveled to his hometown on the outskirts of Wuhan in order to cel-ebrate the Lunar New Year holiday. Whenever surveyors found some-body who had been in Wuhan or Hubei, their policy was to call the community's health service center. The health workers came to Build-ing Nine, where they found that the resident's temperature was 37.1, or 98.8 degrees Fahrenheit. It was within the range of normal, but they tested him for the virus anyway.

"He didn't feel sick," the Party secretary told me. "But it was positive." Later, the man showed symptoms, which meant that the team had caught him at a critical moment—he was likely infectious, but he didn't yet re-alize that he was sick. He spent ten days under observation in the hospi-tal, and then he was quarantined at home for another fourteen days. Because he was isolated so quickly, he didn't infect anybody else.

I asked the Party secretary when we would be able to move in and out of our compound without passes. "I think it will be two fourteen-day pe-riods," he said. He seemed to think in this unit of time, which represented the standard span of the quarantines that were being implemented in China. He estimated that it would be three more fourteen-day units before my daughters returned to school—mid- or late-April. When I asked if there had been much resistance to the pandemic policies, he shook his head. "Ninety percent of the population agrees," he said. "We have some people who think it's not convenient, and they want to go out and play mah-jongg or something. But most people follow the rules."

From what I had seen and heard, he wasn't exaggerating. My former Fuling students disliked the online classes, but they believed they were necessary. My current students seemed to feel the same way. But people in Wuhan, who had witnessed the chaotic early phase of the pandemic, probably had a different analysis. During one exchange with Zhang, the Wuhan pharmacist, I mentioned that most people I knew in Chengdu were supportive of pandemic controls. He wrote back:

> Everyone grumbles a lot, but everyone obeys the rules strictly. It's very contradictory, but it's China. Our cultural traditions dictate our thinking. We will use the word "victory" to describe the final end of the epidemic, although I personally don't like that description.

Xi Jinping had already declared that the country would "defeat the virus." Eventually, President Trump's Twitter feed adopted a similar tone (March 17, 2020: "WE WILL WIN!"). I asked Zhang to explain what he meant, and he responded:

> There is a bad tendency in China right now for the state propaganda department to turn what should be remembered as a sad incident into a comforting one. They are accustomed to using the word "victory" toward everything, the so-called man can conquer nature. I don't think there is joy in such an incident. So many people died, and their families won't think this is a victory whatsoever.

———

One afternoon, I finally entered Building Nine. A strip of plastic had been placed over the elevator buttons, and I pushed the number of one of the higher floors. Local security guards and volunteers had told me the address of the man who had been infected. By now, his mandatory quarantine had long since passed, but people still behaved strangely around the building.

Outside the apartment, there was a rack of shoes, some of them small: at least one child lived here. I knocked on the door. After a moment, a man called out gruffly: "Who is it?"

I replied that I was a neighbor, and that I had a question. The man opened the door. He was middle-aged, with a businessman's paunch. He was smoking a cigarette and he wore clear plastic gloves. He didn't have a mask. I introduced myself and said that I had been informed that a resident of the apartment had been infected.

"Nobody here has had it," the man said.

I tried to put him at ease, explaining that Party Secretary Wang and other health officials had told me that the case had been mild. "I know that the quarantine is finished," I continued. "I just want to learn about what the recovery was like."

"Of course," the man said. "If I were a neighbor, and if somebody had been sick, I'd want to know, too. But nobody here has had it."

"So you've never heard of anybody in this building getting infected?"

"No," he said. I couldn't read anything in his expression, although he was the only unmasked individual I had seen in or around Building Nine. He politely said goodbye and closed the door. On the way down, the elevator reeked of alcohol disinfectant. The following day, more than an hour before the university's noon deadline, I submitted my usual temperature of 36.2, along with the statements. *I have not had contact with people from Wuhan today. I have not had contact with people from Hubei province today.*

On the forty-fifth day of the Chengdu lockdown, my family went out to dinner for the first time. By now, the question of whether it remained a lockdown was becoming hazy. Businesses in the neighborhood had started to open, prioritized according to the mysterious logic of the Party. Barbershops were among the first, perhaps because there was no online alternative. After hair came money—the banks began with limited hours. Then there was food: some restaurants opened at night. During the long weeks of the city suspended, I had often imagined that it would change all at once: the Party would issue a command, and suddenly people would pour out of the high-rises. But the shift turned out to be incremental. It was more like an hourglass turned upside down: day by day, more businesses opened their doors, and slowly the residents trickled out of their fortified compounds. Ariel and Natasha still hadn't interacted with any other children, and there had been no announcement about reopening primary schools.

For our first dinner, we went to a barbecue restaurant next to the Fu River. The hostess shot each twin in the forehead with an infrared gun, and then Leslie and I took our turn. Our names and cell phone numbers were recorded on a clipboard, along with the temperatures that appeared on the gun: Ariel, 36.5; Natasha, 36.2; Leslie, 36.2; me, 36.0.

We sat down and unmasked. This place had always been popular, but it was half full tonight. Across China, the official count was more than eighty thousand confirmed cases and 3,119 deaths. But the rates of increase in both figures had slowed dramatically. Chengdu's last death— its third, total—had happened more than three weeks before. The ages of the three victims had been sixty-four, seventy-three, and eighty, and all had suffered multiple chronic health problems before becoming infected. In another three days, the World Health Organization would officially declare a pandemic.

The restaurant was trying hard. The doors had been thrown open wide, and all lights were blazing; waitresses greeted customers with loud voices. After we ordered, a manager called me over with what I believe to have been a conspiratorial smile, although only his eyes were visible above the mask. He handed me a silver tray with a sprig of flowers, a bowl of glutinous rice, and a red Valentine's-style card. "It's March eighth!" he said.

I had forgotten—International Women's Day.

He pointed at the rice and the card. "It's free," he said. "Write a message to your wife!"

I stared at the red paper. Then I wrote something to the effect that this was the most romantic period we had shared since the 2013 military coup in Cairo. I carried the silver tray back to the table while the masked manager documented the moment by taking pictures with his phone. A waitress brought the bottle of beer we had ordered, and I filled Leslie's and my glasses. Soon, the waitress reappeared with another Tsingtao. "It's free," she said. "Because of the epidemic!" She opened the bottle, and we shared that one, too.

CHAPTER SEVEN

Children of the Corona

May 2020

O N MAY 27, A FEW DAYS BEFORE RETURNING TO CLASSROOM teaching, I was bicycling across a deserted stretch of the Jiang'an Campus when I encountered a robot. The blocky machine stood about chest-high, on four wheels, and it was not quite as long as a golf cart. In front was a T-shaped device that appeared to be some kind of sensor. The robot rolled past me, moving in the opposite direction. I turned around and began to tail the thing at a distance of fifteen feet.

The last time I had been to campus was late February, after the administration informed staff that the spring semester would begin with remote classes. I had hurried to Jiang'an to retrieve some materials from my office, because nobody had any idea how long the campus would be closed. Back then, the virus was still ghostlike: I didn't know anybody who had been infected, and neither did any of my current or former students. It turned out that the date of my last campus visit—February 20—was also the last day that the city of Chengdu reported a new infection from community spread.

By the time I knew somebody personally who had fallen sick, we had entered week four of the semester. That spring, there were two types of time: the slow, predictable progression of the academic term, and the rapid explosion of the virus into the world. During week three, the epidemic officially became a pandemic; by week six, the U.S. death toll had exceeded that of China. That same week, China closed its borders to foreigners, because now there were so many cases outside the country. At the university, I still submitted my daily temperature, along with the usual testimonials, but now these measures seemed hardly relevant. The first infected person I knew wasn't from Wuhan, or Hubei, or even China. He was my literary agent—based in New York City, traveling in London for meetings, sick upon return. In January, William Clark had been among the many U.S.-based friends and relatives who reached out with messages of concern. At the time, he wrote, "We've been thinking of you and the family during the coronavirus outbreak." By week six, I was the one checking in on William and his wife. He responded:

> We're fine, and in Brooklyn. Both of us have lost our senses of smell and taste, but still no fever or difficulty breathing. Our MD friends think we are towards the end of it.

Since then, the time-warp term had continued. In week seven, Wuhan lifted its quarantine; in week ten, the U.S. death toll reached ten times the figure in China. In week eleven, Ariel and Natasha returned to in-school classes; in week thirteen, I boarded a plane for the first time in the post-COVID era. And now, on May 27—week fourteen—I was finally back at Sichuan University, tailing a robot through campus.

I followed the machine until it halted abruptly near some dormitories. An electronic voice called out, "*Daoda zhandian!*"—"Arriving at the stop!" There were no other pedestrians on the street. Most undergraduates hadn't yet returned, and the ones who had were restricted to campus. Every entrance to the university had been equipped with automated turnstiles, infrared temperature gauges, and facial recognition scanners. The scanners had been specially calibrated for masks—earlier that day, when I arrived at the East Gate turnstile, a guard instructed me to keep my face covered while being scanned. My name and ID number popped up on a screen, along with my temperature, and then the turnstile swung open. As a faculty member, I could pass through the gates in both directions, unlike the students. For them, the turnstiles opened only one way: after they entered the walled campus, they couldn't leave.

Now I waited with the robot beside the silent dormitories. Finally, three students approached from different directions, masked and holding cell phones. Each of them entered a code on a touch screen at the back of the robot, and a compartment popped open, revealing a package inside.

One student told me that she had ordered her package through Taobao, the e-commerce site. Before the pandemic, students retrieved their packages at a campus depot, but now the robot was making deliveries. The student said that the machine had telephoned and texted her as it approached the dorm.

For the next half hour, I followed the robot, assuming that eventually it would lead me to its master. Whenever I biked too close, a horn sounded. If I swerved in front, the robot stopped. There was no response when I tried shouting at it. Periodically, the machine pulled over—"*Daoda zhandian!*"—and masked students materialized, clutching phones and making a beeline in my direction. On the deserted campus, it felt like a scene from a horror film: *Children of the Corona*.

At last, the robot parked in front of the campus depot. A worker in a blue vest came out and started loading it with packages. "We have three of these now," he told me. He explained that the robots were a way to reduce potentially infectious contact with students, because depot workers returned to off-campus homes every evening.

I rode across campus and parked the bike next to the College of Marxism. At the entrance to my building, there was another checkpoint with an infrared scanner. I went upstairs and unlocked the door to my office, where a package was waiting on my desk. It contained some tools that the university had provided for my return to in-person teaching: five surgical masks, a pair of rubber gloves, and a box of Opula alcohol prep pads. Despite the three-month absence, the office looked fine. Somebody or something had been watering my plants.

During the early weeks of term, I had tried to adjust to the routine of teaching people I couldn't see. I gave survey questions every class, in order to learn more about the students, and I assigned essays about their lockdown experiences. When they turned on their microphones, I sometimes heard parents or grandparents chattering in the background. Serena's surroundings seemed loudest of all: often I could barely hear her voice over the sound of car engines, horns, and voices. She told me that her building in Nanchong was poorly constructed, with thin walls, and there was a busy road outside. "I think it will fall down in the next earthquake," she said nonchalantly.

Serena shared a small apartment with her grandparents as well as her parents, which was true of a number of students. As China became wealthier, many adults had started living apart from their elderly parents, but multigenerational homes were still common, especially in lower-tier cities. There was a long tradition of such households in China, whose literature is full of claustrophobic domestic scenes. One of the more evocative literary phrases that my daughters learned in school was *sishi-tongtang*, "four generations under a roof." Even the square-edged characters gave the impression of being cramped in a tiny room: 四世同堂.

During my lockdown bike rides, I looked up at the buildings and wondered how everybody was getting along behind the illuminated windows. I started to imagine these scenes much more clearly once I read student essays. The lockdown was the kind of thing that Chinese are good at enduring—many people are accustomed to crowded conditions, and they have a heroic tolerance for everyday annoyances. A number of students wrote about taking cooking lessons from their parents, who then happily ate the meals while offering complaints and criticism between every bite. Grandparents generally awoke at the crack of dawn and socialized remotely, through a special way of using WeChat. For the elderly, it was hard to read text on a phone, so they shouted voice messages and then played their friends' responses at full volume. It was another genre of WeChat theater, a series of phatic statements that unfolded with torturous slowness—*Have you eaten yet? Yes! Have you eaten yet? Yes! Are you at home? Yes! Are you at home? Yes!* Many students described waking up to these conversations.

In Xi'an, a girl named Elaine wrote about how every morning her father stood in the living room and swung a tennis racquet exactly three hundred times, counting every stroke. Mothers danced to loud music; grandparents practiced tai chi. In student essays, the mothers were often pushing some home COVID remedy that they had learned about on social media. A mother might sprinkle vinegar around the apartment, or she would force-feed eggs to her child, because some WeChat thread had claimed that egg-based nutrition counteracts the virus. There seemed to be a parallel pandemic of pontification on the part of patriarchs. Female students were especially skilled at capturing these lockdown sages. "The traits of a place are determined by geographic features," a student named Wenxin, who lived in Chengdu, quoted her father during a long evening at home. He continued: "Chengdu, a basin; its people, shortsighted, with no ambition."

As far as I was concerned, the essays were better than Cheever's enormous radio. The most entertaining COVID *sishitongtang* consisted of idle chatter, intergenerational passive-aggression, and low-grade rumor-mongering and conspiracy-theorizing. One student named Hongyi described a typical evening at home with her parents and grandparents. They watched *So Long, My Son*, a film about the sent-down movement, a Maoist campaign that, beginning in the late-1950s, had forced millions of Chinese urban youths to move to the countryside, where they were supposed to learn from peasants. While this historical drama played out on the screen, and while the current virological drama swept across the globe, Hongyi's family talked and talked and talked:

"You know why the outbreak is in Wuhan?" asked my father. "Because it's the center of transportation where many come and go."

"It sounds like the virus knows how to spread."

"It doesn't, but who knows the virus is not artificial? To tell you the truth, there has been analysis about USA's plotting this outbreak." He announced, brandishing his chopsticks.

"Why? I don't think there's solid evidence for—"

"It's obvious, and [the Americans] have every motivation. You know they have always—"

"OK, that's enough. Your father is often reading these reports," my mother cut in. "No use arguing. It is really a rare case, however."

"Yes, quite rare," my grandma agreed. "I haven't seen so strict management for all the sixty-five years, not even during the 1960s. So rare, once in a lifetime."

"Why not watch the film? I know *So Long, My Son* has won awards in the Berlin Festival."

"OK," my mother answered lightly.

The film was on. My father went out to attend to his garden. I watched how a happy family was shattered by fate and at last got reunited, though submissively, and unwillingly, as a whole.

"What's it about?" Father returned, closed the glass door, and asked.

"About Chinese people affected by [the sent-down movement]. It's quite sad. No one did anything wrong, but everyone becomes victims . . . I don't know what my life would be like if I were born at that time."

"I say it's too complicated, a literary film," my mother commented. "Films that have won awards are like that."

My father uttered nothing more. He walked in to wash his hands, like a concentrating water buffalo. Then very naturally, our gathering was dismissed. I locked my bedroom door.

Essays often referred to conversations about the United States, because the worsening diplomatic conflict also shadowed our semester. During week two, the Trump administration placed new restrictions on Chinese state-owned news organizations in the U.S., effectively expelling half their staff. In week three, a high-ranking Chinese official claimed on Twitter that the United States might have brought the virus to Wuhan. In week four, President Donald Trump started referring to the disease as "the China Virus." That same week, the Chinese Ministry of Foreign Affairs announced that it was canceling the visas of American journalists accredited for *The New York Times*, *The Wall Street Journal*, and *The Washington Post*. The nonfiction students read a short excerpt from *The Souls of China*, a book about religion by Ian Johnson, a *Times* reporter based in Beijing. In class, I mentioned that Johnson's visa had been canceled as part of the U.S.–China dispute.

At the start of the semester, I had left my syllabus open-ended, because I wasn't sure if we would return to campus. The prospect of outside research seemed unlikely, but the government's pandemic controls proved to be more effective than expected. Even the epic patience of these young people finally began to strain under COVID *sishitongtang*. In my week six survey, I asked, "Are you currently allowed to go outside in your community? Are there any restrictions on your movement?" The responses were unanimous: from Yunnan to Jilin, my students were fully mobile. I sent them out to write stories about the pandemic.

During the fall, I had enjoyed the student projects in Chengdu, but now I realized that there were advantages for them researching in their hometowns. They had local *guanxi*: parents connected them with friends or colleagues who were doing interesting things during the pandemic. A freshman named Andy lived near Nanjing, where his family knew somebody who ran a ventilator factory. Andy toured the plant with the boss, who told him that production had increased more than tenfold. A class-mate named Momo, who lived in Liaoning, not far from North Korea, re-ported the opposite trend when she visited a local state-owned tobacco company. Momo's parents were friends with an accountant at the com-pany, who told the girl that business had plummeted during the lock-down. By this point, there were already reports of increased tobacco use in the U.S., because of the stress and isolation of the pandemic. But the social aspect of Chinese smoking meant that without banquets and per-sonal gift-giving, the demand for cigarettes dropped. The accountant told Momo that one of the tobacco company's post-COVID strategies—and, by any measure, an innovative approach to public health—was to give away masks and disinfectant to retailers who purchased cigarettes.

I liked these glimpses of pandemic life from all around the country. In Sichuan, Sisyphos profiled a pharmacist, who said that he had prof-ited nearly one hundred thousand yuan by raising the price on masks in January, before the government issued rules preventing such behavior. A couple of students reported on pet stores going out of business in their communities. In the U.S., the pandemic resulted in a surge of families buying new dogs or cats, but the Chinese response was the opposite. There were many stories about people abandoning pets during lock-down, because they were afraid that animals might harbor the virus.

In so many aspects of the pandemic, the U.S. and China seemed to occupy alternative universes. The American government quickly ap-proved stimulus checks and other measures of temporary economic support, but such policies were minimal in China. In Chengdu, Hongyi shadowed a loan manager at a state-owned bank who was in charge of a new program that supposedly granted deferrals to borrowers who had been affected by the pandemic. Hongyi reported that 370 people in-quired about the program, but the bank approved deferrals for only twenty-two. At another branch, every single applicant was rejected.

In economic terms, individuals were largely on their own. The Party had never allowed the protections of independent unions, and across

China salaries were cut and workers laid off. In April, the country recorded the first economic contraction since the end of the Cultural
Revolution, in 1976. But stimulus policies remained modest: instead of
offering American-style cash payments, the Chinese government preferred to give entrepreneurs some space to figure out their own solutions. In Chengdu, city officials allowed vendors to set up stalls on the
streets. Such vendors had been common in the 1990s, before campaigns
were launched to make the city more orderly. Now the stalls reappeared
all at once, and the evening crowds in my neighborhood reminded me of
how Chengdu felt twenty years ago.

Many vendors told me that they had been laid off from low-level jobs
in factories and other businesses. Even people with white-collar jobs
often found their salaries slashed. When I spoke with one Air China
flight attendant, she explained that she and her colleagues were paid according to flight hours, and the drop in traffic meant that she now received a quarter of her normal salary. For pilots, the reduction was even
more severe. One man who flew for Hainan Airlines told me that for two
months he received less than 10 percent of his usual wage. I had similar
conversations with folks in other industries, but usually they said they
were fine, because they had savings.

They also had low expectations with regard to stability. Prosperity
was still too new for many Chinese to feel complacent or entitled, and
often they didn't perceive themselves as middle class. Americans are famous for self-identifying in the middle. Roughly half of the U.S. population
is middle class, but in some surveys, as many as 70 percent of respondents describe themselves as such. In China, the figure tends to be much
lower. In 2015, the Chinese Academy of Social Sciences surveyed households earning more than two hundred thousand yuan a year—nearly
thirty-two thousand dollars, and almost five times the average urban income in China—but only 44 percent identified as middle class. The figure
was even lower for my former students from Fuling. In 2014, I surveyed
them about their economic situations, and twenty-nine out of thirty

respondents owned at least one apartment and a car. All had stable jobs with good pensions and other benefits. But only eight identified as middle class or higher. The rest—nearly 75 percent—defined themselves with terms that included "poor," "low class," "down class," "poverty class," "proletariat," and "we belong to nothing." In Zhejiang, Willy had an excellent job that paid the equivalent of eighty thousand dollars a year, and he owned three apartments and a car without any debt. For a man raised by illiterate parents on a farm that consisted of a third of an acre, it was a remarkable achievement. But he responded on the survey, "We belong to lower class."

The trauma of having once been poor seemed hard to shake. Members of the Reform generation tended to save money, and they also had plenty of experience dealing with dramatic shifts in policy or circumstance, which helped them weather the pandemic. A student called Cathy lived in northern China's Hebei province, where she profiled an entrepreneur, Chen, who was a friend of her parents. In the 2000s, Chen had built a thriving company that distributed liquor. But sales plummeted after the Party's 2013 crackdown on banquets and other entertainment.

In response, Chen switched to a less corrupting substance: milk. He successfully redefined himself as a milk distributor, but then, when COVID arrived, everything collapsed again. Instead of giving up, Chen doggedly embarked on two months of ten-hour days riding with his delivery crews, talking to the owner of every store on his route. He developed a series of clever promotions that, by the beginning of May, had increased sales to the highest level ever. "In fact, I'm very grateful to the epidemic," he told Cathy. "If not for that, I probably never would have gone to the shops with the salesmen again." Throughout everything, he hadn't changed his company's official name—it still contained the word *liquor*. Because of bureaucratic red tape, it would have been a nuisance to alter the registration. Cathy asked if being called a liquor salesman was a problem for a guy who distributes milk. "They don't look at your name," Chen said. "They look at the things you do."

———

While cadres seemed to have faith in people's economic resourceful- ness, they took the opposite approach to public health. Very little was left to individual choice or responsibility. Any infected person was im- mediately removed from his or her household and isolated in a govern- ment clinic for a minimum of two weeks. On March 28, China effectively closed its borders to foreigners, allowing only citizens to return on the few international flights that were still running. Any Chinese national who did return was subject to a strict two-week quarantine in a state- approved facility.

On official notices around the city, I occasionally saw the Chinese term for social distancing—*anquan juli*—but I never heard anybody ac- tually use these words. Certainly it wasn't practiced in any form. After Chengdu transitioned out of the lockdown, there was no effort to limit the number of passengers on buses and subway cars, and soon they were just as packed as ever. In April, I began to conduct more interviews, and I was surprised to find that people involved in business or diplomacy still shook hands like it was 2019. Mask wearing remained mandatory in- doors and on transport, but it tended to be perfunctory. People some- times holstered the things, or they tugged them below their noses, in the position that the twins and I called the low-rider.

When Ariel and Natasha finally returned to Chengdu Experimental, in early May, their crowded third-grade class was reduced by exactly one student. This had nothing to do with *anquan juli*: the girl had been on vacation with her family in Cyprus when the pandemic struck, and now the family was unable to find a flight back. Inside the classroom, there was some attempt to separate desks, but with fifty-four kids in a modest- size space, any distancing was a game of inches. The school focused on other strategies; at the entrance, they erected a tent tunnel equipped with an infrared temperature scanner. A sign in the hallway listed lyrics to a new song:

Returning to school, what can we do?
Don't be afraid, listen to me.
Wear a mask, study well.
It's possible to protect both you and me.

For a brief period, the mask wearing was enthusiastic. On the first day of music class, Ariel and Natasha were shown how to play the recorder while masked—they lifted the bottom hem and shoved the instrument inside, a kind of reverse low-rider. When I picked up the twins after school, I saw teachers who had their masks rigged up with microphones that were wired to portable speakers on their hips. But after only a week, the Chinese Ministry of Education declared that students no longer needed to cover their faces in low-risk areas, and our school relaxed the rules. Ariel and Natasha reported that their classmates had found a use for discarded masks during lunch: they turned them upside down, like little pouches, and filled them with bones and other food to be thrown away.

The school scheduled regular handwashing breaks, and every afternoon an announcement sounded over the intercom: "Temperature-taking time has arrived!" Each day, my daughters had their temperature taken at least five times. This routine began at six thirty a.m., when the parent WeChat group engaged in something called *Jielong*, or "Connect the Dragon." Dragon connecting was among WeChat's many brilliant innovations for getting Chinese people to engage in high-stress peer-driven data collection for the sake of bureaucracy. Every morning, one designated parent would start the hashtag #Jielong, listing her child's name, student number, and temperature, along with the words "In good health." One by one, other parents jumped in—"Number 21 Li Rongshan, 36.3 degrees, In good health"—lengthening the list with every dragon link. As eight o'clock approached, impatient notes were sent to stragglers: "Number 44 Wang Linxin's Mama, please connect the dragon!"

I feared the dragon. Every morning, I straggled in somewhere around the tail, and occasionally I had to be reminded. For a while, I swore to do better; I glued my eyes to the phone at six thirty a.m., fantasizing about finishing as a top-five dragon connector. But it was impossible; Chinese people were incredibly skilled at this kind of thing, and often there were seven or eight completed dragon links by 6:31. I couldn't type characters fast enough, and if I rushed I made embarrassing foreigner mistakes that were then replicated with each new dragon connection, like an offensive comment on an email chain that keeps bouncing on forever. Finally I gave up and accepted my tail position. The school had informed us that any child with a body temperature of 37.3 degrees or higher had to be tested at a hospital, but I noticed that parents generally reported their kids at 36.6 or lower, so I did the same. I also made sure that Ariel and Natasha had different readings.

My mornings were a mess of fiddling with various health apps, each one designed for a different bureaucratic sinkhole. I was still required to submit my own daily temperature to Sichuan University, along with the outdated promises (*I have not had contact with people from Wuhan today. I have not had contact . . .*). In addition, a QR code with a health report had to be scanned every morning for each daughter. I often felt overwhelmed, not to mention a little odd: during the first month of dragon connecting, I received 1,146 WeChat messages listing the body temperatures of third graders.

I wondered how much of this was theater. Epidemiologists told me that temperature checks, though somewhat useful, represented a crude tool, and they generally believed that social distancing was more effective than mask use. In the United States, there was a common belief that masks were instrumental to the strategy of China and many other Asian countries. But this was mostly because face coverings were so obvious—every news story about the pandemic in China featured a photograph of a crowd of masked citizens. And it was true that average Chinese tended to have a talismanic faith in the protective nature of masks.

But I sensed that the people in charge of policy probably had a different opinion. Two of my Sichuan University students had fathers who worked in important positions in the Chinese Center for Disease Control and Prevention, and both of these students told me that, in private, their fathers downplayed the value of masks as a public-health tool. One boy, whose father was a scientist at the CDC, said that the man referred to masks as "placebos." I suspected that the father was half joking, but his comment seemed to reflect some actual wariness.

In May, I flew to Shanghai to meet with scientists who were working on the pandemic response. One epidemiologist told me there was no question that masks performed well in laboratory experiments. But he noted that face coverings might be less effective as public policy, because people often wore them incorrectly, and their faith in the protection could affect behavior. My impression was that Chinese policymakers considered masks a last-ditch defense, and they certainly didn't rely on them. After the lockdowns had begun in late January, the government never allowed citizens to move freely in a community with significant viral spread, hoping that masks, social distancing, and good judgment would reduce infections.

Instead, the strategy was always to enforce a lockdown until the virus was completely eliminated. At Chengdu Experimental, the school focused on policies that were relatively easy to implement, like the endless temperature checks. I figured that this was probably a way to make parents and children feel safe. Administrators never bothered with more effective but truly disruptive policies—reducing class size, remodeling facilities—because they knew that the virus was not spreading in Chengdu. During my daughters' first month in the classroom, there wasn't a single case from community spread anywhere in the city of sixteen million.

While the government never trusted individuals to set the terms of their own behavior, it did depend heavily on their willingness to work hard. A number of my nonfiction students, including Serena, embedded themselves with neighborhood committees in their hometowns, in order to research papers about the local strategies. Serena told me that before the pandemic, she hadn't even been aware that these organizations existed. In fact, they were part of a Chinese tradition that long predated the Communist era. During the Song dynasty, which ruled from 960 AD to 1279, the imperial government employed local organizations known as *baojia* and *lijia*. This system organized villages and urban neighborhoods into groups of around ten households, with leaders collecting taxes, monitoring neighbors, and reporting on any dissidents or other potential problems. The Ming and Qing dynasties also relied on these cell-like structures, which served as effective links between the grassroots and higher levels of government.

After the revolution, the Party created a similar network of production brigades in the countryside. In urban areas, they developed neighborhood committees, which eventually became instrumental in the monitoring and enforcement of the one-child policy. With the rise of migration and the private economy, the committees became less relevant to many citizens, which was why Serena had been unaware of their existence. But the committees were still there: often, they shrank to a skeleton staff, like ancient organisms gone dormant.

The committees turned out to be the perfect tool for the pandemic. They functioned as the "nerve tips" of the state, according to Benjamin L. Read, a political scientist at the University of California at Santa Cruz who had researched neighborhood committees in the pre-COVID era. The committees allowed the Party to monitor local developments and convey information in both directions, and these structures were easy to ramp up. With new funding, committees could immediately acquire the staff necessary to do things like survey residential compounds.

Of course, these new workers sometimes made mistakes. In Nanchong,

Serena reported that at the end of January, a cadre on her committee had been assigned to survey a Nanchong compound with 1,136 residential units. For two days, the cadre and some subcontractors worked from eight in the morning until midnight, climbing stairways and knocking on doors. But they missed a single apartment. When they knocked, there was no answer, and they failed to leave a note or return for a follow-up.

Soon that kind of error was no longer made. For two months, Serena spent two or three days a week with her committee, and she observed the members becoming more professional. They came to understand their role, along with the stakes of the pandemic. The Chinese press reported that fifty-three members of neighborhood committees died while working to control the virus. Others were fired or chastised for even the smallest mistakes. That's what happened to the Nanchong cadre who missed the apartment—he was forced to write a self-criticism, a long-standing form of Party discipline. It turned out that the apartment contained the first COVID case in the district. The occupant—his surname was Deng—had been taking a shower when the committee members knocked.

At a party a week earlier, Deng had had a long conversation with a DJ, who, it was later learned, had been infected by somebody from Hubei. Deng was thirty-five years old, single, and highly energetic. The details of his movements were posted on a municipal government media site, as well as on various public WeChat channels. In China, there wasn't any nationwide or provincial database that aggregated these case histories. But they were often placed on WeChat by local governments, as a resource for residents.

These histories were incredibly detailed. They used real place names, although given names were obscured: Deng was referred to as "Deng Mou"—essentially, "Deng So-and-so." During the first three days after Deng was infected, he visited a bar, a store, two pharmacies, three gas stations, and six restaurants. His tastes in food were eclectic, ranging from the Long-Boiled Soft Tofu Restaurant next to Fangguokui, to the

Frog and Fish-Head Restaurant on Xihu Street. He got gas at the Sinopec station on Binjiang South Road; he collected clothes at the Junhui Shangpin Dongmen Dry-cleaners. Along the way, he picked up a friend named Huang So-and-so, and he visited his elderly parents at the Agricultural Machinery Compound on Heming Road. He went to work. He got a fever. Post-fever, Deng hopped over to a few more pharmacies, searching for surgical masks, and then he kept going: he picked up Li So-and-so; he visited his elderly parents again; he attended a party at the house of Du So-and-so. On the WeChat account, Deng was the COVID Leopold Bloom of Nanchong, with every step of his urban odyssey recorded in terrifying detail. When was this guy going to stop?

Such meticulous case histories were compiled under the direction of the Chinese CDC. There were about three thousand CDC branches in China, with each branch containing roughly 100 to 150 staff members. Despite these numbers, the Chinese CDC had traditionally been underfunded, like Chinese public health in general. But the CDC was able to tap into the neighborhood committees, and by all accounts the contact tracing and quarantine policies had been highly successful. This was the flip side of what had happened in the early weeks, when the Wuhan government botched almost everything. During that period, Fang Fang had emphasized the systemic nature of China's failure, noting that bureaucratic structures encouraged lower-level cadres to cover up local problems.

But the same bureaucracy played a positive role in the next stage of the pandemic. Government structures served as a kind of scaffolding, the way contact tracing was attached to existing networks of neighborhood committees. Another advantage was timing. At this moment in history, many Chinese were products of an intensely detail-oriented school system, but their families had known poverty in the recent past. People weren't afraid of hard work.

In Shanghai, I met with a twenty-four-year-old scientist named Jiang Xilin, who had been contracted to work on various projects for the CDC and the Gates Foundation. Jiang was in his third year of a doctoral program at the University of Oxford, where he was studying genomic medicine and statistics on a Rhodes Scholarship. In early March, he returned to China, where he helped the CDC with modeling, computer programming, and writing proposals. "The first weekend, I got a call at twelve a.m. on a Sunday evening," he told me. "Nobody said, 'I'm sorry to disturb you so late.' They said, 'Did you get that proposal done?' I said, 'No,' and they said, 'We need that report by noon.'" He quickly became accustomed to such demands. Jiang also learned that if a late-night call went silent, it often meant that the person on the other end had fallen asleep from exhaustion.

By then, many other Chinese citizens were also coming back, because it was clear that the pandemic was being handled poorly in the United States and Europe. It would have been useful to know exactly where these returnees had been, so Jiang wrote a proposal requesting that Tencent, the publicly held company that owns WeChat, provide the IP log-in information for people who came back. "They rejected me because of the data privacy," Jiang said. He was told that Tencent was adamantly opposed to its data being used in this fashion.

Jiang and I were sitting at a small table, and he showed me how our phones automatically sensed each other via Bluetooth. Such information could be used to figure out who had been in close proximity to an infected person. In another CDC work meeting, a colleague of Jiang's suggested using this tool for contract tracing. But her idea was immediately dismissed. "They said, 'This is a violation of data protection. We can't do that,'" Jiang explained. "It was surprising to me."

It surprised me, too. Given the heavy-handed tactics of many lockdown policies, and the mass-scale surveillance equipment that I saw every day, I assumed that the government used any tools available. But there seemed to have been some resistance from prominent tech companies, even the ones who had been commissioned to help with virus control. Tencent and Alibaba both helped the government develop "health code" apps that assisted in monitoring and controlling the virus's spread among citizens. The apps were necessary for travel, and I had installed the Chengdu version on my phone before going to Shanghai. The app was checked at every airport, train station, and hotel along the way, and it listed every place that I visited. I was surprised that this list included Yibin, a city in south-central Sichuan that I had never seen in my life. Recently I hadn't even been within 150 miles of the place.

I mentioned this to one of the Shanghai epidemiologists. "The health code makes a lot of mistakes," he said, laughing. "It's not really that strong." He explained that in many parts of the country, the apps registered a change in the user's location largely through manual data transfer: if the user checked in with his ID at an airport, for example, or if his license plate was recorded at a tollbooth. The epidemiologist noted that the South Korean and Singaporean pandemic phone apps were much more aggressive than the Chinese, in terms of their use of data. Even in Europe, where millions of users had voluntarily downloaded virus-alert apps based on software developed by Google and Apple, these tools used the Bluetooth data that was considered too invasive for China.

The epidemiologist told me that the city of Shenzhen, which was famous for its tech industry, had commissioned the development of a more powerful health-code app. The Shenzhen system combined GPS data and artificial intelligence to alert anyone who came into proximity of an infected person. "But that system was never implemented, even in that city," he said. "It could not get approval from somewhere in the government system because of data privacy." He noted the current Chinese apps did not use GPS data, which would have improved accuracy.

The epidemiologist asked me not to identify him by name, because the Shenzhen government hadn't issued public statements about its project. But he was struck by the way that high-tech solutions had not played much of a role in China's pandemic strategy thus far. "One can argue that what was most useful for COVID was old science," he continued, referring to contact tracing and quarantines. "The methodology is from fifty or seventy years ago. It has not changed."

The CDC policy was that whenever a new case appeared, contact tracers were called immediately, even in the middle of the night. They were given only eight hours to complete the tracing. It was grinding work, but the payoff could be significant. In June, after Beijing had reported no locally transmitted cases for fifty-six days, there was a sudden outbreak at a wholesale produce market called Xinfadi. The place was well managed: masks were required, and anybody who entered the market had to show their health code and have their temperature taken. Even so, more than three hundred people were infected before the first known case came to light. But after that, the government was able to quickly find and isolate other infections, because of all the testing and contact tracing. The city put down the outbreak almost immediately.

Of course, in many other instances the hard work led nowhere. This was another feature of Chinese bureaucracy, which could afford to waste vast amounts of human effort. Deng So-and-so, the COVID Leopold Bloom of Nanchong, whose unchecked eight-day voyage across his city was recorded in excruciating detail, appeared to have infected a grand total of zero people. The tracers never found another positive case anywhere that the man visited. In political terms, this made no difference: one neighborhood-committee cadre in Nanchong was punished for missing the apartment, just as the outbreak in Beijing resulted in six officials being disciplined. Deng himself was never very sick. He spent a week in a coronavirus ward, felt fine, and tested negative. Then, after nearly two more weeks of strict quarantine in a hotel, he tested positive again and returned to hospital confinement. By the time Deng was finally released to the world of the Long-Boiled Soft Tofu Restaurant and the Frog and Fish-Head Restaurant, he had spent sixty-five days in medical isolation. Serena asked for an interview, but a neighborhood-committee member told her that the experience had left Deng too psychologically fragile.

Since arriving in Chengdu, I had tracked security cameras, and I often thought about the ways in which the surveillance state might be functioning. As a teacher of Orwell, I could easily imagine China as a high-tech dystopia, and there were always new devices being introduced, like the package-delivering robots. But I noticed a pattern: at crucial moments, when one might have expected the government to rely heavily on digital tools, the cadres often turned instead to old-fashioned forms of human interaction. The most striking example was the pandemic, but the same thing typically happened when professors were reported for political infractions. In my own case, I hadn't seen evidence that the university reviewed video of my lectures or searched through email and phone communications. Their immediate response had been to talk directly to me and my students. Even when Vincent wrote about the time that he got in trouble for online activity, the most important actions of the security state were face-to-face.

Daniel C. Mattingly, a professor at Yale University, had spent years studying civil-society groups and the ways in which they were controlled, monitored, and co-opted by the Party. In his book, *The Art of Political Control in China*, he writes:

> Press coverage sometimes suggests that mass surveillance, artificial intelligence, facial recognition software, and social credit scores will allow the Chinese state to effortlessly monitor citizens' everyday lives. These are valid concerns, but the reality is that this techno-dystopia has not yet come to pass. When these digital tools reach maturity, the state will still face age-old problems about how to act on the vast amounts of data collected by its information-generating bureaucracies.
>
> For the time being, China still mostly relies on human, not digital, tactics of authoritarian repression and control.

When I talked with Mattingly on a video call, he explained that digital tools are useful for doing things like monitoring communications at scale. "On the other hand, it does a bad job at everything that's not visible through cameras—which is still a lot of life," he said. "When it comes to political thought-work, it's still really useful to have individual people in communities whose job is to take people's political temperature and monitor them for compliance in a really old-fashioned way that stretches back to the Mao era, to the *baojia* system, even."

He noted that the intensely localized nature of most data made coordination difficult. "You can gather a lot of information that is useful for local leaders, but it's harder to figure out how to aggregate it and pass it up the system," he said. These patterns also contribute to the silo quality of Chinese bureaucracy, where one branch might be doing something completely different than another.

"I have a colleague who sometimes asks, 'Is it the Orwellian version of bureaucracy, or is it Kafka?'" Mattingly said. "I think it's usually Kafka. Where the right hand doesn't know what the left hand is doing."

I suspected that the Party's instinctive tendency toward the personal may have been one reason it had lasted so long. In a true techno-dystopia, where life was shaped entirely by the Great Firewall, the surveillance cameras, and the face scanners, the system would have felt unbearable. Certain specific parts of society, like the oppressed Muslim residents of Xinjiang, had reached this point. But for the majority of Chinese citizens, the system still wasn't soul crushing, and there were clear benefits, like in the second phase of the pandemic. Even some of the Kafkaesque moments were part of what made China human.

One evening well into the pandemic, two men stopped by our apartment. They explained that the neighborhood committee had assigned them to check on every foreigner in our compound. By this point, very few non-Chinese remained in the neighborhood, and it was impossible for us to have recently arrived from outside the country, so there was no real disease-control value. But the men had been given their assignment, and they dutifully trooped up to the nineteenth floor to ask the usual questions about nationality, job, body temperature, and contact with Wuhan. Then one man said that he needed to take a cell phone photograph with me. It wasn't necessary to do this with Leslie, apparently because she didn't look like a real foreigner.

After taking the picture, the man removed his jacket and asked if I would pose again in a slightly different part of the living room.

"Do you know why I'm doing this?" he asked with a grin.

Leslie said, "Because you're supposed to come here twice?"

"Duitou!" he said. "Right on!" He explained that they should have come the previous month, but they had missed that visit. I asked if he wanted me to change my shirt. "That would be great!" he said.

For good measure, I also loaned him a jacket that was hanging nearby. We turned and stood with our backs to the balcony. The other main difference with the second photograph was that both of us looked like we were about to laugh.

As we approached the final month of term, a number of student essays mentioned the death of Freud. It took me a while to realize that students were reading Chinese news reports about George Floyd—*Fuluoyide*—and running the name through a machine translator back into English. Floyd, Freud: each name can be conveyed the same way in Chinese characters.

During a class earlier in the semester, a student had typed in the comments box: "Can we see what you look like?" After that, I tried to run my laptop's camera for a short time at the start of every session, hoping to humanize the experience. But I missed interactions in the classroom. A few times, students tactfully asked about events in the United States: the protests in response to Floyd's death; the general failure of American pandemic policies. But such topics had been heavily politicized in the

Chinese state media, and it was difficult to present a more nuanced version to people I couldn't see.

I was surprised that during this period I didn't feel targeted as an American on the street. By now, a significant number of Chinese seemed to believe that the American government had brought the virus to Wuhan, and sometimes they mentioned this in conversation. The same conversations also tended to include comments about how badly the American government had handled the pandemic. I often asked, "If the American government really developed the virus, then why weren't they prepared for it?" Sometimes, people laughed, or they responded by repeating the things that they had just said. But nobody got angry. They weren't under the same pressure as individuals in many other parts of the world, where there was a real chance of catching the virus. Mostly, the Chinese didn't seem particularly invested in these conspiracy theories, and they showed little true curiosity about the origins of the virus. Chinese citizens are accustomed to living with the unknowable, and they also understand that often it's better not to look too closely. Sometimes, I mentioned that I planned to travel to Wuhan during summer vacation, and people invariably thought that I was crazy.

I felt comfortable in Chengdu, but I worried about Ariel and Natasha. By now, they had just one foreign friend left in the city, and her family planned to depart in summer. As the only Americans at Chengdu Experimental, the twins were vulnerable to whatever the other children might be hearing about the United States. For a while, I wondered if administrators might find a tactful way to tell us that Ariel and Natasha could no longer attend, because so many regulations had tightened during the pandemic. But nobody said a word to that effect.

On the last Friday in May, Ariel and Natasha told us that a boy in their class had teased them with some anti-American comments. That week, George Floyd had just been murdered, and the American death toll from COVID was approaching a hundred thousand. Leslie and I explained to the twins that they were bound to hear some remarks during such a time, and the most important thing was that most of their classmates continued to treat them warmly. We never mentioned the incident to the school.

But Teacher Zhang must have noticed. The following Monday, she told the class a story that, in the Chinese way, handled the issue indirectly. She mentioned another news report from the weekend, describing how Elon Musk's California-based company had just launched a manned rocket into space. Teacher Zhang talked about Musk's personal story as an immigrant, and she emphasized the role that American science and education had played in the successful rocket launch. At the end of the story, she said, "Every country has its strong points and its weak points."

In week sixteen, I finally entered the classroom. For more than a month, there had been rumors that undergraduates would return, as they already had in some other provinces. The final decision was left to local officials, and Sichuan University administrators seemed to decide that it wasn't worth the risk. Senior students were called back to take final exams, along with others who had made special requests, but most younger undergraduates were encouraged to stay home. I was disappointed—I had hoped to finally meet the names and voices I had been thinking about all semester. None of my first-year students made it back to campus.

In the end, it became another type of theater: a dress rehearsal. The university introduced the delivery robots and the facial-recognition scanners, but I sensed that these systems were mostly being tested in preparation for the fall. At the moment, the country's policies seemed to have been a success, but the epidemiologists I talked to seemed nervous about a potential second wave of infections.

The first week back, only four students came in person to nonfiction class: Serena, Emmy, Fenton, and Sisyphos. It was like a studio audience—the five of us talked back and forth, but we used headphones and microphones to connect with the others who were still scattered across the country.

A few students had wanted to return but their parents hadn't approved. A girl named Ethel was not allowed on campus because she had traveled to Wuhan for her final research project. She lived in northern Hunan province, close to the border of Hubei. One morning, without telling her parents, Ethel caught a high-speed express train to Wuhan. By this point, the sealed city had officially opened, but Ethel was one of only two people who disembarked at the massive Wuhan station. She walked alone through the cavernous main hallway, and then she caught a subway, which was also deserted. The only other people she saw were security guards at various checkpoints. When she showed her health-code apps, these lonely guards seemed unusually friendly. In Ethel's essay about the experience, she wrote, "I've never heard a security guard say thanks, but this happened twice in the first two hours after I arrived in Wuhan."

Ethel's plan was to have lunch in Wuhan, walk around, and catch an evening train back home. At a pedestrian mall, she passed a row of restaurants. Like many places in China, the restaurants posted staff out in front in order to drum up business. But instead of chanting the usual greeting—*Huanying guanlin*! Welcome to come in!—the hostesses called out, "Everybody on staff has had a recent nucleic acid test!" After Ethel returned home, her health-code app recorded that she had been to Wuhan, and the university declined her request to come back to campus. But she said it was worth it. After more than three months of testifying every morning that she had not been to Wuhan, she had felt a burning desire to go there.

The students who returned to the classroom in week sixteen all had reasons. Emmy was the only person whose family lived in the countryside, and, like Serena, she was tired of being in a home that was loud and crowded. Fenton needed to have dental work done at a university hospital. He wasn't formally enrolled in my class—he had taken it the previous semester—but he decided to attend the last sessions. And Sisyphos, as a senior, was required to return to campus for exams.

Sisyphos was tall, with slightly wavy hair. During online classes, I had sensed that he was shy, and I had never put him on the spot about the origin of his name. But now that we were face-to-face, I asked the question. He reddened slightly and explained that he had chosen the name in high school because he liked the Greek myth.

"So where's the rock right now?" I asked. "Is it high or low?"

Sisyphos brought his hand level with his chest. "It's in the middle," he said.

Before the pandemic, we had planned to spend summer vacations in Colorado, in part so that the twins would not lose their connection to American life. Now we searched for some kind of substitute activity within the borders of the People's Republic, and Leslie discovered a place with a promising name: Walden Farm.

The camp was located outside the city of Mianyang, which probably should have been a warning sign. Of all the places in Sichuan, Mianyang was most famous for rigorous schooling. Mianyang private schools had developed such a reputation that parents in Chengdu sometimes sent their children to board in the smaller city. A number of my engineering students were products of the Mianyang system, and one of my former Fuling students taught in a private school there. Her institution had more than two thousand children in every grade—some of these Mianyang schools had the scale of university campuses.

Nevertheless, any American who sees the words *Walden Farm*, even in close association with the city of Mianyang, is bound to make some positive connotations. Nature, independence, self-reliance—"*We need the tonic of wildness.*" One afternoon, with Henry David Thoreau on the mind, Leslie telephoned the director of Walden Farm.

Very quickly in the conversation, the director mentioned that he had a connection to Peking University. Then he said that some of the children who attended the summer camp had parents who were graduates of Peking University. From that point, the words *Peking University* sounded with increasing frequency, like a stone skipping across the surface of a transcendental pond. Some Peking University graduates had the notion that their children might someday attend Peking University, and so they were searching for an educational experience that, in the spirit of Peking University, would be both challenging and instructive. After last year's session, these parents had complained that campers spent too little time with textbooks. *The mass of men lead lives of quiet desperation.* And that was why, during the upcoming session at Walden Farm, all children would spend at least six hours every day inside the classroom.

"Six hours?!" Leslie said. "Will they do anything outdoors?"

The director said that sometimes the children at Walden Farm might go fishing under the tutelage of a *Da Shi*, a Great Master.

Given the twins' frustration at losing their Colorado summer, we were certain that they did not want to spend six hours a day of their vacation in the classroom. We also had a pretty strong feeling that they wanted to avoid Great Masters. Fortunately, Leslie discovered another company, which had struck upon the concept of establishing summer camps on golf courses that, like River Town Golf, had been shut down during the Xi Jinping anti-corruption campaigns. It was brilliant—these abandoned courses were perfect for summertime kids. And so, after Ariel and Natasha finished their semester, I flew with them to Shanghai, where I hired a taxi, drove west for an hour, crossed a bridge, and ended up on what had once been a luxury resort on an island in the middle of the Maohe River. The staff and other children had already gathered next to an abandoned putting green. The scene was beautiful—the happy kids, the energetic young counselors, the close-cut grass. *I went to the golf course because I wanted to live deliberately.* Before leaving, I took one last look across the fairway at my kids, and then I headed back to Shanghai.

I often wondered what the memories of 2020 would mean to the younger generation: the Children of the Corona. At Chengdu Experimental, the school distributed a handout that encouraged children to keep "New Coronavirus" journals, and Ariel and Natasha took notes almost every day. During the first week, they described the nervousness of other students and teachers. Ariel, who loathed music class, wrote:

> While hiding in the bathroom during music class, a, say, 12-year-old girl came up to me. The first, and only, thing she said to me was: "你一直在成都?" (Have you been in Chengdu the whole time?) I answered: "对." (Yep.) . . . The music teacher is wearing a striped jacket, gray shirt, and black dress pants, plus latex gloves and a blue mask as well as a fake Rolex watch.

I told Ariel that the fake Rolex was a good touch—details matter. I encouraged my own students to keep pandemic diaries, and they wrote end-of-term essays about how their perspectives had changed. "This is the first time that I feel so close to history, and I was actually reporting on it," Serena wrote. "I guess I'll start to keep notes from now on." Spending time with the neighborhood committee had also made her think about her research topics from the previous semester. She realized that in the past the hardworking local officials had also been turned against marginal groups like the Catholics and the gay community, contributing to their oppression. "All of them are good people," she wrote. "They just happen to be in different places, and sometimes in conflicting situations."

Throughout the semester, I had tried to connect with the voices in my headphones, and I knew that such exchanges would become even harder in the future. A number of my Chinese students had abandoned plans to study abroad, and now it was virtually impossible for any young American to come to China. As the pandemic wore on, China and the

U.S. continued to occupy alternative universes. By the time I handed in my final grades, in early July, the U.S. was recording more COVID cases every two days than China had reported during the entire pandemic.

It seemed inevitable that young people on each side of the Pacific would come away with very different lessons. In my students' end-of-term essays, many expressed a renewed faith in government. For my final survey, I asked them to rate their feelings about the future on a scale of 1 to 10, with 10 being the most optimistic. Despite everything that spring—the collapse of U.S.–China relations, the explosion of the pandemic, the death of half a million people worldwide—the average rating was 7.1.

In week seventeen, only three students came in person to the final nonfiction session. Sisyphos was gone; like all seniors, he had finished early. Somehow, Serena, Emmy, and Fenton had learned that my birthday was the previous day, and they threw a surprise party. They ordered balloons, confetti, and a birthday sign from Taobao, and the robot delivered the packages to their dormitories. They also had a cake and a spicy Sichuanese dish called maocai delivered to one of the gates. Serena printed and bound a memory book with messages and photographs from her long-distance classmates. The notes were characteristically self-deprecating:

> I still am not good at writing. Thank you for reading my rough essay (quite a torment to you).

> Before the class, I was afraid because of my poor English. Therefore, I appreciate your patience with my speech in class.

For four months, I had known them only by their voices, their writing, and their research projects. Now, in the pages of the book, I finally saw faces: Cathy, who had researched the liquor-milk man in Hebei;

Hongyi, who had shadowed the Chengdu bank manager; Elaine, who had written about a lesbian bar in Xi'an.

Years ago, my Fuling students had also given me memory books. In those days, none of them owned cameras, and they posed stiffly for the campus photographer—Jimmy in his knockoff Bulls jersey. Now the Sichuan University students dressed up for pictures, which often had been taken before the pandemic, in exotic or scenic locations. Cathy stood in front of the Shanghai Bund, smiling in glasses and a pink blouse. Hongyi, a petite girl with long black hair, posed in front of a lake in the countryside. Patrick wore a striped polo shirt, standing near the top floor of a skyscraper on a sunny day. All the students were smiling, their poses natural, unlike in the photos of old. I wished we had met in person, but it was good to know they were out there somewhere.

 CHAPTER EIGHT

The Sealed City

August 2020

O N MY SECOND VISIT TO THE SITE OF THE FORMER HUANAN SEA-
food Wholesale Market, at the intersection of Development
Road and New China Road, in central Wuhan, I wore a mask and
a pair of sunglasses with a loose frame. It was the last week of August,
and three security guards sat sweating in black uniforms at the entrance to the market. They examined my passport and checked my
temperature: 36.6 degrees. Then they asked me to scan a QR code that
connected to a registration system. The system, though, required a Chinese national ID, and the guards were uncertain what to do with a foreigner. I handed over the sunglasses and explained that they needed to
be repaired.

The previous week, I had taken a reconnaissance walk around the
outside of the market. Huanan was among the most sensitive sites in
Wuhan, because it had been home to the earliest documented clusters
of COVID infections—ground zero, at least as far as public information
was concerned. Since the start of the pandemic, as controversy raged
about possible origins, the Huanan market had been closed to the public. A high blue wall had been erected around the two-story structure.

On my first visit, I was surprised to see that an eyeglass emporium
was open for business in Huanan's second story. I had read countless

articles about Huanan, which had become infamous for the animal stalls
that had been located on the ground floor, along with seafood dealers.
But I had never seen a reference to a second story where glasses were sold.

While walking beside the blue wall, I noticed a man tailing me at a
distance of about fifty feet. He wore sunglasses and a blue surgical mask.
I stopped and fiddled with my phone; the man also stopped. In the early
2000s, when I worked as a journalist in Beijing, I learned to pick out
bianyi, or plainclothes cops, by their sunglasses and military-style crew
cuts. Since the start of the pandemic, the surgical mask had become another plainclothes accessory, because surveillance men liked to hide
their faces and eyes. After I noticed the *bianyi* at Huanan, I walked quickly
away from the market and into a nearby mall. The masked man didn't
follow me.

On my second visit, after the failure of the QR code, I pointed to a
loose hinge on my sunglasses. "This is just a small thing," I said

One of the guards wiggled the frame. "You can go in," he said at last.
"But no photographs."

Another guard was assigned to accompany me. We climbed a steep
flight of stairs, past a freshly painted sign that read "Heguang Eyeglass
Market." The name was new: back in December, it had been the Huanan
Eyeglass City. After everything that had happened—the first reports of
illness in the market, the lockdown of Wuhan, a worldwide death toll of
nearly a million and counting—the owners had decided to rebrand.

There had never been any logic to the Huanan combo: fish downstairs, eyeglasses upstairs. Locals told me that the Huanan second floor
had a history of failed enterprises. It had originally been home to some
karaoke parlors, but there wasn't much nightlife in the area, and the
business failed. Next, somebody tried a wholesale market for children's
clothes, which also went bust. After that, an eyeglass entrepreneur from
a nearby city decided to relocate to Wuhan.

The market was situated in a densely populated part of town, less
than two miles from the Yangtze River. Wuhan's central train station

was nearby, along with a couple of major hospitals. But the crowds of pedestrians vanished as I approached the blue wall: people knew to avoid this place. In Chinese cities, it's not unusual to encounter the site of some disaster or atrocity that has never been properly addressed—after all, Tiananmen Square sits in the heart of the nation's capital. But I had never visited such a location so soon after it became notorious.

The novelist Fang Fang had written about Huanan in early March, when people were speculating about the role that the illegal animal trade might have played in the pandemic. "There are more than a thousand vendors at that market, and the vast majority run legitimate businesses," Fang Fang wrote in her online journal. "Like everyone else in Wuhan, they too are victims here." She continued, "I wonder what the site of the market will become in the future. Some people have suggested turning it into a memorial hall dedicated to this calamity." Then she transitioned abruptly to a description of buying food during quarantine. Like any Chinese writer, she was fully aware of who might be reading, and she knew that there was safety in commerce. She wrote, "I know that the Internet censors won't bother deleting posts about grocery shopping."

The guard escorted me down a long hallway with shops on both sides. It felt like running a gauntlet—I didn't see other customers, and salespeople rushed to their doors, shouting about discounts and half-price specials. The attention clearly made the guard nervous, so I entered the first large shop that was run by somebody with a friendly face. Once I was inside, the shouting died down, and the guard seemed to relax. He waited in the hallway.

The friendly shopkeeper offered me a seat and some water while his assistant tinkered with my sunglasses. I asked about business, and the shopkeeper said that he had stayed in his apartment until April 8 because of the city's quarantine, and then the market reopened on May 12. People in Wuhan often referred to specific dates from the spring, as if they had been burned into their minds. "I tried calling old customers, telling them it's safe," the shopkeeper said. "But of course a lot of them wouldn't come."

He didn't know of anybody in the eyeglass market who had been infected. His assistant, a woman in her twenties, claimed that there hadn't been a single case on the entire second floor. "It wasn't like downstairs," she said. "That's where the disease spread." Later, I saw one Chinese news article indicating that some staff at the upstairs market had been infected, but the story lacked clear details. Throughout the spring, Wuhanphobia had run rampant across China, and now in the city I observed local versions of the same thing. People who lived on the Yangtze's southern bank often pointed out that the virus first spread on the north side of the river, in the area traditionally known as Hankou. Even in the Huanan market itself, there was a dichotomy between the two floors. I wondered if this is what folks are bound to say if you go to any ground zero and walk up a flight of steps: *Nothing happened here. We're fine. It was those people downstairs.*

I asked the shopkeeper about the animal stalls on the first floor. "I never went down there much," he said. "It didn't have anything to do with our business." He told me that there had been an illicit mah-jongg parlor in a hidden location on the first floor. Under the Xi Jinping crackdowns, people had become wary of gambling in public. "It was in a place with bad ventilation," the shopkeeper said. "I heard that four people were playing at one table, and all four got sick."

This sounded like a rumor, but subsequently I met a Wuhan journalist who had visited the mah-jongg parlor. His memories also revolved around precise dates: he had gone to Huanan on December 31, the day before it was shut down. By then, the journalist had heard about a possible virus, and also about some mah-jongg infections. He found the players unfazed by the reports, still gambling for small stakes—the equivalent of ten dollars a hand. "It was next to the public toilet, and you had to climb a ladder to get there," the journalist said. "You wouldn't find it unless you were looking for it. Everybody was smoking and there was no ventilation."

Like most people I interviewed in Wuhan, the journalist asked me not to use his name. On the day that he visited the market, he had seen some wildlife for sale—snakes, wild hares, and some stalls selling organs from slaughtered animals that he couldn't identify. A number of stalls lacked proper signs or licenses, and some owners seemed to have recently left, perhaps because they had heard about an outbreak. The journalist worked for a state-owned paper, which hadn't allowed him to write about the mah-jongg infections, because at that time the local government still hadn't announced that the disease could be transmitted by human contact. "But I personally worried that it was probably spreading between people," he said.

The journalist had returned to Huanan the following day, January 1, after the hazmat teams arrived. He saw them using a detailed list to inspect and sterilize certain stalls, but they wouldn't answer his questions about what they were targeting. Relatively few images of the interior market had been published. By the time I visited, with worldwide infections at thirty-five million and rising, the Huanan market had become a kind of petri dish for the imagination. The most common Chinese conspiracy theory was that the U.S. Army had deliberately seeded the virus during the 2019 Military World Games, which were held in Wuhan that October. Across the Pacific, many Americans believed that the virus had been released, accidentally or otherwise, from the Wuhan Institute of Virology, whose research subjects included bat coronaviruses.

The animal stalls had occupied a tiny part of the market, most of which had been dedicated to seafood and freshwater fish. Wuhan people aren't known for having an appetite for exotic animals, which are much more popular in Guangdong, in the far south. It was also possible that the disease had arrived from somewhere else and then spread in the wet, cool conditions of the stalls. A few Wuhan residents told me that much of their seafood came from Guangdong, and they speculated that perhaps a southerner had unwittingly imported the disease along with some fish. But, like many of the origin theories, this could have been another version of the second-floor perspective: *Nothing happened here. We're fine. It was those people downstairs.*

In the eyeglass shop, I chatted with the owner for most of an hour. There still weren't any other customers, and the security guard outside was getting antsy. The shopkeeper refused to accept money for fixing my sunglasses, and I felt bad, so I bought a new pair for the equivalent of fifteen dollars. I asked about the likely fate of this place. He said that nothing had been decided, but he expected the complex to be demolished and replaced with high-rises. "What else can they do?" he said. "The name is ruined."

Among the dates that had been seared into the minds of Wuhan residents were January 23, the beginning of the *fengcheng*—the sealed city— and April 8, when the restrictions were lifted. Locals had a special word for that day, too: *jiefeng*, or "taking off the seal." Before traveling to Wuhan, I had never heard anybody use this term.

The Wuhan experience was different from that of every other part of China, just as the China experience was different from that of every other country. There was no other large nation where the pandemic's initial effects were so concentrated in a single city. At the time of my trip to Wuhan, Beijing had reported only nine COVID deaths, and Shanghai had seven. In all of Guangdong province—population 113 million—the death toll was eight. Chengdu had only three deaths. The second-hardest-hit Chinese city was a place that few outsiders had heard of: Xiaogan, some forty miles from Wuhan, where 129 people died.

In Wuhan, the official death toll was 3,869, although almost everybody agreed that the actual figure was significantly higher. This lie also distinguished the city from the rest of China. When I talked with foreign diplomats who tended to be skeptical of government statistics, they said that they actually believed the low counts in other cities. Foreign and Chinese scientists told me the same thing, because it would have been impossible to fake China's containment of the virus in the spring and summer of 2020. If COVID-19 had been spreading in major cities, and if large numbers of people were dying or being hospitalized, residents would have known. Cities were so densely populated that hospitals would have been quickly overwhelmed, the way they had been in Wuhan.

Before traveling to the city, I had yet to meet somebody who had been infected. I knew people who had gotten sick in the U.S., but the China side of the pandemic remained somewhat unreal. In January and February, I had experienced the illness mostly through the reports of Fang Fang and other writers in Wuhan. One of these writers, a poet who went by the name Xiaoyin, often described his hometown as "an island," because of the way the virus separated the city from the rest of China. Xiaoyin had posted daily reports on Weibo, where he began every entry the same way: "I'm in Wuhan. Today is the nth day of the sealed city."

Xiaoyin was friends with Zhang, the Wuhan pharmacist I had corresponded with throughout February. In those days, it was still unclear how serious the crisis would become around the world. On February 26, I had asked Zhang what he thought might happen next in the United States. He responded:

How widely will the virus spread eventually? What will be the final consequences? I don't think anybody can answer now. China and America have different cultural, economic, and political situations, even different values.

Now that the city was unsealed, I had traveled there to meet with Zhang and others. In town, I had coffee with an architect named Kyle Hui, whose stepmother had been among the first wave of deaths. She was sixty-five years old, in good health, and she had had no known contact with the Huanan market. Hui had no idea how she got infected; at the time, there weren't any tests for the virus. Other relatives also fell ill, and later, after tests became available, some of these family members were confirmed as positive cases.

Hui's stepmother had raised him from his early teens, and he said that they had been as close as any parent and child. During our interview, he recalled his own litany of dates: on January 4, his stepmother fell ill; on January 11, she was turned away from a crowded hospital; on January 13, she was finally admitted. She died two days later.

"On the eighteenth, she went to the crematorium," Hui said. "I went there, too, and I saw some workers wearing masks, gloves, and protective clothing." He continued, "At that time, there wasn't much news about the disease spreading, but the hospital workers all knew, and so did people at the crematorium." The crematorium had been busy, and there Hui met another family who had lost someone to a flulike illness. At that time, the city's official death toll was only one.

Nobody could say how many people might have died during this initial phase. I met with one infectious-disease physician who handled testing at a large Wuhan hospital, and he believed that the actual toll could be three to four times higher than the government's figure. His guess was that the total was more than ten thousand.

Kyle Hui had grown up in Wuhan, but for years he had lived and worked in Jiangsu province, near Shanghai. After his stepmother's death, he took his wife's parents back to Jiangsu, for safety. They happened to leave Wuhan just before the city was sealed, but in Jiangsu they experienced their own version of the quarantine. Officials from the local neighborhood committee required Hui and his family to stay inside for fourteen days, and the apartment door was sealed with tape from the outside. Hui still had a photograph of the door on his phone. The tape had been printed with the words: "Returned Hubei Resident Home Quarantine." The door was unsealed only when committee members delivered food or collected garbage.

Initially, Hui had an angry confrontation with the cadres, but he decided not to resist the quarantine. "In terms of the big picture, it was correct," he said. But he noted that anybody who had witnessed the early mistakes in Wuhan was bound to feel differently than most Chinese. "Behind every statistic, there's a broken family," he said. "So I can't say whether I'm satisfied or not satisfied with the government."

When we met, Hui was making his first trip back to Wuhan since his stepmother's cremation. Earlier in the year, he had telephoned both the Wuhan mayor's hotline and the local branch of the CDC, in hopes of having his stepmother included in the official count for COVID deaths. But officials responded that it was impossible, because her death certificate listed pneumonia as the cause.

Hui still hadn't told his seven-year-old son that his grandmother was dead. Hiding such information from children isn't unusual in China; a number of my Sichuan University students wrote painful essays about how, when they were small, their parents had lied to them about the death of a grandparent. In this case, the family loss was part of a larger trauma, which seemed to make it even harder to process. "My father wants to tell him, but we haven't figured out how to do it," Hui said.

Since January, they had been telling the boy that his grandmother was sick in Wuhan. Every time the boy wanted to talk with her, they explained that she didn't feel well. During the Lunar New Year holiday, they had given him a traditional gift envelope and said that it was from Grandma. After a while, the boy stopped asking questions. "I think he knows the truth," Hui said.

Throughout my correspondence with Zhang, the pharmacist, I never saw his face. But he wrote long messages, and his words gave me the impression of a man who was both literary and pragmatic. He often described quarantine logistics, but he was also a serious poet. At times, he became philosophical, speculating about Chinese citizens' relationship with authoritarianism:

Traditionally, China was an agricultural country with a large number of peasants, which explains why people have always been so tightly connected to their land. But now China's land is owned by the state, and in a sense the citizens are just renters living in the country. They are fraught with unease. And thousands of years of feudal monarchy, the traditional notion of an emperor's reign, and the ideology of Confucianism have become deeply rooted. All of this forges a natural obedience to authority.

One evening in Wuhan, I planned to meet Zhang, his wife and daughter, and the poet Xiaoyin for dinner. They chose an outdoor fish restaurant near Wuhan's bund, on the northern bank of the Yangtze. The moment I entered the place, I immediately knew which waiting customer was Zhang, even though we had never met in person. He was in his midforties, and his hair was slightly long, like an artist's. Part of a tattoo was visible beneath his short-sleeved shirt.

He said that he hoped I liked fish. "We could barely get fish during the sealed city," he explained. "So now we eat it whenever we can." Xiaoyin said there had been a shortage after the Huanan market was shut down. "One reason was that a major source was gone," he said. "But it was also because people became nervous about fish and seafood, because they associated them with the virus."

At dinner, Zhang's wife remembered that on January 23, her mother called to warn her that the price of meat had suddenly doubled, and on January 27, she spent more than six hundred yuan, nearly ninety dollars, on a relatively small amount of pork. Food often came up in Wuhan residents' memories, and such details had also been prominent in the online diaries.

Xiaoyin explained that he had started his diary because he found it impossible to write poetry in the sealed city. He turned instead to Weibo, where his posts were loose, lively, and wide-ranging. On January 24, the

first full day that Wuhan was quarantined, he described waking up with
a hangover:

> Last night I went out drinking, and today my mind was still disori-
> ented; it seemed like I was still a little drunk. It took me a long time
> to wake up. Then it finally dawned on me that the city had been
> sealed.

Soon, he settled into a rhythm, beginning every day with his trademark opening. On February 7—"I'm in Wuhan. Today is the fifteenth day
of the sealed city"—he expressed anger and sadness at the death of Li
Wenliang, the ophthalmologist who had been punished for warning colleagues about the disease. Xiaoyin wrote: "A monument should be built
for Dr. Li Wenliang in Wuhan. The name of this monument should be
'Rumor Spreaders.'"

That post, like many of Xiaoyin's writings, had been censored. This
became another part of his ritual: often, he spent hours writing a record
that quickly vanished. He told me that no mainland press would consider publishing his diary. After the city's seal was lifted, he collected
files of all his posts and had them privately printed and bound. He presented me with a copy. The volume was 230 pages long, with a stark
white cover: the color of mourning in China. The center featured a black
band with a simple title, also in white: "Wuhan Information."

The only local diary to receive much attention outside China was
Fang Fang's, which was being translated into more than twenty languages. As the novelist gained international fame, there was a Chinese
backlash driven by Little Pinks and hard-core nationalists. They mounted
an online Cultural Revolution–style campaign against the author, accusing
her of being an "American Fifth Column" and an "anti-China bullet." In
Fang Fang's Wuhan neighborhood, somebody hung up large denuncia-
tion posters, and hateful messages were wrapped around bricks and

tossed over the wall of her courtyard home. A prominent tai chi master in Chengdu made a public call for other martial artists to assault the woman. At one point, an anonymous Chinese rapper even composed a diss track, as if he were involved in a street feud with a sixty-five-year-old woman. More than ten million people viewed the song:

What kind of decent person keeps a diary on the internet
Proofreading and translation of a book in just over ten days . . .
And with every drop of ink you cause another national scar.

Zhang and Xiaoyin both knew Fang Fang, although they hadn't seen her recently. She was no longer allowed to appear at meetings or conferences, and she had been banned from publishing. Even her name could not be printed in the state-controlled press. Authorities had instructed her not to accept interviews, especially from foreign outlets. It had become common for average citizens to speak of Fang Fang as a tool of the Americans, which infuriated Zhang and Xiaoyin. "Whenever somebody says something bad about her, I always ask, 'Did you read the diary?'" Zhang said. "Every time the answer is no. The people who attack her don't even bother to read what she writes."

We ordered another round of beers, and Zhang and Xiaoyin returned to the topic of authority. Xiaoyin told a story about a middle-aged *liumang*, or thug, who lived in his compound. When the *liumang* was younger, he used to cause trouble, but now he mostly hung around the street looking depressed. At the start of the pandemic, when the neighborhood committee desperately needed staff, they hired the *liumang* to help manage the compound gate.

"After that, he changed completely," Xiaoyin said. "He worked really hard. He loved wearing the uniform and being able to control people. He was the guy who stood at the gate and pointed the temperature gun at people's foreheads." Throughout the period of the sealed city, which lasted for seventy-six days, the *liumang* reported for work every morning without fail. But once the seal was lifted, the *liumang* was laid off. "He immediately faded back to his old life," Xiaoyin said. "Now I see him hanging out every day on the street, with the same broken-down spirit as before. It's as if nothing happened."

During the crisis, the island of Wuhan replicated its isolation at increasingly smaller levels. There were walled compounds, sealed buildings, and locked rooms. Patients were isolated; suspected exposures were isolated; medical workers were isolated. One nurse told me that she left for work on the morning of February 3 and did not return home until the afternoon of June 7. She was housed in a hotel room, like most workers who interacted with patients. For four months, the nurse communicated with her husband and their five-year-old son only by phone calls and WeChat messages.

In order to create solitude on such a scale, a great deal of construction was necessary. I met a young manager from a building company that renovated 110 hospitals, clinics, schools, gymnasiums, and other buildings. Much of their work involved installing walls, barriers, and special entrances and exits that allowed people to keep away from one another. The company also helped build Huoshenshan, one of two emergency hospitals that were specially constructed to house COVID patients. Huoshenshan, which had a thousand beds, including thirty in an intensive-care unit, became a prime subject of government propaganda, because it was built in roughly ten days. The building-company manager told me that there were seven thousand workers on the site, along with more than a hundred excavators. For a normal building project, he would have had two or three excavators.

The manager, whom I'll call Liu, recruited and oversaw labor. He had often appealed to workers' patriotism, but mostly he paid them well.

Recalling this period, he used a phrase that translates as "Money can make the devil push the grindstone for you." He usually paid unskilled laborers the equivalent of hundreds of dollars a day, because of the risk. The most Liu ever handed over for a week's work, to a carpenter, was fifty thousand yuan, about seven thousand dollars—ten times a normal wage. Even so, recruitment was difficult.

For the sake of speed, Huoshenshan was constructed in zones, and Liu's workers were still finishing the back region while infected patients were being admitted in the front. "A big group of workers fled," he said. "They didn't even claim their salaries." After the hospital had been finished, it was immediately necessary to turn around and go back inside, in order to fix leaks and other problems that resulted from the hurried construction.

At that point, Liu offered the workers the equivalent of a thousand dollars a day, but nobody accepted. He became philosophical when he talked about this time. "The pandemic is like a mirror," he said. "A person can see himself more clearly, both his good qualities and his bad qualities."

He found that the only solution was to put on personal protective equipment himself and accompany the workers into areas with infected patients. "I said, 'If you have a problem, then I have a problem,'" he recalled. "Once I did that, they were willing." In truth, he wasn't convinced that it was safe, and he was relieved that nobody got sick.

Liu said the experience had left him calmer and more patient. He drove more carefully now; he wasn't in such a rush. I often asked Wuhan residents how they had been changed, and there was no standard response. Some expressed less trust in government, while others had increased faith in the national leadership. The nurse who had been separated from her husband and child said that sometimes she missed the simple days when she was isolated in a hotel room and thought about nothing but work. The physician who handled COVID testing at a large hospital told me that he had become fixated on having enough food in his pantry. Nowadays, he always kept at least sixty-five pounds of rice, sixty-five pounds of noodles and pasta, and thirty tins of canned meat. "I have five friends who do the same thing," he said. "But they store even more than I do."

Across Hubei province, the government was offering free admission to nearly four hundred major attractions, in hopes of bringing back tourists. I didn't meet many people from other parts of China, but locals seemed to be taking advantage of the opportunity. When I visited the Yellow Crane Tower, a reconstructed ancient building near the Yangtze, the site was so packed that it was hard to move. Workers told me that daily attendance was capped at twenty-five thousand; that day, the on-line reservation system had filled before noon.

I stayed at the Westin Wuhan Wuchang, on the Yangtze's southern bank. When I checked in, a smiling clerk offered a special post-lockdown deal that allowed me to include the breakfast buffet for the equivalent of an additional twenty-three cents a day. In the elevator, on an endless loop, a screen played a promotional video that featured happy Westin Wuhan scenes: a wedding reception, a chef at work, guests drinking cocktails. Then the footage abruptly shifted to men in gas masks, helmets, and white hazmat suits. They were identified as having come from the Yikang Chemical Company, and they wielded industrial-strength spray machines like flamethrowers. They torched everything in white chemical clouds: reception halls, dining rooms, lounges. On a table, somebody laid out room-key cards in neat rows, like a game of solitaire, and then blasted them with Yikang's best. The soundtrack to these scenes was the song "Love Is Greater," by Amanda Noelle:

Friday night, feeling fine
I'm gonna have a good time.
Raise my hands, watch me dance
Everything's alright . . .

In Wuhan, the official approach to the pandemic was schizophrenic. Cadres and business owners wanted to pretend that nothing had happened, and that their city was normal, but they were also obsessive about protective measures. Wuhan was the most thoroughly tested large city on earth: in the middle of May, in part to boost confidence, the government had tested more than nine million residents in the span of a week and a half. At a time when many cities worldwide were struggling to test even moderate numbers of residents, Wuhan had 321 testing locations around town. The last time the city had reported a locally transmitted symptomatic case had been May 18.

Elsewhere in China, Wuhan's recovery had become a point of national pride. Ariel and Natasha's school gave lessons about Wuhan's protective measures, and in May, during a trip to Hangzhou, I had visited a special exhibit about Wuhan medical workers. But there was nothing in Wuhan itself: no exhibits, no memorials, no propaganda billboards. As far as local cadres were concerned, the recent trauma was as blank as the blue wall in front of the Huanan market. Every morning, I picked up the local newspapers, which ran relentlessly upbeat headlines about the future (*Yangtze Daily*, August 29: STUDENTS DO NOT HAVE TO WEAR MASKS IN SCHOOLS). Movie theaters were open; restaurants and bars had no seating restrictions. At the Hanyang Renxinghui Mall, I saw barefaced kids playing in what may have been one of the last fully functioning ball pits on earth, a sight that, to me, seemed worthy of other headlines (CHILDREN DO NOT HAVE TO WEAR MASKS IN WUHAN BALL PITS).

Wuhan was home to more than a million university students, the second-highest number of any city in China. The students were in the process of returning, and one day I visited Wuhan University with Xiaoyin, the poet. His real job was teaching civil engineering, and he published poetry on the side. Both his parents had also been professors at Wuhan University, and his father had died of a sudden heart attack in May, at the age of eighty-three. "He usually went for a walk every day, but they were indoors during the time of the sealed city," Xiaoyin said. He thought that the period of inactivity had weakened the old man's heart.

Xiaoyin led me along winding paths shaded by parasol and camphor trees. The university is among the oldest in China; it was founded in 1893, when it was known as Ziqiang Xuetang. The words mean "the Self-Strengthening School," a reference to China's struggle against imperialism. During the Second World War, Japanese troops occupied the campus, where they planted cherry trees that still bloom every spring. Xiaoyin took me to buildings that had been designed in the 1920s by F. H. Kales, a young MIT-trained architect who tried to combine elements of Western and Chinese architecture. There had been many such attempts in the early twentieth century, often unfortunate—the worst of West and East. But the Kales buildings at Wuhan University were remarkable. They had lovely lead-glass windows, stone carvings of Chinese-style scrollwork, and graceful, understated Western pillars. The campus was the most beautiful I had seen in China.

"When I came back onto campus after the seal had been lifted, I didn't see a single person," Xiaoyin said. "I thought about how powerful this disease is."

After we stopped at one of the Kales buildings, Xiaoyin asked if I had noticed the only other bystander. I had—sunglasses, surgical mask.

"He's a security agent," Xiaoyin said.

I asked if this was a problem.

"No," he said. "He didn't follow us. Anyway, we're just looking at buildings."

The campus sprawled across a long, steep hillside, and as we approached the bottom, we saw groups of returning students hauling luggage through the front gate. According to university pandemic regulations, the students wouldn't be allowed to leave without making a special application. Most Chinese colleges, including Sichuan University, planned to begin the fall semester with closed campuses.

We stopped to get drinks at a convenience store, where we met two African medical students. Umaro Sow came from Cape Verde, and his friend, Kalaba Mulizwa, was Zambian. I seemed to be the only non-Asian staying at the Westin Wuhan, and of the handful of foreigners I had seen downtown, all were Africans. Virtually every resident from a developed country had been evacuated during the beginning of the pandemic, often on flights organized by embassies or consulates. But many African nations lacked such resources, and their citizens had no option but to remain in the sealed city.

Sow and Mulizwa hadn't left their dormitories during the seventy-six days of quarantine. The dorms were locked from the outside, with university staff delivering food and other necessities. The men said they had been well cared for, but even after the seal was lifted they were still restricted to campus. Today was the first time in more than half a year that they had been granted passes to exit the gates. I asked where they were going.

"McDonald's," Mulizwa said.

"Not me," Sow said. "I want to get some steak. Maybe some chicken. Something grilled."

I said something to the effect that the worst was behind them. Sow grinned and said, "We're still living."

Xiaoyin had told a couple of friends that we were visiting campus, and by the time we approached the front gate, they had told some others. The editor of a literary journal came with their most recent issue, and somebody else brought a couple of books for me to sign. Before long, nearly a dozen of us made our way to a private room at a restaurant off campus.

They were all creative types—writers, poets, painters. Zhang, the poet-pharmacist, came from the other side of town. It reminded me of Chengdu get-togethers: in provincial China, creative circles tend to be close-knit and supportive, especially during a repressive period. After seeing the security agent on campus, I had wondered if police would come to investigate the foreigner. But the only people who intercepted us were the writers and artists. It occurred to me that at least on this particular afternoon, the creative types seemed to be exchanging information more efficiently than the Party did.

Earlier in the summer, I had researched in Yiwu, an eastern city known for its export industry. After a couple of days, the police came to my hotel room to question me, and they made sure that I left the following morning. I had expected similar problems in Wuhan, where I figured I might be forced to leave after a day or two. But over the course of nine days of intensive reporting, I had no contact with security personnel, other than the passing encounters with plainclothes men. Sometimes, I wondered if the police were just as tired as everybody else in the sealed city. But inconsistency was characteristic of the Chinese security state: as always, it helped to think of Kafka as well as Orwell.

At the restaurant, we ate at a large banquet table, and the writers and artists discussed their memories of the quarantine. One professor was a marathoner who had run ten kilometers around his living room every day, measuring the distance with a watch. Others talked about how, after the isolation ended, reunions with friends and associates were complicated.

"If you feel fortunate that you stayed healthy, then you don't want to express this to others," one writer said.

"One of my friends lost his brother," Xiaoyin said. "I used to go see him play the guitar. When I met my friend, I had to be careful what I said. If your family has been lucky, it's better if you don't say anything about it."

"It's also true that if we got sick, we didn't tell anybody," another writer said. "There was some sense that it was your fault if you got infected."

The conversation turned to the origin of the virus. For people around the world, most of whom had hardly heard of Wuhan before the pandemic, it was a mystery how such an apparently obscure place could give rise to such a destructive disease. Locals were less surprised.

"People often say that we have a *matou sixiang*," one writer said. The term means "dock mentality," and he referred to Wuhan's history as a treaty port, one of the cities that had been forcibly opened to foreign trade during the Opium Wars era. "There's always been so much traffic on the rivers, and people tend to be relatively open," he said. "Maybe that's why it happened here."

"Somebody working with seafood could have brought it from the south," Zhang said.

"Maybe it was imported."

"Science is something you can't fabricate. But now we can't trust science, either. Science has also been politicized."

We had been in the private room for more than two hours, and now, from the main part of the restaurant, came the sweet and sour strains of Kenny G's sax playing "Going Home."

"They're trying to rid of us," one writer said, and everybody laughed.

In Wuhan, I never met anybody who believed that the virus had been leaked by the Institute of Virology. The lab-leak theory had been promoted by many in the U.S., including officials at the highest levels of the Trump administration. On May 3, Mike Pompeo, the secretary of state, gave an interview to ABC in which he referred to the institute. "There is enormous evidence that that's where it began," he said. Later in the interview, Pompeo continued: "I can tell you that there is a significant amount of evidence that this came from that laboratory in Wuhan."

Despite such claims, nobody in the American government produced any evidence that the virus came out of the institute. But the speculation continued, in part because the Chinese government remained silent. When I met with the infectious-disease physician who handled testing at a large Wuhan hospital, he told me that his scientist friends had learned not to attempt any research about the origins. "If you propose a research topic that has anything to do with where the virus came from, it's automatically rejected," he told me.

He didn't believe the lab-leak theory, which he found far-fetched. But he also noted that it couldn't be completely ruled out. "Until we know where it came from, we can't say for sure," he said.

In Wuhan, I didn't attempt to visit the Institute of Virology. The lab was located in the city's eastern suburbs, where it was isolated to a degree that made it impossible to stop by without attracting attention. By telephone, I talked with Peter Daszak, a British disease ecologist who was among a number of foreign scientists who had worked closely with the institute. Over a period of sixteen years, Daszak had made repeated trips to Wuhan, where his work focused on bat coronaviruses. He had coauthored more than a dozen papers with Chinese colleagues at the institute. During our conversation, Daszak was adamant that there was no evidence the institute had ever studied a virus that could cause a COVID outbreak.

"Scientists in China are under incredible pressure to publish," he said. "It really drives openness and transparency." He continued, "If we had found a virus that infected human cells and spread within a cell culture, we would have put the information out there. In sixteen years, I've never come across the slightest hint of subterfuge [from scientists at the institute]. They've never hidden data. I've never had a situation where one lab person tells me one thing and the other says something else. If you were doing things that you didn't want people to know about, why would you invite foreigners into the lab?"

Daszak was the president of EcoHealth Alliance, a nonprofit research organization based in New York. EcoHealth had received grants from the U.S. government, and in April, President Trump had told reporters that the U.S. should stop funding research connected to the Wuhan Institute of Virology. Shortly after Trump's comments, the National Institutes of Health canceled a $3.7 million grant that would have supported Eco-Health's research into how bat coronaviruses are transmitted to people.

I asked Daszak why, if he had such faith in the openness of his Wuhan colleagues, the Chinese government had been so closed about the origins and other aspects of the outbreak. He said that science is one thing, and politics something else; he believed that officials were embarrassed about their early mistakes, and so they simply shut down all information. "You're a journalist in China," he said. "I don't know what you would say about the Chinese idea of PR, but I'd say they're pretty terrible."

Even if the government had uncovered evidence that the virus first spread in the Huanan animal stalls, cadres almost certainly would have suppressed it, out of fear of being blamed for negligence. My own experience made me inclined to believe that the Wuhan Institute of Virology would have had trouble maintaining a strict silence about a lab accident that sparked the pandemic. During the chaotic early weeks, information leaked out of Wuhan in all kinds of ways, often through whistleblowers or others who shared key details with the public. Some people did so inadvertently, like Li Wenliang, whose original intention had been to warn only the former classmates in his WeChat group. But others deliberately put crucial information out into the world. The most important example was the virus's genome, which had been sequenced first by Chinese scientists. This data was made publicly available on January 11, and it allowed scientists worldwide to begin studying the virus and developing vaccines.

Nobody in the government had approved the release of the genome. A scientist in Shanghai made the decision on his own, and I met with some of his colleagues in the city. "Somebody in his group said, 'Do we need some kind of approval?'" one scientist told me. "He said, 'I don't care.'"

The scientist was punished professionally, and eventually he changed jobs. But he remained employed, and he was never arrested. When I asked to meet with him, colleagues told me that he didn't want to go public with his story. One scientist compared him to Zhong Nanshan, a prominent pulmonologist who had been instrumental in revealing the government's initial cover-up of SARS in 2003. Afterward, the government recognized Zhong for his service. "The government at that time was smart enough to adopt him as a hero," the colleague told me. "Seize the narrative. But they didn't do it this time."

As a result, the Shanghai scientist had never been recognized in either the Chinese or the foreign press. One colleague had attended a dinner at which the scientist got tipsy and complained about how some Chinese officials now cited the sequenced genome as an example of their supposed willingness to share information. "He said, 'That was my decision, and I got punished for it!'" the colleague told me.

There were many such figures, often unknown. Somebody at the Chinese CDC had leaked an internal government report about animal stalls at the Huanan market, which helped foreign scientists analyze patterns in the early spread. Given the inconsistencies of Chinese bureaucracy, as well as the confusion of the initial outbreak, I wasn't surprised by the lack of control over information. And Chinese scientists, many of whom had been trained overseas, generally felt a deeper obligation to their field and to their data than they did to the Party. It seemed unlikely that highly educated people at the Institute of Virology would have known about the escape of a deadly new virus and then said nothing, either intentionally or accidentally, while the disease killed thousands in their hometown over a period of weeks. Even a quiet warning to friends probably would have blown up, as it did with Li Wenliang.

But the lab-leak theory would never disappear without definitive proof for another source. All that existed was circumstantial evidence, which over time seemed to point to the animal trade. In February 2022, *Science* published a preprint of a paper that analyzed the pattern of early known infections in Wuhan. The previous year, the lead author, Michael Worobey, a prominent Canadian evolutionary biologist, had called for scientists to take the lab-leak theory seriously. But Worobey's subsequent research convinced him that the animal trade was by far the most likely culprit. On Twitter, he summarized the group's findings: "We found that cases in December were both nearer to, and more centered on, the

Huanan market than could be expected given either the population density distribution of Wuhan, or the spatial distribution of COVID cases later in the epidemic. Its epicenter was at the market."

Nevertheless, polls showed that an overwhelming majority of Americans believed the lab-leak theory. People were also inclined to assign blame for China's early mistakes, although this seemed much less common among American scientists. "I tend to take a charitable view of countries that are at the beginning state of epidemics," Jennifer Nuzzo, an epidemiologist at the Johns Hopkins Center for Health Security, told me, when we spoke on the phone. Referring to the virus's ability to spread asymptomatically, she said that it was unrealistic to expect that any country could have stopped it at the source. "I've always believed that this thing was going to spread," she said.

Wafaa El-Sadr, the director of ICAP, a global-health center at Columbia University, also had a broader perspective on the issue of origins. She told me that we might never know the true starting point, because it's hard to trace a chain of infections back to the source. El-Sadr noted that after nearly forty years, scientists still don't know the exact origin of HIV. They had come to the consensus that it most likely started through the bush-meat trade in Africa—the first human was probably infected with HIV after coming into contact with a primate or primate meat. For El-Sadr, HIV and COVID both reflected a larger trend, the encroachment of people on the natural world. "We are now living through two concomitant massive pandemics that are the result of spillover from animal to human hosts, the HIV and the COVID pandemics," El-Sadr wrote to me in an email. "Never in history has humanity experienced something along this scale and scope."

From the Wuhan perspective, the historical significance wasn't unprecedented. Big things had always happened in the Yangtze town. The opium-selling Westerners had built their bund in Wuhan, and the revolution that toppled the Qing had started in Wuhan, and the invading Japanese had planted their cherry trees in Wuhan. In this sense, the city's story even had a moral. First, during an era of Western domination, a provincial town is forced at gunpoint to open to the outside world; and then, more than a century and a half later, in an age of intense globalization, the same city returns the favor by sparking a worldwide pandemic.

Early in the year, when I had corresponded with Zhang, he often expressed anger toward the government. On February 26, he wrote: "My personal opinion is that the government has always been careless and suppressed dissent. Because of this, they lost a golden opportunity to control the virus."

When we met in person, Zhang said that some of his anger had passed. As the virus swept across the world, and as mistakes were made by advanced countries like the U.S., Zhang realized that control of the disease was harder than he had expected. Near the end of my time in Wuhan, we had dinner again. I asked what he would do now if he found himself in Li Wenliang's position: working in the hospital and aware of an outbreak of some unknown disease. Would he post a warning online? Contact a health official? Alert a journalist?

Zhang thought for a moment. "I would tell my close friends in person," he said. "But I wouldn't put anything online. Nothing in writing."

I asked if such an event would turn out differently now.

"It would be the same," he said. "It's a problem with the system."

He explained that Chinese authoritarianism creates two dynamics. Local officials are inclined to cover things up, but higher-level leaders also have the capacity to act quickly and effectively. In Zhang's opinion, China was destined to fail at the beginning of the crisis and then do better in the next stage.

Zhang found it strange that after the trauma of the sealed city had passed, and after the virus had exploded around the world, so much in his hometown remained unchanged. Recently, he had updated his eyeglass prescription at the same store he had been using for years. He found it in the same stall in the same building, on the second floor of the Huanan market, behind the high blue wall. Even the shopkeeper and the staff were the same. The main difference was that prices had plummeted, because business was so bad. "Usually I would bargain, but this time I felt a little embarrassed," Zhang said. "I didn't bargain at all."

On one of my last days in Wuhan, I met with Fang Fang. Given all the restrictions that had been placed on the writer, I had assumed that she would decline my request for an interview. But she agreed, and rather than choosing a private residence or some other quiet place, she sent the address of a fashionable café in a busy part of town. We were seated at a conspicuous table that faced the entrance.

Fang Fang was a tiny woman with dyed black hair and the friendly, crinkled eyes of a grandmother. But she had presence—after she swept into the café, the hostess immediately recognized her. She was a regular; the server knew the type of tea that the writer liked. After sitting down, Fang Fang presented me with two signed books. One was *Soft Burial*, a novel that had been banned three years earlier. I had brought a book of my own, and we exchanged the gifts.

"I already read your book about Fuling," she said. "But there's something I wanted to ask. Did you know that Wuhan is called 'river town'?"

When Fang Fang was two years old, her family moved to Wuhan, and since then she had never lived anywhere else. Her real name was Wang Fang; as a young writer, she had chosen Fang Fang as her pen name. She had published more than a hundred books, both fiction and nonfiction, and almost all of her material came from Wuhan or the surrounding region. Before the pandemic, Fang Fang had been the classic example of a provincial writer. She was famous in Wuhan, and somewhat less famous in China as a whole, and not famous at all outside the country. None of her books had appeared in English translation before *Wuhan Diary*. That was the risk of a provincial writer: the career is built inside the city, and inside the city is largely where the career stays.

Ironically, the sealing of Wuhan was the act that thrust Fang Fang out into the world. An estimated fifty million people had shared her online diary, which remained popular even after Weibo suspended her account. Other Chinese writers and tech people helped her find ways to distribute posts on social media, and soon the outside world noticed. HarperCollins acquired the U.S. rights, and Michael Berry, a professor of contemporary Chinese cultural studies at UCLA, began translating the book before Wuhan was even unsealed.

Fang Fang was far from a dissident. She wasn't a Party member, but she had held positions in Party-controlled organizations, including the Hubei Writers' Association, where she once served as chair. In *Wuhan Diary*, she criticized officials who lied and bumbled in the early weeks, but she also gave full credit for subsequent policies that were effective. Nevertheless, Chinese public opinion turned against her, and her decision to publish overseas was viewed as the act of a traitor. The book was not allowed to be published on the mainland. Fang Fang donated all foreign profits to the families of frontline medical workers who had died in China, but state media did not report on her generosity.

Originally, HarperCollins planned to use the English title *Wuhan Diary: Dispatches from the Original Epicenter*. The reaction online was intense because of the controversy over the origins of the virus, and the publisher quickly changed the subtitle to "Dispatches from a Quarantined City." But even those five words caused trouble. Chinese nationalists micro-analyzed the word *dispatches*, claiming it was evidence that Fang Fang and Michael Berry were agents of the American government. On WeChat, Berry received thousands of angry messages, often alluding to China's past humiliations:

You think we are still in the year 1840 and this is the fall of the Great Qing Empire? You white devil, feasting on the flesh of man and drinking human blood, the eighteen realms of hell were created especially for you!

One day, somebody sent a message to Berry: "If you ever set foot in China again I will kill you." Ten minutes later, the individual wrote again:

Sorry, I had too much to drink, I shouldn't have said that.

———

At the café, Fang Fang told me that she had timed her Weibo diary with censors in mind. She noticed that the firewall's guardians didn't seem to work as much after midnight, which was when she usually sent out dispatches. "Normally the posts would get deleted after nine o'clock in the morning," she said. Like any shrewd Chinese, she had considered the ways in which bureaucracies function. "I think that the people who do those jobs go to work at eight thirty," she explained. "First they have a meeting, and then they start working around nine." The early-morning window gave people time to read the posts and create screenshots.

Fang Fang referred to her attackers as "ultra-leftists," and some of the most prominent critics had also attacked *Soft Burial*. The novel describes the Land Reform Movement, which was launched by Mao in 1946 and included intense violence against former landowners. Fang Fang viewed *Soft Burial* and *Wuhan Diary* as part of the same endeavor: both books resisted the Party's attempts to control the past. "I think China should admit to historical mistakes," she told me. "We have to learn from our mistakes. You have to face it—don't deny it." She continued, "Why are there so many so-called Little Pinks and Wolf Warriors in China? They don't even know about the Cultural Revolution. Our history textbooks don't mention it."

Fang Fang said that two local cadres had visited and tried to persuade her to withdraw the overseas publication of *Wuhan Diary*. They implied that her pension from the Hubei Writers' Association might be at risk. "I said, 'If you cancel my pension, I'll sue you,'" she told me.

At the age of sixty-five, with stature in the Chinese literary world, Fang Fang was bolder than most younger writers could have dared to be. She hadn't asked for permission to accept my interview. "They told me not to talk with foreign journalists," she said. "But you're a writer, not a journalist. So I decided that I would meet with you." This was mostly wordplay—as a teacher, I wasn't registered as a *jizhe*, a journalist. But I had been registered this way in the past, and China had no official designation for a *zuojia*, a writer.

At the café, a number of customers recognized Fang Fang and said hello. She seemed remarkably upbeat for a writer who had been silenced. But she knew how the Party worked—it tried to handle the past in the same way that it handled the virus. Throughout the Communist era, there had been many moments of quarantined history: the Land Reform Movement, the Cultural Revolution, the massacre around Tiananmen Square. In every case, an initial silencing was followed by sporadic outbreaks of leaked information. Fang Fang was confident the same thing would happen in Wuhan.

Until recently, she had been scheduled to teach a writing class at Wuhan University. "I was planning to organize students to do an oral history," she said. "I was going to have them interview the medical workers who came to Wuhan." University officials had been supportive, but finally they asked Fang Fang to delay until a future semester, because of the attacks. She still had faith in the young, despite the Little Pinks and the ultra-leftists. Recently, she had been consoling a writer in her thirties who had also been banned. "I said you have to be patient," Fang Fang told her. "I believe it won't be like this forever."

When we finished our conversation, I escorted her outside. She smiled and shook my hand before leaving. Later, I looked at the books she had signed. After nearly forty years of writing about the same river town, her inscription couldn't have been simpler:

Fang Fang
Summer, 2020
Place: Wuhan

CHAPTER NINE

Involution

September 2020

A T THE BEGINNING OF SEPTEMBER, THIRTY MILLION UNIVERSITY students returned to in-class instruction. Virtually all Chinese colleges began the semester with closed campuses, and they used cell phone apps, infrared scanners, and other high-tech strategies to enforce pandemic policies. Throughout the summer, students and staff at Sichuan University had been required to fill out a daily health questionnaire through the university's app.

While reporting in Wuhan, I initially avoided opening the app, because it would tell cadres where I was. Shortly after noon on my first day in the city, I received a WeChat message from a SCUPI administrator. It was arranged neatly into three lines, in English, like the work of a somewhat beleaguered modernist poet:

Daily Health Report

By 12 P.M.

Please

The administrator was the same friendly young woman who had been chasing me for body temperatures since the start of the pandemic.

I felt bad, because I knew that she was being hounded by somebody else, and that person was being hounded by somebody else, and so on up the chain. After the first day in Wuhan, I capitulated. Every morning, I opened the app and submitted what I had come to think of as my signature body temperature: 36.2 degrees. By now, that figure seemed as fundamental to my personhood as the name and number that appeared on my passport, and also like those things, my temperature never changed. If anybody at the university noticed that I had been in Wuhan, they didn't say anything.

In September, the various tools that had been tested the previous spring on the Jiang'an Campus were now implemented in full force. Three robots rolled between dormitories, delivering packages, and each campus gate had been equipped with infrared thermometers, automated turnstiles, and face scanners. If a scanner registered the face of a student trying to exit, the turnstile wouldn't budge. Only faculty and staff were allowed to leave.

One evening during the first week of term, I used my face to exit the East Gate, in order to have dinner. On the way to a restaurant, I followed the campus wall, where I saw some undergrads who were in the process of sneaking out. They had found a spot without surveillance cameras, and somebody had parked bike-share vehicles on both sides of the wall. By stepping upon the seat of a bicycle, a student could reach the top of the barrier and swing over.

That semester, students referred to escaping campus as *fanqiang*, "climbing the wall." This was the same term that was used to describe the act of using a VPN to evade the Great Firewall. I was accustomed to computer language that derives from the physical world—going viral, or searching the web, or emptying trash on a desktop. But the term *fanqiang* had moved in the opposite direction. In the past, Chinese students found ways around a virtual wall, and now they climbed a real one.

There was another prime *fanqiang* location at the southern end of campus. A narrow section of wall consisted of horizontal metal bars that were perfect for climbing, and for a while students scrambled over with impunity. Then the university sent a crew of maintenance workers who covered the bars with thick layers of some kind of slow-drying paint. The gooey substance was bright red and it stained the hands and clothes of anybody who tried to *fanqiang*.

I received wall-climbing updates from various students, including Serena. This semester, she wasn't in my class, but periodically we met on campus. On September 20, Serena showed me a series of three photographs from the southern fence. In the first photograph, a half dozen students are at various stages of clambering over the bars. All students are masked, like people breaking out of a prison or an insane asylum.

The second photograph was taken after the university tried the slow-drying paint. Students countered by covering the gooey bars with paper or cloth, and sometimes they wore cheap disposable gloves that were ordered online and delivered by the robots. In Serena's second photograph, blood-red napkins, towels, and other materials litter the ground in front of the fence, like bandages discarded in the wake of some terrible massacre.

The third photograph continued the general theme of a standoff that, having started with face scanners and infrared thermometers, is deteriorating into increasingly low-tech tactics. In this image, the ground has been cleaned up, and the slow-drying paint has been removed, and the masked students are no longer hanging from bars. Nearby, a security guard in a black uniform sits outside the wall. The man's arms are crossed and he stares at the empty fence.

For days, the university posted guards at the *fanqiang* spot. These figures never budged: each sat with his back to the outside world and his eyes fixed on the fence. When it rained, he held an umbrella. There hadn't been a single locally transmitted COVID infection in Chengdu for more than half a year, but the rumor was that the cadres wouldn't risk opening Jiang'an until the National Day holiday had been safely celebrated.

The campus wall stretched for more than four miles, and it didn't take long for students to find other *fanqiang* locations. Meanwhile, various fast-food apps figured out spots along the fence where deliverymen could park their mopeds and hand off packages. Clusters of kids gathered around the fence at dinnertime, waiting for the moped men to squeeze bags of McDonald's between the bars, like rations at a refugee camp.

Finally, on September 24, a full week before the People's Republic celebrated its seventy-first anniversary, the cadres gave in. They announced that students were allowed to leave campus. All gate infrastructure remained in place—the scanners, the automated turnstiles—but now the student faces worked in both directions. On lower campus, the robots stayed busy, humming back and forth between dormitories.

That fall, Ariel and Natasha began fourth grade. They still had Teacher Zhang: in China, instructors typically accompany the same class from year to year, building a relationship over time. The previous June, along with their classmates, the twins had been presented with gold pins that signified their membership in the Young Pioneers, the Party's organization for schoolchildren. On specially designated days, the twins wore the pins and the red scarves. Sometimes, they returned home complaining about a class with anti-American undertones, or a heavy-handed textbook lesson about China's territorial claim to the Spratly Islands. Leslie and I always told them the same thing: they should be respectful, because they were guests at the school, but they had no obligation to believe everything they were taught.

Once, in a speech at Peking University, Xi Jinping described the project of educating young people in core socialist values as similar to "fastening buttons on clothes." He said, "If the first button is fastened wrong, the remaining buttons will be fastened wrong." Leslie and I found that there was no need to deliberately counteract the propaganda, because our daughters' buttons were wrong from the start: they seemed to have an instinctive distrust of the political lessons. In any case, the material was hardly inspiring. The class known as Morality and Rules ostensibly taught schoolchildren to love the Party, but like many of the other minor subjects, it employed a text with a strange hodgepodge of lessons. I had assumed that the twins would be drilled in stories about the Opium Wars or the Japanese invasion, but there was surprisingly little history in their curriculum. I learned that such material tends to be covered more heavily in subsequent years. During third and fourth grade, the political class focused more on how to behave in society. One section of the twins' textbook was titled "Teacher, You Are Working Hard," and it required them to hand-copy the instructor's weekly schedule.

In addition to inculcating such Confucian values, the text of *Morality and Rules* featured the usual cautionary tales about childhood disasters. Terrible things often happened during summer vacation, when kids were not strictly monitored or scheduled. According to *Morality and Rules*, there had been a recent vacation when seven middle school students drowned in a river in Shandong. During the same summer break, five elementary school kids drowned in a pond somewhere in Henan. Meanwhile, in Heilongjiang, seven students played on the banks of a river, where four of them drowned. The specificity of these numbers made me suspect that we were drifting toward a math problem, but the fast-moving current of *Morality and Rules* was capable of veering abruptly from the tragic to the mundane. "I am a picky eater," one boy said, in another chapter that featured cartoon children delivering self-criticisms. "This is not good for my body, so in the future I will correct it." Another child remarked, "I don't play on windowsills or slide down bannisters, that way I don't fall and get hurt."

In English class, the teacher often asked Ariel and Natasha to model pronunciation by reading lessons aloud. The twins loved this, especially if the material involved injury, pain, and momentary lapses in judgment that resulted in lifelong consequences. One lesson in the English text had been divided into sections labeled "Fun Time" and "Story Time."

It was hard to tell the difference—both fun and story seemed equally dreadful. When the twins read aloud, they always used a hectoring tone:

FUN TIME

Don't throw things out the window. It's dangerous. You might hurt someone.

Don't cook here. It's dangerous. A small fire can become a big one.

Be careful! Look out for cars. Don't go against the traffic.

Don't open the door for a stranger. It's dangerous.

STORY TIME

What are you doing, Little Bear?

I'm lighting firecrackers.

Be careful!

Ow! That hurts.

Don't run down the stairs.

Ouch! My arm hurts. I am having a bad day.

Look out! A bike is coming.

My leg hurts. I can't walk.

We are taking you to the hospital.

Oh, dear! I am having a bad day!

In addition to the long parade of children who paid dearly for stupidity and carelessness, the English text also featured innocents trapped in circumstances beyond their control. One very short story reminded me of Hemingway. Like "The Snows of Kilimanjaro," it featured a mountain, an airplane, and terse dialogue:

Mary and her mother are flying over the mountains in a small plane.

Suddenly there is a loud noise. The plane has a problem! It crashes.

Mary's mother is hurt. She says, "Mary, I can't move. We need help."

Mary has a good idea. She writes SOS with her feet in the snow.

Also like Hemingway, there were stories in which characters drank too much. One chapter of *Morality and Rules* featured a boy named Anran, who accompanies his parents to a birthday dinner. At dinner, the father gets drunk and then tries to drive home. The lesson featured the kind of parent-child role reversal that seemed oddly common in China. "Father, after drinking you absolutely cannot drive!" Anran says firmly. "Please get a *daijiaren* to drive us home!"

The *daijiaren* was one of many brilliant innovations of the Reform era. China has a zero-tolerance policy for alcohol, and even a single drink can result in the suspension of a driver's license. On DiDi, China's most popular ride-share app, you could summon a man who showed up at your car on a folding bicycle. He folded the bike, put it in your trunk, drove you home, parked your vehicle, charged a fee of a few bucks, and then pedaled off to the next drinker. It was amazing how quickly these guys materialized—on any given Friday night in downtown Chengdu, there seemed to be at least two *daijiaren* per city block. You could track them on DiDi's map: little dots of sobriety drifting through downtown.

I admit that after acquiring my Chinese license, I also became a faithful *daijiaren* consumer. But this didn't mean that the service needed endorsement from Morality and Rules. Regardless, Natasha and Ariel seemed to ignore all of it. By fourth grade, they had learned the most important lesson that Morality and Rules has to offer, which is that Morality and Rules is the least important academic class in a Chinese school. After the twins noticed classmates using the period to surreptitiously catch up on other homework, they did the same. Ariel told me that she kept the *Morality and Rules* text open with her math book inside. She also used the period to *zoushen*, a term that translates directly as "the spirit walks away"—to daydream. My Sichuan University students described similar activities in their own mandatory political courses.

It was one of many mixed lessons in a Chinese school. When politics is omnipresent, it becomes a kind of background noise, and students learn to tune it out. The cadres hoped to create a patriotic younger generation, and there seemed to have been success with the Little Pinks. But my impression was that a much larger percentage of young Chinese chose to disengage entirely from politics. It probably wasn't unintentional: for the Party, creating a large cohort of apolitical children wasn't the worst possible outcome of Morality and Rules.

In any case, the art of disassociation has a long history. The twins' fourth-grade language text included the story of Liu Yuxi, a poet and government official in the early ninth century, during the Tang dynasty. In the text, Liu takes a principled stance against corruption and is relegated to a remote place called Hezhou, where a petty superior repeatedly demotes Liu. With each demotion, the poet's lodgings are reduced with bureaucratic specificity: from three floors to three rooms, then to one and a half rooms, and finally to a dilapidated hut. At every step, Liu finds his own way to *zoushen*—he gazes out the window and writes a verse about the view and the disconnect with what's inside his mind. Rather than turning against the state, Liu simply bides his time, an early example of educated acquiescence. The story concludes by noting that, more than a thousand years later, Liu's poems are still alive, while the petty superior is *yipou huangtu*—"a handful of yellow earth":

> *Facing the mighty river, and watching the white sails float past,*
> *My body has been demoted to Hezhou, but my heart still defends*
> *my beliefs. . . .*

Poetry was among the many positives that outweighed the nonsense. In language class, students memorized characters and wrote essays, but they also engaged with verse that had been the heart of Chinese culture for centuries. By fourth grade, Natasha and Ariel had memorized dozens of classic works by Li Bai, Du Fu, and others. Virtually all educated Chinese learn certain poems by heart, like "A Gift to Wang Lun," which Li Bai wrote in the eighth century, after saying farewell to a friend:

李白乘舟将欲行 　　*Li Bai chengzhou jiang yu xing,*
忽闻岸上踏歌声。 　　*Huwen anshang ta gesheng.*
桃花潭水深千尺 　　*Taohua tan shuishen qian chi,*
不及汪伦送我情。 　　*Buji Wang Lun song wo qing.*

Such a poem is relatively easy to memorize: four lines of seven characters each, a total of twenty-eight syllables. A Shakespearean sonnet is five times longer—140 syllables. But even a short string of characters in classical Chinese can convey a great deal:

I, Li Bai, embark on a boat, ready to set sail,
When suddenly from the shore came a melodic farewell.
The depths of Peach Blossom Lake, a thousand feet below
It's still incomparable, O Wang Lun! To the love that you bestow.

As a boy, Li Bai lived near Chengdu, which was also home to Du Fu, the other most famous poet of the Tang. The same dynasty produced Xue Tao, yet another Chengdu resident, who was one of the great women poets of ancient China. Ariel and Natasha's class memorized one of Xue Tao's poems, and there was a monument to the woman less than a mile from our home, on the banks of the Jin River. It was hard to imagine a better environment for children to connect with literature. Where else in the world can a ten-year-old schoolgirl read a twelve-hundred-year-old poem, knowing that it came from another woman in her same city, writing in the same language?

The class memorized about a dozen poems per semester. Periodically, Teacher Zhang used a random-number generator to pick a student, who then had to stand and recite a poem. If the student made mistakes, she lost points on a board that tracked behavior and academic performance. Girls and boys in the top ten were eligible to serve terms as *xiao zuzhang*, "small-group leaders," who were responsible for managing classmates.

From the beginning, we emphasized to Natasha and Ariel that grades didn't matter. The goal was to learn Chinese; it made no difference where the twins stood in any kind of class ranking or exam. But whereas we never needed to counter the political propaganda, we found it much harder to handle the issue of competition. No matter what we said, Natasha and Ariel cared about their scores.

And despite everything that was hard about being a latecomer to the school system, there were also some advantages. Chinese characters are so difficult that they tend to slip away: even while children learn new words, they constantly forget others that need to be reviewed. For Ariel and Natasha, everything was still fresh, whereas the other fourth graders were dealing with their first significant wave of forgotten characters. When children made errors, teachers sometimes pointed out that Cai Cai and Rou Rou were writing correctly. During parent-teacher conferences, Teacher Zhang sometimes mentioned the twins' progress.

For other parents, this opportunity was too good to pass by. When I picked up the girls after school, it wasn't unusual for a mother or father to approach me with their child in tow. "Look at Cai Cai and Rou Rou," the mother would say. "They just started learning Chinese, and they're already better than you!" Next to her, the poor kid stood tired from the long day, his Young Pioneer scarf knotted sloppily like a Friday-night drunk's necktie. "You need to study Cai Cai and Rou Rou's example!" the mother would berate the boy. "Work harder!"

This happened so often that I wondered whether it was the reason why we had been admitted to Chengdu Experimental in the first place. The twins were the perfect cudgel, a two-headed staff available to parents and teachers alike. I often thought about how in America this would have been a recipe for disaster: take two children from a country that has essentially become a national enemy and then relentlessly browbeat the native kids about how they can't measure up. But Ariel and Natasha's nationality seemed irrelevant in this context. The parents didn't care where the twins came from, or what the Trump administration was currently doing; they were focused on something far more important: the traditional Chinese respect for education. If Rou Rou and Cai Cai could be used to motivate their classmates, that was all that mattered.

Remarkably, other kids didn't seem to resent the twins. I almost would have sympathized if children had responded with bullying, but those poor boys with the twisted scarves absorbed the parental scolding and moved on. In China, childhood criticism is essentially environmental, an element of the natural world; abuse rolls off the backs of kids like water from a duck. And from an early age children develop the traditional reverence for education. The best students in a Chinese class also tend to be the most popular, which was part of what motivated Ariel and Natasha. The things that might be important for popularity in America—athletics, social dominance, being cool—mean very little in a Chinese classroom.

During the fall, Natasha became the first of the twins to serve as *xiao zuzhang*, a small-group leader. Soon Ariel was also granted the honor. It clearly made them proud, but I could also see that small-group leadership was basically unpleasant. *Xiao zuzhang* had the responsibility of deducting points for bad behavior, and they also corralled homework and in-class assignments. Periodically, teachers organized head-to-head competitions between small groups, which then recited Tang poetry or solved rapid-fire math equations. It was stressful to be in charge of a group, and we told the twins that they could simply decline the position. But the honor meant too much. The Party failed miserably every time it attempted to indoctrinate Natasha and Ariel with clumsy propaganda, but the system was far more successful with competitions and titles.

When the class studied Li Bai's eternal poem about departure, friendship, and sadness, the other students taught Ariel and Natasha an alternative version. The twins came home with this second verse diligently memorized:

李白乘舟要拉屎   *Li Bai chengzhou yao lashi,*
忽然发现没带纸   *Huran faxian mei dai zhi,*
勇敢伸出大拇指   *Yonggan shenchu da muzhi,*
抠抠屁股全是屎。   *Kou kou pigu, quan shi shi.*

The meter and rhyme were perfect, with everything conveyed eloquently in those twenty-eight syllables:

I, Li Bai, embark on a boat and have to take a shit,
When suddenly I discover that I have no paper,
Bravely I stretch out my thumb
And dig and dig into my butt—O, all of it is shit!

When I mentioned this poem to former students, they recalled different versions from their own childhoods. In some poems, Li Bai plumbs the depths of memory, emotion, and shit, because his true friend Wang Lun has provided a generous gift of toilet paper. Other verses feature the Lake of Peach Blossoms being used as a Li Bai bidet. Willy could still recite the poem that had been popular in the rural school he attended more than thirty years ago:

李白乘舟去拉屎   *Li Bai chengzhou qu lashi,*
坐在船上忘带纸   *Zuo zai chuanshang wang dai zhi,*
桃花潭水深千尺   *Taohua tan shui shen qian chi,*
水洗屁股当草纸。   *Shui xi pigu dang caozhi.*

I, Li Bai, travel by boat to take a shit,
But sitting on the boat I realize that I forgot paper,
However deep the Lake of Peach Blossoms may be,
It rinses my ass as well as any straw paper.

These shit-show shadow classics impressed me almost as much as the Tang verse in the fourth-grade textbooks. Imagine if American schoolchildren knew poetry well enough to appreciate scatological versions of Andrew Marvell or John Donne! For me, there was also relief in the irreverence. Despite the strict discipline of the classroom, and the wooden lessons in Morality and Rules, these students engaged in play that mocked the material they were taught.

On the whole, the kids seemed remarkably well-adjusted. We organized occasional get-togethers of a dozen or so girl classmates at our apartment, and the group dynamics were different from what I had observed among American girls of similar age. The Chengdu students didn't form cliques or deliberately exclude others, and there was never any mean-girl drama. In part, this seemed to reflect the fact that Chinese girls of ten or eleven typically don't engage in the kind of preteen behavior that is common in America. And the cultural emphasis on the group means that Chinese children learn to compromise and accommodate. Despite the fact that most kids had no siblings, they didn't behave like spoiled brats.

The problem was never whether the girls could get along—it was whether they could get together. Scheduling a playdate required weeks of WeChat messaging with parents, because of endless *buxi,* or supplemental courses, and other activities. These routines had become so entrenched that parents seemed befuddled by the possibility of unstructured play. Once, Leslie invited a classmate over on a weekend afternoon, and the girl's mother sent a somewhat panicked message asking if they could go to the science museum instead. She wanted a destination with a clearly defined educational purpose; otherwise, what would the girls possibly do, and what would they learn?

At every small party, the kids played in the courtyard of our compound, organizing their own games. Parents often commented on how nice it was to see the girls so happy. But over the course of two years, nobody else in the twins' friend group organized a similar gathering. It simply wasn't done; children were too overscheduled, and parents were too narrowly focused on education. Many mothers had quit their jobs in order to manage the single child, a pattern that was unheard of a generation earlier. Of the women I taught in Fuling during the 1990s—around a hundred total—there wasn't a single one who didn't work full-time after having children. But now it was becoming more common in China, in part because of new prosperity, but also because of educational pressure.

Eventually, we stopped hosting parties, because scheduling was too difficult. Some parents seemed to recognize how unhealthy it was to keep their children so busy. Once, Leslie and I had dinner with the parents of a classmate of the twins. When the conversation turned to education, the father said that he hated enrolling his daughter in *buxi* courses, but he felt helpless. "That's the way all parents feel," he said. "It's too competitive. But if you want your child to have a chance, you have to do all this stuff."

For Chinese parents, the most terrifying specter—even worse than free time, or summer vacation, or children playing around random bodies of water in Henan and Heilongjiang—was the *gaokao*, the college-entrance examination. In terms of cultural impact, it's the successor to the old imperial civil-service tests. High school seniors sit the *gaokao* at the end of their final year, and the possibility of failure haunts everybody. This was one reason why Leslie and I had moved to China while our daughters were still in elementary school—we figured this would be early enough to avoid the malign influence of the *gaokao*. But the system had become so competitive that even small children felt the pressure. At Chengdu Experimental, as in all Chinese schools, each semester ended with a week of final exams. Even in third grade, these exams were grueling: one hundred minutes for language, and ninety minutes each for math, science, and English. The children were trained like endurance athletes, and Ariel and Natasha became much better at focusing. But they also talked about the pressure, and they picked up random *gaokao* details. At the beginning of fourth grade, the math teacher announced to the class that if they hoped to enter Tsinghua University in eight years, they would need to score at least 649 on the *gaokao*.

When the twins reported these remarks, I had to stop myself from saying: *That sounds low for Tsinghua.* As a teacher of first-year composition, I acquired all kinds of eclectic information about the *gaokao*. The first crop of students told me that as part of the exam the previous spring, they had been instructed to handwrite an English letter apologizing for missing volleyball practice. Such bizarre topics were typical of the English essay component of the *gaokao*.

Given the low quality of English texts in public schools, it was amazing that so many of my students spoke and wrote the language well. But they had generally acquired this facility outside the official system. Many had relied on private tutoring, or they had diligently taught themselves from whatever materials they could find, as Serena had with her episodes of *Gossip Girl*. They rarely learned as much from school lessons, which often wasted time on useless skills like handwriting. One first-year student wrote an essay about an English font that had been designed by a famous school in the city of Hengshui, in Hebei province:

> If a candidates' writing looks neat and clear, [exam graders] will tend to give them high marks. Hengshui Middle School first discovered this phenomenon, and it has invented a special font for students to use in the Gaokao, which is known as the "Hengshui font." The main parts of letters are very round, and the extended straight lines are as short as possible. All the letters must be the same height and the space between words is very narrow. At present, most Chinese high schools require students to practice this font, and Hengshui copybooks have become very popular, some online stores can sell 2,000-plus Hengshui copybooks in one month. However, apart from being neat, Hengshui font is not necessarily aesthetically pleasing. It exists specifically for the Gaokao. Once [the exam] is over, candidates will throw the copybook aside and restore their original writing habits.

Every September, many first-years still used the Hengshui font out of habit. Sometimes I received an in-class assignment so neat that it looked as if it had been produced by a machine. But students generally allowed those rounded Hengshui letters to deflate not long after they entered university. The font was one of many small tricks that were mastered for the *gaokao* and then promptly discarded. Key subjects like math and language still represented the core of the exam, but it had become so competitive that a top student needed to work the margins with peripheral skills like handwriting. And the *gaokao* score was all that mattered for admission: apart from a few scattered exceptions, Chinese universities didn't consider grades, recommendations, or extracurricular activities.

One attraction of SCUPI was that its cutoff *gaokao* score was lower than that of other departments at Sichuan University. This was justified because most SCUPI students would eventually enter Pittsburgh or other foreign institutions where Chinese exam scores weren't important. In order to be admitted to SCUPI in the fall of 2019, a student in Sichuan needed to score 632 points out of 750—a figure that placed them in the top 6 percent of test takers in the province. The next-lowest cutoff at Sichuan University was 649, which allowed a student to enter less prestigious departments, including Water Resources, Sanitation Testing and Quarantine, and Marxism. The English department, in contrast, had a cutoff of 660. Econ was 663, Mathematics 667: tiny divergences in score could result in completely different subjects and career paths. Every year, roughly ten million Chinese students take the exam, and only about 1.6 percent qualify to enter 985 universities. One first-year student told me that her high school instructor in populous Guangdong had repeatedly invoked a mantra: With every point you gain on the *gaokao*, you pass a thousand competitors.

The Sichuan University website listed departmental cutoffs, and status was measured accordingly. Everybody looked down on Marxism—despite the Party's attempts to glorify theory, it was telling that aspiring Marxists occupied the same low *gaokao* rung as future sanitation testers. SCUPI was also considered to be lower tier, and students complained about being disrespected by other departments. The ultimate campus elite, the Brahmins of Sichuan University, studied at the School of Stomatology. At first, this mystified me—why such a fuss about oral medicine? My students spoke with a mixture of envy and resentment about the stomatologists, who seemed to excel at everything on campus. Their department even won the highest honors at the "Praise the New China and Sing the New Era" singing competition before National Day.

I learned that the stomatology department at Sichuan University's West China School of Medicine was recognized as the best in China. Their *gaokao* scores were truly stunning: in order to enter the department's program in clinical medicine, a student needed 696, almost thirty points higher than a math major. Stomatologists existed on such a higher plane that they avoided interacting with other undergrads. Serena told me that if a stomatologist was asked about his major, he might coyly avoid answering, like a humble-brag Harvard grad who says he went to school "in Boston."

Most students seemed traumatized by the *gaokao* experience. One boy wrote a personal essay about being hospitalized for stress-related heart trouble, and several others reported that they had considered suicide. A couple of them mentioned that the private school in Hengshui, in addition to developing its nationally famous font, had also installed guardrails around the balconies of the teaching building, in order to prevent students from jumping.

Even after the exam, the stress didn't end. Some of the most vivid *gaokao* essays described the traditional celebratory banquets that families held after results were announced. These meals were prime opportunities for disappointment, second-guessing, recrimination, and all-around passive-aggressive behavior. One student compared her family's banquet to a famous scene in the epic *Romance of the Three Kingdoms*, in which Xiang Yu hosts a meal in order to attempt an assassination of the hero Liu Bang. The student explained that although she had tested into Sichuan University, she was as vulnerable as Liu Bang because she had a cousin who had made it into an even better school. She described the way in which older relatives made physical comparisons:

"One centimeter taller" means "more promising," "no pimples on the face" means "self-discipline," every simple feature has a meaning and needs to be compared.

In one first-year composition class, I surveyed students on how they had reacted to learning their *gaokao* scores, and seventeen out of eighteen reported that they had been disappointed. Leslie and I sometimes joked that in America, every child is a winner, while in China, every child is a loser. The glass was one-tenth empty; failure seemed built into people's expectations. During my second year at SCUPI, I had a student who called himself Darker Liao. The English name was perfect—Darker was a quiet, slightly morose presence in the classroom, but he wrote brilliantly. His first essay consisted of thirty-five hundred scathing words about his high school math teacher. At Darker's post-*gaokao* banquet, this teacher materialized like the ghost of Banquo, lambasting the boy in front of parents and relatives. "With your intelligence, you could have gone to a better school," he said. "Now what? Well, that's what happens when you didn't listen to me."

The instructor was a charismatic figure, and initially Darker had fallen under his spell:

> My attitude towards the teacher could not be said to be respectful, but rather of worship, which even reached a level of madness. Every time I saw him, I always made a big bow with my body bent to nearly 90 degrees, which also often caused embarrassment to my classmates. When handing in my homework, I always handed it with both hands. I even wrote my affirmation and praise of his teaching measures in my weekly diary. . . . Now to think of it, if the teacher had told me to commit suicide, I probably would have done it.

Darker's tragic flaw, as fatal as Macbeth's ambition, was that as a senior he pursued a hobby in robotics. The boy might as well have been snorting methamphetamine or dabbling in online porn, as far as the teacher was concerned. He ordered Darker to drop the robotics and focus entirely on *gaokao* prep, but the boy decided that he could do both. The teacher began mocking and criticizing Darker in front of his peers. One day, after enduring a withering series of remarks, Darker finally saw his idol with new eyes. He titled his essay "Silk Thread":

I looked at my limbs and found that there were countless silk threads tightly wrapped around them. I looked at [the other students] and they were also wrapped with silk threads. Some of them nodded their heads and looked at the headteacher with adoring eyes just like me before, when I couldn't see the silk threads; some of them looked at me with a funny expression, as if they were laughing at me to see the silk threads now. I looked along the silk threads and found that their ends were in the hands of the headteacher.

————

In my second year, I surveyed more than sixty students about whether they believed the *gaokao* and the college-admissions process should be significantly changed. A clear majority—61 percent—favored retaining the system. During in-class debates, the results were similar, and, in another instance of educated acquiescence, students often wrote argumentative essays supporting the status quo. One boy even coughed up my favorite transition:

We cannot give up eating for fear of choking, we should treat *gaokao* dialectically. On the whole, its advantages far outweigh its disadvantages.

The most common reason for supporting the *gaokao* was that numbers are incorruptible. A rich man could buy a Porsche or a luxury apartment, but he couldn't buy his kid's way into stomatology at Sichuan University. The only advantage could be found in paying for better high schools and more *buxi* classes, but even those avenues required hard work. On the whole, it was much easier to game the admissions system in the United States, which was one reason why many wealthy Chinese had started sending their children to America for high school.

In this and in many other issues, the students impressed me as realists. These only children weren't spoiled, but they also weren't fresh-faced and wide-eyed. They seemed to believe that the world was too flawed for idealism, and they accepted the fact that childhood included large amounts of stress and grinding work. In nonfiction class, a student named Sarinstein chose a ten-year-old Chengdu schoolboy as the subject of his profile paper. Sarinstein interviewed the boy and his parents, and he followed him to school and observed some of his *buxi* classes. Sarinstein was a physics major, and he had been educated in the Mianyang schools that were famous for intense preparation. He had created his portmanteau English name because he admired both Sartre and Einstein.

While Sarinstein personally connected with the individualism of the French philosopher, he acknowledged that such values have little place in China. In his profile of the ten-year-old, he observed that the school seated children in the classroom from front to back according to exam scores. Again, Sarinstein was capable of holding two contradictory ideas at once: he disliked this practice, but he saw it as a necessary evil. In an email exchange about his profile, he wrote:

> In China, education is the most important tool for class mobility, therefore accentuating *fairness,* everyone looking at the [exam] score; western education is more of a tool for vested interests' class to keep a grip on their advantages, therefore emphasizing *justice.*
>
> The very nature of China's education is an elimination mechanism, a selection mechanism, rather than a mechanism for talent cultivation. China's system cannot afford individualized education, caring for one's all-around and healthy growth. . . . Our system is merely a machine helping the enormous and somewhat cumbersome Chinese society to function—to continuously supply sufficient human resources for the whole society. It is cruel. But it is also probably the fairest choice under China's current circumstances. An unsatisfying compromise. I haven't seen or come up with a better way.

My own response was also contradictory. Sarinstein's conclusion might be dispiriting, but the clarity of his analysis was remarkable. Despite being a physics major, he wrote better in English than most American college students. I admired the discipline and tough-mindedness of such students, and I had to respect the system that had produced them. But I also sympathized with their fatalistic view of competition and achievement. They often spoke of *neijuan*, or "involution," which had become a touchstone term for their generation. Involution refers to a point at which intense competition produces diminishing returns—one friend described it as the sensation of running on a hamster wheel.

Helplessness was part of the feeling. Students recognized how much effort they wasted on things like the Hengshui font, but they also believed that if this or any other aspect of the exam were reformed, it would be replaced by something else that was equally competitive and draining. In one in-class debate, a first-year student argued that admissions offices should also consider extracurricular activities like volunteer work. After he was finished, a classmate stood up to give a counterargument. "If you add volunteer work, then you are just adding more things and you are adding more pressure," he said. "If you do one hundred hours of volunteer work, then I'll do two hundred. And then you'll do three hundred."

During my second year, I surveyed more than sixty students about the pressures they had felt during high school. When I asked if they had suffered from stress, 75 percent said yes. For the next question—Did your parents put too much pressure on you?—the response was virtually the opposite: 78 percent said no. This also seemed characteristic: these students recognized the flaws in the system, but they didn't blame anybody for creating or perpetuating this system. They rarely exhibited the young rebel's desire to tear down the world of his parents.

If anything, they were deeply sympathetic toward the older generation. Young people generally had a weak knowledge of sensitive political events like the Cultural Revolution and the massacre around Tiananmen Square, but they had a much better grasp of recent economic history. From their parents' stories, they knew something about how it had felt to be poor and then suddenly enter a brand-new world of opportunity, risk, and struggle. Even as young people hated competition, they respected the role that it had played in their parents' rise.

In the fall of 2020, a nonfiction student named Yin Limei interviewed her mother about her work history. In the 1990s and early 2000s, the woman's *danwei*, or work unit, had been a state-owned grain wholesaler in remote Yunnan province. The work atmosphere had been profoundly noncompetitive; employees had few opportunities for advancement, and the inefficient grain bureau was propped up by the government. Inevitably, the changes that were happening elsewhere in China finally descended upon the grain wholesaler. Yin Limei described the stoic response of her mother and her colleagues when they learned that their old life was over:

> One day at the end of 2004, the Grain Management office held a staff meeting. At this meeting, all employees were formally notified that their work *danwei* would be abolished. . . . I asked my mother if any of them had any overreactions at the meeting, and she told me no. It seemed that they knew everything, or maybe nothing. No one was surprised, and no one was angry. After the end, everyone did not communicate too much, and everyone acted as if this was just a normal meeting.

Yin Limei's mother was roughly the same age as my Fuling students, whose classroom environment had also been relatively noncompetitive. All of them had been admitted based on *gaokao* scores, but in those days most high schools hadn't yet reached a stage of intense strategy and preparation. My Fuling students never wrote essays about their exam experience, and I never heard them refer to a specific score or cutoff. Students sometimes described the joy they had felt at learning that they would enter university, but they didn't describe the process itself. For a teacher, there was no equivalent of the Hengshui font, the stomatology elite, or the other random *gaokao* details that I picked up twenty years later at Sichuan University. The exam came up so rarely that I didn't mention it in *River Town*.

Much later, I learned that Emily had considered sitting the *gaokao* again. She was young for her grade, and her teachers and parents believed that she could probably test into a better university if she studied for another year. This practice eventually became more common—a number of my Sichuan University students had spent an extra year working to improve their scores. But Emily decided against it, because she was satisfied with basically any college. As a student, she never talked to me about her grades in my class, which was typical. Adam and I quickly realized that the kids in our sections weren't motivated by scores, and we rarely put numbers or letter grades on assignments. Students were satisfied with general encouragement and feedback, and grades seemed to make no difference to their futures.

After accepting the government-assigned teaching jobs, they entered a working world that operated under the old system. But changes were on the horizon, just as they had been for Yin Limei's mother. Among the Fuling students, the handful who migrated were the first to experience intense competition, although sometimes they didn't recognize it as such. Anry, the student who traveled to Shanghai in the wake of his older brother's dynamite accident, said that he felt better after joining the migrants in the city square. His initial reaction was a sense of solidarity: at that moment, he didn't see the others as competitors. "Everybody else was doing the same thing," he remembered, years later. "So I thought that I would be fine."

Over time, Anry's perspective on competition changed. He thrived at DBTel, the Taiwanese company where he found his second job. He liked the sensation of rising in the company's hierarchy, and he realized that it helped to enroll in night courses. In 1999, the factory began manufacturing cell phones for Motorola, and the American company requested that some Chinese employees receive training in management. Anry was one of twenty employees selected for the course. In a sense, this represented the second phase of Anry's formal education in American culture and practices. The first phase had occurred courtesy of the U.S. government, through the Peace Corps volunteers in Fuling. Now, in the second phase, Anry was educated by an American corporation.

In 1986, an engineer at Motorola had developed a quality-control management system called Six Sigma. According to the theory, a person who correctly follows a rigorous Six Sigma process should be able to manufacture a product with a statistically infinitesimal chance of defects. Six Sigma became so successful that in the 1990s it was picked up by other large American firms, including General Electric and Honeywell. By the end of the decade, as manufacturing moved across the Pacific, Six Sigma was introduced to some Chinese factories.

At Anry's plant, Motorola provided instructors who were both American and Chinese. The course met twice every week for a year and a half. It was given an American-style abbreviation, QSR: Quality System Review. The goal was to prepare the twenty employees so that they could implement Six Sigma and then teach the practices to everybody else at the factory.

For Anry, Six Sigma had the force of a religious awakening. The early part of his working life had been essentially passive: he left Sichuan because of his brother's tragic accident; he went to Shanghai because a fellow villager happened to be there; he accepted whatever jobs he could get. But now he started to grasp the importance of system, process, and competition. Suddenly, he had agency—by working hard, he had distinguished himself enough to be chosen for the Six Sigma course.

The factory was massive, with more than eight thousand employees, but the culture quickly changed. Anry and the other Six Sigma students implemented rigid protocols for manufacturing, and they held seminars. During the workday, they instructed assembly-line staff. They introduced

new terminology like ppm, or "parts per million." In America, Six Sigma
had a quality target of 3.4 ppm—an average of 3.4 defective products out
of every million produced. In 1999, before Anry's company introduced
the Six Sigma course, the factory averaged more than five thousand defective products for every million. By 2001, that figure was twenty. In the
span of only two years, they had reduced manufacturing errors by 99.6
percent.

Anry couldn't believe how quickly a factory of such size could change.
His own conversion was also complete, and that year he embarked on a
new career as a Six Sigma evangelist. He left DBTel, set up a private consulting business, and went on the road. He traveled to factories across
the eastern provinces—Jiangsu, Zhejiang, Anhui, Shandong—and gave
presentations about the American management system.

"They didn't have any clear work instructions," Anry remembered of
the factories, years later. "They didn't have official documents. Workers
just relied on experience. It was all trial and error, and people learned
things directly from others, by word of mouth. I told them that you have
to define your parameters, you have to document your operations. You
need work instructions. You need standards. You need basic process
control."

Anry's consulting company thrived, and he hired a half dozen employees. He bought a car and an apartment, and he no longer worried
about money. Over time, during follow-up visits to factories, he observed
the ways in which their standards and safety had been dramatically improved by Six Sigma. He saw himself as a teacher of foreign ideas—in
that sense, he was fulfilling the mission of his original training. Instead
of applying the English language that he had learned from Peace Corps
volunteers, he was spreading Motorola's management ideas.

He rarely returned to Sichuan, although he still sent money to his
disabled brother every month. He stayed in close contact with two of his
roommates from the Fuling dormitory, North and Youngsea. All three
boys had come from poor rural backgrounds, and none of them had been

particularly good students in my class. But they stood out by virtue of charisma and appearance, especially Youngsea. He was strikingly handsome, with blue-black hair, large round eyes, and a high, aquiline nose. In a class populated entirely by Han Chinese, Youngsea looked almost as if he belonged to a different ethnic group. Like Anry, he was a poetic soul who flouted the college rules against dating. Youngsea successfully wooed a girl in the Chinese department, writing her poems in the classical tradition. He had chosen "Youngsea" for his English name because it was literal translation of his Chinese *biming*, or pen name.

Youngsea was only the second person to enter college from his remote village in northeastern Sichuan. After graduation, he accepted the government-assigned teaching job at a middle school near his hometown, where he earned the equivalent of a little more than thirty dollars a month. Hoping to supplement this income, Youngsea bought two cheap keyboards and set up a private night course in typing at his school. People had started to hear about the importance of computers, and dozens of parents signed up their kids for Youngsea's course. He taught in assembly-line fashion. Behind each keyboard, twenty students lined up, and when they got to the front, they had two minutes to practice typing. After the time was up, Youngsea sounded an alarm, and another child took his turn. Tuition for each class was the equivalent of about twenty-five cents. There was so much interest that Youngsea soon earned more money from the private course than he did from his full-time job.

Initially, the cadres at the school didn't know how to respond to Youngsea's success. It wasn't yet common for children to take *buxi* supplemental classes, but families were starting to have enough disposable income to afford such things. Initially, the cadres did what cadres usually do when confronted with anything new—they banned the class. They told Youngsea that he couldn't engage in a sideline endeavor on school property. But parents complained, and other officials noted that entrepreneurship was being encouraged across the country; after all, this was exactly the kind of thing that Deng Xiaoping had wanted. Soon, the school reversed its position, and the children returned to Youngsea's assembly-line typing class.

After a year, Youngsea had saved some money, and he transferred his teaching job to a training institute in Fuling. He began dating a woman who was so beautiful that she seemed out of place in the small city. "Everywhere she went, men would proposition her and harass her," Youngsea remembered, years later. The woman, whom I'll call Lin, worked at a shop where the boss's younger brother became so infatuated with her that she felt unsafe. Every afternoon, Youngsea sent two students from his institute's martial-arts department to escort Lin home. But he realized that this was a short-term solution. "I knew that the only way to keep her was to become a big boss," he said. "If I was a boss, she could work with me, and men would leave her alone."

At the training institute, a retired teacher in her sixties was impressed by Youngsea's energy and drive. When he told her about his dream of becoming a boss, the retired teacher offered to lend him the equivalent of more than a thousand dollars. It was 2000, and successful entrepreneurs in small cities like Fuling had started buying cell phones, so Youngsea opened a shop downtown. Lin helped manage the store, and the business thrived. Her beauty was one foundation for success—when men saw the woman, they often stopped to browse phones.

In less than four months, Youngsea paid off the loan from the retired teacher. He had taken a leave of absence from the training institute, but now he quit for good, in order to focus on business. In addition to cell phones, his shop stocked other electronic devices, including walkie-talkies. Initially, Youngsea thought that the walkie-talkies were outdated, but then they started flying off the shelves.

It took him a while to figure out what was happening. Construction companies used walkie-talkies to communicate on building sites, where workers typically didn't have cell phones. Every time a company expanded, it hired more workers, and the workers needed more walkie-talkies. Invariably, the company returned to the same dealer, in order to buy devices that operated on the same frequency. In the early 2000s, it seemed that every Chinese construction company was growing at an explosive rate, especially in the region of the Three Gorges Dam.

Youngsea realized that he had stumbled onto every entrepreneur's fantasy: a fast-growing market niche that was completely unexploited. "It was possible to make so much more money from walkie-talkies than cell phones," he remembered. "But nobody else knew this. I was the first one to figure it out in Fuling." He opened a second shop, and within a year he had saved more money than he had ever imagined. Soon, another competitor set up a walkie-talkie business in Fuling. "We had battles!" Youngsea said happily, when he remembered this time. "It was like a real fight, with each of us trying to find an edge. But I had started first, and he was never able to catch up."

Later in life, Youngsea described this period in terms that were almost fable-like. The competition was intoxicating: he loved figuring out his business rival's strategies and finding ways to counter them. Initially, Youngsea's main motivation had been a desire to protect his girlfriend, but as time passed, and as he grew richer, it was as if money numbed this desire. "What we had was true love," he said. "But at that time the drive for money was stronger than anything else. She was going back and forth from home to the shop, working constantly. We bought an apartment and a car together. We were so busy; I was doing business all the time."

When Lin wanted to have a child, Youngsea resisted. "I thought it wasn't the right time," he remembered. New opportunities kept cropping up; it didn't make sense to start a family yet. He expanded into Chongqing, where walkie-talkies led him to other high-demand products: alarm systems, video intercoms, parking-lot management systems. Each new success seemed to lead Youngsea to another product. He bought and sold real estate; he set up a construction company. In downtown Chongqing, he began to erect billboards that he rented out to advertising agencies.

Periodically, Lin talked about marriage and a child, but Youngsea always put it off. By the time he was finally ready, five years after they started dating, a businessman from out of town had begun to pursue Lin. Initially, Youngsea didn't take the threat seriously. By now, he was a millionaire many times over, and he had overwhelmed every business competitor in Fuling and Chongqing. It took him by surprise when, at the height of his success, Lin left him.

For Youngsea, the fable had two endings. As a businessman, he won; as a lover, he lost. In his mind, these outcomes were connected: he believed that Lin had left him because he was too distracted by the demands of building his conglomerate. Years later, he spoke openly about his regret, but there was also a sense of fairness. He had deserved to win in business, just as he had deserved to lose in love. In both cases, there was a clear connection between his actions and the final outcome. Youngsea's realization was similar to that of his friend Anry: there is agency in competition.

Like other members of the Reform generation, Youngsea and Anry had grown up without anything that resembled a faith. When their parents were young, Maoism effectively functioned in this way, and people worshipped the leader and the Party with a religious fervor. But the Cultural Revolution and other disastrous policies mostly ruined this belief. After 1978, when China began to transition to its new economy, the ideological vacuum was slowly filled by other things: materialism, nationalism, even traditional religion.

In the 1990s, I avoided mentioning religion in the classroom because students couldn't seem to take it seriously. They impressed me as true atheists—this part of their Marxist indoctrination seemed to have been highly effective. But over time, these ideas changed. Some of the more adventurous students, like Emily, explored exotic faiths—for a while in Shenzhen, she attended Baha'i meetings. Willy, who also liked foreign ideas, joined a Christian church in Zhejiang.

Even the more conservative students reconsidered their atheism. In 2016, my annual survey focused on faith, and twenty-seven out of thirty-three respondents said that they believed in God. Twenty-eight believed in *baoying*, the Buddhist concept of karmic retribution. A clear majority—twenty-three—had visited a place of worship during the previous year. "I am a Party member, so I am not allowed to do that," one woman wrote, and then continued, "But I like going to the Buddhist temple."

Unlike the Abrahamic religions, the traditional Chinese concept of faith didn't emphasize exclusivity. This centuries-old pattern seemed to reassert itself among my students. In Zhejiang, Willy joined the Christian church, but he also went to Buddhist temples, and eventually he decided that he preferred the latter. "I think the Chinese local God works much better than Jesus," he wrote on my survey. He explained that he seemed to have better luck when he was visiting the temple. Such pragmatism was typical among former students, who also tended to be flexible. "I want to believe in Jesus, but there is no church here," one woman wrote. "So I have to believe in the Chinese God."

They often perceived religion in competitive terms. The issue wasn't whether an individual felt a call from God; it had more to do with how each religion measured up in terms of accessibility, effectiveness, and community. In truth, the bedrock faith of their generation was competition. People who grew up during the Reform years believed in striving, and they believed in self-improvement. In a fast-changing world, competition provided both structure and meaning, process and outcome. It wasn't much different from *baoying*, karmic retribution. This was the agency of individuals like Anry and Youngsea: they believed that decisions have consequences, and that people often get what they deserve. As with many faiths, the respect for competition was passed on to the next generation, which was one reason why my Sichuan University students were so tolerant of the *gaokao* and other brutal educational practices. They complained about involution, but deep inside they believed the same thing as their parents: that the world was made for strivers.

———

Even when members of the Reform generation succeeded, they rarely rested on their laurels. For one thing, they were often responsible for managing the competitive strategies of less fortunate family members. This was especially true for favored younger siblings like Willy and Anry, whose educations had benefited from the sacrifices of elder brothers. Willy's two older brothers both became laborers, and he monitored their careers closely. In 2008, during the financial crisis, Willy helped his middle brother move to Zhejiang. Many of Willy's students had entrepreneur parents, and he was able to use this network to help his brother get established as an air-conditioner repairman.

Initially, the job was good, and the brother eventually took his new trade back to Sichuan, where third- and fourth-tier cities were growing fast. After five years, Willy sensed that the air-conditioner trade was played out. In the intensely competitive environment of post-millennium China, people had to stay nimble, and Willy decided that his brother should enter the elevator trade. He explained his thinking in an email to me:

> During hot weather, many people can endure without air condition-
> ing, and in winter, the usage of air conditioners in Sichuan is even
> less. So I told [my brother] that regardless of residents' financial sit-
> uation, elevators must be installed. When the elevator is out of
> order, it needs to be repaired immediately. Moreover, regular eleva-
> tor maintenance is necessary for safety. After a person owns a car,
> they can often ignore it, not care for it, and neglect its maintenance.
> However, it is different for elevators. They require constant atten-
> tion.

In 2013, Willy's brother took the advice, and he learned the elevator trade by working on a repair crew. For a number of years, he earned a decent living, but then his income began to decline. In the past, Willy would have guided him to a new specialty, but now it had become harder to find promising trades, because every field was devolving into *neijuan*.

In Fuling, North also suffered elevator involution. In 2019, when I first visited, North had building sites all around the city, with relatively few competitors. By July of the following year, more than a dozen new elevator companies had sprouted up. North complained that many of these outfits made lowball bids and then cut corners. It had also become more difficult for North to negotiate with residents, especially those who lived on lower floors. These individuals paid nothing for a new elevator, because they wouldn't use it, so they generally agreed to a project. But they had a tendency to change their minds as construction proceeded. After an elevator was installed, upper-floor property values increased dramatically, whereas those of the lower floors changed relatively little. The downstairs people couldn't bear to look up and see their neighbors getting benefits.

In July, North took me to a project that was having problems. It was almost finished—next to the building, the new shaft of glass and steel was gleaming in the morning light. A week earlier, some lower-floor residents had deliberately sabotaged the project's electric supply, in order to halt construction on the final touches. There had been angry confrontations with upstairs neighbors, who called North for help.

When we arrived, a man in his forties took out a tape measure and started complaining about the size of the elevator's entrance. Then he claimed that everybody would get stuck with high electricity bills. "And what about maintenance?" he said.

"Neither has anything to do with you," North said. "If you use the elevator, you pay. If you don't use it, you pay nothing."

The man swore in dialect: "The devil's own uncle knows! We are talking about those people upstairs—what if they sell their apartments, or if the elevator has to be fixed?"

"Since you aren't using the elevator, none of those things concern you," North said calmly. He produced a document with a state seal. The top read, in large letters: "Building Project Permit."

"Everything has been approved," North said. "You can see it here."

A woman in her thirties wearing a pink T-shirt began to shout at North. "You have made your mistakes!" she said. "A prime minister's belly should be broad enough for a boat!" The phrase basically means: Be magnanimous.

North spoke gently and pointed to the permit; after a while, the man took out the tape measure again. For most of an hour, the argument continued, with each side flourishing its prop to onlookers. Finally, the woman in the pink T-shirt stalked off, and the crowd began to dissipate. "If you have any problem, you can always call me," North said. He held up the permit again. "But all of this has been approved. It's all legal."

He had parked his Volkswagen nearby, and we got back into the car. The vehicle still looked new, and there was still a sheet of cardboard on the passenger-side floorboard. While driving, North told me that the argument had all been a performance intended to prepare for further negotiations. Now he would have to go door-to-door on the upper floors, figuring out how much people would be willing to pay their downstairs neighbors to stop interfering. "But they won't push it too far," he said. "That woman is a government official."

The woman in pink hadn't mentioned her job, but North had discovered earlier that she was a cadre. His strategy was to learn as much as possible about residents' backgrounds. The woman's status emboldened her to a certain point, but it also reduced her appetite for serious conflict. At such a sensitive time, nobody wanted to be seen as a problem.

In some ways, involution had been perfect for the pandemic. Years of ever-intensifying competition had taught people to work hard, and they were willing to engage in repetitive tasks like the health reports, the door-to-door surveys, and the contact tracing. When North argued with the residents, nobody wore a mask, but there was no fear of contagion, because disease control had been so effective. There were few places in the world where life felt as normal as it did in China that summer.

Most citizens took pride in the fact that their country had recovered so quickly after the initial disaster in Wuhan. Sometimes, though, I met a thoughtful individual who worried about the precedents that might get established. In Shanghai, I interviewed Gary Liu, a prominent economist and the founder of the National Affairs Financial Review Institute, a private think tank. Liu feared that the pandemic justified authoritarian structures, and he saw it as a black-swan event that could, in the long run, move China in the wrong direction. "The pandemic is a very exceptional situation," he said. "You can't make a long-term conclusion based on an exceptional situation."

In a broader sense, I wondered how long people could sustain the work routines that had been common even before the pandemic. North had already enjoyed a long and productive career, and he had sent his son off to college, but he was still working as hard as somebody in his twenties. Anry and Youngsea were doing the same thing, despite all their success. People sometimes referred to *tangping*, or "lying flat," a kind of disengagement that was supposed to be a counterpoint to involution. But I saw little evidence that citizens were committed to *tangping*. From my experiences at Chengdu Experimental and Sichuan University, it seemed clear that future generations were also being trained to tolerate intense competition and work.

Of course, these were both elite institutions, at least by provincial standards. But similar patterns seemed true at lower levels. That year, a girl in my nonfiction class researched a profile of a middling student at a middling high school in a fourth-tier Sichuanese city. The student was preparing for the *gaokao*, and she clearly had no chance of testing into anything close to a 985 or 211 university. Her practice scores were mediocre, and she couldn't afford *buxi* tutorials; the instruction at her school wasn't very good. Nevertheless, the girl sat in front of her books for hours every day, doing whatever she could to grind it out. The equivalent student in America was probably spending very little time on academics; she would be enjoying herself with friends or engaging in hobbies or extracurriculars. In my opinion, this was one of the biggest differences between China and the United States. In China, the intensely competitive environment seemed standard across all groups: from elite to lower class, from childhood to middle age.

And poverty was still recent enough that many Chinese had yet to shake the psychology of financial insecurity. Even after people became successful, they often maintained significant contact with working-class issues through their extended families. It wasn't surprising that a relatively wealthy man like Willy continued to describe himself as "lower class," because he remained responsible for family members who were in fact poorly educated and economically marginal. Periodically, Willy sent updates about the brother who worked with elevators:

> During the Spring Festival, he called me from the construction site and told me that one of his coworkers fell from the sixth floor of an elevator shaft and lost consciousness immediately. Later, I found out that the elevator installation company didn't provide them with any accident insurance or anything. I was worried that the worker would die. However, he was intensely treated and didn't seem to suffer any disabilities, but the compensation for the injured worker still hasn't been settled.
>
> Now, my second brother is a contracting person for installation work. He has a team of five people, including his own son, my nephew. I'm always concerned about their safety awareness, so when I call them, I frequently remind them to prioritize safety.

Anry told me that one reason for his obsession with Six Sigma was the way it reduced accidents in Chinese factories. In the United States, it had become common to view China in narrowly competitive terms, and Americans were infuriated by the way that business, technology, and ideas had crossed the Pacific. For somebody like Anry, though, these transfers seemed almost humanistic, because they drastically reduced poverty and danger. Having applied American concepts to Chinese manufacturing, Anry had witnessed how quickly things improved, but he also knew that it still wasn't good enough. His third brother, the one who had quit school in order to support Anry's studies, worked at a Shanghai factory that produced computer cases and cables. One day, Anry's brother was repairing an injection-molding machine when there was a high-voltage malfunction. He was electrocuted and died instantly.

After the accident, Anry shut down his consulting business. He had been happy in Shanghai, but he was still supporting his disabled eldest brother, and now there had been another family tragedy. Anry decided it was time to move closer to relatives.

In Chongqing, he found a well-paying job as a quality-control auditor with the International Automotive Task Force, a group of companies that seek to improve auto-parts manufacturing. Anry enjoyed the work, which allowed him to apply his knowledge of Six Sigma and factory consulting. He also liked using English to communicate with people involved in auto parts around the world. He no longer used the name Anry—it sounded too strange to foreigners, who would never understand the poetic anger that had once inspired a young man trying to escape rural poverty. Nowadays, he called himself Allen, after Allen Iverson. Like many Chinese basketball fans of his generation, he admired the American guard as a scrappy, undersize player who had overcome adversity.

 CHAPTER TEN

Common Sense

November 2020

AT SICHUAN UNIVERSITY, THE ONLY STUDENT PUBLICATION THAT was not under the oversight of the Party was called *Changshi*, or "Common Sense." The name had been chosen, in part, as an homage to the famous pamphlet written by Thomas Paine shortly before the American Revolution. The Sichuanese *Common Sense* had been founded in 2010, which happened to be the final phase of a relatively open period that ended, in 2012, with the accession of Xi Jinping to the nation's leadership.

During the early Xi years, *Common Sense* was one of a handful of truly independent campus journals. All of these publications were at select 985 universities that were far from the political center of Beijing: Fudan University, Zhejiang University, Sun Yat-sen University, Wuhan University, and Sichuan University. As time passed, and as the political climate became more repressive, some of these publications went dormant, while others struggled to find writers and distribution. Only *Common Sense* thrived—it was by far the most vibrant of any independent student publication in China.

One key to survival was lack of formal structure. The magazine had no masthead, and the publication schedule was erratic. All bylines were fake. Sometimes, an article was attributed to "Jun Jun," which was actually a cat that belonged to a student. *Common Sense* didn't maintain an office or a website, although writers used a WeChat channel to recruit staff and distribute stories.

A degree of disorganization could be advantageous when dealing with Chinese authority. Daniel C. Mattingly, the Yale professor who studied grassroots politics, had analyzed a number of villages in southern China that tried to fight government land expropriations. Mattingly discovered that when villages relied on more formal structures, like traditional lineage associations, they were actually less likely to mount successful resistance. Established organizations created easy targets for the Party, which was experienced at intimidating and co-opting leaders. In contrast, villages that lacked such groups actually did a better job of fighting land grabs. Mattingly wrote: "This is the power of leaderless collective action in China: it is not that no one initiates it, it is that it *appears* that no one does."

A similar pattern could be observed at Sichuan University. In September, when undergraduates succeeded in ending the period of the closed campus, it wasn't because they organized a student government or formed a leadership committee that met with Party officials. Instead, students got their way because too many of them were independently hopping over walls and getting fast-food orders squeezed between the bars of the fence. At some level, the cadres feared the young, which is generally true in any authoritarian system.

Common Sense also followed a public strategy of leaderless action, although there was clearly enough structure at the magazine to get things done. Staff writers occasionally reached out to me with invitations to events or meetings. During my first semester on campus, a *Common Sense* staffer had been involved in the play based on *1984*, and she was the one who asked me to attend the performance. At the end of that semester, *Common Sense* writers invited me to speak at a conference that marked the publication's tenth anniversary. They held the event at a discreet site off campus, and more than fifty people attended, including alumni as well as current students. The staff presented me with copies of old issues, many of which had provocative covers. One magazine from 2011 featured a photograph of two men holding hands, along with a headline: "Comrade, Are You OK? A Record of the Gay Community Around You and Me."

Nowadays, it was too risky to print magazines, and *Common Sense* existed only online. Whenever a new issue appeared, the WeChat channel posted a QR code that could be used to download stories. Issues were also distributed via pdf, which was a common way for underground writers to publish in China.

Every semester, one or two *Common Sense* staffers took my nonfiction class. None of them mentioned the affiliation in their applications, and sometimes I didn't learn about a student's connection until I saw her at a *Common Sense* event. When I taught Serena, she wasn't connected to the magazine, but she became a staffer during her senior year. She was growing more interested in journalism, and another student invited her to join. Like many of her peers, Serena impressed me as largely disengaged from politics. But she was curious and adventurous, and she seemed thrilled by the illicit energy of *Common Sense*.

Serena told me that the vast majority of staff writers were women. Of the few men who wrote for the magazine, a large percentage seemed to be gay. There weren't many writers majoring in journalism. Again, this was partly an issue of structure: inside the journalism department, professors and staff could monitor students more closely, and they advised undergraduates to stay away from *Common Sense*. Journalism majors were aware that their job prospects could suffer if they were caught writing something sensitive for the magazine.

Despite the apparent lack of leadership at *Common Sense*, there was in fact a chief editor. She was a graduate student in the humanities, and when we met for an interview, she told me that she didn't intend to become a journalist in the future. Like Serena, the editor didn't seem particularly political, and she shrugged when I asked about the magazine's connection to Thomas Paine. "I haven't read that book," she said. "I just know it had something to do with social problems." In the trick-mirror world of Chinese censorship, the fact that the woman was not an obvious candidate for an underground publication made her an obvious candidate for an underground publication. She told me that editors usually held the position for short terms, which made it harder for authorities to figure out who was in charge.

Some *Common Sense* alumni had become successful in journalism and other fields, and they quietly contributed the minimal funding necessary to run the magazine and host periodic events. The chief editor told me that some faculty members at Sichuan University were also supportive. When I asked why the authorities hadn't tried harder to shut down the magazine, she said that for the most part writers didn't push too far.

"We can't make a big change," the chief editor told me. "But maybe we can change small things, like some problems on campus. I'm pessimistic, but I think there are some small things we can do. Sometimes we have an article that's read by fifty thousand people."

Periodically, Serena stopped by my office to discuss *Common Sense* projects. That year, she wrote a number of stories about campus issues that had been kept out of Party-controlled publications. One piece featured an undergraduate who had filed a lawsuit against the university for low-quality cafeteria food. It became the most popular *Common Sense* story of the semester, with more than fifty thousand downloads.

In order to report, Serena relied on subterfuges that were standard at the publication. Writers never used their phones to contact people, and they didn't give out their real numbers. Instead, they set up fake accounts on social media sites. Sometimes, a writer interviewed two or three individuals and then turned them into a composite character, in order to protect identities. *Common Sense* staffers also regularly interviewed people without telling them that they were being interviewed. Such practices would be considered highly unethical at a foreign publication, and in a way, it was terrible training for a young journalist. But this was the nature of reporting in an authoritarian climate. When risks are high, and when the people in charge don't have to follow clear rules, a reporter can justify almost any kind of evasion.

Every semester in nonfiction, I gave a lesson about Georg Simmel, a founding figure in the field of sociology. In 1908, Simmel, who was German, published an influential essay called "The Stranger." The title refers to an outsider who comes to a community:

> His position in this group is determined, essentially, by the fact that he has not belonged to it from the beginning, that he imports qualities into it, which do not and cannot stem from the group itself.

The stranger might be somebody with a different nationality, ethnicity, or faith. Simmel, who came from an assimilated Jewish family, describes the European Jew as a "classical example" of the stranger. He also mentions traders who come from outside a neighborhood. A man who delivers packages or picks up garbage can play the role of a stranger, and so can a migrant worker. Sometimes, people tell things to the stranger that they wouldn't tell their relatives, friends, or neighbors. The stranger is in the community, but not of the community:

> He is not radically committed to the unique ingredients and peculiar tendencies of the group, and therefore approaches them with the specific attitude of "objectivity." But objectivity does not simply involve passivity and detachment; it is a particular structure composed of distance and nearness, indifference and involvement.

I reminded my students to be alert to strangers while reporting. In Egypt, I had written about Chinese traders in remote Muslim communities, because their roles and observations were so unusual. Migrants like Anry, Youngsea, North, and Willy, all of whom had made the transition from country to city, from poverty to prosperity, were also strangers. Stranger status was probably one reason why young women and gay men were more likely to gravitate toward *Common Sense*. These individuals were somewhat alienated from traditional structures of power and authority, which made them more willing to view the system critically.

Of course, I was also a stranger. At Sichuan University, *Common Sense* staffers sought me out, and others told me things because they knew that I wasn't part of the system. But my outsider status also made it hard to give advice. My role was temporary: at any given moment, I might feel the weight of authority, but I could always leave China. When Serena talked to me about *Common Sense*, I advised her not to internalize the reporting strategies that would be unacceptable at most publications. But I had no easy solutions. In the U.S., a university education in journalism is partly about establishing a foundation of responsibility and idealism. For a young Chinese writer, though, lessons in cynicism tend to come early.

That fall, a nonfiction student named Katherine wrote about her experience as a summer intern. Katherine was a journalism major, and her internship was at a state-run television station in Beijing, where she assisted a young on-camera correspondent. The correspondent was pretty and ambitious, and she had already perfected the standard state-television presentation: heavy makeup, fake smile, and a gaze that never wavers even in the midst of the most dishonest Partyspeak.

As an intern from a provincial university, Katherine was also a stranger, and she noticed things that surprised her. Despite the young television correspondent's public success, her daily life seemed marginal. She lived in a run-down apartment on Beijing's Sixth Ring Road, in the distant suburbs, and her base salary wasn't even five hundred dollars a month. She earned much of her income through payoffs for stories that were basically corrupt promotions. This arrangement was so crude that Katherine quickly learned the mechanics. For a public-relations story, the subject paid the station, which in turn gave a fee of about seventy dollars to the correspondent and the cameraman. They split the money sixty-forty. The correspondent earned slightly more because she had to do a little preparation work.

Near the end of summer, Katherine overheard the correspondent arguing with her superior at the station. The young woman wanted to pursue a more critical story, but the superior flatly refused. Later in the day she was sent out to do another paid puff piece.

After the internship, Katherine returned to Chengdu, and she occasionally corresponded by text with the correspondent. The woman began to open up, and Katherine noticed a certain sadness beneath the polished exterior. In her essay, she quoted from one of their text conversations:

"To be honest, the first time I saw you, I was a little scared of you."

"I understand. After all, our daily work always has a sense of something plastic. News production today is not the same as it was ten years ago."

"Do you hate those daily tasks?"

"I definitely don't like it. I also have my journalistic ideals."

"Then why are you doing this?"

She sent a message that ended in italics.

" *'May your choices reflect your hopes, not your fears.'* —*Nelson Mandela*."

———

When I started at Sichuan University, I planned to take a break from writing. I agreed to a relatively heavy teaching load, and I intended to use any free time to do research in Fuling and other places around the region. I figured that after two or three years I would transition back to writing full-time. But all those plans were upended by the pandemic and the conflict between the U.S. and China. By the second half of 2020, there were only about thirty American journalists left in the country, because so many others had been expelled.

My own status was hard to define. Because I wasn't currently registered in China as a journalist, I wasn't targeted by the expulsions. It was possible to evade the issue with language: in Wuhan, Fang Fang made a point of describing me as a *zuojia*, not a *jizhe*—a writer rather than a journalist. But there was no guaranteed protection for a foreign professor who also wrote about current events. I could teach nonfiction, but that didn't mean that I was approved to practice nonfiction.

After the pandemic began, I decided to research and publish stories. As the country whipsawed through the initial effects of the virus, my articles prompted anger from both sides. During the first phase of the pandemic, I described the mistakes in Wuhan, the death of Li Wenliang, and the problems of remote schooling, and some Chinese nationalists attacked me online. A couple of months later, when I wrote about how subsequent policies had succeeded in eliminating the virus in most parts of China, criticism came from outside, with foreigners claiming that I served as a Party propagandist. After that, the pendulum swung again, and Little Pinks expressed outrage that I reported in Wuhan. Michael Berry, Fang Fang's American translator, subsequently published an account of the ways in which the novelist and others were attacked by ultra-nationalists. These radicals often took a competitive approach to the pandemic, taking pleasure in American failures. Berry quoted some of the comments that appeared on Chinese social media:

No matter how many writers like Michael Berry and Peter Hessler that the American fascists hire, their words will never be able to bring back the 210,000 lives that have been lost.

In the Chinese system, it was unclear who should take responsibility for my writing. Sichuan University and SCUPI were in charge of my teaching, but these institutions had no history of oversight for foreign journalists. That role fell to the Information Department at the Ministry of Foreign Affairs, but the Information Department didn't handle teachers. Within the bureaucracy, I was somewhere between different silos, and there was always a chance that nobody would do anything. One question was whether online attacks would become insistent enough to motivate officials to action. Pressure could come from both sides: even vocal critics of Chinese government oppression might say things that made such oppression more likely. At the start of the fall semester, Geremie Barmé, a prominent Australian sinologist, published an online essay in which he attacked me for not being critical enough of the Party. Barmé highlighted my legal exposure:

> I would suggest that Mr. Hessler is to my understanding engaging in unaccredited reporting, something that, strictly speaking, is illegal in China.

By making such a comment, Barmé may have put subtle pressure on the university and SCUPI. The more that people thought about my status, the more likely it was to cause a problem. But throughout the second half of 2020, nobody from the university called me in for a conversation. During the summer, after police in Zhejiang questioned me about my reporting, I learned that they notified the university. But no dean or Party official ever mentioned it. Every day, I hoped the silence would continue.

During this period, I stayed in touch with diplomats at the U.S. consulate in Chengdu. The consulate was situated to the south of downtown, in a complex that had been completed in 1994. Back then, rice fields bordered the consulate walls, and the main six-story building, a residential

complex, was the tallest structure in the area. During the early years of
the Peace Corps, volunteers were sometimes invited to the consulate for
Thanksgiving dinner or Fourth of July parties. For us, it felt like an American oasis in the city's southern hinterlands.

Since then, Chengdu's population had more than doubled. The consulate remained essentially unchanged, although its tallest building was
no longer used because it was deemed unsafe after the Great Sichuan
Earthquake of 2008. Outside the consulate walls, the rice fields were long
gone; nowadays the complex was shadowed on three sides by high-rises
of twenty or more stories. It was the architectural equivalent of the way
I felt when first-year students stood up and loomed over me. In all respects, the Americans were getting shorter in China.

For U.S. diplomats in the People's Republic, 2020 had been the worst
year in recent memory. In January, the Trump administration had abruptly
ended the Peace Corps program; not long after that, they also shut down
Fulbright exchanges to China and Hong Kong. During the pandemic, the
State Department evacuated all family members and nonessential personnel. Meanwhile, the trade war was ongoing, and journalists on both
sides were expelled, and officials from each country blamed the other for
the pandemic. For American diplomats, the job had become basically
impossible.

In July, the Trump administration ordered the closure of the Chinese
consulate in Houston. The U.S. accused the consulate staff of spying,
and the Chinese were given seventy-two hours to vacate the Houston
premises. The announcement was made on a Tuesday. All year, the nations had followed a pattern of tit-for-tat diplomacy, which meant that
on Friday morning, after the seventy-two hours expired, the Chinese
were bound to retaliate.

On Thursday evening, I sat down with a diplomat from the American consulate. We met in a bar a couple of blocks from the compound.
Earlier that afternoon, the *South China Morning Post*, an independent
Hong Kong newspaper, had reported that the Chinese were going to shut

down the Chengdu consulate. But nobody in the government had confirmed the news, and the diplomat wasn't convinced that the Chinese had made their decision.

He said that under normal circumstances the U.S. would not have closed the Chinese outpost in Houston. "They were spying there," he said. "But everybody is spying. That's not new." Usually, if such activities become egregious, the host country might call in consulate staff for an angry dressing-down. "You can do something like that, to send a message," the diplomat said. "Or you can expel a handful of diplomats. There are many other things you can do before closing the consulate."

He believed that the upcoming U.S. presidential election had probably been a factor. The Trump administration included a number of staunch China hawks who wanted a more aggressive policy toward the People's Republic, and now they realized that their time might be limited. "The window is closing," the diplomat said. "Six months from now we will potentially have a new president."

The U.S. had recently arrested a number of Chinese citizens on accusations of spying, and the State Department was concerned that there could be retaliation. "I worry that Chinese will start going after Americans here," the diplomat told me. "They'll say, 'These people are clearly spies, or they're doing something that's not in line with their visa status.'" He continued, "There's not much we can do to stop that. That worries me. The last thing I'd like to see is somebody sitting in a Chinese jail like Michael Spavor and Michael Kovrig."

Spavor and Kovrig were former Canadian diplomats who had been engaged in business in China. At the end of 2018, they had been arrested on what seemed to be trumped-up charges of espionage. It was another tit-for-tat move, this time in response to a Chinese citizen who was currently being held in Canada for extradition to the U.S.

The diplomat told me that he and his colleagues had been asked to come up with a list of American citizens who could be targets. The possibilities were dwindling, because so many foreigners had left. He mentioned the name of a former State Department employee who was currently doing business in Shanghai. "He could be at risk," he said. Then he paused and looked up. "You could be at risk." He continued, "I don't think that anybody cares about what you're writing. It's just that you are here and there are messages to be sent."

We ordered another drink. The bar was dead; in the past, it had been a popular hangout for foreigners. The diplomat told me that he had wanted to meet before the seventy-two hours expired. "I might be really busy tomorrow," he said, laughing.

I thanked him, and I said that I hoped the Chinese would choose a different target than the Chengdu consulate. But he responded that this wouldn't necessarily be a good thing. If the Chinese wanted to escalate, they might shut down the large American consulate in Hong Kong.

Before saying goodbye, he repeated the warning. "I hate to recommend that you leave China," he said. "But I don't know if I would feel safe if I were you."

Early the next morning, staff at the U.S. consulate noticed an increased police presence on the street outside. On a typical day, five or six Chinese officers were on patrol, but this morning there were fifteen to twenty. In Chinese, the street was called Lingshiguan Lu—"Consulate Road."

Around nine thirty, consular staff observed some figures standing on the roof of a neighboring high-rise. The figures appeared to be security officers. They were looking down at the American compound.

At ten o'clock, the police closed Consulate Road. By now, the American diplomats assumed that they had been chosen as the target of China's retaliation, but the Ministry of Foreign Affairs waited another two hours before issuing a statement. "The current situation between China and the U.S. is something the Chinese side does not want to see," the statement read. "The responsibility lies entirely with the U.S. side." The Americans were given seventy-two hours to vacate the premises in Chengdu.

After the news broke, I biked over to Consulate Road. There were about thirty uniformed officers, along with others who were obviously plainclothes: crew cuts, sunglasses, surgical masks. I had a mask, too— nowadays I wore one whenever I hoped to stand out less as a foreigner. In front of the consulate, a few dozen citizens had gathered, taking pictures. The moment I pulled out my phone, a plainclothes cop was at my side.

"You can't take photographs," he said.

"They're taking photographs," I said. "I'm just doing the same thing."

"*You* can't," he said.

I put the phone away. I walked up and down the street, but the plainclothes man followed closely, so I headed home. Over the next three days, I made periodic visits to Consulate Road, where the crowd of citizens grew larger. People took selfies at the front gate, which was decorated with the official seal of the United States. One afternoon, I heard a woman tell her companions to hurry up with their photos so that they could make it to Dujiangyan, a historical site outside the city. They told me that they were on vacation from Wenzhou, and they had added the doomed American consulate to their tourist itinerary.

The police kept the crowds moving. One day, somebody set off a string of celebratory fireworks in the middle of Consulate Road, and the video went viral, but officers didn't allow it to happen again. I never saw people chanting or carrying anti-American signs. It would have been easy to encourage such activities, but Chinese officials seemed to have decided to keep the scene as controlled as possible.

Inside the compound, the staff was engaged in a protocol known as a destruction plan. The Americans had always minimized the number of classified documents on-site, but there were other papers that needed to be destroyed: calendars, personnel records, visit schedules, anything with names of local contacts. Eight industrial-size paper shredders were staffed by twenty people, who took turns feeding documents into the machines. Another group of employees smashed computers, telephones, and other telecommunications equipment that posed a security risk. Even the pieces of these things wouldn't be disposed of in Chengdu. All broken communications equipment would be packed up and transported by a secure bus to the embassy in Beijing, where American officials would decide what to do with the pieces.

In Houston, the Chinese had followed their own destruction plan, and the exchange had the ritualized air of a particularly wasteful sport. Each event was timed, and there was one home game and one away game. When you were home, you collected whatever you could for propaganda. In Houston, U.S. security agents tailed Chinese consular staff on visits to the Home Depot, where they purchased barrels in which to burn documents. The Home Depot detail was leaked to the American media, which also ran news stories with images of smoke plumes rising from the consulate's courtyard.

In Chengdu, the neighboring high-rises had always posed a security risk. Now the Chinese government arranged cameras on the roof and upper floors, in order to live stream all activity in the consulate's courtyard. Later, the American diplomat told me that one goal was to complete the shredding before the clock ran out, so that they wouldn't have to use fire. "They were clearly set up to get a shot of us burning documents," he said.

Somebody came up with the idea to commission banners that would be visible for the live stream. They hoped that the message—*Ganxie Chengdu*, "Thank you, Chengdu"—would convey a more dignified image than the courtyard fires in Houston. But they knew that any American staff would be followed, so they had the order made at a print shop by a Chengdu resident. Just before the banners were supposed to be ready, the resident was taken into custody and interrogated. She was held for seven hours.

Before the Chinese left the Houston consulate, they had secured the doors and poured glue into the locks. That also made the news—footage of American security officers battering down the front entrance. The staff at the U.S. consulate in Chengdu decided to leave everything open, in order to avoid such images. They finished the shredding well before the deadline. The only paper products left intact were classic novels and other books that had been part of the lending library at the consulate's American Center. The center had been open to Chengdu citizens, who could check out books, join reading groups, and attend cultural events.

Shortly after dawn on the third day, with more than three hours left on the clock, the last American diplomats in Chengdu unlocked the front door. Then they departed out the back in unmarked vehicles. The Chinese live stream seemed to miss that shot, or maybe they determined that it wasn't useful; for whatever reason, it never appeared on state-run media. Nobody ever saw the thank-you banner, either. There was no public record of what Chinese security officers did with the various things they found inside the vacated building, which included, lined up neatly on a shelf, more than a dozen copies of *The Catcher in the Rye*.

The China hawks in the Trump administration had advocated a policy called "decoupling." The goal was for the United States to separate itself from China, especially in the realms of economics and technology, although there was also a desire to reduce diplomacy and person-to-person exchanges. The hawks believed that since the beginning of the Reform era, most benefits of U.S.–China contact had gone to the People's Republic, where prosperity only strengthened the Communist Party.

Initially, the pandemic seemed to accelerate the process of decoupling. The Chinese export economy collapsed, and even after the lockdowns ended it was unclear whether there would be a recovery. Near the end of April, I had met with Li Dewei, an entrepreneur in Chengdu who manufactured sport shoes that he sold on Amazon. Like many Chinese manufacturers, Li targeted the American market, where he typically made more than 70 percent of his sales. But his business was decimated when the virus struck America. The month before I visited, Li had laid off fifty workers—a third of his Chengdu staff.

He told me that things would have been even worse if not for the stimulus checks sent out by the Trump administration. Because Li sold directly to Amazon customers, he could track sales closely. "We check the statistics every day," he said. "After the American government started issuing the money, the next day we saw an increase in sales." By the time of my visit, two weeks into the stimulus program, Li's American sales had almost doubled, although they were still down from normal.

Li had recently discussed strategy with his business partner and other export entrepreneurs. They had concluded that June 2020 would be a critical month. "If by June the virus is totally under control in the U.S. and the E.U., then we can rebound to the normal level," Li told me. But he and the others concluded that the U.S. and other Western countries probably would not handle the pandemic well. Li was also concerned about the ongoing political conflict. His solution was to reduce his American exposure, and he started manufacturing shoes to be sold in China. In his own small way, Li Dewei planned to decouple.

His headquarters were situated in southern Chengdu, not far from the university, and that year I stopped in periodically. Li's background was modest: his mother and father had both grown up on farms, and neither attended university. They had started out as assembly-line workers in a rug factory, and eventually they started a small rug manufacturer of their own. Profits were spent on educating Li and his two siblings. All three children went to college, and Li graduated from Sichuan University. He was a trim, sharp-eyed man in his midthirties, with a serious demeanor that made him seem older.

Over the course of 2020, three things about Li impressed me most. One was that his initial prediction about the pandemic's economic effects turned out to be wrong. The second was that he had no hesitation in abandoning plans that were based on this prediction. In May, he told me that he was having trouble selling in China—like so many domestic markets, the shoe business had reached a point of involution. Meanwhile, Li's American sales continued to recover. In July, he abruptly decided to give up on the Chinese market.

Li concluded that he had been correct about U.S. pandemic failures, but he was wrong about the effects. Now he believed that the worse things were in America, the better his sales would be. "A lot of businesses are closed," he said of the U.S. "People are afraid of going to shops, because of infections, so they want to buy online." His experience seemed common across China: in July, exports rose 7.2 percent compared with the same month a year earlier. At a time when the rest of the world was struggling with the virus, China was booming.

The third thing that impressed me about Li was his ability to understand the American market with zero personal contact. He had never visited the United States, and his spoken English was modest; we always communicated in Mandarin. But he read English well, and he used a VPN to skirt the firewall and access sites like Google Trends. "It would help to go to America, but from the internet we can learn a lot," he said. "America is a free place—so much information is open. That's different from China."

From a distance, Li had developed certain ideas about the U.S. "My thinking is that Americans don't save much," he told me, after describing the way that sales increased in response to stimulus payments. "Whenever they have money, they'll spend it."

He always knew the most recent COVID statistics. On July 2, when I visited his office, he rattled off the number of Americans who had been infected. "Two million six-hundred-and-fifty thousand," he said. "Every day it goes up another thirty to forty thousand. These are not optimistic numbers." He also knew the number of shoes he was shipping to America every day: three thousand pairs. "The U.S. government has been sending out more money recently," he said.

I told him that he was mistaken—there hadn't yet been a second stimulus program. But Li swore that government money was reaching consumers: he could see the impact in sales. The following day, I received an email from the young woman who was renting our family's house in southwestern Colorado. She had sent me a list of things that had appeared in our mailbox, including a CARES Act debit card labeled "Economic Impact." It was in the amount of thirty-four hundred dollars.

I learned that during the past couple of weeks the government had been sending debit cards to citizens who had been missed in April, often because their bank information wasn't on file. Previously, I had wondered why we hadn't received a stimulus check, but I was too busy with life in China to look into it. Now I realized that if I wanted to keep updated on the U.S. government's payment schedule, I could always go to southern Chengdu and ask Li Dewei.

Later, I interviewed Scott R. Baker, an economist at Northwestern University who studied spending habits during the first phase of the pandemic. Baker analyzed high-frequency bank-transaction data for more than thirty thousand consumers, in order to understand the effects of the stimulus program. He observed that during this period Americans spent less on durables; most purchases were for inexpensive items, including the kind of products that often came from China.

I mentioned Li Dewei's post-stimulus sales. "I'm not surprised that he sees that surge so clearly," Baker said. "We see that the majority of spending that does happen goes out in the first week or so after receiving the check." In economic terms, the notion of decoupling seemed like a fantasy. Even during a period of terrible relations and strict pandemic controls, an entrepreneur in Chengdu could tell instantly when the American government sent out checks, because some of that money went into his pocket.

At every session of nonfiction class that October, a boy named Jerry sat in the front row wearing a baseball cap that read "Trump: Keep America Great." Trump's Chinese name begins with "chuan," the same character that appears in Sichuan. "I think that Trump has a special place in Sichuanese hearts because his name starts with 川," Jerry wrote in an email, when I asked where he had found the hat. He said that on Taobao it had cost the equivalent of three dollars, including robot delivery. Jerry referred to Trump as *Chuan Jianguo*, an ironic nickname that paired the president's name with a Communist-era patriotic moniker—essentially, "Make-China-Great-Again Trump." The idea was that despite Trump's anti-China bluster, his lack of strategic thinking would ultimately benefit the People's Republic.

I talked about the election in both of my classes that fall. The subject no longer felt as fraught as it had in 1996, when Adam and I angered the Fuling cadres. Back then, our own insensitivity was partly to blame—it was disrespectful to fill out American ballots in class. But that era had also been much closer to the Tiananmen Square protests of 1989. Nowadays, there hadn't been a significant pro-democracy movement in China for more than three decades, and few citizens seemed to take the possibility seriously. I often wondered if average people would even want to have the right to select their own national leader. In 2017, during my annual survey of former students, I asked if China should become a multiparty democracy, and 73 percent said no. Fewer than 10 percent expected a significant change in China's political system during the next decade.

Many respondents commented that China had been successful under the current arrangement, and they feared that a multiparty system would mean conflict and inefficiency. Other reasons were more cynical:

We already have one corrupt party. It will be much worse if we have more.

No, one corrupt party is enough. We cannot stand more.

We have seen America with multiparty, but you have elected the worst president in human's history.

At Sichuan University, some of my current students followed the election coverage on Fox News. In a detail that was unlikely to appear on any of Fox's promotional materials, the station's website was not blocked by the Communist Party. Anybody who wanted access to CNN, *The New York Times*, and other major American sources had to climb the firewall, but Fox was left untouched, apparently because the Chinese government deemed it unimportant. Students liked watching Fox because they didn't have to go through the hassle of using a VPN.

In class, I showed images from my reporting in Zhejiang province the previous summer. I had visited an entrepreneur named Li Jiang, who had first gone into business in 1995, producing the red Young Pioneer scarves that my daughters and other schoolchildren wore. In 1997, Li expanded into Chinese flags, because Hong Kong returned that year and demand was high. That became Li's pattern: he rode any geopolitical wave that brought the most business. In 2001, after 9/11, he produced mostly American flags for export, and since 2016 he had been making Trump flags and banners. "If people want it, we make it," Li told me. On his desk, a small gay-pride flag sat next to one featuring the face of Muhammad Ali Jinnah, the founder of Pakistan.

I visited another flag manufacturer called Johnin, where a young manager named Jin Gang gave me a tour of the assembly lines. Dozens of women sat at sewing machines stitching flags that read "North Dakota for Trump," "Keep America Great," and "Trump 2024." When I saw the last banner, I wondered if Jin Gang knew something about the future that I didn't. He shrugged and said that all designs were generated by customers. "That's what they asked for," he said.

In class, the students laughed at the assembly-line pictures. On a survey, I asked if the election mattered to them personally, and the majority responded in the affirmative:

> I care about the result because it will affect whether I go to the United States, you know, visa, international student policy, etc.

The most important reason is that it will affect my future plan of studying abroad. Moreover, it will influence where China and America will go in the future—whether they will stick into the cold war.

Also, now the politicians are not as polite as they were in the past. I want to see how crazily the failed candidate's party will behave.

That last comment came from Vincent. He was now a sophomore, and he had enrolled in my nonfiction class. The pandemic hadn't changed his plans for the future: he still intended to study in the United States, where he swore that he would exercise his right to purchase a firearm. When I polled students on who they believed would win the election, Vincent was among the minority who said Biden. Across my classes, 54 percent predicted that Trump would win.

Most other people I talked to seemed to agree. During one of my meetings with Li Dewei, he told me that he thought Trump would win. "He does things badly, but there are some people who like that," he said. When I asked if Li had a personal preference, he said no. "I don't think it's important who gets elected," he said, explaining that even the Trump trade war didn't affect his business. In response to the tariffs, Li had simply raised his Amazon prices by 15 percent. "The tariff is paid by the customer," he said.

Every day, Li combed through Amazon reviews of his shoes. He described this as a *jiaoliu*—an exchange or conversation—and he took pride in how quickly he responded. Early in the pandemic, many American reviewers mentioned slow delivery, so Li contracted with a more expensive but reliable shipping service. When a number of customers complained about shoes with a narrow toe box, Li had some adjustments made at the factory.

He sold his shoes for about thirty dollars per pair, under dozens of brand names. Some of these brands sounded vaguely pedestrian—Feetmat,

Troadlop—whereas others were etymological puzzles: Biacolum, Bengbobar, NYZNIA, Zocavia, Zocania, Zonkim. On Amazon, if a consumer
studied the listings closely, pieces of the puzzle started to connect. The
Feetmat Men's Non Slip Gym Sneakers Lightweight Breathable Athletic
Running Walking Tennis Shoes looked exactly the same as the Biacolum
Men's Running Shoes Non Slip Gym Tennis Shoes Slip Resistant Air Knitted Sneakers Walking Workout Sport Shoes, which in turn appeared
identical to the Troadlop Men's Running Shoes Non Slip Shoes Breathable Lightweight Sneakers Slip Resistant Athletic Sports Walking Gym
Work Shoes.

I came to think of this language as Amazonglish: awkward but basically intelligible, redundant but highly searchable. Product descriptions
often had just enough accuracy to sail past a computerized grammar
check. Troadlop: "The rubber outsole can anti-slip performance." Zonkim: "The fashion knitted upper will keep your feet away from the wet
condition, and create a dry environment for your feet during moving."

One word that never appeared in Amazonglish was *China*. Li described his research as a *jiaoliu*, but the exchange consisted of two one-
way streets. Chinese products went to America, and American money
and information went to China. Nearly half of the top sellers on Amazon—
those with more than a million dollars in annual sales in the U.S.—were
based in China, but they generally didn't advertise their location. They
had figured out that, at least in the low-end market, brand recognition
didn't matter. It was smarter to flood the website with obscure trade-
marks, in order to dominate search results. This was why Li's brand
names were so strange: anything unusual was more likely to be approved quickly by the U.S. Patent and Trademark Office, which typically
rejects a name that's too close to an established brand. Feetmat was brilliant, and so were Troadlop, Bengbobar, Zocavia, and Zocania. Nikey
and Adijas, on the other hand, would have been terrible ideas.

Baker, the economist at Northwestern, had told me that Americans with less money in their bank accounts were more likely to spend stimulus checks quickly. These were Li Dewei's target customers, and his *jiaoliu* gave him glimpses into what the pandemic felt like for lower-income Americans. In reviews, these shoe customers rarely mentioned exercise, sporting events, or leisure activities. They seemed much more likely to wear Feetmat or Troadlop at workplaces that required them to stand. Sometimes they referred to jobs that vanished, along with other problems:

May 6, one-star review:

They were late. Then they were stolen off my porch. I would like a refund immediately.

May 16, one star [on account of "non-slip" tread]:

I'm a cook at dennys and I almost busted my face just from water on our kitchen floor! Super scary!

June 14, five stars:

I got them for work but just found out my work won't be opening back up but I still like them.

July 13, five stars:

Bottom tread doesn't last very long. I was only chased by the police twice while wearing these and they're down to half the tread life!

August 1, one star:

Bought two pairs, didn't return because of the whole pandemic thing (was honestly afraid to get them in mail *nervous chuckle*)

On Google Trends, Li noticed that many Americans were carrying out searches using the word *pet*. "Pet clothes, pet toy, pet health," he told me. "I can tell that this is a good market right now." By the time of the election, Li had registered a new brand, Pemily12, with the U.S. Patent and Trademark Office. He opened a website that sold pet products to American consumers. Google Trends had identified "pet clothes" as a particularly common search topic, so Li contracted with a factory in the south that manufactured tiny sweaters for dogs. On his website, he explained the brand in Amazonglish:

Why is Pemily?

This is a combination of pet family

Why is it 12?

12 = 12 month = 1 year = forever

Why is Pemily12?

pemily12 means we will always be a family

———

After Trump refused to accept the results of the election, I devoted a couple more classes to the American political system. We discussed the electoral college and the way results are announced by the media, and I described the tradition of a losing candidate acknowledging defeat. Students seemed well-informed, and if they were enjoying any schadenfreude, they kept it to themselves.

In general, these young people didn't seem particularly self-righteous. Every semester, I taught *Animal Farm* to first-year students, and one assignment required them to write about the character they most iden-

tified with. The most common choice was Benjamin, the donkey who is
skeptical of the new farm but keeps his thoughts to himself:

> When the power status between myself and the other party is too
> far apart, I don't think there is a need to hit a rock with a pebble. Of
> course, I still admire those who are brave enough to resist, but I per-
> sonally may not take this risk.

> As a Chinese saying goes, *huocongkouchu*, which means that all
> one's troubles were caused by his tongue. We have two eyes, two
> ears, two hands, but only one mouth, which just tell us that we
> should observe more, listen more, do more, and speak less.

> His character shortcomings are similar to mine. He saw the essence
> of pig rule but did not oppose Napoleon's outrageous autocratic be-
> havior. He didn't dare to express his political views boldly like Snow-
> ball, and he didn't dare to challenge Napoleon. . . . This is a kind of
> cowardice or selfishness. I am very similar to him in this respect, I
> only care about a small group of people who come into my heart.

After Benjamin, the second most common choice was Boxer. In Orwell's novel, Boxer is a hardworking and slow-witted horse who always
obeys Napoleon's leadership. Near the end of the novel, after overwork
has ruined Boxer's health, he is sold to a knacker who will kill the horse
and process the corpse. Critics consider Boxer to be an allegory for the
Russian working class, which supported the Communists during the
revolution and then paid the price in suffering. Some students saw themselves in this tragic figure:

> I am a person without independent thinking, too. I often believe
> what others say to me, and I always complete the work given by other

people without any personal thinking. If I am one of the animals in the farm, I will believe the word said by the leader such as Snowball and Napoleon. . . . Maybe I will be brainwashed by Napoleon and finally become the animal who does whatever Napoleon orders me to do. In the end, I will be put away by Napoleon.

The students could be brutally honest about themselves, and they entertained few illusions about the Chinese system. It was vastly different from my experience in the 1990s, when the people in my classroom generally came across as young and naive. In those days, I constantly had to remind myself that I wasn't much older than my students. "It was easy to laugh at their ridiculous names, or smile at their childlike shyness," I wrote in *River Town*, "and it was easy to dismiss them as simple young people from the simplicity of the countryside. But of course nothing was farther from the truth—the Sichuan countryside is not simple, and my students had known things that I had never imagined." At the time, the students seemed young because they were entering a brand-new world, which had been true for every generation of modern Chinese. Time and again, young people had been thrown into the maelstrom of overwhelming change, whether it involved war or revolution, politics or economics.

But the students at Sichuan University were old souls. They knew how things worked; they understood the system's flaws and also its benefits. They were entering the same environment in which their parents had worked—for the first time in modern history, China had been both stable and prosperous for a period that was longer than an undergraduate's memory. As a middle-aged teacher, my perspective had changed: now I had to remind myself that my students weren't as old as they seemed. When a sophomore like Hongyi wrote about her parents' generation, and about the society that she would someday inherit, she could be completely cold-eyed:

My parents were born in the 1970s, and I think they now fit into the lower middle class in China. They are characterized by firm patriotism and nonchalant cynicism. They strongly support the People's Republic of China, not by praising the Chinese government, but by criticizing foreign governments. They refuse to use Apple products, decline to travel to Japan, and dismiss Trump as crazy and malicious. Yet they seldom admire China with passion. They have witnessed corruption in Chinese bureaucracy as well as injustice in society, which they are not able to redress, so they always say, "Things are just like that." . . .

I think my generation, born in the age of the Internet, is puzzled and somehow depressed by the conflict between Chinese beliefs and Western ones. Propaganda about liberty and reason prevails on the Internet while propaganda about patriotism and Communism prevails in the textbooks. Youngsters are mostly attracted by the former, but when passing exams and pursuing jobs, they should bear in mind the latter, and in practice in China, more often than not, the latter functions better.

———

After the U.S. diplomat warned me about the possibility of getting arrested, Leslie and I discussed various scenarios. We concluded that if there was trouble with my writing, the Party would probably find a quiet way to get us out. Perhaps my contract at the university wouldn't be renewed, or visas would be canceled. The more dramatic possibilities seemed unlikely, at least in our estimation. The most recent pattern was that the Chinese matched American diplomatic moves, but they rarely initiated, and lately they seemed wary of accelerating the conflict. During such a complicated period, there was also a good chance that nobody would take initiative, and the wheels of bureaucracy would keep turning, and I would be left alone. In the end, I decided to continue publishing stories.

Of course, it was all guesswork. Nobody could really make sense of the U.S.–China relationship, or the strange ways in which ideas and products moved back and forth. One Chinese student might wear a Trump hat to class, celebrating the president's connection to Sichuan, while others used Thomas Paine's title for their samizdat publication. For a Chinese manufacturer, Young Pioneer scarves could lead to Trump banners, and a Chengdu entrepreneur could engage in such intense commercial *jiaoliu* that he knew the exact day when American customers received their stimulus checks. But all of these tiny points of contact didn't necessarily add up to a larger portrait of sympathy and understanding. I often reminded myself how much diplomatic strategy and subterfuge had been employed by both sides on an unseen banner with the words "Thank you, Chengdu."

On New Year's Eve, I held my last nonfiction class of the term. I asked the students a question: For you, was 2020 a good year or a bad year?

Earlier in December, the campus had been closed again. As the weather grew colder, China experienced a few COVID outbreaks, which usually originated with citizens who had quarantined after returning from abroad. In Chengdu, an elderly person handled contaminated garbage near a quarantine facility, initiating a chain of infections. The first case was reported on December 7, and in the following five days, the city tested more than two million residents. Despite having had no infections since February, and only 143 total cases, Chengdu had 141 testing locations—a ratio of almost one facility for every non-imported symptomatic infection since the start of the pandemic. All told, thirteen new cases of community spread were reported that month.

Nobody at the university was infected. But the old systems returned: security guards monitored the weak spots in the wall, and student faces no longer moved the turnstiles at the gates. Across Chengdu, there were a few targeted lockdowns, but our neighborhood and most of the city remained normal. Ariel and Natasha's school never closed. In the middle of the outbreak, Chengdu opened five new subway lines.

Almost 70 percent of my students responded that it had been a good year. But they were still old souls—even when things went well, they struggled to make sense of the system's contradictions. In nonfiction class, Vincent wrote:

> During the period of staying at home, I was aware that there are too many problems of the China political system, and I started to think about how to solve it—at least, what I can do for the country. During the pandemic, I sometimes felt really depressed by the country when I read the news that the doctors were sacrificed, people lost their relatives and other disappointing news. I was so angry about our government. . . . I felt so sad about the Party and the country at that time.
>
> But after things got better, and after seeing other countries' worse behaviors, I changed my idea about China and the Party. Although I know there are still too many existing problems in China, I am convinced that the socialist system is more advanced especially in emergency cases.

Li Dewei also reported a good year. Feetmat, Troadlop, and the other shoe brands had enjoyed their best holiday sales ever, with the year's total revenues increasing by about 15 percent compared with 2019. Pemily12 was thriving, and Li believed that his entrepreneurial future might involve pet beauty products marketed to Americans.

"It will be just like beauty products for people," he said, when I visited him early in 2021. He showed me a picture of a dog wearing false eyelashes. "We haven't started this yet," he said. "But we can see that other people are making this product. Maybe in two or three years it will be a big market."

For Jin Gang, the flag manufacturer in Zhejiang, the year had been more difficult. The closure of major sporting events in Europe had affected his business. But after January 6, when the American Capitol was stormed, there was a spike in orders for Trump banners. Jin sent pictures of the three most popular new designs that he was currently manufacturing:

TRUMP 2024: THE REVENGE TOUR

TRUMP 2024: TAKE AMERICA BACK

TRUMP 2024: SAVE AMERICA AGAIN!

Every Monday, Ariel and Natasha tied their red Young Pioneer scarves, put on the gold pins, and went off to school as Cai Cai and Rou Rou. Sometimes they complained about not being able to visit Colorado, and they missed our cat, Morsi, who was being cared for by our tenant. But increasingly that life felt distant. One afternoon, the twins found an abandoned kitten on the banks of the Fu River. They took him in and named him Ulysses, because he was also far from home. In the Chinese way, they also immediately gave the cat a nickname: Yu Yu.

That was the best way to cope—one reality here, one reality there. Certain family photographs hung in both our homes, and some pieces of IKEA furniture were also duplicated. In Colorado, our black Honda CR-V was parked in the barn; during the fall, we bought another black Honda CR-V for Chengdu. Our Chinese Honda had been manufactured in Wuhan, and we called it the COVID car. Even the assembly lines in the sealed city had had a good year: Honda reported that in 2020, automobile sales in China increased by almost 5 percent over the previous year. When I drove to campus, I parked the COVID car in the basement of the College of Marxism.

CHAPTER ELEVEN

Generation Xi

Spring and Summer 2021

WHEN EMILY WAS IN HER LATE TEENS, SHE HAD A RECURRING nightmare about her brother. In the dream, the boy is much younger than Emily, and they are playing on a high balcony. Emily's brother faces her and grips her hands. Holding tight, he walks up her legs, step by step, and then he flips over backward, the way that small children sometimes do with adults. On one of the flips, Emily loses hold, and her brother tumbles off the balcony.

She had this nightmare for years before the suicide. Later in life, she believed that the dream must have reflected the helplessness she felt while trying to support her brother. She didn't talk about such feelings with her parents, and for a long time she avoided telling her son, Tao Tao, how his uncle had died.

Emily also rarely told Tao Tao stories about her college years or her time as a migrant in Shenzhen. These memories weren't painful, but she doubted that they had much value. "In those days I was very passive," she told me once. "I wasn't making my own decisions—I was just reacting. Even going to work in Shenzhen wasn't really an active decision. It was just that I didn't want to stay in Fuling." She continued, "I think that I was passive until Tao Tao was born. And then I started reading books about how to raise children, and I developed my own ideas about what was right and wrong. I made my own decisions. That's when I began really reading. Before that, I didn't read carefully."

Migrants of Emily's generation often described an initial lack of direction. Her former boyfriend Anry had also felt passive and unprepared for city life, and he had been forced to leave the countryside by circumstances beyond his control. Over time, many of these individuals were forged in the crucible of competition. They learned to work hard, and they figured out how to improve their skills and knowledge. Emily, though, cared little for status and material progress. Even within her own family, she observed that such things didn't necessarily lead to fulfillment. Her father had become a highly respected professor, but he didn't seem satisfied. And Cousin Liu, despite his enormous wealth, had responded with ambivalence.

After Cousin Liu became rich, he hosted a grand celebration every Lunar New Year holiday at the mansion he had built in his home village. The party was attended by relatives from across the region, along with business associates and government cadres. Cousin Liu and the other rich men would play mah-jongg late into the night.

In the 2010s, Cousin Liu made a real estate investment in northern China that went bust, and his net worth dropped significantly. He was still rich, but now the annual parties became less grand, and fewer businessmen and cadres showed up. Emily noticed that her cousin seemed wistful, and sometimes he talked about morality and religion. Throughout everything, the rich man's mother remained essentially unchanged. She still farmed the fields outside her luxurious home as if she were a peasant.

Early in 2021, during the Lunar New Year holiday, Cousin Liu celebrated his fiftieth birthday with another party. Afterward, Emily wrote me a long message:

Hi, Happy Spring Festival! I have been thinking of writing to you since the day when Mr. Biden won the presidency. I like the president's daughter, for she seems to be a nice person, so the father might be a nice guy, too. Hope that he can make things right.

We have been stuck in Chongqing this break. We visited families in the countryside; attended my rich cousin's 50th birthday party; and drove to see rock carvings in Dazu, where Tao Tao asked me something about Buddhism and other religions. I told him that I didn't know much but I thought the essence of all religions was the same: love, kindness, generosity . . . and he listened seriously. Travelling with the boy is getting more and more interesting, I thought.

As the boy shows great interest in poems written by Rabindranath Tagore and Kahlil Gibran, I guess he might love to read more poems or philosophy books. I bought both kinds, he is more attracted by the latter. He is now reading *The Big Questions* by Robert C. Solomon and is addicted to it. He reads and thinks. I read it, too, but I can't understand it easily. I try to keep an open mind to different ideas, but my former knowledge and experience sometimes block me. I think it's good for the boy to read this book and try to figure out his own way of looking at things before he receives too many ideas from other people.

My brother was interested in philosophy too when he was at Tao Tao's age, but he didn't have access to such good books, and I didn't understand what he was trying to say.

Like most Chinese, Emily had great faith in education, but her belief was of a different sort. Nowadays, education was another form of competition, a way for children to strive for class rank and *gaokao* scores. Emily's perspective was broader: she believed that an ideal school also teaches values, empathy, and self-awareness. Part of her respect for education was an understanding that schooling can also damage a child. In Emily's opinion, this was what had happened to her brother. The local system had been too rigid and cruel for a talented but unorthodox mind.

She recognized certain echoes of her brother in Tao Tao. Unlike his uncle, Tao Tao was popular with classmates, and his grades were excellent. But he had a similar instinct for nonconformity, and he asked hard questions about society and politics. During one of my spring visits to Fuling, I had dinner with Emily, and she told me that sometimes she struggled to respond to her son.

"I don't know what to say when he asks me questions," she said. "I don't want him to end up like those students in Hong Kong."

By now, the protests in the former British colony had long since been suppressed, with a number of student activists arrested. "Is that because you think they're wrong?" I asked. "Or because they get punished?"

"Because they get punished," Emily said.

Recently, a teacher had chided Tao Tao for breaking some trivial school rule. The boy responded, "I follow the rules that are reasonable, but not the rules that are unreasonable."

After the exchange, the teacher called Emily. "I can see by the things that he writes that his thinking is not the same as the other children," the teacher said. "Tell him that he can think these things, and he can even write them in essays for my class. But actually doing these things is something else."

The teacher's tone wasn't angry or aggressive. In fact, she went out of her way to be gentle. It was clear that she was worried for the sake of Tao Tao, and not for the sake of the rules. This kind of protective attitude about politics was common in China. Even people in positions of authority often did little things to help others navigate the system, and the level of decency could be surprising. Sometimes, it was possible to forget that this was actually one way in which the system was sustained. For most people, it was an article of faith that nothing important could be changed, and that the goal was simply to avoid problems at the individual level.

I asked Emily what she said to Tao Tao after the conversation. "I told him that the country isn't perfect," she said. "And maybe in the future you can do something to make it better. But for now you have to be in the system."

In little more than a year, the boy would enter high school, and it was becoming harder to hide things from him. Not long before my visit, an older cousin told Tao Tao what had happened to his uncle. Instead of keeping quiet, Tao Tao went directly to Emily.

"He asked me, 'Why did my uncle kill himself?'" Emily said. "I didn't know what to say." But she discovered that once the subject had been broached, it wasn't as difficult as she had expected. "I said that there were some things that my brother didn't talk about," Emily explained. "He needed to talk about them, and we should have helped him. But we didn't know how to do that at the time. I told Tao Tao that if he ever has anything that worries him, he should tell us."

The conversation seemed to put Tao Tao at ease. He appreciated his mother's honesty, and he liked hearing what she said about his uncle's personality and interests. Afterward, Emily realized that it was one of the first times that talking about her brother made her feel better.

During spring, I visited Fuling as often as possible. It was easier now with the COVID car, and I went for long drives through the river valleys of the Yangtze and the Wu. In the 1990s, I had explored these areas on foot, sometimes with a pack and a tent. My favorite walks were out the back gate of the college, where rice terraces had been carved atop the steep eastern bank of the Wu. They were like mirrored staircases—each step was a flooded paddy, reflecting the color of the sky. In the afternoon, farmers were busy in the fields, weeding crops or replanting rice seedlings. Children sat on the cement threshing platforms in front of their homes, doing homework. In *River Town*, I wrote:

> On sunny afternoons there was a child on virtually every platform—
> Fuling schools assigned an enormous amount of homework, and the

students did it with remarkable diligence, even if they were from un-educated peasant families. I had come to recognize this as perhaps the characteristic that I admired the most about the local people: they had a great respect for education, and it was easy to feel good about teaching in a place like that.

Nowadays, the mirrored staircases were gone, and I never found any-body growing rice. Farmers told me that the crop was too labor inten-sive. For the hard work of maintaining terraces and transplanting rice, young hands were best, but all the young hands had left long ago for the cities. Those children on the threshing platforms had learned their les-sons well.

Invariably, the few farmers I met were elderly. Their ambitions had dwindled, along with their numbers. They tended small vegetable plots, and they no longer maintained the intricate web of footpaths that I re-membered from the past. High above the Wu, where the rice terraces had been most spectacular, the staircases had collapsed into long, slop-ing fields overrun with weeds.

I had photographs from my walks as a young man, and sometimes I hiked up and tried to replicate an image from the same vantage point. It was almost impossible, because the surroundings had changed so much. In the 1990s, I had been struck by all the ways in which the countryside was shaped by human labor—it was a lived-in landscape, a place whose fields and pathways felt as intimate as the furniture of an old house. But now I saw that neglect could be as powerful as hard work. The shape of certain hillsides had changed dramatically, and trees had sprung up ev-erywhere. In the past, farmers rarely let anything grow to more than a few feet, because they couldn't afford the shade; every patch of fertile soil needed to be used for maximum efficiency. But now some sections of hillside had turned into small forests. Often, when I tried to retake an old photograph, I found the view blocked by trees. Similar changes had happened across China, which, in 2004, had become a net importer of agricultural products. Since then, even more young people had moved to cities, and even more land was left fallow. The People's Republic, once the most populous agrarian country on earth, was now the world's largest importer of food.

I had better luck with photographs from the summit of Beishanping. Atop the mountain, the views were still clear, and I was able to re-create a number of shots that looked down across the Yangtze to the heart of the city. When I placed the pictures side by side—1996 on the left, 2021 on the right—the differences began at the top, with the sky, and proceeded all the way down to the bottom of the river. In the old pictures, the sky was gray and textured, like a dirty piece of fabric draped atop the horizon. In those days, pollution was terrible, because of poorly regulated industry in the heart of the city. As a Peace Corps volunteer, I had suffered chronic sinus infections, and I was infected with tuberculosis, a disease that was widespread in the river valleys. In the 2000s, the government shut down or relocated the downtown heavy industry. Friends told me they noticed an immediate improvement in respiratory health.

In the new pictures, the air is clear and blue, and it's possible to see distant ranges of mountains that weren't visible in the 1990s. Beneath the sky, the heart of the city is laid out across the long hillside of the Yangtze's southern bank. When the photographs are paired, the new version of Fuling seems to have nothing to do with the old, because there are so many gleaming high-rises. But closer inspection reveals a palimpsest: beneath the new development, an underlying pattern of old streets and alleyways remains intact. Fuling was never demolished wholesale; this wasn't a case of state-directed destruction and rebuilding. Instead, the changes happened at the most local level: street by street, building by building, individual by individual. Somebody made money and put up a new structure or a row of shops; soon, a neighbor followed suit. Meanwhile, the streets and even their names remain the same: People's Road,

Construction Road, Prospering China Road. Some names, like Ink-Washing Road, refer to neighborhood industries that are long gone. Like so many things in China, it feels like a contradiction: everything has changed; nothing has changed.

At the bottom of the new photographs, where the city meets the Yangtze, the river is bordered by a concrete dike that rises 160 feet. The dike appears as a long band of white beneath the high-rises, as if the city has hiked up its skirts at the river's edge. The Yangtze in these photos is wider than it used to be in the old images, and the surface is still and glassy, with mirrored reflections of towering buildings. In the old pictures, the river reflected nothing; the pre-dam water moved too fast for that. Boats of all sizes used to skim along the surface, ranging from tiny fishing sampans to squat passenger ferries. From a distance, docks look like floating leaves scattered around the juncture of the two rivers.

In new pictures, almost all the docks are gone, and so are the boats. Over the years, commercial fishing on the Yangtze was steadily restricted, until a total ban was enforced at the start of 2021. Long before that, virtually all passenger ferries went out of business. The two rivers, like the terraced rice fields above their banks, have essentially been abandoned.

Some of the old Beishanping photos were taken in winter. Before the dam, the level of the Yangtze dropped during the cold months, revealing small islands and strips of sandstone. The most famous of these rocks was called the White Crane Ridge. It appeared in the old photographs as a pale, delicate line in the river, running parallel to the southern bank. In the 1990s, the site was managed by the local antiquities bureau. Every winter, after the ridge emerged, the bureau posted a worker named Huang Dejian to the site. Huang sat at a small wooden desk, dressed in a surplus People's Liberation Army greatcoat. That was his *danwei*—an official work unit surrounded on all four sides by the rushing Yangtze.

Fishermen still lived on the water in those days. During winter, a couple of itinerant families docked their sampans near the White Crane Ridge, where they charged three yuan, about thirty-five cents, to ferry visitors to and from the southern bank. As a Peace Corps volunteer, I went there a few times every winter, and Huang Dejian would explain the history of the ridge. More than twelve centuries ago, somebody had carved a pair of swimming carp into the stone, which then began to serve as a hydrological gauge. Boatsmen heading downstream could stop on the ridge, compare the water level with the fixed line of the twin carp, and know what to expect from the rapids in the Three Gorges.

Eventually, people started recording annual water levels and inscribing them into the ridge. The earliest dated carving was from 763 AD, during the Tang dynasty. Over time, it became a tradition to mark the annual appearance of the stone carp with an inscribed verse. Various poets and calligraphers were posted to government jobs in Fuling, occasionally as a punishment for some political misstep, and each writer left his mark on the stone. All told, more than three hundred thousand characters decorated the ridge.

Huang Dejian had effectively memorized this text, like the schoolchildren with their Li Bai verses. During my time in the Peace Corps, I purchased a book about the ridge, and I used to bring it on my visits. If I asked about a certain carving or a poem by a famous calligrapher, Huang could find it immediately. He was a friendly man in his thirties with close-cropped black hair and ears that protruded like those of a Daoist sage. He often looked tired, with heavy bags sagging beneath his eyes, and I figured this was the outcome of spending long winter days on the cold rock. But Huang was endlessly enthusiastic. One of his favorite inscriptions was situated near the western edge of the sandstone, where four characters read 惟汶永年: "The River Runs Forever." The calligrapher, Shu Changsong, hadn't been particularly famous, but the writing was beautiful, in the graceful curves of a style known as "running grass."

When I lived in Fuling, everybody knew that the site was doomed. The first stage of the dam was scheduled for completion in 2003, with the water level in Fuling rising about 150 feet. After that, the White Crane Ridge would disappear forever. But there seemed to be little urgency about the impending loss. Locals rarely went there; on many visits, I was the only one on the rock with Huang. For my tutorials in Chinese, I studied any local articles I could find about the ridge, and on January 1, 1998, the *Chongqing Evening News* reported on a proposal to enclose the ridge in some kind of underwater museum.

Friends at the college scoffed at the idea—they said the government was always promising things that it couldn't deliver. Fuling, after all, was a town without a single traffic light. Huang Dejian was among the few people I knew who was hopeful about the underwater museum, although he didn't know anything more than what was described in the *Chongqing Evening News*. Every time we discussed the issue, Huang was shivering at the wooden desk, like a punished schoolboy who had been sent to the wide-open hallway of the Yangtze Valley. I figured that for somebody in Huang's position, any kind of indoor museum was likely to inspire some magical thinking.

The newspaper article also mentioned another, less ambitious proposal. As an alternative to the underwater museum, officials suggested commissioning high-quality rubbings of the carvings that could be displayed after the ridge was flooded. In *River Town*, I predicted that this was the most likely outcome:

> To them, this would undoubtedly be the more practical solution—the region simply didn't have the sort of resources necessary to build an underwater exhibition chamber, and the White Crane Ridge didn't mean much to the average Fuling resident. . . . Experts estimated that within ten years of the dam's completion the silt and sand of the new reservoir would erase all twelve centuries' worth of carvings.

In the new photographs taken from the summit of Beishanping, the delicate line of the White Crane Ridge has vanished. But two large concrete tubes are visible on the southern bank, where they run directly into the water. Above the concrete tubes, it's possible to make out the blocky shape of the White Crane Ridge Underwater Museum.

The museum opened full-time in 2010. The first time I visited, in March of the following year, I was greeted by Huang Dejian. Huang had been named director of the museum, and his face was still the same: the close-cropped hair, the Daoist ears. The bags under his eyes seemed to have grown even heavier, so my theory about the Yangtze cold, like my prediction for the museum, turned out to be wrong. All told, the government invested the equivalent of more than thirty-four million dollars into the project. Huang explained that the riverbed posed so many technical challenges that the museum had been designed by a professor at the Institute of Rock and Soil Mechanics at the Chinese Academy of Sciences.

Instead of the PLA greatcoat, Huang now wore a gray suit with a red tie. He carried two cell phones, one for work and another for personal use. The work phone rang incessantly, with a ringtone that featured a woman's voice. "*Jia you! Jia you! Jia you!*" she said. "*Go! Go! Go!*"

Each concrete tube contained an escalator, one going down, the other up. Huang led me to the one that went down. Inside the tube, the escalator was encased in a sheath of steel. Huang and I descended steeply, and after half a minute he remarked that we had dropped beneath the surface of the Yangtze. There was still a long way to go; the escalator was more than three hundred feet long. The image that came to mind was that of a giant steel straw dipped into the muddy river.

At the bottom, Huang led me through an open door with heavy airlock latches. "We can shut that door if there's any kind of leak," he said. We were now 130 feet underwater. Ahead of us stretched a long, curved viewing gallery with portholes that resembled the windows of a submarine.

The ridge lay just outside the portholes, illuminated a ghostly green by spotlights. Huang led me down the viewing gallery, pointing out carvings, just like in the old days. He showed me the twin carp, and then we stopped at the old favorite: "The River Runs Forever." The characters had been arranged vertically on the rock, and the last one—年—trailed off in a long line like a dagger. I remembered tracing the 年 with my finger atop the dry ridge only thirteen years earlier.

Near the end of the tour, I asked Huang if he ever looked at the ridge and felt a sense of loss. He shook his head. "They weren't able to do this at the Aswan Dam in Egypt," he said, noting that Egyptian authorities had to move relics before they were flooded. "It makes me proud," he said. "I don't have any feeling of loss when I come here; I feel like it's a success."

He said that more visitors came nowadays, and the most important thing was that the carvings remained intact. And that was true—it was still the same artifact, the same river, even the same man who used to sit shivering behind his wooden desk. Same story, too: nothing had changed; everything had changed.

We took another walk through the viewing gallery. I paused at each porthole, trying to remember the way the carvings used to appear. Several times, Huang Dejian's phone rang, and the woman's voice called out: "*Go! Go! Go!*" Here at the bottom of the Yangtze, beneath twenty fathoms of sluggish water, the cell phone coverage was excellent.

During the spring school holiday, we took the COVID car to western Sichuan. These were Tibetan regions, high in the Himalayas, and we followed switchback roads to mountain passes. Ariel and Natasha commented that the route was *yangchangxiaodao*, a poetic phrase they learned in school. It means "winding road," but the literal translation is more vivid: "a road like sheep intestines."

Chinese phrases often refer to food—people may have left the farms, but the language has not. I liked seeing Chinese through my daughters' eyes. In school, they learned that stalagmites are *shisun*, "stone bamboo shoots," while stalactites are *shizhongru*. The first character is "stone," and the last is "breast": the image is that of milk dripping down from the ceiling. For "cheek by jowl," the twins wrote *jiquanxiangwen*, another farming phrase: "chickens and dogs can hear each other." Bad traffic is *cheshuimalong*, "carts flowing like water and horses like dragons." An "old yellow ox" is a hardworking person who never complains. To refer to somebody as a *habagou*—a Pekingese dog with its nervous, snuffling face—is to call him a sycophant.

When we traveled, people invariably asked the same question: "Who's the *jiejie*?" In America, the most common twin query is: "Are they identical?" But the Chinese didn't seem to care so much about that. Their question probably reflected the language, which specifies whether a sibling is older or younger. Ariel, the elder by a minute, was *jiejie*, "big sister," while Natasha was *meimei*. The school also distinguished according to birth order, giving Ariel a class number that was one digit ahead of her one-minute *meimei*.

Like girls around the world, Natasha and Ariel listened to Taylor Swift. They acquired information about the singer inside the firewall, on Mandarin websites, and for searches they used her Chinese nickname: Mei Mei. But this wasn't the *mei* that means younger sister, or the *mei* that means beautiful. For Swift, the Chinese used a more obscure *mei*: "mold, mildew." This also seemed characteristically Chinese, a way of cutting to the chase: the singer might be young and beautiful, but she often sang about love gone bad.

After the challenges of the first year, it was a relief to see Ariel and Natasha so comfortable with the language. By staying in China, we had avoided the nightmare of remote schooling, and now we decided to remain for at least another year. At the end of March, I wrote Minking Chyu, the dean of the SCUPI program, and asked to renew my contract.

I figured that it should be a formality; the director of my program wanted me to stay, and the administration had given me a teaching award. It was difficult to bring in new foreign instructors, because of China's pandemic controls.

But Chyu responded with a curt message, explaining that the institute had no need for my services: "We have some prospects so far and a previous colleague who left us a couple of years ago will likely rejoin us again this fall." The dean, who was a naturalized American citizen and lived in Pittsburgh, had not visited Chengdu since the start of the pandemic. I hadn't heard anything about recruiting, so I checked with the director of my program, who was also American. He confirmed that they weren't in the process of finding new teachers, and he suggested that I write the dean again, in case there was some long-distance misunderstanding.

This time, Chyu added a different explanation. He referred to the fact that my one-year contract had already been renewed once:

> As you might know that under the Chinese labor law, the third signing will make the contract/employment permanent, which could void the short-term nature of the appointment and put both sides at risk.

Why had the reason changed? And why was all of this handled in such coldly bureaucratic language, without a personal conversation? I checked with an administrator at the university, who said that the labor law was intended to protect young academics from getting strung along on temporary contracts. He told me that it should be easy for the university to find a way to keep me on.

Chyu's email also claimed that SCUPI needed to prioritize long-term hires. I figured there was one way to see whether this was true: I offered to sign a long-term contract, and I said that I was willing to teach more courses if necessary. In truth, the last thing I wanted was more work, but I had a pretty good idea what would happen next. I made the offer through the director of my program, because the dean had been so uncommunicative with me. Early the next morning, the program director informed me that the decision was final. He said that the dean wouldn't hire me under any circumstances.

Afterward, Leslie and I quietly started preparing to leave China. I didn't tell my current students, because I wanted their semester to be as normal as possible. But I was curious about the decision. On campus, I asked around discreetly, and two professors told me that they had heard that political pressure was to blame.

During the past year, there had been various Chinese social media attacks on my writing, and a significant one occurred around the time I applied for renewal. A commentator under the pseudonym Lin Yiwu had posted a four-thousand-character screed on an open WeChat channel. Among other things, Lin took issue with the fact that I had met with Fang Fang in Wuhan. He also didn't like the way I mentioned parking the COVID car in the basement of the College of Marxism. A number of Little Pinks had been angry about that detail—in a way, it was gratifying to see that readers were alert to symbolism. Using my Chinese name, Lin Yiwu wrote, "Mr. Ho Wei understands neither Marx nor contemporary China."

The post was read more than sixty thousand times. Some anonymous commentators became influential, because they published things that were edgier than what appeared in the state media. For the government, it was a balancing act—ultranationalism was useful, but it could also lead to extreme xenophobia and unrealistic demands. In this case, the online attack had not been censored, which suggested that authorities tacitly approved.

The Sichuan University professors told me that when staff members were publicly attacked or criticized, mid-level administrators had to file internal reports. During the past year, whenever I published a story that created some controversy, the bureaucrats had been forced to produce reports, and now they wanted to eliminate the problem. But there hadn't been a direct command from the top, according to the people I talked to. It wasn't necessary, because the system generated so much nervousness that individuals generally erred on the side of caution. "*Tianwei bukece*," one professor explained, using a phrase that translates as "Heavenly might can't be measured." He continued, "You have to guess what the exact order is."

This professor had been disciplined in the past for political problems of his own. He told me that he wasn't surprised the university wanted to get rid of me. "It's a safe move," he said. "They could keep you here, but they'll have to file reports, and they'll have to have meetings again and again with people from the provincial government. That's how the bureaucratic system works."

It had been years since the professor had been disciplined, but his email and social media accounts were still monitored closely by administrators. He didn't blame them for doing their job. "It's dirty work, but they have to do it," he said. "I tend to believe that nobody enjoys this kind of work. The system has kidnapped everybody."

On the first day of class each semester, I asked students to write their Chinese and English names, their majors, and their outside interests. That spring, a nonfiction student called Lyndon introduced himself:

> I have used "Lyndon" for a while. I think my name comes from a former U.S. president and most importantly, it sounds just like my Chinese name. But I [want to] abandon it because it makes me sound TOO OLD!!!

I had a lot of old names that final semester. Ethel, Alfred, Flora, Carl, Albert, Rita, Henry—we seemed to be traveling back in time, to names that could have come from my parents' generation. There was a Bruce, too, a handsome industrial engineer who rode a motorcycle in his free time. He had taken his English name from Bruce Lee. For nonfiction class, Bruce researched a Chengdu motorcycle club, and then he proposed another motorcycle-oriented paper about a road in the Himalayas that had served as a key supply line during the Second World War. In the proposal, Bruce wrote:

> Lexi Road was built in 1942, with a total length of 525 kilometers. It links Leshan and Xichang. It was built by the Kuomintang government for the War of Resistance Against Japanese Aggression. The construction conditions of the road were very difficult and many workers died. . . . I'm going to go there by motorcycle tomorrow and return to Chengdu on Sunday.

I was glad to have one last round of research projects. The system hadn't kidnapped everything, at least not yet; over the course of nearly two years, nobody from the administration had meddled with my syllabus or the students' reporting. Like every group I taught, the last-semester undergrads were industrious at finding stories in the odd corners of Chengdu. One boy shadowed a cosmetic surgeon who was doing facelifts at a large clinic, and another student spent a day working in a warehouse for a subsidiary of Taobao. Rita researched the American Airlines Gym, which turned out to have nothing to do with American Airlines. As always, the students were alert to scam artists and phonies, and they seemed to relish the way the most disturbing story could begin in the most innocent fashion.

Lyndon wrote about what happened after he adopted a cute kitten named Kiki. He found the pet on a university bulletin board, where it was being offered by an undergrad at another Chengdu college. In the story, the other undergrad is called Tian Dahan, and initially he met Lyndon only once, in order to exchange the kitten. Kiki was in good health, and for roughly half a year Lyndon had no further contact with Tian Dahan. Then one morning he received a text message with an embedded video of the young man masturbating.

Five minutes later, Lyndon's phone rang. The call came from somewhere in Myanmar. Lyndon quoted the conversation in his paper:

"Are you the owner of Kiki?" somebody asked in Chinese, on the other side of the phone.

I paused. "*Kiki*? That's the name my cat's last owner gave him."

"That's right. Then you must know Tian Dahan? Did you see his video? Tell him to give me my fucking money! And tell him I will let everyone see his small dick if he doesn't respond." The man yelled angrily, and then hung up.

There was a name for this sort of thing: *luoliao*, or "naked chat." Naked-chat scammers were often Chinese living outside the country, where they operated with impunity. They enticed a young person into having phone sex, usually with women posing as eligible singles. In the middle of the sex, there was an apparent connection problem, and the scammers sent a new link. The link secretly installed software that downloaded all WeChat contact information from the victim's phone. Then the scammers went through the contacts one by one, sending a video of the phone sex and threatening the victim with more humiliation if he or she didn't pay up.

In the case of Tian Dahan—not his real name—Lyndon had been low on the list of WeChat blackmail priorities. By the time the naked chatters got around to the guy who had adopted Tian Dahan's cat, they had already sent the video to most of the young man's friends and relatives. After the Myanmar call, Lyndon reached out to Tian, who agreed to meet.

When they met in Chengdu, Tian sheepishly said that he had paid the naked chatters well over a thousand dollars. But they kept contacting more people from Tian's address book, so he finally told his parents and the police. In the end, pretty much everybody he knew had received the video. He explained that he had been a soft target. "I've never had a girl-friend," he told Lyndon, sadly. He regretted spending all his time either studying or watching suggestive videos on TikTok. "Seeing these videos every day has deepened my fantasy of sex," he said.

When Lyndon read the story aloud in class, the other students nod-ded knowingly. They told me that at the start of the school year, all un-dergrads had been required to scan a QR code that linked to a detailed warning about naked-chat scams.

Old names, old souls—was it any surprise that these students came across as wary, cautious, knowing, cynical? I thought of them as prema-turely aged, and even their sense of time was accelerated. That spring, a first-year engineering student named Milo wrote about a Chongqing auto-parts factory that he had visited eight years earlier, for an elemen-tary school project. Milo decided to return to the same factory for my class, but when he got there, he found the site abandoned. It turned out that the company had upgraded to a different location, because business had flourished.

After Milo made it to the new site, he was struck by how much older the boss looked. The man was only in his forties, but his face was worn and haggard; he explained that success required frequent travel and many alcohol-fueled banquets. Milo quoted the boss: "I had no time to take care of my family. My kids do not understand me and even dislike me, since I seldom show up. What's more, after drinking so much alco-hol, I sometimes have a terrible stomachache."

On the factory floor, Milo met a foreman who said that automation had reduced the workforce by a third. Production had become far more efficient and profitable, but it was also stressful, and the foreman cut off the conversation so he could return to work. Milo titled his essay "Fare-well, Old Factory." He concluded:

Everyone in the society must try their best to follow the world's trends. This is a colorful and fascinating world, but this is also a cruel world. If you are not good enough, you will be eliminated without a trace of pity.

Sometimes, I read a paper that made me think: This kid is only nineteen years old. As a teacher and a writer, I believed in getting young people off campus, where they could ask questions and think hard about their own society. But occasionally I wondered whether students were gaining awareness and agency, or whether they were simply being demoralized. As usual, I had no easy answers, although I took comfort in the fact that the students always seemed energized by their reporting. And then, during the first week of June, while motorcycling along the army-built road in the southeastern Himalayas, Bruce was run over by a thirteen-ton Shanqi-brand dump truck.

I had never considered the possibility of a student getting hurt or killed while doing research. The vast majority of projects were in the city, where the worst-case scenario seemed to be a student getting detained by the police or disciplined by campus authorities. I required proposals in part so that I could identify potential risks and steer them to safer ground. But Bruce's proposal wasn't politically sensitive, so I had approved it without much thought.

The weather was perfect on the morning he set out. He rode an FB Mondial bike with a 125cc engine, and he planned to travel for three days. He carried a backpack, along with another bag that was strapped to the stylish Italian motorcycle. For a long stretch, Bruce followed the Dadu River into the Himalayas. The banks of the Dadu are steep, and in some places the road narrows to little more than a single lane. On the second day, Bruce continued west on an even smaller road. It switchbacked to higher elevations, following a route as twisted as sheep intestines.

The accident happened on one of the *yangchangxiaodao* turns. The driver of the Shanqi dump truck, who may have been overtired, had drifted across the median. Meanwhile, Bruce approached on a blind curve at a speed of approximately thirty miles per hour. By the time he saw the truck it was too late. The trucker slammed the brakes; Bruce skidded and lost control of the bike. He slid directly underneath the moving truck, between the front and middle wheels.

I didn't learn about the accident from the police, or the emergency medical services, or anybody at the university. It was characteristic of these diligent and uncomplaining students that the news arrived in the form of a polite request for an extension:

June 7, 2021

Dear Prof. Hessler,

I had an accident on my way to the Lexi Highway. I was turning a corner when I was hit by a truck. Now I have a fracture in my left hand and a piece of flesh has been grinded off my left hand. Then the ligaments and nerves were damaged, and the whole left hand was immobile. My left foot was also injured. It was badly bruised. The whole foot was swollen and couldn't move. I'm in hospital now. I'll have to stay in the hospital for a while before I can come back. So I may not be able to write the article about the Lexi Highway. I don't know what to do now. Can I write the article at a later date? Because I can't do my research right now. And it's really hard for me to type with one hand.

Best wishes,
Bruce

In nonfiction class, Lyndon, Alfred, Rita, Henry, and the rest of the old-sters sent get-well notes to the hospital in Chongqing. Periodically, I checked in on Bruce by email. I told him repeatedly not to worry about the assignment, but he insisted on writing. Slowly, as his injuries healed, he produced a description of the accident:

> All I could recall is that I was turning a corner on a mountain road, and I was going up, and the truck was going down, and the road was narrow. The truck had crossed the center line and I didn't have time to get out of the way because I couldn't react when a huge object came towards me. The next thing I remember is being crushed under a truck. It was no doubt very lucky this time, the truck came to a halt. From the pictures of the scene, I can see that the tire of the truck just hit my head, and I can't imagine what would have happened without the helmet.

Bruce's other good fortune had been that the Shanqi truck was un-loaded. At full weight, the vehicle wouldn't have stopped so quickly, and the massive wheels would have crushed the boy. Instead, the undercar-riage dragged Bruce across the road, and the middle left tire slammed his helmet. But the truck did not roll over him. It screeched to a halt with Bruce pinned to the asphalt.

> I couldn't feel my left foot and my left hand, and I thought at the time that if I survived, I might lose my left hand and my left foot. After a while, I heard someone was yelling "Back the truck up!" . . .
> It was midday in June, and the sun was beating down on the tar-mac. Laying on the ground, I felt the sun was baking me. I managed to remove my helmet with my right hand. There have already been

crowds surrounding the spot. I shouted for help, but no one dared to step forward. The truck driver was busy taking pictures. I cried desperately.

"The gas is leaking!" a voice came out from the crowd. The fuel tank of the motorbike had been damaged. With a more desperate emotion, I shouted harder for help, but still no one dared to come forward. For a moment I was utterly disappointed with the indifference of the watchers.

At Chinese accidents, onlookers are often reluctant to help. A classic scam of the Reform era, and one that long predates naked chat, involves people who fake injury and then extort money from any bystander who tries to help. Even if somebody is clearly hurt, witnesses tend to be wary. Bruce lay beneath the truck for a long time before somebody finally approached him:

A middle-aged man came up to me and told me not to panic. He said, "It was the engine oil."

"Is my hand still there?" I kept repeating my question. "It is fine," the man answered. I tried to move the fingers of my left hand and luckily, I found it could be moved.

The most serious injury turned out to be a fracture of the left wrist. Bruce's other injuries healed quickly, and he returned to campus for the end of semester. When he entered the classroom for our final nonfiction session, his arm in a cast, the other students applauded.

Many of Bruce's SCUPI classmates, including Vincent and Rakim, planned to transfer to schools in the United States that summer. Even before the accident, Bruce and his parents had decided to wait another year before he went abroad, because of the pandemic. Now he found that his perspective on life had changed.

One ordinary night after my injury, I lay in bed, unable to fall asleep. The night in the early morning was very quiet, at that moment I burst into tears. Suddenly I felt how good life is, how good to be alive.

Back to the Jiang'an Campus, I sat in the splendor of the sunset in front of the library. Mallards swam slowly across the lake and egrets darted across the sky. Some people were walking by the lake, others were sitting on the grass and reading. Seeing these beautiful scenes, I couldn't help but be moved. The ordinary life is full of beauty and vitality.

———

In May, I started receiving requests from students who wanted to study nonfiction in the fall. I explained in private emails that I was leaving the university, and near the end of the month, one student shared this information on a WeChat group that included some *Common Sense* staffers. From there, things proceeded as they often did in the world of Chinese social media. Somebody took a screenshot and posted it on Weibo. Then the post was removed by censors, but not before more screenshots had been taken. Soon, I was receiving phone calls and messages asking for comment. I wrote a short statement confirming that my contract had not been renewed, which was posted by a friend on Douban, another social media site. This time it took less than an hour for the censors to remove the statement. But that was long enough for the post to be forwarded 230 times, along with an untold number of screenshots.

All of this occurred on May 30. The following day, the state media happened to report on a speech that Xi Jinping made to the Political Bureau of the 19th Central Committee. In the speech, Xi emphasized the need for writers and others to communicate eloquently the details of life in China. *People's Daily* reported his words under the headline: "Xi Jinping: Tell Chinese Stories Well, Spread Chinese Voices Well." The article's torrent of Partyspeak was probably the best illustration of why the Communists had trouble telling stories well:

> Accelerate the construction of Chinese discourse and Chinese narrative systems. It is necessary to use Chinese theory to interpret Chinese practice, use Chinese practice to sublimate Chinese theory, and create new concepts, new categories, and new expressions that integrate China and foreign countries. . . . Help foreigners realize that the Chinese Communist Party is truly striving for the happiness of the Chinese people, and so that they understand why the Chinese Communist Party can do this, why Marxism works, and why socialism with Chinese characteristics is good.

On social media, some commentators remarked that if Xi Jinping were truly interested in storytelling, it might have been a mistake to expel so many resident foreign writers and journalists. Serena told me that *Common Sense* wanted to write an article about the issue, and I was contacted by others, including reporters at Xinhua, the state-run news agency. During June, some professors at other universities quietly reached out to ask if I might be interested in applying for a job. I sensed that people were testing the boundaries, trying to figure out how far they could go with Xi's speech. I politely declined the invitations, because the political climate seemed too tense and uncertain. This month, Xi might promote better storytelling, but who had any idea what he might say next month?

Of all the gods in the Chinese political firmament, Xi Jinping felt the most remote to me. It was different from the 1990s, when students had referred so often to Mao and Deng that these figures seemed almost familiar. During my first semester in Fuling, I had asked students to write about their heroes, and Mao was by far the most popular public figure, followed by Deng and Zhou Enlai. Nobody chose an entrepreneur or business leader. One boy wrote:

Of course, Mao had a lot of mistakes, but one flaw cannot obscure the splendor of the jade. . . . So I think Mao Zedong fully deserves a worthy [spot] in the world's history. I am afraid only Lenin and Churchill can compare with him.

Like most foreigners in China, I felt no affection for Mao. But Deng was a more complicated figure. At times, his policies had been brutal, including the violent crackdown on protesters around Tiananmen Square in 1989. But Deng had also initiated the Reform era, and as a Sichuanese he possessed qualities that I recognized in many of my friends and students. Deng was unassuming, direct, and pragmatic, and he was tough-minded, surviving repeated purges during the Cultural Revolution. His only son was permanently paralyzed after a fall from an upper-story window during some kind of struggle with radical Red Guards.

Xi Jinping's family also suffered greatly during the Cultural Revolution. His father, a respected figure in the first generation of Communist leaders, was purged and beaten repeatedly. At the age of thirteen, Xi was denounced as a counterrevolutionary by a mob in Beijing, and even his mother was forced to participate in the taunting. One of Xi's sisters was tormented until she committed suicide.

But Xi's reaction to this experience seemed very different from Deng's. Deng clearly recognized the risk of one man holding too much power, and after he rose to become China's paramount leader, he gave local leaders and citizens a leeway that they had never enjoyed under Mao. Xi, on the other hand, seemed more traumatized by the specter of Red Guards than by Mao. He feared street protests and organized groups, and he believed in consolidating authority. He distrusted private business to the point where many of the country's most successful entrepreneurs, including Jack Ma, the founder of Alibaba, had become targets of state investigations or other forms of authoritarian pressure.

For all Xi's power, he remained a cipher at the personal level. His face and words were everywhere, and citizens had become skilled at responding to even the most obscure speech or directive. But there seemed to be no emotional connection, especially among the young. I came to think of my Sichuan University students as belonging to Generation Xi, because they had grown up entirely under the leader's authority. But I noticed that they almost never mentioned his name. Over the course of four semesters, I couldn't remember any student bringing up Xi in class. I reviewed every paper I had received, more than five hundred total, and the leader was mentioned only twenty-two times, usually in passing.

In the classroom, I found little evidence of increased nationalism. The main exception was the incident at the end of 2019, in which I had been reported on social media for my editing comments on John's argumentative essay. Ever since, I had wanted to talk with John to try to learn what happened, but I never saw him in the hallways of the institute. A number of times, I considered reaching out on email or WeChat. But with all the other stresses of the final semester, I decided to wait until I was gone from China.

Other than the *jubao* scare, I had never had an uncomfortable political interaction with a student at Sichuan University. In my experience, the students of twenty-five years earlier had been much more nationalistic, and much less aware. Today's students also seemed less inclined to join the Party. In Fuling, many of the brightest and most charismatic kids had been recruited for Party membership, but my talented students at Sichuan University tended to resist such overtures. When I talked to them about it, they said that membership was irrelevant to the careers they hoped to have.

In a closed system, it's difficult to study such trends, but some Chinese social scientists have pursued the topic. Li Chunling, perhaps the country's leading sociologist, has carried out many surveys of young Chinese. In her 2021 book, *China's Youth*, Li describes a tendency for high income and higher education to correlate with reduced national identification. Large-scale surveys have also shown a pattern of less interest in joining the Party. But Li emphasizes that this is not necessarily a sign of youthful dissidence. "They see Western democratic institutions as better than China's current systems," she writes. "But they see little value in immediately instituting a Western-style democratic order, because China's current situation seems to demand the institutions that it has."

Li also writes that, with regard to highly educated young Chinese, "simple propaganda-style education will not be effective." This seemed true in my experience, ranging from the Morality and Rules class at Chengdu Experimental to the mandatory political courses at Sichuan University. In five sections of first-year composition, I gave the same assignment that I had given two decades earlier, when I asked students to write about their heroes. At Sichuan University, the most common choices were scientists and entrepreneurs. Steve Jobs was popular—in one class, two different boys had given themselves the English name Steve in honor of the Apple founder. Students also liked pop stars, athletes, and actors. Out of the sixty-five students who wrote about heroes, four chose Mao, three wrote about Deng, and one selected Zhou Enlai. Only one chose Xi Jinping, which left China's leader tied with Eminem, Jim Morrison, Lionel Messi, and George Washington. The student who chose Washington wrote, "The reason why I admire him most is that he gave up his political power voluntarily."

In June, I taught George Orwell for the last time. I had used his writings in class every semester, and even my former students from Fuling occasionally mentioned the British writer. Emily sent a long letter explaining that Tao Tao had recently read *Animal Farm*, *1984*, and Aldous Huxley's *Brave New World*, which had inspired her to do the same. She wrote:

After finishing them, it seemed that I could understand more about what happened during those 10 horrible years [the Cultural Revolution], and about what is happening now. Under the joyful and prosperous covers, something unpleasant is going on without people's [awareness].

When we came back to school this autumn, we are told that our school had a much more powerful wi-fi which covers the whole campus, we could use it for free but we should be careful not to spread any negative information, because the school authority and the Fuling Education Committee can see whatever we put on internet.

For the final assignment in first-year composition, I asked students to reimagine *Animal Farm* at Sichuan University. Some wrote pandemic versions of Orwell. In one boy's story, the campus is closed, and students' faces no longer open the turnstiles, which inspires the young people to rise up and take over the university. A different student wrote about something she called "studentism." This political movement was based on two principles:

1. Anyone who stops you from leaving campus is an enemy.

2. Anyone who helps you get out of campus is a friend.

They had a knack for creating brilliantly dystopic bureaucratic rules. In another story, students are strictly banned from drinking soda, which is available only to Mr. Hessler, who sits in his air-conditioned office sipping Diet Pepsi and making negative comments on essays. One boy wrote about an undergraduate mob that penetrates the administrative office in charge of grades. The rebels plan to hack the computer and raise everybody's marks—but then, in the final scene, they discover that surveillance cameras are still operating.

A boy named Carl wrote about the hierarchy of *gaokao* scores at different departments. In his story, a revolution creates a new system in which all students are equal, but some are more equal than others:

> Without teachers, the undisciplined people give up studying completely, while the self-disciplined people work harder every day, especially the people from the West China College of Stomatology. Although they said there was no discrimination, the students at Pittsburgh Institute were about 15 points worse than those of other colleges of Sichuan University in the college entrance examination.

Carl's story ends with the stomatologists embarking on successful careers, while other students fail to get jobs, thus destroying the university's reputation.

In the various fictional dystopias that became twentieth-century classics, there were different ways of controlling and distracting citizens. In *1984*, the authoritarian state depends on continuous war and rewritten history, while *Brave New World* uses sex and the drug called soma. In *We*, the early Russian novel, a regime employs the surgical removal of human imagination. But none of these futuristic stories anticipated what the People's Republic would become in the twenty-first century. There was no fictional world that combined authoritarianism and censorship with economic success, freedom of movement, and improved education. And no novelist had predicted how useful competition can be in a repressive state. For most of my students, the greatest fear wasn't surveillance cameras, or revised history, or any of the other instruments that are typically associated with state control. The students feared one another—they worried about all the other talented young people who were also striving for grades and jobs. When competition becomes as powerful as faith, it also functions, in Marxist terms, as an opium of the people. Most young Chinese I knew were too numbed and too distracted by the struggle for success to think hard about the big picture.

———

Near the end of the semester, the *Common Sense* staff invited me to meet at a private residence downtown. A couple of writers, including Serena, were researching an article about the various online attacks that seemed to have contributed to the university's decision to let me go. The meeting was attended by about twenty students, only three of whom were men. This was another aspect of Chinese university life that wasn't quite Orwellian. Orwell's fiction is marked by a pronounced misogyny, including some descriptions in *1984*: "It was always the women, and above all the young ones, who were the most bigoted adherents of the Party, the swallowers of slogans, the amateur spies and nosers-out of unorthodoxy." My experience was the opposite: on average, young Chinese women seemed much less nationalistic and much more open to different ideas than the men.

At the meeting, we talked for most of an hour. One woman asked me to compare the political climate to that of Fuling twenty years earlier, and I mentioned the way students used to talk about leaders. "Mao and Deng felt like real individuals," I said. "I don't get any sense of personality from Xi. He almost feels like a robot. I think that he embodies the system."

Another woman asked about my impression of their generation. I said that young people often seemed risk-averse, because they were only children who felt pressure to succeed. They were also much better educated and more aware of the outside world than previous generations had been. "But I don't know what this means for the future," I said. "Maybe it means that they figure out how to change the system. But maybe they just figure out how to adapt to the system." I looked at the young faces around me. "What do you think?"

"We will adapt," one woman said, and several others nodded.

"It's easy to get angry, but easy to forget," another woman remarked.

But Serena, who was sitting toward the back of the group, said, "We will change it."

In Serena's final year, she had decided to become a writer. She was accepted to a graduate program in journalism at Fudan University, one of the best institutions in China. In June, I attended her graduation ceremony in the Foreign Language Studies Department. This year's ceremony was closed to parents, because of COVID restrictions.

The graduation was scheduled for eleven o'clock, but in the Chinese way, it started ten minutes early. Three hundred students were seated on cheap plastic stools in a cramped lecture hall on the fifth floor of the building where I taught. Speeches were delivered in turn by an administrator, a professor, and a student. All three of them kept their remarks brief, and they made no reference to current events, social issues, or even the experience of completing college during the pandemic. Each speaker made a rote statement about the history of Sichuan University, and they mentioned the importance of alumni staying in touch. Their main goal seemed to be to exit the stage as quickly as possible. Afterward, students lined up, walked briskly to the front, and received their diplomas while loudspeakers played "The Athlete's March," a song that accompanies mandatory calisthenics at Chinese schools. From start to finish, the graduation took exactly thirty-three minutes. At the end, rather than using Kenny G, an administrator shooed everybody out by barking into a microphone: "*Biye kuaile!*" (Happy graduation!)

In a culture with a two-millennia tradition of valuing education, at the best university in the province, the event had all the pomp and circumstance of a vaccination campaign. There were far more elaborate graduation ceremonies at nursery schools in the United States. But this was also the Chinese way: the point was the process, not the achievement, and people weren't inclined to ceremony.

Afterward, Serena and a few of my other students celebrated with bowls of noodles in the cafeteria. The dining hall was full of people in caps and gowns, carrying plastic trays and eating quickly. The students talked to me about their plans: Anna was going to graduate school in the Netherlands, and Fenton was bound for the London School of Economics. He had also been accepted at USC, which he would have preferred. But his parents insisted that he go to England because they were concerned about U.S.–China relations. "They worry that if there's a war, the Chinese students in America won't be able to leave," Fenton told me.

Serena hoped to wrap up some final *Common Sense* stories before moving to Shanghai. Her most recent piece had been about a Sichuan University student who, earlier in the semester, had suddenly died in his dormitory room. The death seemed to have been the result of some undiagnosed medical condition, but the story was kept out of the state press. The *Common Sense* report had caused a stir on campus.

"The counselors were looking for the person who wrote it," Serena said.

"Did they figure it out?" I asked.

"If they did, I wouldn't be here today," she said, laughing. "They thought it was somebody in the journalism department."

We took pictures at the ceremonial gate on the upper end of campus. I told the students that I had to get my car and drive back to the city for another appointment. "Did you park under the College of Marxism?" Fenton asked. It had become a running joke because of the online vitriol from Little Pinks.

Recently, as part of Serena's reporting for *Common Sense*, she had tracked down Lin Yiwu, the pseudonymous writer who had attacked me. He wouldn't tell her his real name, but he agreed to talk. His job had nothing to do with media; he was a young man who had had a short career as a lawyer in London and Beijing, and now he worked as a translator. He wrote nationalistic screeds in his free time. It seemed remarkable that such people could help shape public discourse, but this was one outcome of heavy censorship. Lin Yiwu told Serena that he was pleased that the university had let me go. "It's good that he's leaving, because he's too old," he said. "He should go back to America and think more carefully about what he writes."

As part of her story, Serena wanted to interview Minking Chyu, the SCUPI dean. I advised her not to follow the usual *Common Sense* practices of surreptitious reporting. I explained that Chyu was an American and SCUPI was a joint program, and thus it was appropriate to approach the dean openly, the way a journalist would in the United States.

Serena took my advice. She sent an email to Dean Chyu, requesting an interview. Within hours she was called in to be questioned by university administrators.

On campus, Serena was led into a room with her academic counselor and a Party official. The counselor was a woman, and the official was a man, and they proceeded in classic good cadre / bad cadre fashion. The counselor referred gently to Serena's excellent academic performance, but the official was stern-faced. "Did you already get your diploma?" he asked. When Serena said yes, the official mentioned that she could be expelled from alumni associations.

A couple of weeks later, when we met to talk about the incident, Serena told me that the bad cadre wasn't nearly as bad as he could have been. She believed that if the incident had happened a little later the officials wouldn't have even bothered with the interrogation. "Today is the day when my face disappears," she explained. She meant that she was now officially finished at Sichuan University, so the turnstile scanners no longer recognized her, and she wasn't a responsibility of the administration.

But at the time when she contacted Dean Chyu, she was still living in the dormitory, so officials felt compelled to do something. With regard to the bad cadre, Serena said: "He was just doing his job." She also performed her role: she began to cry, and she promised not to write anything about me or my job status. She later said that it was easy to cry in such situations.

During the interrogation, the cadres scolded Serena for daring to approach Dean Chyu for an interview. From the way the cadres talked, Serena believed that somebody from SCUPI had reported her, although it was never explicit—it may have been simply coincidence that she was interrogated a few hours after contacting the dean. It was also possible that the authorities had been monitoring her email. Either way, I felt terrible. I should have warned her not to investigate, and it was a mistake to suggest that she approach the dean directly, in the American fashion. I had forgotten one pattern of institutional exchange, which is that sometimes, if a foreign organization is in China, and if it comes under some kind of pressure, members may behave according to the worst local practices. *The system has kidnapped everybody.*

Later, after I returned to the United States, I contacted Dean Chyu to request an interview in order to clarify what had happened with my job. He replied in an email that he was too busy. Later, when he was contacted by fact-checkers at *The New Yorker*, he claimed that I had never expressed interest in signing a long-term contract, and he said that he had made plans to replace me before the pandemic began.

I also reached out to the University of Pittsburgh, asking to talk about the long-term goals of the SCUPI program in China. The university's response was exactly like that of a Chinese institution. Initially, a Pittsburgh spokesman seemed helpful, but then, after a number of delays, he declined the interview request.

The day after Serena's interrogation, she had sent an email:

I will write about this "forbidden" topic 30 years later when things are better. I have an outline that I really like. . . .

Remember the last time when we talked at *Common Sense*? You asked us if we thought we would change the country in the future. I said yes. I was being very optimistic. Now I become much more realistic after hours of "education" yesterday. I feel like growing up a bit. But I will not give up.

———

On the twins' last day at Chengdu Experimental, Leslie and I picked them up early. Teacher Zhang and the other children had prepared a farewell video that featured clips from school activities: students doing math sums, reciting poems, and engaging in science experiments. After the video was finished, classmates came to the front one by one, giving small gifts and saying goodbye. One pudgy boy with a crew cut invited Cai Cai and Rou Rou to visit him at his home, and he recited a long address: street, building, entrance, floor, apartment number.

Teacher Zhang spoke last. "These two years have been very long," she said to the twins. "There was one period when we were at home because of the pandemic. But you always kept learning, and all of our students can learn from your example. The most important thing, though, is our friendship."

In some respects, having Ariel and Natasha in public school had been the most challenging part of our time in Chengdu. Leslie and I had had previous experience with almost everything else: in the past, both of us had lived and worked in China for more than a decade. But we had never had children in a Chinese public school, and the adjustment had been nearly as hard as what I remembered from the Peace Corps.

But in other respects the school experience had been completely simple. After Natasha and Ariel were enrolled, there were no *guanxi* games, and nobody asked us for favors or gifts. We were never charged a single yuan in tuition. There was no nervousness about my writing or nationality, and nobody cared if I was attacked online by pseudonymous blowhard lawyers. Chengdu Experimental continued to welcome the twins during the pandemic, and their schooling was much less disrupted than it would have been in the United States. The Chinese way could be frustrating, but it could also be wonderfully straightforward. As long as our daughters did their work, and as long as they came to class prepared to learn, they were treated the same as every other child. The school was one of the few parts of my Chengdu life that had never been complicated by politics.

On Natasha and Ariel's first day, they had cried when I picked them up. At the time, it seemed impossible that they could ever learn the language and fit into the Chinese system. Teacher Zhang's comment on the last day was accurate—it had been a long two years. I knew that no matter what we did in the future, the Chengdu experience would stay with Ariel and Natasha for the rest of their lives.

After the classroom presentation, the children applauded, and we left. Teacher Zhang escorted us down the hallway. Leslie and I told her how grateful we were for all her help. "Cai Cai and Rou Rou never could have done this without you," Leslie said. Teacher Zhang waved off the compliments, and she knelt and hugged each of the girls. They cried, like they had on the first day, and this time Teacher Zhang cried, too.

Leslie, Natasha, and Ariel, along with Ulysses the cat, were scheduled to leave in early July. I planned to stay a while longer, in order to take a final trip down the Yangtze Valley. Less than a week before my family's flight, Yang Guang, the deputy director of Sichuan University's foreign-affairs office, asked if we could talk.

We met at a café near the old campus of Sichuan University, on the northern bank of the Jin River. Yang was in his early fifties, and he spoke fluent English; he had a doctorate in American studies. He explained that for seven years he had managed the Sichuan University–Arizona State University Center for American Culture. The center had been one of the many attempts by American universities to collaborate with Chinese institutions. Yang said that for years the center had been successful in hosting visiting scholars and special lectures, but some of the funding came from the U.S. State Department, which ended support at the start of the Trump administration. In 2017, the center was closed, and Yang was transferred to the foreign-affairs office. Lately his job consisted of dealing with abandoned or canceled exchanges.

"Because of the bad relations between our two countries, many of these programs have to stop," he said. "I hope that in the future these kinds of programs can continue."

While talking, Yang nervously crumpled a piece of paper in his fingers. He mentioned that his office had not been involved with the refusal to renew my contract, but now they wanted to know if anything could be done. "That's why I'm here today, to see if there's a possibility of having you work at Sichuan University for a longer time," he said.

I said that three months earlier, I had offered on three different occasions to stay on at the university, but each time I had been rejected. "I was told by some people at the college that administrators were worried about public criticism of my writing," I said.

Yang answered slowly. "I know there was an article attacking you in the spring," he said. "There are these kinds of attacks. But my understanding is that this is just a voice. There are so many different voices. I don't think it's so important. Anybody has the right to express their ideas."

I told Yang that it seemed strange that Dean Chyu had avoided speaking with me directly, and that his behavior made me suspect political pressure.

"He was in America during this time," Yang said, speaking carefully. "He did not know the whole situation here." (Later, when contacted by a *New Yorker* fact-checker, Yang denied saying this.)

I thanked Yang for reaching out, and I explained that my family was leaving in six days; it was too late to reconsider our departure. Yang seemed relieved. I couldn't tell if the offer was sincere, but it seemed clear that the university wanted to lay the blame on Chyu. My guess was that either Chyu had misread signals or, more likely, there had been some blowback after the negative press about my departure.

I had brought one of my China books, and I gave it to Yang. A few years earlier, he had written a book about American activities abroad, and now he presented me with a signed copy. The English title read: *The Role of Government: A Liberalism Perspective on American Cultural Diplomacy.*

We stood up to leave, and Yang mentioned that he had an appointment on the old campus, to shut down the former Peace Corps office. The American staff had left the previous year, but a few Chinese employees had stayed on in order to complete various bureaucratic tasks associated with ending the program. Today the building was officially being transferred back to Sichuan University. I asked Yang if I could accompany him, and he agreed.

We walked to the East Gate and had our faces scanned. Inside the turnstile, we passed a large red banner that had been erected in honor of the next anniversary, which would be commemorated later that summer:

WARMLY CELEBRATE THE 100TH ANNIVERSARY OF THE FOUNDING OF THE CHINESE COMMUNIST PARTY

A local Peace Corps employee named Liu Haishu was waiting in front of the former headquarters. Yang explained that the handover required representatives from three organizations: the National Assets Office, Sichuan University, and the Peace Corps. Usually, an American government official would have been present, but the consulate had been closed for more than half a year. Today, Liu would represent the American agency, along with another local employee, Hu Yi.

Two women and a man arrived from the National Assets Office. Liu unlocked the door and we followed him inside. The assets officials took their time, inspecting the contents of each room and taking photographs. "The air-conditioning units will be handed over, too," Liu told them. On the third floor, we passed a map of China with red strings attached to the various places where volunteers once served: Fuling, Leshan, Mianyang, Guiyang, Lanzhou—dozens of towns across the southwest. The strings used to connect to the names of current volunteers; now they hung slack from the wall.

I asked Liu how long he had worked there. "Nineteen years," he said. "What did you do?"

"Multiple jobs. IT specialist, financial assistant, director of management and operations."

I had heard that Chinese staff of both the Peace Corps and the consulate had had trouble finding new jobs, because of their former connection to the American government. I asked Liu if he had had any luck. "No," he said. "It's a little hard."

At the end of the tour, Liu handed over 350 keys, for the various doors in the building. The three representatives signed a form testifying to the transfer. Finally, Liu produced the chop, or ink stamp, that had been used by the Peace Corps on all official documents. The red stamp was engraved in both languages with the euphemistic title that had been adopted more than a quarter century ago, when the words *Peace Corps* were still tainted by Maoist propaganda:

美中友好志愿者

U.S.–CHINA FRIENDSHIP VOLUNTEERS

After the chop was handed over, Yang announced that the transfer was complete. We chatted for a few minutes on the sidewalk outside, and I asked Liu if any volunteer possessions remained in Chengdu. He said that he still had a diamond ring in his apartment. Two volunteers had gotten engaged in Zhangye, a remote city in Gansu province, and the en-

gagement ring had been in their apartment when everybody was evacuated at the start of the pandemic. Chinese staff had mailed most
possessions back to the U.S., but the ring was too valuable.

"We aren't allowed to ship anything worth more than a thousand
dollars," Liu said. "I don't know how we'll get it to them. I don't even know
if they're married by now."

On the way back to the East Gate, we passed the red banner commemorating the founding of the Communist Party. Yang stopped before
the gate and shook my hand. "I want to reiterate that you are very welcome at Sichuan University," he said. I thanked him and said that I
couldn't have been happier with my students. At the turnstile, I had my
face scanned, and then I walked out of the university for the last time.

After my family flew to Colorado, there was a period when I was alone
in the apartment beside the Fu River. The place was silent except for one
of my least favorite sounds on earth, the shriek of packing tape being un-
wound. Every day, I boxed up possessions, and whenever that became
unbearable I went out in the city. A few times, I drove to southern
Chengdu to see Li Dewei. His Amazon sales had continued to boom during the pandemic, and in early July his company moved into a massive
new office. Li planned to increase his staff by a factor of four.

Sometimes we had dinner with Li's entrepreneur friends, most of
whom had also figured out ways to access the American market from
Chengdu. One friend, Zhang Shuyu, had started a company called Dreams-
painter. Zhang used a VPN to run an Instagram account that allowed
Americans to commission acrylic portraits based on photographs of loved
ones. Zhang had developed a network of Chinese artists, each of whom
could complete a large painting in five to ten days, for around five hundred dollars.

Most commissions involved dead people or pets. Apparently, there
were many Americans who wanted a painting of a departed grandfather

holding a grandson he had never met, or a picture of one dog that had died alongside another dog that was living. Customers sent photographs of the various subjects, and the artists merged them into a single image that made it appear as if everybody were still alive and together. Often, there was something slightly off-kilter about the way people stood next to one another, or placed a hand atop a pet's head. But customers seemed satisfied. "I started it only half a year ago, but it's doing really well," Zhang said.

During my sunnier moments, I thought of this as the last bulwark of U.S.–China friendship. The Peace Corps was gone; the Fulbright program had ended; the consulate was closed; most American journalists had been expelled; there were essentially no more functioning exchange programs in China. But at least some Chinese artists were painting dead Americans and their dead dogs.

In the evening, I met friends, students, or colleagues for farewell dinners. I settled into a routine: every night, I drove the COVID car, parked near a restaurant, and had dinner and drinks. Afterward, I opened the DiDi app and called a *daijiaren*. In about seven minutes a man in a helmet appeared on a collapsible bicycle. He put the bike in the back of the COVID car, took the keys, and drove me home.

After a string of evenings that ended with strangers on collapsible bicycles driving me back to an empty apartment, I decided that it was time to head off for the Yangtze Valley.

I followed new highways to the Three Gorges Dam. In the old days, the journey from Fuling took three days on a boat; now it was possible to drive the distance in little more than six hours. The dam was situated at the western edge of Hubei province, where it had been turned into a sprawling tourist destination. Even from the viewing platforms, it was impossible to grasp the scale of the structure: forty stories tall and a full mile across. On the afternoon I visited, there was a steady drizzle, and everything around me seemed to be some shade of gray: the sky, the river, the rain, the dam. It was the largest concrete structure on earth.

One part of the site was called the River Closure Memorial Park. The park commemorated November 9, 1997, when the Yangtze had been diverted in order to make way for the construction of the dam's retaining wall. I had watched the diversion live on television in my Fuling apartment. On that day, Jiang Zemin gave a speech in which he declared: "It vividly proves again that socialism is superior in organizing people to do big jobs."

The park displayed some of the original equipment, like artifacts from a long-lost age. Rusting yellow bulldozers with balloon tires were arranged neatly on a green lawn, along with scattered concrete tetrahedrons that had been used to block the river. None of the park's historical displays referred to Jiang or to his speech. This was true throughout the dam site: I could find only one thing connected to Jiang, a modest display of his calligraphy. Otherwise, every reference to a leader involved either Mao Zedong or Xi Jinping. At the dam and other tourist sites across China, Xi was consolidating history the same way that he had consolidated power.

For a week, I visited Fuling students in various settlements that had been built to replace flooded communities. The driving was often difficult, because cities had been designed in the early 2000s, before people realized how prevalent automobiles would become. In Wushan, at the entrance to one of the gorges, there were daily traffic jams between the upper and lower parts of town, and it was hard to find parking. Usually I left the COVID car at the hotel and walked.

A former student named Yancy taught at the best secondary school in upper Wushan. When we met for dinner, Yancy told me that teaching jobs had become so scarce that his school recently had ninety applicants for a single opening. "When we were young, it was so easy to find a job," he said.

As with so many other things, Yancy and the rest of his teaching cohort had enjoyed good timing. They had entered the profession when the country's population was still relatively young, and when education was being expanded on a massive scale. But now the demographics had turned. In Yueqing, the Zhejiang city where Willy had prospered for twenty years in private schools, he saw trouble on the horizon. He wrote in an email:

> The education situation in the coming years is a bit worrying, especially for private schools. After about six years, the number of students will sharply decrease. For example, currently there are over 15,000 new students in Yueqing's first year of junior high, but in six or seven years, there will only be around 3,000 or 4,000. This means many schools will face a shortage of students, and the government will undoubtedly protect its public schools.

———

While driving through the Three Gorges, I stopped to visit Jimmy. Many years ago, Jimmy and his wife had owned a hotel and restaurant in Jiangkou, but that town was long ago underwater. Along with tens of thousands of people from the surrounding area, Jimmy and his family had been relocated to the new city of Yunyang. It was situated about twenty-five miles away from their old home, on the steep northern bank of the Yangtze.

Like some of the new river towns that had been constructed across previously uninhabited mountainsides, Yunyang had an unbelievable assortment of stairways. In the spring of 2011, I had visited Jimmy, who took me to see the new town's centerpiece, a broad public staircase with more than nineteen hundred steps. It was stark white and straight as an arrow; the thing ran like a spine through the center of this vertical city. Standing at the bottom and gazing at the antlike figures on the upper reaches was enough to make me dizzy.

Years later, I recognized that this had been a special window in Yang-tze time: postdiluvian but pre-elevator. Everybody still trudged up steps, and Jimmy and his wife had recently bought a sixth-floor walk-up at the top of a building next to the Yangtze. The penthouse was prime real estate, and it reflected how well the couple's hotel and restaurant had done in their previous hometown of Jiangkou. Since then, Jiangkou and the surrounding region had been flooded by the dam, but Jimmy and his wife didn't seem to mind. She had figured out new opportunities in the tech industry, and by 2011 she had become HP's head sales representative for that stretch of the Yangtze Valley.

Over the following decade, things continued to go well for the couple. Their daughter, Chen Xi, headed off to graduate school in Manchester. When I visited in 2021, Jimmy's wife was driving a gold Mercedes-Benz, and the couple was still adept at figuring out new angles. Recently, they had responded quickly to a new Xi Jinping campaign. In 2018, the leader had made a speech in which he referred to the issue of schoolchildren straining their eyes from overwork. One of Xi's phrases—"protect our children's eyes together, give them a bright future"—was picked up by various propaganda organs. In 2021, the government announced a project called Guangming Xingdong, or "Operation Light." It was a typical response: rather than reducing schoolwork, they simply turned up the lights. Immediately after the campaign was announced, Jimmy and his wife opened a small factory that manufactured high-quality light fixtures for classrooms. When I visited, business was booming, and forty-five employees were staffing the assembly line.

The only thing that hadn't worked out for Jimmy was elevators. The couple's penthouse apartment still had beautiful Yangtze views, but now they were getting older, and they were tired of walking up six flights of stairs. Some local companies specialized in attaching elevators, like North's business in Fuling. But Jimmy's building was situated in a way that made such a project impossible. He told me that they would eventually move to a new home.

As always, Jimmy was in a good mood. That was one constant among Fuling students: over the years, in annual surveys, I had often asked them to rate their feelings about the future, and the responses were consistently optimistic. They were in many ways a blessed generation. The Reform years had taught them how to be pragmatic, resourceful, and fearless, and even the ones who had been dealt a difficult hand seemed to make the best of the situation. When I stopped in Fuling, I was amazed to find that Lu Yong was still doing relatively well despite his lung cancer. The experimental drug had continued to be effective; on the day we met, Lu Yong looked thin and pale, but he was just as cheerful as Jimmy.

One morning, Emily and I had a long conversation in downtown Fuling. She told me that finally, in her late forties, she had come to understand her own strengths and weaknesses. "My weakness is that I'm not very good at logical thinking," she said. "But my strength is intuition. With Tao Tao, I often feel that something is right, but everybody else says it's wrong. If I follow my intuition, it always seems to turn out to be correct."

During the previous semester, Tao Tao had excelled academically, and he had been invited to attend a selective summer session. The course prepared children for the upcoming high school entrance examinations. Tao Tao hoped to test into a prestigious Chongqing school known for both excellence and being relatively progressive. But Tao Tao told his mother that he didn't want to attend the summer classes.

Friends and family advised Emily to ignore the boy's wishes. The session cost little, and it was both an honor and an advantage. "I personally thought that he should go," Emily said. "It's not that long, only twelve days, and the teachers are really good. But he didn't want to do it. He said that this should be vacation, and he wanted time off. I decided to respect his wishes."

Tao Tao spent the summer reading freely and ignoring most of the school's recommended assignments. The following year he tested into the prestigious high school anyway.

During my last days in Fuling, I spent as much time as possible in the countryside. It felt like a lost world—along with the old campus, the fields and the farmers' paths reminded me most vividly of the way things used to be. A single local ferry still crossed the Yangtze, and one morning I walked from my hotel and took the boat. At the base of Beishanping, I found the stone staircase that visitors used to hike on weekend trips. Many of the steps were overgrown with weeds, and trees had grown tall on old terraced fields that farmers no longer tended. But it was still possible to climb the mountain's southern face.

After reaching the long, flat summit, I followed another path with clear views of the city and the rivers. The path ended near the edge of River Town Golf. The bronze bull and matador were still frozen in the same position, and the replica Siegestor arch was starting to look weathered. The luxury hotel and the villas had never been finished. Nearby, somebody had tried to turn one section of the golf course into an imitation Mongolian grassland where visitors could pay to ride horses. There were still some advertisements featuring smiling people in ethnic costumes, but the horses were gone, and the Mongolian grassland idea, like every other attempt at moneymaking on this doomed mountain, had been abandoned.

Only two parts of the golf course still attracted visitors. One was the former fairway where vendors sold drinks and mutton skewers, and the other was a large water hazard. Fishermen liked to go to the water hazard in the mornings and afternoons. I chatted with a couple of the men who were standing with their rods, and then I rested in the shade. It was a quiet, peaceful site; I always enjoyed stopping here during Fuling visits. Lots of writers had their stories adapted into movies and television shows, but I didn't know anybody else with a book that became a failed golf course.

One warm morning, I drove across the Yangtze and picked up a former student named Grant. He had grown up in the countryside west of Fuling, and I had always wanted to see his home village. On the way, we stopped by the rural school that Grant attended as a child. It was situated atop a hill, at the site of a former Buddhist temple. Like many rural religious institutions, the temple had been converted to a school after the Communist revolution.

Grant had been only the second child from his village to make it into college. After graduating, he excelled as a teacher, and now he worked at the best high school in Fuling. "When I was in elementary school here, we had three classes per grade," he said, while we visited the empty schoolyard. "Now there's only one small class." He speculated that eventually the government would close the school, a process that had been happening in rural China on a scale that was almost unimaginable. According to the central government, beginning in 2000, China had shut down an average of sixty-three elementary schools every day for a full decade.

This area was called Lidu: Li's Crossing. Grant explained that the name came from a legend that Li Bai had crossed the Yangtze here during one of his many exiles. The Tang poet had always liked watery landscapes; he was the one who first nicknamed Wuhan "river town." But my mind's image of Li Bai had been permanently contaminated by fourth-grade doggerel. Whenever I heard about Li Bai crossing the Yangtze, or floating past Wuhan, or doing anything with a body of water, all I could think about was shit:

> *But sitting on the boat I realize that I forgot paper,*
> *However deep the Lake of Peach Blossoms may be. . . .*

The roads grew smaller as we approached Grant's village. Traditionally, residents had farmed corn, soybeans, and vegetables, but now most fields were fallow. Grant's house stood three stories tall behind a large threshing platform. He tried the front door—locked. "I actually don't have a key," he said with a laugh. He walked down a hill to get a spare from one of the few neighbors who still lived here.

Grant's parents had rebuilt the structure in 2000, thinking that at least one of their three children would stay in the village. But all of them had migrated, and now Grant and his siblings returned only once a year, for the Lunar New Year holiday. Both parents had been dead for more than a decade. Grant and I walked through the silent house, where certain objects—a thermos sitting on a table, a pair of pants draped over a bed—gave the impression that residents had departed just yesterday.

Outside, Grant pointed to a beautiful white-fig tree that he had planted as a teenager in 1991. Ten years ago, a developer offered more than a hundred dollars for the tree, in order to replant it in one of Fuling's new suburbs. But Grant declined for sentimental reasons. He said that developers often scouted these areas for healthy trees to uproot. In rural China, where the scale of exodus was almost biblical, this was the final stage: in the beginning, the people migrated, and then the trees followed.

I drove back toward town. When we passed the old elementary school, Grant told a story about a former classmate who had come from one of the village's poorest families. "They had three sons and one daughter, and all of them had bad clothes," he remembered. "He was a terrible student. He used to look up to me, because I was the top student."

Grant's classmate dropped out before middle school. As a young teenager, he headed off to Shanxi province, in the north. The boy worked as a laborer in a rock quarry, and then he continued to mining jobs, along with a younger brother. "Eventually, he started opening his own mines," Grant said. "That was during a time when there was a lot of illegal mining. They were doing things that you can't do anymore. He made a lot of money, and he came back here and started a construction company."

The company currently had the equivalent of a fifteen-million-dollar contract to build a new section of highway. Grant had invested in the project, and he received a significant dividend every month. Despite their disparate paths, he and the classmate remained close. "Sometimes we get together and play mah-jongg," Grant said. He noted that his friend's two children had both tested into highly ranked universities.

Grant fell silent, and I thought the story was finished. But then he spoke again. "His younger brother died in one of those mines," he said quietly. "That was early in his time there, before he became a boss. There was an accident." He paused again. "I remember when it happened; the family was so upset. I think my friend always felt some responsibility."

For the Reform generation, even the most spectacular success stories were often accompanied by some kind of sadness or loss. This side of the experience was usually left unspoken, the way it was for Emily's family. When I talked with Anry about his life, he told me that his oldest brother was never able to work again after the dynamite accident. The disabled man was eventually divorced by his wife, and he now lived in a full-time care facility in Chongqing. The second brother died suddenly, of illness, in 2008, and the third had been electrocuted on the Shanghai assembly line. Of the four siblings, Anry was the only one who was both alive and healthy.

For his friend and classmate Youngsea, the sadness had been the loss of Lin, his first love, who never returned after breaking up with him at the height of his success. Lin married the other businessman, with whom she had two children, although they eventually divorced. Nowadays, Youngsea was happily married to a middle school teacher. Like Anry, he had married late enough that he was able to have two children legally. Youngsea told me that he had never tried to contact Lin. "It's better that way," he said.

The last time I saw Youngsea, Anry, and North that spring, we made a pilgrimage to the old campus. In downtown Fuling, we met at a hot-pot restaurant for lunch. North joined us, and his former roommates asked about the elevator business. "It's OK," North said. "Just the usual problems." Anry had told me in private that he thought things were likely to get harder for North. "He started the business too late," Anry said.

As the broth boiled in the hot pot, the old friends talked about the past.

"The toughest generations were those who grew up in the sixties, seventies, and eighties," Youngsea said.

"Those of us who grew up in the countryside had no *guanxi*," Anry said. "Nobody in the city helped us. Everything depended on ourselves."

With their chopsticks, the men fished delicacies out of the pot—thin-sliced beef, golden-needle mushrooms. The conversation turned to food.

"When I was five or six, that's when we were the poorest," North said. "We never had enough to eat."

"I can remember people eating leaves," Anry said. "They used to boil them in a soup. My family didn't do that, but our neighbors did. They ate from the *huangjingshu*."

In English, *huangjingshu* is the Chinese chaste tree, a plant known for its dense foliage.

"We had meat once every half month," North said. "And we had it at the Lunar New Year."

After the meal, all of us climbed into Youngsea's black Mercedes S350. A year earlier, he had bought the car, which was manufactured in Germany, for more than $150,000. Driving through downtown Fuling, he pointed out the site of his original cell phone shop. He still owned the business, but long ago he had handed over management to his younger brother. In recent years, Youngsea's firm had continued expanding into manufacturing, advertising, and building bridges and roads. His latest venture involved the construction of more than twenty huge billboards, about half of them digital, in downtown Chongqing.

The Mercedes cruised east across the Wu River. As usual, the entrance to the old campus was unguarded. Youngsea drove past the fading propaganda:

THE PEOPLE'S CITY IS BUILT BY THE PEOPLE
THE PEOPLE'S CITY SERVES THE PEOPLE

BUILD A HYGIENIC CITY
CREATE CULTURED URBAN CITIZENS

BUILD A NATIONAL CIVILIZED CITY
AND A NATIONAL HYGIENIC DISTRICT

I AM AWARE, I PARTICIPATE,
I SUPPORT, I AM SATISFIED

He parked at the library. We took pictures in front, like in the old days. During the past two years, China's property sector had started to contract, and friends in Fuling had told me that they didn't expect the old campus to be sold anytime soon. After finishing the library pictures, we continued on foot to the broken-down building where I used to live. The trees on the roof seemed to have grown thicker, and sections of the concrete exterior were crumbling away. The three former students looked up in silence.

"It's hard to believe that this was where the highest officials lived," Anry said. "It seemed so nice to us in those days."

Before heading back to the Mercedes, North walked around the building and studied the stairwell's exterior wall. "You could put an elevator there," he said.

The Uncompahgre River

Summer 2023

I N SOUTHWESTERN COLORADO, NEAR THE BANKS OF THE UNCOM-
pahgre River, my family returned to the home we hadn't seen for two
years. Before moving to Chengdu, we had planted some aspen trees,
which had grown taller, and now we planted some more. The Honda that
was parked in the barn was the same color as the Honda that I used to
park beneath the College of Marxism. There was also a large Egyptian
cat named Morsi. A number of years ago, Leslie had carried Morsi from
Cairo to Colorado, and this time the twins lugged Ulysses home from
Chengdu.

Once the cats were together, it was clear that they did not get along
in a specific way. The Chinese cat liked the Egyptian cat, but the Egyptian cat did not like the Chinese cat. Everywhere the Egyptian cat went,
the Chinese cat followed, but if he got too close, there was a brief and very
one-sided fight. Eventually, the cats worked out an acceptable distance
of about fifteen feet. In tandem, as if tied together on a string, they
hunted mice and pocket gophers in our pasture.

The window of my study overlooked the pasture and the Uncompahgre River Valley. While writing, I often thought about the Chengdu apartment on the nineteenth floor, and I remembered the view of the Jin River.
For some reason, I often envisioned the way Chengdu had looked on the

night of the earthquake, at the start of the pandemic: the city suspended
and the silent river, its surface slick with lights.

One day in Colorado, I reached out to my former student John. Ever
since the *jubao* incident at the end of 2019, I had wondered what really
happened. Now I sent John a long email and a screenshot of the bulletin-
board posts that had accused me of anti-China teaching. John responded
almost immediately:

> I'm astonished, and to be honest, I have never known what had hap-
> pened to you until I received this email. . . . I am deeply sorry for
> that, and I would like to find out who is behind this, so I would like
> to talk to you about this matter.

Within hours, we were connected by video. John looked the same,
and we chatted for a while about how things were going. Then, speaking
slowly, he apologized again. "I didn't know about this," he said. "I remember I heard from classmates that you had been reported by somebody.
But I didn't know the reason."

He said that he had a Weibo account, but he used it only to follow
others—he didn't post. He remembered my editing comments on his
essay, but he claimed to have no idea how the remarks became public.

Back in Chengdu, I had discussed the incident with a handful of
trusted students and fellow professors. One teacher who knew John had
told me that the boy didn't seem like a Little Pink. The teacher suggested
a possible scenario that was similar to what Serena had imagined. Both
of them thought that perhaps another student had seen the essay, or
heard details from it, and then wrote the attacks.

On the video call, John said that he had mentioned my editing comments to his roommates in the dormitory. He had also taken the paper
to SCUPI's writing center, where other students and tutors may have

seen it. From the expression on John's face, and from his willingness to talk, I believed that he was telling the truth.

"Actually, after you gave the comments on the paper, I was a little upset," he said. "I totally agree with you about the comments, if we don't consider the politics. But I had to consider the politics, because I am under a certain circumstance in China. Your comments were against the traditional politics."

I asked what in particular had upset him.

"The sovereignty," he said.

During the conversation, he never said the word *Taiwan*. Instead, he used various indirections: *sovereignty, certain circumstance, certain situations*. Like most young Chinese, John had been trained to avoid trouble, and part of his mind didn't want to touch the sensitive language. He said that back in 2019, when he had heard that I was involved in some kind of *jubao* situation, he had done nothing to try to learn what had happened. Some of his classmates had told me the same thing. They had been aware of rumors that I was in trouble, but they didn't respond with any particular curiosity. This made sense: any student in China learns that there are moments when he asks no questions. *Certain circumstances, certain situations.*

John thanked me for reaching out, and he said again that he harbored no resentment about my comments on the essay. "Actually, if I am American I would totally agree with you," he said. "But I'm not."

I asked if he would have the same reaction now.

"Yes," he said. "It's not that the comments are wrong. It's just the feelings."

Before leaving Chengdu, I had gathered my students' contact information, the same way I had in Fuling twenty-three years earlier. This time, the young people were heading much farther afield. By 2023, the English names from my classroom had scattered across the world: Anna in

Nijmegen, Fenton in London, Michelle in Oxford, Elaine in Hong Kong, Tim in Lubbock, Damien in Munich, Sarinstein in Singapore. During my lectures on Georg Simmel, I used to say that if I were a young Chinese writer I would consider going to Africa, because of all the Chinese who had migrated there for business and diplomacy—strangers in a strange land. Two of my most talented students went in that direction, in order to research and write: Yidi to Sierre Leone, Serena to Algeria and Tanzania. For Serena's first professional long feature, published in the *South China Morning Post*, she profiled a Chinese entrepreneur who had been named an honorary chieftain of the Yoruba tribe in southwest Nigeria.

Many SCUPI students transferred to the University of Pittsburgh, and I visited them at their new home. In a Chinese restaurant near the Pitt campus, I had dinner with Bruce, who was healthy and happy. He hadn't ridden a motorcycle since the accident near the Dadu River. Vincent joined us for the meal; he was also living in Pittsburgh. After two years in the American city, Vincent had acquired a SIG Sauer P365 pistol, a SIG Sauer P320 pistol, a 12-gauge Winchester shotgun, a SIG Sauer MCX Rattler, a 16-inch AR-15, and an AK-47.

He had also joined the Presbyterian Church and decided to stay in the United States. He told me that after arriving in Pittsburgh, he began to read seriously about the massacre around Tiananmen Square and other sensitive events. "My ideas changed a lot in the first few months," he said. "It was a matter of being in a free environment, and being able to access whatever I wanted."

I mentioned that at the end of the fall semester of 2020, Vincent had written positively about the government's approach to the pandemic. "Young people are like this in China," he said. "They tend to support the system. I was not opposed to the Party then." His views on sovereignty had also changed dramatically, and now he believed that Xinjiang should be independent. "When I was in China, I thought that all news about Xinjiang was fake, created by foreigners," he said. "Most young Chinese people feel that way, even the ones who are here and can access other information." Vincent said that the more that he thought about China's recent past, the more convinced he was that he could never return to live in a society with so many political restrictions.

He had also been dismayed by the final phase of the pandemic, when China adhered to its strict "zero-COVID" policy long after it was no longer necessary. After Vincent posted some critical comments on social media, he was attacked online by nationalists, and his parents in China were warned that their son could get in trouble. He decided to stay permanently in the United States. The majority of my former students who were living abroad still intended to return to China eventually. But several had told me that they planned to settle in the United States or Europe. This seemed to be part of a larger trend—the young referred to it as *runxue*, or "run philosophy." There were signs that some young Chinese, especially those who were highly educated, were trying to emigrate.

In the end, the Chinese government's performance with COVID could be divided into three phases, each with a different lesson. The first phase, in Wuhan, reflected the shortcomings of a heavily censored media, as well as a system in which local officials were inclined to cover up problems. The second phase showed more positive aspects of the Chinese bureaucracy. During this period—the longest of the three—the government developed a coherent and effective nationwide strategy, which benefited from decades of improvement to the educational system. In retrospect, it had been my family's good fortune that we happened to be in China during this time.

It also turned out to be our good fortune that we were forced to leave before the third phase. By the end of 2021, it was clear that zero-COVID was much less effective against the weaker but more contagious Omicron variant. Nevertheless, the government failed to adjust, and many cities, including Chengdu, suffered long lockdowns. Children in most parts of the country studied remotely for weeks at a time. One lesson from this final phase was a reminder of the system's rigidity and its tendency toward Kafkaesque bureaucracy. But it also showed what happens when too much power is placed in the hands of one individual who ignores strong evidence and good advice.

When zero-COVID was finally abandoned, in December of 2022, the change happened in response to a series of leaderless movements. Angry citizens held spontaneous demonstrations in Chinese cities, and a number of protests occurred at universities, including Sichuan University. In March, a brave student hung a propaganda-style banner in the heart of the Jiang'an Campus:

THIS IS THE SICHUAN UNIVERSITY
OF STUDENTS AND TEACHERS

NOT THE SICHUAN UNIVERSITY OF BUREAUCRATS

After the cadres gave up on zero-COVID, they sent almost all students home, knowing that infections would sweep across campus. But students at Sichuan University's West China School of Medicine were required to stay, because their services were badly needed at the institution's overburdened hospital. On December 14, a West China medical student died of a sudden cardiac event after finishing a long shift. The university refused to release many details about the death, and the story was kept out of the state press.

The staff at *Common Sense* began to research the incident. After one writer interviewed some classmates of the dead student, he was interrogated by counselors at the university. It became clear that the authorities had been monitoring the WeChat feeds of everybody associated with the publication. The university demanded detailed confessions, along with promises that the students would no longer be associated with *Common Sense*. Twelve years after the publication had been founded, it was effectively shut down.

Later, one student wrote me:

> I was quite depressed and fearful that time since nowhere inside the great firewall is safe for us to discuss. All our information is visible for them. We have stopped our work and *Common Sense* has not posted any reports since then. I even doubted the meaning of writing—if it can't be published and read by others, what does it mean for myself?

———

When I heard from former Fuling students, relatively few seemed very upset by the lockdowns. They generally lived in third- and fourth-tier provincial towns, which suffered less than major cities like Shanghai, Beijing, and Chengdu. Their teaching jobs were stable, and they were of a generation that tended to be tolerant of sudden shifts in policy. I had noticed that, over the years, their initial enthusiasm for Xi Jinping seemed to have waned, but their comments tended to be measured, and few seemed to want a major political change. While living in Sichuan, I had often found myself repeating the same mantra: *Nothing has changed; everything has changed*. On one side, there was the outsider's perspective: if the Chinese had been able to initiate so much social, economic, and educational change, then why couldn't they do the same thing with politics? But the logic was equally strong on the other side. Many Chinese, especially in the provinces, believed that political stability had been necessary in order to make all the other changes possible.

It seemed different, though, for the young. My Sichuan University students were much angrier about the lockdowns, which they often described as having fundamentally altered their perspectives. Sometimes, I wondered if the traditional "educated acquiescence" would hold true for their generation. One young man wrote from Europe:

> Most significantly, it has changed my opinions about "revolt" and "demonstration." I think Chinese should more often seek their rights through demonstrations, even though demonstrations in China have been equated with "revolt." . . .
>
> At some point, I am so disappointed in the domestic situation. Not only the government, but also the normal people. The patriarch is there but the protesting voices are so low. The working conditions are still inhumane, while everyone chooses to swallow the bitterness. . . .
>
> My friend who only wants to get richer says, "[Since] we are not able to change these situations, I'd rather think of ways to tolerate them."
>
> This is pathetic.

From Fuling, Emily reported that her students had suffered from the isolation of the lockdown period, but now they seemed to be recovering. She sent updates about her son:

> Sometimes when I look at Tao Tao, I have a strange feeling that this is my brother, especially when we talk about philosophy.
>
> Talking honestly about my brother's death with Tao Tao is good for both of them. You can't lie to Tao Tao because he won't stop if he doesn't get the truth. And it's not a shame for my brother.

Tao Tao was thriving in his new high school, which encouraged more critical thinking. Emily sent the transcript of a speech that Tao Tao had written for English class. The speech was titled "Should We Talk Back to Our Parents and Teachers?"

> There are also some more benefits of talking back. A German psychologist once said that those teenagers who are able to debate with seniors have more potential in their lives. They have better logical and critical thinking, problem-solving, communicating and social skills, which will help them do better and be successful in their career.

———

From Fuling to Chengdu, from 1996 to 2021, one thing that didn't change was my feeling toward the people I taught. I had great faith in them—I admired their diligence and their toughness, and I sympathized with their struggles. Each generation had inherited a system for which they were blameless, and they did the best they could with what they had. But the challenges for a young person in the 1990s, although formidable, had also been clear-cut and attainable: get educated, move to the city, escape poverty. Thirty years later, the problem runs deeper: something fundamental about the system needs to change. I still have great faith in the young, but I sense that their future will be more complicated.

I thought of them as Generation Xi, although this was a title they never would have used by choice. When I visited former students in Pittsburgh and other cities, I noticed that even in America they tried not to say the Chinese leader's name. Once, after meeting a former student in California, I sent her a note asking about this tendency. She wrote back:

> I do find myself avoiding mentioning Xi's name directly in California, even in private conversations and in places where I generally feel "safe." It's weird when I actually think about it. . . . I guess it's a

thing that has been reinforced millions of times to the point that it just feels uncomfortable and daunting to say his full name, as it has too much association with unrestrained power and punishment.

In the summer of 2023, I sent out a letter to former students from Sichuan University, and I included survey questions about their lives. When I asked what they worried about most, out of forty-seven responses, three specified the possibility of war with Taiwan. Another three mentioned politics. Only one student said that environmental issues concerned her the most. By far, the majority of answers were personal, and more than half mentioned job opportunities or issues with graduate school. This seemed to be another lesson that they had learned well, that there's no point in concerning yourself with big questions and systemic flaws.

I was most struck by responses to a simple query: "Do you want to have children eventually?" Most people who answered said no, and the trend was especially clear for women. Of the twenty-four women who responded, eighteen did not want children—a total of 75 percent. One explained:

From my observations in the UK and Europe, I think that Chinese children are more stressed and profoundly confused, which will continue. We are already a confused generation, and children's upbringing requires long periods of companionship and observation and guidance, which is difficult to ensure in the face of intense social pressure. The future of Chinese society is an adventure and children do not 'demand to be born.' I am worried that my children are not warriors and are lost in it.

———

We enrolled Ariel and Natasha in the rural public school near our home. At Chengdu Experimental, they had been the only Americans, and now in their Colorado school the twins were the only students of Chinese descent. Nearly a century earlier, their great-grandfather had traveled through the state, visiting mines. There were so few Chinese in Colorado that in his diary he recorded a rare encounter, on April 13, 1927:

> In the afternoon I went with the friend by car to Denver. The snow was heavy and the temperature below freezing. I went to the YMCA and then to Mandarin Chop Suey for dinner. There was a half-Chinese waitress who was very pretty and cute, only 16 years old.

In Colorado, Cai Cai and Rou Rou continued to follow the Chinese curriculum for language and mathematics. Twice a week, the twins stayed home from Colorado school and connected by video with a tutor in Chengdu. They still battled Chinese math problems:

> A certain number, when divided by 3, leaves a remainder of 2; when divided by 4, leaves a remainder of 3; when divided by 5, leaves a remainder of 4. What is the smallest that this number could be?

During the first week of school in Colorado, Ariel had to stop herself from crossing her arms neatly on the desk, placing both feet on the floor at all times, and standing up whenever teachers called on her. During the third week, the school bused all students and teachers to a lake at an elevation of nearly ten thousand feet, where they camped for three days. Midway through the semester, Natasha announced that her favorite class was shop. She and her classmates began the term by fixing tables and chairs in the library, and later they learned how to change an automobile tire. One morning, the teacher showed them how to use an extension ladder. He opened the ladder, propped it against the side of the shop building, and had the children take turns climbing up. High on the Uncompahgre Plateau, beneath the dome of a clear blue sky, Natasha was thrilled to stand on the roof without any rails.

Acknowledgments

For more than a quarter century, I have been fortunate to hear from my Chinese students. Our conversation began in the classroom, first in Fuling, on September 2, 1996; and then again in Chengdu, on September 4, 2019. But I've also received countless letters, emails, and survey responses from former students after they finished school, and I'm grateful that they stayed in touch. For quotations in this book, I contacted the authors for permission, and I have identified them by English or Chinese names according to their preference. In the few cases in which somebody requested a pseudonym, I have mentioned it in the text.

I also want to thank the many students who helped me contact and stay in touch with their peers, especially Willy, North, and Serena. Adam Meier, my former Peace Corps site mate, has also worked hard to continue the dialogue that we started with our students more than twenty-five years ago.

In 1998, after finishing a draft of *River Town*, I sent the manuscript to Emily. Her comments were invaluable, and since then we have had an ongoing conversation about the issues of writing about China. We have also exchanged many letters and messages about education, and Emily's various perspectives—as a former student, as a current teacher, as a parent—have informed my writing. I am grateful to her and to Tao Tao for their generosity in allowing me to write about their experiences.

Three of my books have been translated into Chinese by Li Xueshun, who was a colleague at the Fuling college in the 1990s. With each translation, Xueshun took great care to capture the language of the moment and the place. Without these books, it would have been much harder for non-English speakers to understand what I was trying to do as a writer in China. I hope that someday it will be possible for Xueshun to translate this book and the others that have not yet appeared on the mainland.

The years that I taught at Sichuan University turned out to be more challenging than expected, because of both the pandemic and the political climate. I am grateful to the hardworking people who handled day-to-day administration at SCUPI, including Zoey He, Euphy He, Alex Sun, Jingjing Wang, and Gavin Tang. I was also fortunate to have wonderful colleagues in the English department: Areum Jeong, Shijie Wang, Emily O'Dell, Yumei Li, David Jeffrey, John Rhym, and Yoo Young Ahn.

In Chengdu, Harry Wu was a great friend who helped with all sorts of things, ranging from the COVID car to introductions to entrepreneurs. Tzu-yi Chuang Mullinax welcomed us during our initial time in the city, and her hospitality and friendship made that period much easier. Michael Meyer, another former Peace Corps volunteer turned writer, alerted me to the possibility of teaching at SCUPI, and I am especially grateful for the introduction to his former student, He Yujia. Yujia's research and general good advice proved to be invaluable, especially during the pandemic. Mostly, I am thankful to Yujia and her husband, Eric, for their friendship.

Jiang Xueqin helped Leslie and me navigate the primary school landscape in Chengdu, and he gave excellent advice with regard to Chengdu Experimental. The leadership at the school could not have been more welcoming—a remarkable act of generosity during a period of troubled U.S.–China relations. For us, Teacher Zhang will always represent everything that's good about Chinese education, and her attention and compassion made it possible for Natasha and Ariel to transition into the school. Teacher Yu, the math instructor, was remarkably dedicated, and Tracy, the English teacher, was very good at involving the twins in lessons. During the first year, they also benefited from tutoring in Mandarin by Jean He and Rachel Mei. We've been grateful that Rachel has been willing to continue online classes since we returned to Colorado, despite the fourteen-hour time difference.

During the early period of the pandemic, it helped to correspond with Zhang, the pharmacist in Wuhan, who wrote frequently despite the pressure of being a front-line medical worker during the crisis. Later that summer, when I visited Wuhan, Zhang and the poet Xiaoyin were generous in showing me the city and in talking about their memories from the spring. It was a joy to spend time with their circle of friends—a glimpse of creative energy in a city that had recently suffered so much trauma. In Chengdu, my understanding of pandemic economics benefited from repeated visits to Li Dewei, the Amazon entrepreneur. Dewei's introductions to others in the export industry were also helpful.

I had a number of long phone conversations with Jennifer Nuzzo, an epidemiologist who at the time was at the Johns Hopkins Center for Health Security, and Wafaa El-Sadr, the director of ICAP, a global-health center at Columbia University. Both scientists were patient with my uninformed questions, and they helped me consider China's experience in a larger perspective. Throughout my time in Chengdu, I frequently corresponded with Ian Johnson, whose careful reading also helped shape this manuscript. It meant a great deal to be in conversation with Ian during a time when I was professionally isolated.

Doug Hunt was the first person to see a draft of *River Town*, and since then he has been a faithful reader, a careful editor, and a dear friend. I appreciate his comments on this book, and it was also helpful to be in conversation while I was writing from China.

I am deeply grateful to Willing Davidson, my editor at *The New Yorker*, and to David Remnick, for doing everything possible to help me report and write from China during the pandemic. I also want to thank Han Zhang, Hélène Werner, Dennis Zhou, Madelyne Xiao, Nina Mesfin, and Yinuo Shi, for their diligent fact-checking of my various *New Yorker* stories.

William Clark has been my agent since the Jiang Zemin era. Thank you for representing this book and all the others. At Penguin Press, I have been fortunate to work with Scott Moyers. It's a long journey from Cairo to Chengdu, but Scott followed me all the way and had faith in this book. It's also been a pleasure to work again with Mia Council, whose patience and attention to detail have been invaluable.

Thanks to my sister, Angela Hessler, whose beautiful maps have been such an important part of my books since *Oracle Bones*.

And Leslie—certain shared Chengdu moments will always stay with me. The first day of school, the night of the earthquake, the first post-lockdown meal. . . . Your good judgment and calmness under pressure made it possible for us to navigate this difficult period.

Leslie and I moved to Sichuan with two nine-year-olds who spoke hardly a word of Mandarin. Natasha and Ariel, 柔柔和采采. This book is dedicated to you and to your transformation.

Ridgway, Colorado
December 2023

Notes

CHAPTER ONE: REJECTION

3 **title was Introduction to Journalism and Nonfiction:** I chose the course title in May 2019. Administrators at SCUPI collected student applications and submitted them to me by email on June 5, 2019.

6 **she sent a long email:** Serena's message was sent September 13, 2019.

8 **only one out of every twelve:** In 1996, the rate of admission to higher education was 8.3 percent. "'Du daxue dengyu hao gongzuo' shi WTO shidai hongli, rujin huanjing yibian" 读大学等于好工作"是WTO时代红利，如今环境已变 ["'Attending College Equals a Good Job' Was a Bonus in the WTO Era, but Now the Situation Has Changed"], *Baijiahao*, June 12, 2023, https://baijiahao .baidu.com/s?id=1768497089507271164&wfr=spider&for=pc.

8 **China's population was 83 percent rural:** From World Bank population figures: https://data .worldbank.org/indicator/SP.RUR.TOTL.ZS?locations=CN.

9 **"In China, passing an entrance examination":** This student's writing was in response to an assignment in writing class on September 20, 1996.

9 **"My mother was a peasant":** From a student's homework assignment in writing class during the National Day holiday, on October 1, 1996. I asked students to compare their ideas about China with those of their parents.

11 **"The children show no interest":** From a letter postmarked October 14, 2001.

12 **"In 1999, a charming girl":** From Jimmy's letter, postmarked December 25, 2002.

12 **I am now going to Fujian:** From a letter postmarked February 2, 2007.

13 **more than a quarter of a billion rural Chinese moving:** Daniel Griswold, "*China's Great Migration: How the Poor Built a Prosperous Nation* by Bradley M. Gardner," *Cato Journal* 28, no. 1 (2018): 311.

13 **China's population officially became majority urban:** From World Bank figures, which listed China's population as 49.49 percent rural in 2011. See https://www.macrotrends.net/countries /CHN/china/rural-population.

13 **nearly eight hundred million:** According to the World Bank's International Poverty Line. See https://www.worldbank.org/en/news/press-release/2022/04/01/lifting-800-million-people -out-of-poverty-new-report-looks-at-lessons-from-china-s-experience.

13 **"For three years, I did not eat and sleep well":** From a response to the survey I emailed to former Fuling students on October 1, 2014.

14 **long journey from Colorado to Fuling:** I visited Fuling from March 10 to 11, 2018. The conversation with my friend was on March 11.

15 **"They talked about big people and big events":** From an email sent by Emily on April 29, 2011. In *River Town*, I used the pseudonym Anne for Emily, because of uncertainty about how the book would be received. In *Oracle Bones* and all other subsequent writings I have used the name Emily.

16 **"Of course, Xi Jinping is the one I admire":** I emailed the survey to students on January 24, 2017.

20 **"I had no idea about the man":** Giselle's essay was submitted on September 24, 2019.

21 **"My father was born in 1972":** This essay was for my first-year composition class. It was submitted on March 15, 2020.

21 **"My parents were born in rural Shandong":** Fenton's essay was submitted on December 30, 2019.

22 **study in *The Lancet*:** "Height and Body-Mass Index Trajectories of School-Aged Children and Adolescents from 1985 to 2019 in 200 Countries and Territories: A Pooled Analysis of 2181 Population-Based Studies with 65 Million Participants," *Lancet* 396 (2020): 1511–24, https://www.thelancet.com/action/showPdf?pii=S0140-6736%2820%2931859-6.

23 **speech about Chinese education at Peking University:** Jiang Zemin's speech marked the anniversary of the May Fourth Movement and was delivered on May 4, 1998. For full text, see: http://www.reformdata.org/1998/0504/4551.shtml.

24 **to 51.6 percent:** According to Ministry of Education figures. See Section 6 (高等教育), "2019 nian quanguo jiaoyu shiye fazhan tongji gongbao" 2019 年全国教育事业发展统计公报 ["2019 National Statistical Bulletin on Educational Development"], May 20, 2020, http://www.moe.gov.cn/jyb_sjzl/sjzl_fztjgb/202005/t20200520_456751.html.

25 **"For the Long March Singing Contest":** Peter Hessler, *River Town: Two Years on the Yangtze* (New York: HarperCollins, 2001), 4.

26 **story on the university's website:** Zhang Jie 张洁, "'Lizan xin Zhongguo, chang xiang xin shidai'—qingzhu Zhonghua Renmin Gongheguo chengli 70 zhounian Sichuan Daxue jiaozhigong hechang bisai juxing" '礼赞新中国，唱响新时代'—庆祝中华人民共和国成立70周年四川大学教职工合唱比赛举行 ["Praise the New China and Sing the New Era: Celebrating the 70th Anniversary of the Founding of the People's Republic of China, Sichuan University Holds a Faculty and Staff Choral Competition"], September 22, 2019, https://www.scu.edu.cn/info/1207/11553.htm.

27 **per capita GDP:** According to the World Bank, China's per capita GDP was $156 in 1978 and $10,144 in 2019. See https://www.macrotrends.net/countries/CHN/china/gdp-per-capita.

28 **"My mother used to hand in all her money":** Serena's essay was in response to an assignment to write about her parents' generation. It was submitted on June 22, 2020.

29 **"gay bathroom":** The students submitted research proposals on October 22, 2019.

CHAPTER TWO: THE OLD CAMPUS

33 **three-year institution:** The Chinese term for this kind of college is 专科学校. When I taught in Fuling, the official name of the college was 涪陵师范（高等）专科学校.

33 **Yangtze Normal University:** The Chinese name is 长江师范学院.

35 **my first trip back to Fuling:** I visited Fuling from September 12 to 14, 2019.

36 **"He was sent to Guang'an":** From an email sent on January 10, 2011.

37 **urban population was around 185,000:** The figure was 185,900 in 1996, according to the Chongqing government. Chen Zhiping, ed. 陈治平主编, "Chongqing tongji nianjian" 重庆统计年鉴 ["Chongqing Statistical Yearbook"] (中国统计出版社, 1997), 42, https://www.zgtjnj.org/navibooklist-N2006080076-1.html. In 2019, the urban population was 512,800, according to the Fuling government. "2020 nian Fuling qu tongji nianjian (jiexuan)" 2020 年涪陵区统计年鉴(节选) ["2020 Fuling District Statistical Yearbook (Excerpt)"], September 8, 2020, http://www.fl.gov.cn/bm/tjj/zwgk_46564/tjxxbf/sjzl/tjxx_tjnj/202209/t20220908_11092050.html.

41 **"When my parents were of my age":** Emily wrote this for a homework assignment in writing class during the National Day holiday, on October 1, 1996.

41 **"I don't know much about the history":** From an email sent on March 23, 2023. At Emily's request, I have not included Cousin Liu's full name.

45 **Robert Hilliard, who had been born in Fuling in 1943:** I interviewed Robert Hilliard in Toronto on April 16, 2022. His father was Irwin Hilliard, and his great uncle was Robert McAmmond. For

details about Fuling in the 1940s I have also relied on "The China Times: Six Years in a War Zone Among a Gentle People," the unpublished memoir of Mary Crawford, another Canadian missionary who lived in the city. Robert Hilliard provided a copy of the memoir.

45 **"This is a frank record"**: *China White Paper: August 1949*, vol. 1 (Stanford, CA: Stanford University Press, 1967), IV, https://archive.org/stream/VanSlykeLymanTheChinaWhitePaper1949 /Van+Slyke%2C+Lyman+-+The+China+White+Paper+1949_djvu.txt.

46 **"Farewell, Leighton Stuart!"**: Mao Tse-Tung, "Farewell, Leighton Stuart!" in *Selected Works of Mao Tse-Tung*, vol. 4, ed. Maoist Documentation Project, https://www.marxists.org/reference /archive/mao/selected-works/volume-4/mswv4_67.htm.

47 **why the Peace Corps was based in Sichuan**: Daniel Schoolenberg, "The Inside Story of the Peace Corps in China," China Project, September 30, 2021, https://thechinaproject.com/2021 /09/30/the-inside-story-of-the-peace-corps-in-china.

48 **"The Indians living in America"**: Zhang Kuiwu, ed. 张奎武（主编）, Ying-Mei gaikuang xia 英美概况:下 [*Survey of Britain and America*, vol. 2] (Jilin: Jilin kexue jishu chubanshe 吉林: 吉林科学技术出版社, 1988), 42.

49 **"it also opened up fresh ground"**: Zhang, Ying-Mei gaikuang, 45.

49 **"Constitution of 1787 established the dictatorship"**: Zhang, Ying-Mei gaikuang, 64.

49 **"Most New Englanders"**: Zhang, Ying-Mei gaikuang, 15.

49 **"For example, 'draw one'"**: Zhang, Ying-Mei gaikuang, 216.

49 **"Homosexuality is a rather strange social phenomenon"**: Zhang, Ying-Mei gaikuang, 252.

49 **"The most important reason"**: Zhang, Ying-Mei gaikuang, 256.

51 **"Not long after you became my teacher"**: During this period, Emily sent her letters via fax, from the office where she worked in Shenzhen. I no longer have the paper copy of this fax, but it was recorded in my notes on June 29, 1999.

51 **"I hate political cant"**: From a fax sent on July 9, 1999.

55 **"I don't think about success"**: Wang Guozhen 汪国真, "Reai shengming" 热爱生命 ["Love of Life"], Wang Guozhen shijingbian 汪国真诗精编 [Collected Poems of Wang Guozhen], (Wuhan: Changjiang wenyi chubanshe 武汉: 长江文艺出版社, 2014), 98. Translation is mine.

55 **"I now know that I had been a frog in a well"**: From a letter postmarked September 28, 1998.

56 **"I'm working in a small village"**: From a letter postmarked January 21, 2000.

57 **"Nowadays there is a boy who is hunting"**: From a letter postmarked May 6, 1999.

57 **"Last winter, I was married with a doctor"**: From a letter postmarked December 20, 2000.

57 **"What makes me happy"**: From a letter postmarked November 15, 2004.

57 **"[After] graduating Fuling Teachers College"**: From a letter postmarked April 22, 2000.

58 **"I called Anry the other day"**: From a fax sent on November 7, 1999.

61 **North took me to a project site in Fuling**: We visited the site on November 9, 2019.

62 **Kenny G's saxophone**: Dan Levin, "China Says Goodbye in the Key of G: Kenny G," *New York Times*, May 10, 2014, https://www.nytimes.com/2014/05/11/world/asia/china-says-goodbye-in -the-key-of-g-kenny-g.html.

64 **official agreement with the Peace Corps**: Peace Corps, "U.S. and China Sign Peace Corps Agreement; Accord Reached During Presidential Visit," news release, June 29, 1998. For a copy of the agreement, see: https://worldjpn.net/documents/texts/USC/19980629.T2E.html.

65 **demanded that the Peace Corps permanently relocate**: Office of Senator Rick Scott, "Sen. Rick Scott Releases Four Proposals to Help Bahamas Recover After Hurricane Dorian," news release, September 5, 2019, https://www.rickscott.senate.gov/2019/9/sen-rick-scott-releases -four-proposals-help-bahamas-recover-after-hurricane-dorian.

65 **senator issued another statement**: Office of Senator Rick Scott, "Sen. Rick Scott: Peace Corps Ignored Demands to Get out of Communist China," October 9, 2019, https://www.rickscott.senate .gov/2019/10/sen-rick-scott-peace-corps-ignored-demands-get-out-communist-china.

65 **agency's goals**: For the Peace Corps goals, see https://www.peacecorps.gov/about/#:~:text=To %20promote%20world%20peace%20and,on%20the%20part%20of%20Americans.

65 **"I didn't even see any foreigners"**: From an email sent on February 17, 2020.

67 **"Adam gave us a cassette"**: Richard (代强) wrote these comments in a Chinese essay that was posted online on August 30, 2016. The essay was titled "Jilu shidai yu rensheng yidu 'Jiangcheng,' zhongshi wenzi de liliang" 记录时代与人生:读《江城》, 重识文字的力量 ["Recording Time and Life: Reading *River Town* and Realizing the Power of Words"]. The website no longer exists.

CHAPTER THREE: THE NEW CAMPUS

69 **ceremony that was held:** The matriculation was September 6, 2019.

70 **This edition had been published in India:** George Orwell, *Animal Farm* (New Delhi: Rupa Publications India Pvt. Ltd., 2019).

73 **"Soon, many pupils began to cry":** From an essay submitted by a nonfiction student on March 23, 2020.

73 **"My English teacher even told us":** From an essay submitted by a first-year composition student on November 16, 2020.

74 **more than forty hybrid programs in China:** This estimate is from the Cross-Border Education Research Team (C-BERT); see https://www.cbert.org/intl-campus.

74 **in 1996, 42,503 Chinese were enrolled:** Todd M. Davis, ed., *Open Doors 1996–1997: Report on International Educational Exchange* (New York: Institute of International Education), 9, https://files.eric.ed.gov/fulltext/ED417651.pdf.

74 **two thirds of the country's passport holders:** Cheng Li, "China's Millennials: Navigating Socioeconomic Diversity and Disparity in a Digital Era," in *China's Youth: Increasing Diversity amid Persistent Inequality*, Li Chunling (Washington, DC: Brookings Institution Press, 2021), 5.

74 **more than 372,000 Chinese at American institutions:** "Student Mobility Facts and Figures 2022: China," Open Doors, https://opendoorsdata.org/wp-content/uploads/2023/07/OpenDoors_FactSheet_China_2022.pdf.

75 **more than 80 percent of Chinese students returned:** "Vast Majority of Chinese Students Return Home after Studying Abroad: MOE," Xinhua News Agency, September 20, 2022, https://english.news.cn/20220920/38d7b612ced14c5a9aa37216c721051a/c.html.

75 **started developing the Great Firewall in 1998:** The firewall was originally known as the Golden Shield Project (金盾工程), and the first phase was initiated in 1998. Sonali Chandel et al., "The Golden Shield Project of China: A Decade Later: An In-depth Study of the Great Firewall," *2019 International Conference on Cyber-Enabled Distributed Computing and Knowledge Discovery (CyberC)*, 111–92, https://www.acsu.buffalo.edu/~yunnanyu/files/papers/Golden.pdf.

77 **the equivalent of sixty million dollars:** "Sichuan University–Pittsburgh Institute," Swanson School of Engineering, University of Pittsburgh, https://www.engineering.pitt.edu/scupi.

77 ***"Pride and Prejudice*, by Jane":** In the fall semester of 2019, I taught two sections of first-year composition. The two students who chose *Pride and Prejudice* and *The Merchant of Venice* were in the section that answered this question on September 20, 2019. The other responses are from the section that answered on September 9, 2019.

78 **"They raised us like they raised pigs":** I emailed the survey to former Fuling students on October 1, 2014.

79 **I'll call him Vincent:** At the student's request, I have not used his real English name. Vincent's essay about the police interrogation was submitted on October 17, 2019.

83 **"Moreover, because some instructors":** Vincent's argumentative essay about military training was submitted on December 5, 2019.

84 **I surveyed all my classes:** In the fall semester of 2019, out of 42 students who were surveyed, 37 had no siblings—a total of 88 percent.

86 **"Actually my mother was once pregnant":** From an assignment in nonfiction class to write about their parents' generation. This essay was submitted on January 8, 2020, at the end of the fall semester.

86 **One Chinese survey from 2014:** Xing Wang et al., "Changes in the Prevalence of Induced Abortion in the Floating Population in Major Cities of China 2007–2014," *International Journal of Environmental Research and Public Health* 16, no. 18 (2019): 5, https://www.ncbi.nlm.nih.gov/pmc/articles/PMC6765927/.

87 **"Abortion is nothing sensitive":** From an email on December 3, 2023.

87 **"I think my mom was pregnant":** From an email on September 1, 2022.

87 **Almost all said no:** The survey was emailed to students on February 2, 2016. There were 33 respondents, one of whom already had a second child. Of the others, only 2 out of 32 were considering having a second child—6 percent.

89 **"I got Nora registered officially":** From an email on August 24, 2014.

89 **"By the way, [a former classmate's] wife":** From an email on March 19, 2012.

89 **I called to congratulate him:** We spoke by telephone on October 31, 2012.

93 **"What confuses me":** Vincent's paper about the marriage corner was submitted on November 16, 2019.

96 **"His friend just sat":** The student's paper was submitted on November 17, 2019.

97 **"The devil came!":** Serena's paper was submitted on November 9, 2019.

98 **the Peace Corps sent a same-sex married couple:** The couple was sent to China in summer of 2015 and served until summer of 2017.

99 **79 percent of my first-year students:** In the fall semester of 2020, I taught one section of first-year students. On December 31, 2020, as part of a survey to prepare for a debate class, I asked for their opinions on same-sex marriage. Out of 19 students, 15 believed that same-sex marriage should be legal in China.

99 **"They're open-minded in many things":** From an assigned writing on generational differences, nonfiction class, spring semester of 2020. This student submitted the essay on June 22, 2020.

99 **my annual survey of former Fuling students:** The survey was emailed on September 22, 2021. Out of 31 responses, 26 opposed the legalization of same-sex marriage. Of the 16 women, 12 opposed.

99 **former student named Grant:** I visited Grant on May 18, 2021.

100 **less than 15 percent of gay Chinese:** "Being LGBTI in China: A National Survey on Social Attitudes towards Sexual Orientation, Gender Identity and Queer Expression," United Nations Development Programme (Beijing: Information for United Nations Development Programme, 2016), 26, https://www.undp.org/sites/g/files/zskgke326/files/migration/cn/UNDP-CH-PEG-Being-LGBT-in-China_EN.pdf.

101 **class called Economics of Love and Marriage:** The course title was 爱情婚姻经济学, and it was taught by 张引颖 (Zhang Yinying).

101 **Family Inheritance Law:** The course title was 亲属继承法, and it was taught by 张晓远 (Zhang Xiaoyuan). I interviewed Zhang on June 28, 2021, when he told me the results of his in-class survey, which have not been published.

104 **"business is operated on WeChat":** Yidi's paper was submitted on December 2, 2019. She read it aloud in class on December 4, 2019.

CHAPTER FOUR: CHENGDU EXPERIMENTAL

109 **Number 54 Zhang Xingcai:** Ariel's Chinese name is 张兴采 and Natasha's is 张兴柔.

112 **delegation of Chinese scholars visited:** Wang Rui, "John Dewey's Influence on Chinese Education" (PhD diss., Northern Illinois University, 1993), 4, https://www.proquest.com/openview/8f73d65a3790eb4f9e69f845ed33e885/1?pq-origsite=gscholar&cbl=18750&diss=y.

112 **the world's oldest standardized test:** Yingyi Ma, *Ambitious and Anxious: How Chinese College Students Succeed and Struggle in American Higher Education* (New York: Columbia University Press, 2020), 173.

112 **title of Dewey's first lecture in China:** Jessica Ching-Sze Wang, *John Dewey in China: To Teach and to Learn* (Albany: State University of New York Press, 2007), 16.

113 **"Bankers and editors frequent his residences":** Sun Youzhong, "John Dewey in China: Yesterday and Today," *Transactions of the Charles S. Peirce Society* 35, no. 1 (1999): 69–88.

113 **"in which what is best in western thought":** Sun, "John Dewey in China," 76.

113 **"early leaders of the CCP":** Elizabeth J. Perry, "Educated Acquiescence: How Academia Sustains Authoritarianism in China," *Theory and Society* 49 (2020), 5.

114 **young Mao Zedong mentioned in letters:** Sun, "John Dewey in China," 77.

114 **"Thus we will not provoke":** Sun, "John Dewey in China," 77.

114 **One of these figures was Hu Yanli:** Material about Hu (胡颜立) comes from the following article: Zhang Hongxia 张红霞, "Minguo Chengdu laile wei Jiangsu ren, gengyun 12 nian liuxia yi suo bainian mingxiao" 民国成都来了位江苏人，耕耘12年留下一所百年名校 ["During the Republican Era, a Jiangsu Native Comes to Chengdu and Works Hard for 12 Years, Leaving the Legacy of a Century-Old Famous School"], Chuan guan xinwen 川观新闻, October 28, 2018, https://page.om.qq.com/page/OKlbMcQ7uSE2669rXitXHNug0.

115 **all first graders begin the march to literacy:** The first-grade first-semester text used by Chengdu Experimental was: Zong Zhu, ed. 总主编, "Yuwen: yi nianji, *shangce*" 语文：一年级，

上册 ["Language: First Grade, Volume One"] (Beijing: Renmin jiaoyu chubanshe 北京：人民教育出版社，2016).

115 **opening page of the language text:** Zong, "*Yuwen*," 2–3.

118 *Feng li tong xing dian*: Leslie T. Chang, *Factory Girls: From Village to City in a Changing China* (New York: Spiegel and Grau, 2009), 129.

120 **More than a third of the Chinese students:** Chang, *Factory Girls*, 135.

120 **"China still does not have a person":** Chang, *Factory Girls*, 134.

120 **"Harbin's transport is very convenient":** This entry, like others that did not appear in *Factory Girls*, is from the unpublished diary of Zhang Shenfu. The diary was translated by Leslie T. Chang and 何宏玲 (He Hongling). They translated three volumes: the first is from January 1, 1926, to December 31, 1926; the second is from January 1, 1927, to June 10, 1927; and the third is from February 10, 1940, to December 30, 1940. These are the only volumes of the diary that survived; others are presumed to be lost.

120 **"If China wants to become prosperous":** Chang, *Factory Girls*, 135.

121 **"President Wilson thought":** Shenfu's diary, vol. 1, March 8, 1926.

121 **"My personal conduct must be honorable":** Chang, *Factory Girls*, 133.

121 **"The youth society in America":** Shenfu's diary, vol. 1, January 9, 1926.

122 **"In the morning I went to the factory":** Shenfu's diary, vol. 1, April 26, 1927.

122 **"In the morning I went into the No. 72 mine":** Shenfu's diary, vol. 1, May 22, 1927.

123 **"In 2009, the total number of migrant workers":** Liu Jian, Sun Qiping, and Zhang Dan, eds. 刘坚、孙企平、张丹主编，"Shuxue san nianji, shangce" 数学：三年级，上册 ["Mathematics: Third Grade, Volume One"] (Beijing: Beijing shifan daxue chubanshe 北京：北京师范大学出版社，2014), 21.

124 **"The class has 18 boys and 18 girls":** Liu et al., Shuxue, 9.

124 **"While multiplying one two-digit number":** Wan Zhiyong, ed. 万志勇主编, Huanggang xiaozhuang yuan: zuoyeben: san nianji shuxue, xia 黄冈小状元：作业本：三年级数学(下) ["Little Straight-A Students of Huanggang: Homework Book: Third Grade Math (Second Semester)"] (Beijing: Longmen shuju 北京：龙门书局), 32. (This was the homework book that accompanied the main math text.)

125 **"[Every four years] there is a year":** Jian et al., "Shuxue," 69.

125 **"Out of 1900, 1996, 2018":** Wan, "Huanggang," 58.

125 **"Out of 1800, 1960, and 2040":** Wan, "Huanggang," 55.

125 **"I was looking through a calendar":** Wan, "Huanggang," 54.

126 **"Math is virtue":** The math teacher made this remark at the parent-teacher conference (家长会) on January 12, 2020.

126 **"Long Yiming started to do his homework":** Wan, "Huanggang," 56.

128 **"Since Mussolini's rise":** Shenfu's diary, vol. 1, January 3, 1926.

128 **"Read Mussolini's good-will speech":** I have Frank Dietz's diaries from October 28, 1929, to June 19, 1931.

130 **"You should supply the University at Peking":** Colman James Barry, *Worship and Work: Saint John's Abbey and University, 1856–1980* (Collegeville, MN: Liturgical Press, 1980), 307.

131 **"the problem of the tail":** Teacher Zhang made these comments at the parent-teacher conference (家长会) on July 3, 2021.

131 **typical American primary-school teacher:** For a discussion of the difference between the American generalist approach and Chinese specialization, see Lenora Chu, *Little Soldiers: An American Boy, a Chinese School, and the Global Race to Achieve* (New York: HarperCollins, 2017), 285–87.

133 **"Bill—8 years old—foot hurts":** Wu Xin, Larry Swartz, and Beth Levy, eds. 吴欣主编, "Yingyu: san nianji, shangce." 英语：三年级，上册 ["English: Third Grade, Volume One"] (北京：人民教育出版社，2014), 33.

134 **careless children often drowned:** Lu Jie, ed. 鲁洁总主编, "Daode yu fazhi san nianji, shangce" 道德与法治：三年级，上册 ["Morality and Rules: Third Grade, Volume One"], (Beijing: Renmin jiaoyu chubanshe 北京：人民教育出版社，2018), 56.

134 **apparently friendly aunties:** Lu, "Daode yu fazhi," 64.

134 **"But he suffered extensive burns":** Lu, "Daode yu fazhi," 50.

135 **"One might have expected":** Perry, "Educated Acquiescence," 9.

136 **political campaigns attacking Dewey:** Sun, "John Dewey in China," 83.

137 **Japanese arrested Father Clougherty:** "Looking Back: Aug. 15, 1963," *Georgia Bulletin*, August 15, 2013, https://georgiabulletin.org/news/2013/08/looking-back-aug-15-1963/.

137 **"These few years have passed":** Chang, *Factory Girls*, 141.

138 **"To die for my duty":** Chang, *Factory Girls*, 144.

138 **"Those people who sing":** Shenfu's diary, vol. 1, January 19, 1926.

139 **American philosopher's view of reform:** Wang, *John Dewey in China*, 65–70.

140 **In the 2021 survey:** The survey was emailed to former students on September 22, 2021. Of the 31 respondents, 8 had worked at the same school since graduation.

140 **"China's education is like junk food":** This was from the 2016 survey, which was emailed to former students on February 2. These two comments were in response to an open-ended question about what they would like to change about their lives. Six mentioned education, in terms of wishing that they could change the material they taught.

140 **In 2017, I asked former students:** This survey was emailed on January 24, 2017. When asked about China's greatest success in the previous decade, 13 of 30 respondents cited improved transportation. The next most common response was improved living standards, which was mentioned by six.

141 **"I decided not to use 'guanxi'":** Emily's description of her 2009 job interview was sent by email on April 11, 2011.

142 **"Yesterday afternoon, when I saw students":** From an email on February 24, 2011.

142 **"One day on a bus":** Email, February 24, 2011.

143 **"Dear Mr. Hessler, How are you?":** From an email on May 29, 2009.

144 **funeral was attended by more than ten thousand:** Chang, *Factory Girls*, 147.

144 **Beijing tram line:** Chang, *Factory Girls*, 384.

145 **"I feel sad every time":** From an email on May 15, 2004.

145 **"Neill believed that 'not to interfere'":** From an email on October 13, 2011.

147 **"Last Saturday when we were having dinner":** From an email on December 11, 2020.

CHAPTER FIVE: EARTHQUAKE

149 **literature professor named Tang Yun:** Javier C. Hernández, "Professors, Beware. In China, Student Spies Might Be Watching," *New York Times*, November 1, 2019, https://www.nytimes.com/2019/11/01/world/asia/china-student-informers.html.

149 **law-school teacher from another institution:** I interviewed the professor on June 15, 2021.

150 **tweet by Peidong Sun:** Sun's Twitter account was @Peidongsun1.

151 **"To have Ho Wei teaching in our institute":** The bulletin-board posts were removed so quickly that I never saw them on the original location. By the time I taught my class that evening, the posts were being distributed via screenshot on Weibo, Twitter, and other social media sites.

151 **engineering major named Tim:** Tim's paper was submitted on December 6, 2020. The group he wrote about is on Douban (豆瓣), a social media site, and it is called 抠门男性联合会 (Koumen nanxing lianhehui). See https://www.douban.com/group/562227.

152 **she visited a Porsche dealership:** Anna's paper was submitted on December 6, 2020.

152 **"[Ho Wei] spoke w/o restraint":** This translation was posted by a Twitter user with the handle @LutherFreeman12.

153 **"This generation of young people":** The Weibo posts in this section were quickly censored, but I recorded them with screenshots. This comment was from an account with the username 咖啡提神奶茶续命.

153 **"The students at Sichuan University":** This post was from an account with the username 过期小饼干.

153 **"The students who reported Ho Wei":** This post was from an account with the username 王恺同学.

153 **"The main reason is not":** This post was from an account with the username 民科专家老王的室友.

153 **"I took a poetry appreciation class":** This post was from an account with the username 电气玉.

153 **"Each person has different values":** This post was from an account with the username 林师博马克two.

154 **state-published text,** *A Handbook of Writing*: Peter Hessler, *River Town: Two Years on the Yangtze* (New York: HarperCollins, 2001), 99.

156 **"It's not accurate to say"**: The draft of John's paper was submitted on November 30, 2019. My editing comments were made on December 7.

158 **Leslie visited the nonfiction class:** This class was on October 16, 2019.

158 **"I remember once Leslie"**: Serena's email was on January 15, 2022.

159 **"Introduction to Mao Zedong Thought"**: 毛泽东思想和中国特色社会主义理论体系概论.

159 **"Research on Xi Jinping Thought"**: 习近平新时代中国特色社会主义思想研究.

159 **"Only by taking the socialist core values"**: Scott's essay was submitted on December 1, 2019.

163 **to an NPR correspondent:** Rob Schmitz posted a message on his Twitter account (@rob_schmitz). See https://twitter.com/rob_schmitz/status/1205393826333876225?s=46&t=iKK5bAp61NXI0X -NyJXaVg.

163 **my department held a meeting:** The meeting was on December 27, 2019.

166 **For the first class after the attack:** The class was on December 16, 2019.

167 **Xinhua Winshare:** I visited the bookstore on July 19, 2021.

168 **dramatic performance of *1984*:** I attended the performance on December 23, 2019. All quotations are from the play's script, which was given to me by one of the student authors.

171 **"I'm glad you told me"**: May's letter was postmarked May 3, 2000.

172 **"We can meet at my home"**: From WeChat correspondence on December 5, 2019. I visited May and Lu Yong on December 7.

173 **leading cause of cancer death:** Maomao Cao and Wanqing Chen, "Epidemiology of Lung Cancer in China," *Thoracic Cancer* 10, no. 1 (2019): 3–7.

174 **I made a trip to the Three Gorges:** I visited Jimmy in Jiangkou on November 5, 2002.

174 **"Everything has two sides"**: Jimmy's letter was postmarked December 25, 2002.

174 **I have to take medicine:** From a letter postmarked April 7, 2003.

176 **I asked the question again in 2021:** The survey was emailed to students on September 22.

176 **I am a good man:** These quotes were in response to the 2016 questionnaire, which was emailed to former students on February 2.

177 **China's divorce rate has more than tripled:** In 2000, China's rate of divorce was 0.96 per thousand population per year, which rose to 3.09 by 2020. See https://www.statista.com/statistics /279449/divorce-rate-in-china/. In comparison, the U.S. rate is 2.9 per thousand population per year. See https://factsanddetails.com/china/cat4/sub20/entry-4334.html.

177 **I have a boyfriend:** The first comment was from an email sent on January 27, 2001; the second comment was from a letter postmarked December 25, 2006; and the third was in response to the 2021 survey.

182 **her perspective was one of "white superiority"**: Sheila Melvin, "The Resurrection of Pearl S. Buck," *Wilson Quarterly* (Spring 2006): 28.

182 **"There was no railroad"**: Hessler, *River Town*, 3.

182 **"I think no one would like"**: From a fax on August 12, 1999.

183 **"In the first chapters"**: From a fax on November 7, 1999.

183 **changed the title to *Jiangpan Cheng*:** This translation was for internal use and was never published. Somebody who worked on the project showed me a copy. The title was 江畔城.

183 **local map that misprinted the characters:** The map labeled the mountain 白山坪, or "White Flat Mountain," when it should have been 北山坪, "North Flat Mountain." The map was "Fuling diqu jiaotong lüyoutu," 涪陵地区交通旅游图, published by Chengdu ditu chubanshe 成都地图出版社, July 1, 1995.

184 **"With a distance of time"**: From an email on April 29, 2011.

184 **I would never have picked up:** From a reviewer with the username Alexandra, November 15, 2022.

184 **"Some of the ethnocentric views"**: From a reviewer with the username John Tipper, September 26, 2022.

184 **"I heard it's kinda cringe"**: From a reviewer with the username Amy, January 24, 2023.

185 **an interview with Li Piaohai:** I interviewed Li on September 18, 2014. The Chinese name of the development was 御临江山.

186 **banned the construction of new golf courses:** Austin Ramzy, "China Cracks Down on Golf, the 'Sport for Millionaires,'" *New York Times*, April 18, 2015, https://www.nytimes.com/2015/04/19 /world/asia/chinas-crackdown-on-corruption-targets-golf-a-sport-for-millionaires.html.

187 **in 2018, there still weren't any holes:** I visited River Town Golf on March 11, 2018.
189 **fifty-nine people in the city:** Sui-Lee Wee and Vivian Wang, "China Grapples with Mystery
    Pneumonia-Like Illness," *New York Times*, January 6, 2020, https://www.nytimes.com/2020/01
    /06/world/asia/china-SARS-pneumonialike.html?searchResultPosition=1.
190 **nearly sixty-year history of the Peace Corps:** Peter Hessler, "Broken Bonds," *New Yorker*, March
    16, 2020. See https://www.newyorker.com/magazine/2020/03/16/the-peace-corps-breaks-ties
    -with-china.
192 **During our phone interview, the senator:** I interviewed Senator Rick Scott by phone from
    Chengdu on February 13, 2020.
193 **"Farewell, Peace Corps in China":** Pan Gongyu 潘攻愚, "Meiguo zai hua 'Heping Dui,' zouhao,
    busong" 美国在华 '和平队', 走好, 不送 ["Farewell, Peace Corps in China, We Won't See You
    Off"]. Guanchazhe wang 观察者网, January 20, 2020, https://www.guancha.cn/pangongyu
    /2020_01_20_532304.shtml.
194 **Tom Rogan wrote approvingly:** Tom Rogan, "U.S. Rightly Ends Peace Corps Mission in China,"
    Washington Examiner, January 19, 2020, https://www.washingtonexaminer.com/opinion/us
    -rightly-ends-peace-corps-mission-in-china.
194 **China had an official total of 11,791:** These figures are from China's National Health Commis-
    sion. See http://www.nhc.gov.cn/xcs/yqtb/202002/84faf71e096446fdb1ae44939ba5c528.shtml.
194 **Chengdu tightened its lockdown policies:** The city's first lockdown restrictions were issued on
    January 24, 2020; see http://cdwjw.chengdu.gov.cn/cdwjw/c135633/2020-01/31/content_957c
    840eccec4877bbc844cf328d9438.shtml. After the first week, these restrictions were tightened;
    see http://cdwjw.chengdu.gov.cn/cdwjw/c135633/2020-01/31/content_2d7bb94972d240cf848f
    434856653ba0.shtml.
195 **earthquake struck the northeastern outskirts:** See https://earthquaketrack.com/quakes
    /2020-02-02-16-05-42-utc-5-2-9.

CHAPTER SIX: THE CITY SUSPENDED

199 **On the twenty-seventh day:** February 19, 2020. For more on the lockdown phase in Chengdu,
    see Peter Hessler, "Life on Lockdown," *New Yorker*, March 23, 2020.
200 **most packages I counted:** This was on February 27, 2020.
202 **Party official at SCUPI had distributed:** This message and the replies were sent on January 28,
    2020.
203 **Li posted a screenshot of the report:** Tan Jianxing 覃建行, "Xinguan feiyan 'chuishao ren' Li
    Wenliang: Zhen xiangbi pingfan geng zhongyao" 新冠肺炎"吹哨人"李文亮：真相比平反更重要
    ["The New Coronavirus 'Whistleblower' Li Wenliang: The Truth Is More Important Than Re-
    dress"], Caixin 财新, January 31, 2020, https://web.archive.org/web/20200131074029/http://
    china.caixin.com/2020-01-31/101509761.html.
204 **Wang told Chinese state media:** Jeremy Page, Wenxin Fan, and Natasha Khan, "How It All
    Started: China's Early Coronavirus Missteps," *Wall Street Journal*, March 6, 2020, https://www
    .wsj.com/articles/how-it-all-started-chinas-early-coronavirus-missteps-11583508932.
204 **"But right now what I want to say":** Fang Fang, *Wuhan Diary: Dispatches from a Quarantined
    City*, trans. Michael Berry (New York: HarperCollins, 2020), 20–21.
204 **more than fifty million readers:** Michael Berry, *Translation, Disinformation, and Wuhan Diary:
    Anatomy of a Transpacific Cyber Campaign* (Cham, Switzerland: Palgrave Macmillan, 2022), 16.
205 **"The only things I can pay attention to":** Fang, *Wuhan Diary*, 119.
205 **"The reason I like Wuhan":** Fang, *Wuhan Diary*, 85.
206 **"Right now everyone in this city":** Fang, *Wuhan Diary*, 66.
206 **"To my dear internet censors":** Fang, *Wuhan Diary*, 77.
208 **more than twenty-two million college students:** From the Ministry of Education: "Yi shuzihua
    zhuli jiaoyu qiangguo jianshe" 以数字化助力教育强国建设 ["Using Digitization to Help Build a
    Powerful Country in Education"], February 11, 2023, http://www.moe.gov.cn/jyb_xwfb/xw_zt
    /moe_357/2023/2023_zt01/fzzs/202302/t20230211_1043749.html.
208 **180 million schoolchildren:** From the Ministry of Education: "Guanyu tongchou anpai guojia
    zhong xiao xue wangluo yun pingtai he Zhongguo jiaoyu dianshitai tigong zhong xiao xuesh-
    eng xuexi ziyuan de gonggao" 关于统筹安排国家中小学网络云平台和中国教育电视台提供中小学

生学习资源的公告 ["Announcement on the Arrangement of National Primary and Secondary School Cloud Platforms and China Educational Television to Provide Learning Resources for Primary and Secondary School Students"], February 14, 2020, http://www.moe.gov.cn/jyb_xwfb/xw_zt/moe_357/jyzt_2020n/2020_zt03/yw/202002/t20200214_421069.html.

209 **"Physics, finance, and economics":** Sisyphos was responding to a series of questions I gave students on the first day of class, on February 25, 2020.

209 **"In my point of view":** This quote is from the draft of Rakim's argumentative essay, which was submitted on May 23, 2020. *The New York Times* began capitalizing Black on July 2, 2020. Nancy Coleman, "Why We're Capitalizing Black," *New York Times*, July 5, 2020, https://www.nytimes.com/2020/07/05/insider/capitalized-black.html#:~:text=Decades%20later%2C%20a%20monthlong%20internal,and%20cultures%20of%20African%20origin.

209 **I asked if students personally knew anybody:** During the spring semester of 2020, I taught one section of nonfiction and two sections of first-year composition, and I surveyed all students on the first day of class. The first-year classes began on February 24 and 25, and the nonfiction class began on February 24. Of the 56 students, 17 reported that they had not gone outside their compounds during the previous month.

210 **"I was reading news":** This is from a first-year student's essay that was submitted on March 5, 2020.

210 **On the thirty-ninth day:** This was March 2, 2020.

212 **only 143 cases had been reported:** On February 20, 2020, the last locally transmitted case was reported by the Chengdu government, for a total of 143: http://cdwjw.chengdu.gov.cn/cdwjw/gzdt/2020-02/21/content_29c16ddd2a0842ca9883a39fbbf0e20e.shtml. Chengdu next reported a case on March 4, but this case was imported, not locally transmitted: http://cdwjw.chengdu.gov.cn/cdwjw/gzdt/2020-03/05/content_114bd8c4b4404c2cac7d142ada6157ad.shtml.

212 **Rakim wrote an essay:** Rakim submitted the essay about his grandmother on March 20, 2020.

214 **three different occasions:** Volunteers surveyed us at our apartment on January 28, February 11, and February 26. On February 11 they told me about the case in Building Nine.

215 **"My personal opinion":** From a WeChat message on February 26, 2020.

215 **"Our basic needs are met":** From a WeChat message on February 24, 2020.

215 **"People who spend a lot of time":** From a WeChat message on March 1, 2020.

216 **"Ping Ping: I calculated":** Wan, "Huanggang," 68.

216 **more than 220 million children:** Guanghai Wang et al., "Mitigate the Effects of Home Confinement on Children During the COVID-19 Outbreak," *Lancet* 395, no. 10228 (2020): 945–47, https://www.ncbi.nlm.nih.gov/pmc/articles/PMC7124694.

217 **"As for the classes online":** From a WeChat message on March 13, 2020.

217 **"their kids are *shenshou*":** From a phone conversation on March 12, 2020.

217 **had jumped out:** My friend in Fuling reported hearing about the attempted suicide on March 10, 2020.

218 **leading cause of death among young people:** Li Xinling 李新玲, "Zhong xiao xuesheng zisha shuju bu gai cheng yanjiu jinqu" 中小学生自杀数据不该成研究禁区 ["Research on Suicides of Primary and Secondary School Students Should Not Be a Forbidden Zone"], Zhongguo qingnian bao 中国青年报, May 30, 2014, http://zqb.cyol.com/html/2014-05/30/nw.D110000zgqnb_20140530_1-02.htm.

218 **suicide in Hebei province:** "Kebei! Hebei yi xuesheng shang wangke bu jiji bei xunchi tiaolou qingsheng, fumu huihen chui de tongku" 可悲! 河北一学生上网课不积极被训斥跳楼轻生, 父母悔恨捶地痛哭 ["How Sad! A Student in Hebei Province Was Scolded for Not Being Active in Online Classes and Committed Suicide by Jumping off a Building, His Father and Mother Beat the Ground and Cried Bitterly in Regret"], Baijia hao 百家号, March 4, 2020, https://baijiahao.baidu.com/s?i=1660231339930242864&wfr=spider&for=pc.

218 **boy eventually died:** The friend reported that the child died from his injuries on March 16, 2020.

218 **"Some of them have been terrified":** Emily's email was from February 27, 2020.

219 **"I was optimistic":** Emily's email was from March 13, 2020.

219 **"When I told my colleagues":** Emily's email was from March 15, 2020.

220 **"But one thing clear":** Fang, *Wuhan Diary*, 96.

220 **When I met with the local Party secretary:** I met with Wang Yi (王怡) on March 7, 2020. The neighborhood committee was 锦官驿街道水井坊社区.

222 **"Everyone grumbles":** From a WeChat message on March 1, 2020.
222 **"defeat the virus":** "Xi Jinping: Zai tongchou tuijin xinguan feiyan yiqing fangkong he jingji she-hui fazhan gongzuo bushu huiyi shang de jianghua" 习近平：在统筹推进新冠肺炎疫情防控和经济社会发展工作部署会议上的讲话 ["Xi Jinping: Speech at the Meeting on Coordinating the Deployment of New Coronavirus Epidemic Prevention and Control and Economic and Social Development"], Xinhua 新华, February 23, 2020, http://www.xinhuanet.com/politics/leaders/2020 -02/23/c_1125616016.htm.
222 **"There is a bad tendency":** From a WeChat message on March 4, 2020.
223 **I finally entered Building Nine:** This was March 7, 2020.
224 **more than eighty thousand confirmed cases:** On March 8, 2020, the total number of reported cases in China was 80,735: http://www.nhc.gov.cn/xcs/yqtb/202003/f2c83db9f73d4be5be0dc 96af731813c.shtml.
224 **ages of the three victims:** According to Chengdu government reports, one death occurred on January 29, and two more on February 15. "Sichuan tongbao 3 lie xinguan feiyan siwang binglie, xiangxi bingqing gongbu" 四川通报3例新冠肺炎死亡病例，详细病情公布 ["Sichuan Reports 3 Deaths from the New Coronavirus, Detailed Patient Reports"], Jiankang Sichuan 健康四川, February 20, 2020, https://www.sohu.com/a/374558572_116237.

CHAPTER SEVEN: CHILDREN OF THE CORONA

228 **"We've been thinking of you":** William Clark's email was on January 28, 2020.
228 **"We're fine, and in Brooklyn":** William's email was March 24, 2020.
231 **Elaine wrote about:** Elaine's essay was submitted on March 5, 2020.
231 **"The traits of a place":** Wenxin included her father's comment in a research paper that was submitted on May 25, 2020.
232 **"You know why":** Hongyi's essay was submitted on March 5, 2020.
233 **week six survey:** I surveyed the three sections on March 30 and 31, 2020.
233 **Andy lived near Nanjing:** Andy and Momo submitted their research papers on April 24, 2020. For more about this semester and the government's approach to the virus, see Peter Hessler, "How China Controlled the Virus," *New Yorker*, August 17, 2020.
234 **Sisyphos profiled a pharmacist:** Sisyphos submitted his profile on April 24, 2020.
234 **people abandoning pets:** "Yiqing qijian bei yiqi chongwu zengduo, duo de chutai guanli gui-fan" 疫情期间被遗弃宠物增多，多地出台管理规范 ["Abandoned Pets Increased During the Pandemic, and Many Places Introduced Management Regulations"], Renmin ribao 人民日报, April 28, 2020, https://baijiahao.baidu.com/s?id=1665171871258770863&wfr=spider&for=pc.
234 **Hongyi shadowed a loan manager:** Hongyi submitted her story on May 29, 2020.
235 **man who flew for Hainan Airlines:** I interviewed the Hainan Airlines pilot by telephone on July 24, 2000.
235 **as many as 70 percent:** Emmie Martin, "70% of Americans Consider Themselves Middle Class—but Only 50% Are," CNBC, June 30, 2017, https://www.cnbc.com/2017/06/30/70-percent-of -americans-consider-themselves-middle-class-but-only-50-percent-are.html.
235 **only 44 percent identified as middle class:** "Tamen wei shenme bu yuan chengren ziji shi zhongchan?" 他们为什么不愿承认自己是中产？["Why Don't They Recognize That They Are Middle Class?"], Sou hu 搜狐, April 10, 2017, https://www.sohu.com/a/133094881_422109.
235 **I surveyed them about their economic:** I emailed the survey to students on October 1, 2014.
236 **Cathy lived in northern China's Hebei:** Cathy submitted her profile on May 29, 2020.
239 **I received 1,146 WeChat messages:** This was the total number of messages from May 15, 2020, when parents were first asked to submit temperatures, to June 12, 2020.
240 **One epidemiologist told me:** We met in Shanghai on May 22, 2020.
241 **local organizations known as** *baojia* **and** *lijia*: Daniel C. Mattingly, *The Art of Political Control in China* (Cambridge, UK: Cambridge University Press, 2020), 155–57.
241 **"nerve tips" of the state:** Mattingly, *Art of Political Control*, 158.
242 **Serena reported:** Serena began researching her neighborhood committee in late February 2020 and submitted her paper on April 24, 2020.
242 **municipal government media site:** "Shunqing xinzeng 1 lie! Nanchong leiji quezhen 30 lie fu xinzeng 1 lie huodong guji" 顺庆新增1例！南充累计确诊30例 附新增1例活动轨迹 ["There Is 1

New Case in Shunqing! A Total of 30 Cases Have Been Diagnosed in Nanchong, and the Activities of the New Case Are Attached"], Nanchong bobao 南充播报, February 7, 2020, https://h5 .newaircloud.com/detailArticle/10424168_16599_jrsq.html?source=1.

244 **Jiang Xilin:** We met in Shanghai on May 21, 2020.

245 **one of the Shanghai epidemiologists:** This was the scientist I met on May 22, 2020.

247 **"Press coverage sometimes suggests":** Mattingly, *Art of Political Control*, 181–82.

248 **I talked with Mattingly:** We spoke via Zoom on February 17, 2023.

248 **One evening well into the pandemic:** The two men stopped by on January 4, 2021.

251 **In week sixteen:** The first class back on campus was the evening of June 8, 2020.

252 **Ethel caught a high-speed express:** Ethel's story was submitted on May 29, 2020.

255 **"While hiding in the bathroom":** Ariel's journal entry was from May 8, 2020.

255 **"This is the first time":** Serena's essay was submitted on June 21, 2020.

256 **U.S. was recording more COVID cases:** I submitted grades on July 5, 2020. The total number of new cases in the U.S. was 54,846 on July 4 and 45,374 on July 5. See https://covidtracking.com /data/national/cases.

256 **average rating was 7.1:** The three classes submitted their surveys on June 22 and 25, 2020, and a total of 52 students answered this question.

CHAPTER EIGHT: THE SEALED CITY

260 **On my second visit:** My first trip to the Huanan market was on August 22, 2020, and I returned on August 28. For more details about my reporting in Wuhan, see Peter Hessler, "The Sealed City," *New Yorker*, October 12, 2020.

261 **"There are more than a thousand vendors":** Fang Fang, *Wuhan Diary: Dispatches from a Quarantined City*, trans. Michael Berry (New York: HarperCollins, 2020), 219.

262 **some staff at the upstairs market had been infected:** "Wo zai Wuhan Huanan haixian shichang loushang mai yanjing" 我在武汉华南海鲜市场楼上卖眼镜 ["I Sell Eyeglasses on the Second Floor of the Huanan Seafood Market"], Xinhua 新华, February 22, 2020, https://baijiahao.baidu.com /s?id=1659193132000695871&wfr=spider&for=pc.

262 **Wuhan journalist who had visited the mah-jongg:** We met in Wuhan on August 28, 2020.

264 **The second-hardest-hit Chinese city:** These statistics are from the health commission of Hubei province. "2020 nian 5 yue 31 ri Hubei sheng xinguan feiyan yiqing qingkuang" "2020年5 月31日湖北省新冠肺炎疫情情况" ["May 31, 2020, Hubei Province COVID-19 Pandemic Situation"], Hubei sheng weisheng jiankang weiyuanhui 湖北省卫生健康委员会, June 1, 2020, http:// www.hubei.gov.cn/bmdt/ztzl/fkxxgzbdgrfyyq/xxfb/202006/t20200601_2372980.shtml.

264 **official death toll was 3,869:** This was the figure reported by the Wuhan government.

265 **architect named Kyle Hui:** I met Kyle Hui in Wuhan on August 21, 2020.

266 **infectious-disease physician:** I met the physician in Wuhan on August 24, 2020.

268 **"Traditionally, China was an agricultural":** From a WeChat message on March 4, 2023.

268 **One evening in Wuhan:** We met in Wuhan on August 23, 2020.

269 **"Last night I went out drinking":** From Xiaoyin's unpublished journal. Xiaoyin 小引, Wuhan xiaoxi 武汉消息 ["Wuhan Information"], January 22, 2020–April 15, 2020, 4.

269 **"monument should be built":** Xiaoyin, Wuhan xiaoxi, 51.

270 **prominent tai chi master:** Michael Berry, *Translation, Disinformation, and Wuhan Diary: Anatomy of a Transpacific Cyber Campaign* (Cham, Switzerland: Palgrave Macmillan, 2022), 110–11.

270 ***"What kind of decent person":*** Berry, *Translation, Disinformation, and Wuhan Diary*, 104–5.

271 **One nurse told me:** I interviewed the nurse in Wuhan on August 23, 2020.

271 **young manager from a building company:** We met in Wuhan on August 22, 2020.

272 **Money can make the devil:** The Chinese phrase is 有钱能使鬼推磨.

273 **Yellow Crane Tower:** I visited the site on August 27, 2020.

274 **tested more than nine million:** Wenxin Fan, "Wuhan Tests Nine Million People for Coronavirus in Ten Days," *Wall Street Journal*, May 25, 2020, https://www.wsj.com/articles/wuhan-tests -nine-million-people-for-coronavirus-in-10-days-11590408910.

274 **special exhibit about Wuhan medical workers:** I visited the exhibit on May 21, 2020, at the China National Silk Museum in Hangzhou.

274 **STUDENTS DO NOT:** Liu Jia 刘嘉, "Xiaoyuan nei xuesheng wu xu peidai kouzhao" "校园内学生无

需佩戴口罩" ["Students Do Not Have to Wear Masks in Schools"], Changjiang ribao 长江日报, August 29, 2020, 2.

274 **second-highest number of any city:** Guangzhou has the most university students.

274 **visited Wuhan University:** I visited the campus on August 25, 2020.

277 **police came to my hotel room:** This was in Yiwu, on July 31, 2020.

279 **I talked with Peter Daszak:** We spoke by phone on September 11, 2020.

280 **some of his colleagues in the city:** I met with the group of scientists on November 10, 2020.

281 *Science* **published a preprint:** Michael Worobey et al., "The Huanan Seafood Wholesale Market in Wuhan Was the Early Epicenter of the COVID-19 Pandemic," *Science* 377, no. 6609 (2022): 951–59, https://www.science.org/doi/10.1126/science.abp8715.

281 **"We found that cases in December":** Worobey's tweet was on December 26, 2022, https://twitter.com/MichaelWorobey/status/1497610918712078336.

282 **overwhelming majority of Americans believed:** Aaron Blake, "How the COVID Lab Leak Became the American Public's Predominant Theory," *Washington Post*, March 16, 2023, https://www.washingtonpost.com/politics/2023/03/16/lab-leak-theory-polling.

282 **"I tend to take a charitable view":** I spoke by phone with Jennifer Nuzzo on July 10, 2020.

282 **Wafaa El-Sadr, the director of ICAP:** I spoke by phone with Wafaa El-Sadr on May 8, 2020. Her quote is from a follow-up email on May 9.

283 **"I would tell my close friends":** Zhang and I met for dinner in Wuhan on August 27, 2020.

284 **I met with Fang Fang:** We met in Wuhan on August 26, 2020.

285 **Fang Fang donated all foreign profits:** Berry, *Translation, Disinformation, and Wuhan Diary*, 68.

286 **"You think we are still in the year 1840":** Berry, *Translation, Disinformation, and Wuhan Diary*, 78.

286 **"Sorry, I had too much to drink":** Berry, *Translation, Disinformation, and Wuhan Diary*, 79.

CHAPTER NINE: INVOLUTION

290 **One evening during the first week:** August 10, 2020.

292 **"fastening buttons on clothes":** Xi Jinping's speech was May 4, 2014. "Xi Jinping: Qingnian yao zijue jianxing shehui zhuyi hexin jiazhiguan" 习近平：青年要自觉践行社会主义核心价值观 ["Xi Jinping: Young People Should Consciously Practice the Core Values of Socialism"], Renmin ribao 人民日报, May 5, 2014, http://cpc.people.com.cn/n/2014/0505/c64094-24973220.html?ivk_sa=1024320u.

293 **hand-copy the instructor's weekly schedule:** Lu Jie, ed. 鲁洁总主编, Daode yu fazhi: san nianji, shangce 道德与法治：三年级，上册 ["Morality and Rules: Third Grade, Volume One"], (Beijing: Renmin jiaoyu chubanshe 北京：人民教育出版社，2018), 36.

293 **seven middle school students drowned:** Lu, Daode yu fazhi, 56.

293 **"I am a picky eater":** Lu, Daode yu fazhi, 51.

294 **"Don't throw things out the window":** Wu Xin, Larry Swartz, and Beth Levy, eds. 吴欣主编, Yingyu: si nianji, shangce 英语：四年级，上册 ["English: Fourth Grade, Volume One"] (Beijing: Renmin jiaoyu chubanshe 北京：人民教育出版社，2014), 55–56.

295 **"Mary and her mother":** Wu et al., Yingyu, 46–47.

295 **boy named Anran:** Lu, Daode yu fazhi, 55.

296 **story of Liu Yuxi:** Qu Yixian, ed. 曲一线主编, "5*3 tiantian lian: Xiaoxue yuwen, si nianji, shangce" 5*3天天练：小学语文，四年级，上册 ["5*3 Practice Every Day: Elementary School Language, Fourth Grade, Volume One"] (Beijing: Shoudu shifan daxue chubanshe 北京：首都师范大学出版社, 2015), 91–92.

297 **"I, Li Bai, embark on a boat, ready to set sail":** The English translation by He Yujia of the Li Bai poem "A Gift to Wang Lun" is used by permission.

304 **"If a candidates' writing":** This student essay was submitted on December 5, 2019.

305 **top 6 percent of test takers:** These figures are for students who were in the 理科生 (science) track, since all engineering students had this background. In 2019, according to the Sichuan Educational Examination Authority, a total of 260,034 students took the exam, of whom 15,684 scored 632 or higher. See https://www.sceea.cn/Html/201906/Newsdetail_1032.html.

305 **next-lowest cutoff at Sichuan University:** The gaokao cutoff scores for departments are from the university website: https://zs.scu.edu.cn/info/1101/2062.htm.

305 **only about 1.6 percent:** The figure for 2019 was 1.62 percent. "Zhaxin zhenxiang! Zuizhong

neng jin 985 de haizi jin 1%, 50% de haizi jinbuliao gaozhong, 80% de haizi wuyuan benke" 扎心
真相！最终能进985的孩子仅1%，50%的孩子进不了高中，80%的孩子无缘本科 ["The Distress-
ing Truth! Only 1% of Children Make It into 985 Universities, 50% Can't Make It into High School,
and 80% Can't Go to University"], Pengpai xinwen 澎湃新闻, June 6, 2020, https://m.thepaper
.cn/baijiahao_7716786.

305 **Their department even won the highest honors:** Zhang Jie 张洁, "'Lizan xin Zhongguo, chang
xiang xin shidai'—qingzhu Zhonghua Renmin Gongheguo chengli 70 zhounian Sichuan Daxue
jiaozhigong hechang bisai juxing" '礼赞新中国，唱响新时代'—庆祝中华人民共和国成立70周年
四川大学教职工合唱比赛举行 ["'Praise the New China and Sing the New Era'—Celebrating the
70th Anniversary of the Founding of the People's Republic of China, Sichuan University Holds a
Faculty and Staff Choral Competition"], September 22, 2019, https://www.scu.edu.cn/info/1207
/11553.htm.

306 **personal essay about being hospitalized:** This essay was for nonfiction class and was submitted on April 6, 2021.

306 **installed guardrails around the balconies:** Liu Xingwang, 刘兴旺, "Hengshui erzhong jiaoxue-
lou an 'tielong' yin zhengyi, xiaofang: buneng yingxiang tiaosheng he miehuo" 衡水二中教学楼
安"铁笼"引争议，消防：不能影响逃生和灭火 ["The 'Iron Cage' Installed in the Teaching Building of Hengshui Number 2 Middle School Has Caused Controversy, Fire Department: It Cannot
Affect Fire Escape and Fire Fighting"], Pengpai xinwen 澎湃新闻, April 22, 2014, https://www
.thepaper.cn/newsDetail_forward_1323714.

306 **"One centimeter taller":** This essay was submitted for nonfiction class on October 12, 2020.

306 **seventeen out of eighteen:** I surveyed this section of students on December 10, 2020.

307 **"My attitude towards the teacher":** Darker Liao was in first-year composition, and he submitted his essay on April 6, 2021.

308 **I surveyed more than sixty students:** I asked about the *gaokao* in three classes: nonfiction and
first-year composition in the fall of 2020, and then another section of first-year composition in
the spring of 2021. The question was answered by a total of 61 students, of whom 38 did not want
significant changes to the *gaokao*.

308 **"We cannot give up eating":** From a first-year composition essay in the unit on argumentation.
This essay was submitted on May 25, 2020.

309 **ten-year-old Chengdu schoolboy:** Sarinstein submitted his profile on May 10, 2021.

309 **"In China, education is the most important tool":** From an email on May 14, 2021.

310 **In one in-class debate:** This debate was on October 18, 2019.

310 **I surveyed more than sixty students:** I surveyed three classes: nonfiction, on November 26,
2020; first-year composition, on November 25, 2020; and another section of first-year composition, on April 29, 2021. A total of 63 students were surveyed, of whom 47 reported suffering from
stress during high school. Forty-nine said that their parents had not put too much pressure on
them.

311 **"One day at the end of 2004":** Yin Limei submitted her story on December 21, 2020.

314 **more than five thousand defective products:** These figures are from a series of interviews with
Anry, ranging from early 2021 to 2023. For more background on Anry and his classmates, see
Peter Hessler, "Going Up," *New Yorker*, January 3 and 10, 2022.

319 **In 2016, my annual survey:** The survey was emailed to students on February 2, 2016.

320 **"During hot weather":** Willy's email was sent on May 26, 2023.

321 **North took me to a project:** We visited the site in Fuling on July 7, 2020.

323 **Gary Liu, a prominent economist:** I met Gary Liu in Shanghai on November 9, 2020.

323 **profile of a middling student:** The profile was submitted on April 24, 2020.

324 **"During the Spring Festival":** Willy's email was sent on May 25, 2023.

CHAPTER TEN: COMMON SENSE

327 **independent campus journals:** "Duli xiaoyuan meiti de shengmingxian" 独立校园媒体的生命
线 ["The Lifeline of Independent Campus Media"], Changshi 常识, September 23, 2015, https://
mp.weixin.qq.com/s/K1VPIPwJFDabpZDL1ZTcOg.

328 **"This is the power of leaderless collective action":** Daniel C. Mattingly, *The Art of Political Control in China* (Cambridge, UK: Cambridge University Press, 2020), 93.

329 **"Comrade Are You OK":** "Tongzhi, ni hao ma?" 同志，你好吗? ["Comrade, Are You OK?"], Changshi 常识, July 2011, 6–15.

329 **there was in fact a chief editor:** We met in Chengdu on July 2, 2021.

331 **"His position in this group":** Georg Simmel, *The Sociology of Georg Simmel*, ed. and trans., Kurt H. Wolff (Glencoe, IL: Free Press, 1950), 402.

331 **"He is not radically":** Simmel, *Sociology of Georg Simmel*, 404.

332 **Katherine wrote about her experience:** Katherine's profile was submitted on November 16, 2020.

334 **"No matter how many writers":** Michael Berry, *Translation, Disinformation, and Wuhan Diary: Anatomy of a Transpacific Cyber Campaign* (Cham, Switzerland: Palgrave Macmillan, 2022), 146.

335 **"I would suggest that Mr. Hessler":** Geremie R. Barmé, "The Good Caucasian of Sichuan & Kumbaya China," *China Heritage*, September 1, 2020, https://chinaheritage.net/journal/the-good-caucasian-of-sichuan-kumbaya-china/.

336 **diplomat from the American consulate:** We met in Chengdu on July 23, 2020.

336 **had reported that the Chinese:** Teddy Ng, "China 'Set to Shut U.S. Consulate' in Response to Houston Closure, and Denies COVID-19 Is a Factor," *South China Morning Post*, July 23, 2020, https://www.scmp.com/news/china/diplomacy/article/3094336/us-consulate-chengdu-prime-target-china-retaliation-over.

339 **protocol known as a destruction plan:** Details about the destruction plan and the closing of the consulate are from a series of interviews conducted with Americans who were involved in these events. The two main sources were interviewed on August 12, 2020, and March 3, 2021.

340 **U.S. security agents tailed Chinese consular staff:** Anna Fifield et al., "China Pledges to Retaliate after U.S. Orders Closure of Its Consulate in Houston," *Washington Post*, July 22, 2020, https://www.washingtonpost.com/world/asia_pacific/china-vows-to-retaliate-after-us-orders-closure-its-consulate-in-houston/2020/07/22/41e5c6ea-cbf1-11ea-99b0-8426e26d203b_story.html.

342 **"We check the statistics every day":** I met with Li Dewei in Chengdu on April 24, 2020. Subsequent meetings during the initial phase of the pandemic were May 14 and July 2.

344 **I interviewed Scott R. Baker:** We spoke on the telephone on January 2, 2021.

345 **China should become a multiparty democracy:** I emailed the survey to former students on January 24, 2017. When I asked if China should become a multiparty democracy, 22 of 30 respondents said no. I also asked if they expected a significant change in China's political system during the next decade, and 2 said yes.

346 **entrepreneur named Li Jiang:** I visited Li Jiang at his stall in the Yiwu wholesale market on July 31, 2020.

346 **flag manufacturer called Johnin:** I visited the Johnin factory in Shaoxing, Zhejiang, on August 1, 2020. For more details about the manufacture of Trump flags, and Li Dewei's business, see Peter Hessler, "Manufacturing Diplomacy," *New Yorker*, March 15, 2021.

347 **54 percent predicted that Trump would win:** On October 29, 2020, I polled two classes: nonfiction and first-year composition. Out of 32 students in nonfiction, 17 predicted that Trump would win. Out of 20 first-year students, 11 predicted Trump.

347 **"He does things badly":** I talked with Li Dewei about the election on September 25, 2020.

348 **Nearly half of the top sellers on Amazon:** John Herrman, "All Your Favorite Brands, from BSTOEM to ZGGCD," *New York Times*, February 11, 2020, https://www.nytimes.com/2020/02/11/style/amazon-trademark-copyright.html.

349 **May 6, one-star review:** These reviews were all of a Feetmat sneaker: https://www.amazon.com/Feetmat-Athletic-Running-Walking-Sport/dp/B07D16L5NG/ref=sr_1_1?dchild=1&keywords=feetmat&qid=1603615294&sr=8-.

351 **"When the power status":** The first two quoted responses were from students in the fall semester of 2020. They submitted their essays at the end of term, on January 5, 2021. The third quoted response ("His character shortcomings") was from the spring semester of 2021, submitted on July 2, 2021.

351 **"I am a person without independent thinking":** This essay was submitted on January 5, 2021.

352 **"It was easy to laugh":** Peter Hessler, *River Town: Two Years on the Yangtze* (New York: HarperCollins, 2001), 22.

353 **"My parents were born in the 1970s":** Hongyi submitted this essay on July 2, 2020.

354 **tested more than two million residents:** The total number of people tested in the five-day span was 2,170,372, according to an online report by Chengdu Television: Xie Cong 谢聪, "Kangyi qi tian: Pidu qu de zhou yu ye" 抗疫七日：郫都区的昼与夜 ["Seven Days of Fighting the Epidemic: Pidu District Days and Nights"], Chengdu dianshitai shenniao zhi xun 成都电视台神鸟知讯, December 17, 2020, https://www.sohu.com/a/439053285_814888.

355 **Chengdu opened five new subway lines:** The lines were opened on December 18, 2020. "China's Chengdu Opens 5 New Metro Lines," Xinhua, December 18, 2020, http://www.xinhuanet.com /english/2020-12/18/c_139600493.htm#:~:text=CHENGDU%2C%20Dec.,metro%20system %20to%20558%20km.

355 **Almost 70 percent:** There were 29 students in class on January 31, and 20 said that 2020 had been a good year.

355 **"During the period of staying at home":** Vincent submitted his essay on January 6, 2021.

355 **"like beauty products for people":** I visited Li Dewei on February 27, 2021.

356 **Jin sent pictures:** Jin Gang sent the images on WeChat on January 20, 2021.

356 **Honda reported that in 2020:** Shunsuke Tabeta and Takashi Kawakami, "China's Auto Market Survives 2020 with Just 2% Dent," *Nikkei Asia*, January 7, 2021, https://asia.nikkei.com/Business /Automobiles/China-s-auto-market-survives-2020-with-just-2-dent.

CHAPTER ELEVEN: GENERATION XI

358 **"Hi, Happy Spring Festival!":** Emily's email was sent on February 23, 2021.

360 **I had dinner with Emily:** This conversation was on May 16, 2021.

361 **"On sunny afternoons":** Peter Hessler, *River Town: Two Years on the Yangtze* (New York: Harper-Collins, 2001), 352.

363 **net importer of agricultural products:** Zongyuan Zoe Liu, "China Increasingly Relies on Imported Food. That's a Problem," Council on Foreign Relations, January 25, 2023, https://www .cfr.org/article/china-increasingly-relies-imported-food-thats-problem.

363 **world's largest importer of food:** Jayson Beckman et al., *China's Import Potential for Beef, Corn, Pork, and Wheat*, U.S. Department of Agriculture Economic Research Service, Economic Research Report No. 310, August 2022, https://www.ers.usda.gov/webdocs/publications/104541 /err-310.pdf.

365 **"The River Runs Forever":** Ren Zhenxue, ed. 任祯雪主编, "Shijie diyi gudai shuiwenzhan: Baiheliang" 世界第一古代水文站：白鹤梁 ["The Number One Ancient Hydrometric Station: The White Crane Ridge"], (Beijing: Zhongguo Sanxia chubanshe 北京：中国三峡出版社, 1995), 55.

366 *Chongqing Evening News* **reported:** Tao Qing 陶青, "Baiheliang ti ke: Baohu fang'an te dingduo" 白鹤梁题刻：保护方案待定夺 ["White Crane Ridge Inscriptions: Protection Plan to Be Determined"], Chongqing wanbao 重庆晚报, January 1, 1998, 3.

366 **"To them, this would undoubtedly":** Hessler, *River Town*, 107.

367 **The first time I visited:** I visited the White Crane Ridge Underwater Museum on March 23, 2011. See Peter Hessler, "Return to River Town," *National Geographic*, March 2013.

370 **Chyu responded with a curt message:** I sent an email requesting an extension of my position on March 30, 2021, and Chyu responded with an email on April 1. I wrote again on April 9, and Chyu emailed his second explanation on April 12. Then I offered to sign a long-term contract and teach additional classes, and the director of my program relayed this request to Chyu on April 17. The following day the director told me that Chyu had declined the offer.

371 **Lin Yiwu had posted:** Lin Yiwi 林一五, "He Wei shi 'waiguo youren,' nali bu duijin?" 何伟式'外国友人,'哪里不对劲 ["What's Wrong with Ho Wei as a 'Foreign Friend'?"], March 30, 2021, https://mp .weixin.qq.com/s?__biz=MzI0MzAzNjk2Nw==&mid=2651659123&idx=2&sn=a03f6b61dbd 024d818c4057518ac9ad7&chksm=f28a9d3bc5fd142d3a9ce8a33bf969eb7f3e53acf238af0fc5a9 e5cd6b3597d3cae4b8c3bf6d&mpshare=1&scene=1&srcid=0331SyHSOCE4Or92FBf2fAn8 &sharer_sharetime=1617177388389&sharer_shareid=a3a92d28bd5d33ee5183941eb754be1c &exportkey=AddUhR4ndk3RbqIb%2Bqy8NZU%3D&pass_ticket=xvdt75CCr9vFq%2B19i QlaCHZkS4CEFQ%2Bbdw0jipFjDO6QZUw9zv0iJzAhU07KzqZ6&wx_header=0#rd.

372 **"I have used 'Lyndon'":** The first day of class was March 11, 2021.

373 **Lexi Road was built in 1942:** Bruce's proposal was submitted on May 25, 2021.

374 **"Are you the owner of Kiki?":** Lyndon's paper was submitted on May 10, 2021.

375 **Chongqing auto-parts factory:** Milo's paper was submitted on May 8, 2021. For more details about the Sichuan University students and the political climate, see Peter Hessler, "A Bitter Education," *New Yorker*, May 16, 2022.

378 **"All I could recall":** Bruce submitted his paper on July 8, 2021.

379 **our final nonfiction session:** The last class was on the evening of July 1, 2021.

380 **posted by a friend on Douban:** The statement was posted to Douban on May 30, 2021, by He Yujia, under her username, 仙境兔子不忘记.

380 *People's Daily* **reported his words:** "Xi Jinping: Jiang hao Zhongguo gushi, chuanbo hao Zhongguo Shengyin" 习近平：讲好中国故事，传播好中国声音["Xi Jinping: Tell Chinese Stories Well, Spread Chinese Voices Well"], Haiwai wang 海外网, June 3, 2021, https://baijiahao.baidu.com /s?id=1701503556700154128&wfr=spider&for=pc.

382 **"Of course, Mao had a lot of mistakes":** In writing class, I asked Fuling students to write about their heroes midway through the fall semester of 1996. Out of 22 students who wrote about public figures, 15 chose political leaders: 7 Mao Zedong, 4 Deng Xiaoping, and 4 Zhou Enlai. This survey is described on pages 132–33 of *River Town*.

383 **belonging to Generation Xi:** This term is not used in China, where the cohort of my Sichuan University students is known as *linglinghou*, or "post 00s." Western writers occasionally use the term; see: Stephanie Studer, "Young Chinese Are Both Patriotic and Socially Progressive," *The Economist*, January 23, 2021, https://www.economist.com/special-report/2021/01/21/young -chinese-are-both-patriotic-and-socially-progressive.

383 **more than five hundred total:** I reviewed all papers from every course I taught at Sichuan University: four sections of nonfiction and six sections of first-year composition.

383 **high income and higher education to correlate:** Li Chunling, *China's Youth: Increasing Diversity amid Persistent Inequality* (Washington, DC: Brookings Institution Press, 2021), 298–300.

384 **less interest in joining the Party:** Cheng Li, introduction to *China's Youth*, 17.

384 **"They see Western democratic institutions":** Li Chunling, *China's Youth*, 313.

384 **"simple propaganda-style education":** Li Chunling, *China's Youth*, 306.

384 **In five sections of first-year composition:** I asked about heroes in two sections of first-year composition in fall of 2019, two sections in spring of 2020, and another section in spring of 2021.

385 **"After finishing them":** Emily's email was from September 27, 2020.

385 *Animal Farm* **at Sichuan University:** These essays were assigned as part of the portfolios that students prepared at the end of term. Carl and the others submitted the essays on July 2, 2021.

387 *Common Sense* **staff invited me:** We met on the evening of June 22, 2021.

387 **"It was always the women":** George Orwell, *1984* (New York: Signet Classic, 1983), 12.

388 **I attended her graduation ceremony:** The departmental graduation was held on June 5, 2021.

390 **Serena was led into a room:** The officials spoke with Serena on June 23, 2021. We had a longer conversation about the incident on July 5, the day she officially left the university system.

391 **He replied in an email:** Chyu's email was on April 29, 2022. The University of Pittsburgh declined my interview request on the same day.

391 **"I will write about this 'forbidden' topic":** Serena's email was on June 24, 2021.

392 **last day at Chengdu Experimental:** This was June 29, 2021.

393 **We met at a café:** I met Yang Guang and visited the former Peace Corps headquarters on June 28, 2021.

395 *The Role of Government*: This book is in Chinese, with an English title printed on the cover. The Chinese title is different: Yang Guang 杨光, "Zhonghua wenhua zouchu qu beijing xia: Meiguo duiwai wenhua jiaoliu Zhong de zhengfu juese yanjiu" 中华文化走出去背景下：美国对外文化交流中的政府角色研究 ["Background for Chinese Culture Going Global: Research on the Government's Role in U.S. Cultural Exchanges Abroad"] (Chengdu: Sichuan daxue chubanshe 成都: 四川大学出版社, 2018).

398 **On the afternoon I visited:** I went to the Three Gorges Dam on July 11, 2021.

399 **"It vividly proves":** Seth Faison, "Set to Build Dam, China Diverts Yangtze While Crowing About It," *New York Times*, November 9, 1997, https://www.nytimes.com/1997/11/09/world/set-to-build -dam-china-diverts-yangtze-while-crowing-about-it.html.

399 **former student named Yancy:** I visited Yancy and Jimmy separately on July 10, 2021.

400 **"education situation in the coming years":** Willy's email was on July 16, 2023.

400 **in the spring of 2011, I had visited Jimmy:** I went to Yunyang on March 26, 2011.

402 **Emily and I had a long conversation:** We met on July 14, 2021.

404 **former student named Grant:** I visited Grant's village on July 15, 2021.

404 **average of sixty-three elementary schools:** The statistic on closed rural schools is from the central government website. "Shi nianjian nongcun mei tian xiaoshi 63 suo xiaoxue: nongcun jiaoyu zouxiang hefang" 十年间农村每天消失63所小学: 农村教育走向何方 ["During the Past Ten Years, an Average of 63 Rural Elementary Schools Have Closed Every Day: Where Will Rural Education Go?"] Zhongyang zhengfu menhu wangzhan 中央政府门户网站, November 20, 2012, https://www.gov.cn/jrzg/2012-11/20/content_2270579.htm.

407 **pilgrimage to the old campus:** We visited the campus on May 17, 2021.

EPILOGUE: THE UNCOMPAHGRE RIVER

410 **my former student John:** I emailed John on April 4, 2022, and he replied that same day. We spoke by video call on April 5.

412 **Serena's first professional long feature:** Li Yijuan, "Joining the Tribe," *Post Magazine*, August 12, 2023; see https://www.scmp.com/magazines/post-magazine/long-reads/article/3230814/first-chinese-chief-africa-does-he-and-others-him-wield-any-real-influence.

412 **dinner with Bruce:** I had dinner with Bruce and Vincent on November 2, 2022. Vincent's comments about his decision to stay in the U.S. are from an interview in Colorado on May 8, 2023.

413 *runxue*, **or "run philosophy":** Li Yuan, "'The Last Generation:' The Disillusionment of Young Chinese," *New York Times*, May 24, 2022, https://www.nytimes.com/2022/05/24/business/china-covid-zero.html.

414 **THIS IS THE SICHUAN UNIVERSITY:** The banner was hung on the morning of March 22, 2022, and it had been removed by the afternoon. The message was: "川大是全体师生的川大，不是全体官僚的川大."

414 **a West China medical student died:** Lü Xucheng 吕煦成, "Yiqing xia, buyuan liu zao yiyuan de gui pei shengmen" 疫情下，不愿留在医院的规培生们 ["During the Pandemic, Graduate Students Who Do Not Want to Stay in the Hospital"], Xin lang wang 新浪网, January 18, 2023, http://k.sina.com.cn/article_6724296968_190cca108001012rpk.html#.

415 **"I was quite depressed":** From an email on September 17, 2023.

416 **"Most significantly, it has changed":** This was in response to a question in a survey that I sent to former Sichuan University students on June 2, 2023.

416 **"Sometimes when I look at Tao Tao":** From an email on August 30, 2023.

417 **"There are also some more benefits":** Emily sent the speech by email on October 29, 2022.

417 **"I do find myself avoiding mentioning Xi's name":** From an email on December 5, 2023.

418 **more than half mentioned job opportunities:** The total was 26 out of 47.

418 **Most people who answered said no:** Including both men and women, 23 out of 40 who answered the question did not want children. There were also 7 who said they were unsure and didn't respond yes or no. Six of these 7 were women.

419 **"In the afternoon":** Zhang Shenfu's diary, vol. 2, April 13, 1927.

419 **certain number, when divided by 3:** Lu Jinling, ed. 路进玲责任编辑, "Ketang jinglian: Shuxue wu nianji: shangce" 课堂精炼：数学五年级：上册 ["Classroom Training: Fifth Grade Math: Volume One"] (Beijing: Beijing shifan daxue chubanshe 北京：北京师范大学出版社, 2019), 37.

Index